OXFORD HISTORICAL MONOGRAPHS

Time and Work in England 1750–1830

HANS-JOACHIM VOTH

CLARENDON PRESS · OXFORD

OXFORD
UNIVERSITY PRESS

Great Clarendon Street, Oxford OX2 6DP

Oxford University Press is a department of the University of Oxford.
It furthers the University's objective of excellence in research, scholarship,
and education by publishing worldwide in

Oxford New York

Athens Auckland Bangkok Bogotá Buenos Aires Calcutta
Cape Town Chennai Dar es Salaam Delhi Florence Hong Kong Istanbul
Karachi Kuala Lumpur Madrid Melbourne Mexico City Mumbai
Nairobi Paris São Paulo Shanghai Singapore Taipei Tokyo Toronto Warsaw

and associated companies in Berlin Ibadan

Oxford is a registered trade mark of Oxford University Press
in the UK and certain other countries

Published in the United States
by Oxford University Press Inc., New York

British Library Cataloguing in Publication Data
Data available

Library of Congress Cataloging in Publication Data
Data available

ISBN 0-19-924194-5

1 3 5 7 9 10 8 6 4 2

Typeset in Ehrhardt
by J&L Composition Ltd, Filey, North Yorkshire
Printed in Great Britain
on acid-free paper by
Biddles Ltd, Guildford and King's Lynn

ACKNOWLEDGEMENTS

THIS book is about the use of time, and I owe an immeasurable debt to the many individuals who have generously given me of their time. The Oxford dissertation that formed the basis of the current manuscript was supervised by Richard M. Smith and John Landers. They and my examiners, Charles H. Feinstein and E. A. Wrigley, were a constant source of suggestions, helpful criticisms, and encouragement. From them as well as my college supervisor, Avner Offer (who read most of the manuscript during a short stay in Venice), I hope to have learned what it means to be a scholar. My supervisor at the European University Institute, Albert Carreras, gave crucial guidance and support. Mary MacKinnon kindly read an early draft.

The manuscript of this book is arguably one of the better-travelled pieces of writing. I started work on the idea behind this manuscript at St Antony's College, Oxford, while studying for the Master of Science in Economic History. The dissertation project that followed from the Master's thesis on the abolition of holy days in England and Austria was first pursued at the European University Institute, Florence. After one year in Italy, I returned to Oxford, where Nuffield College had elected me to a funded studentship. My greatest debt, both intellectually and in terms of access to resources, is to the Warden, fellows, and students of Nuffield. The manuscript of the dissertation largely finished, I took up a Research Fellowship at Clare College, Cambridge, in the following year. The doctorate was completed in the summer of 1996, and won the EHA's Gerschenkron Prize for the outstanding thesis in international economic history as well as the EHES's Gino Luzzatto Prize for the best dissertation. After a year at McKinsey & Co., Germany, I returned to academia, visiting the Economics Department, Stanford University. My hosts, Paul A. David and Gavin Wright, generously gave help and advice. The Social Science History Institute at Stanford, under the stewardship of Steve Haber, provided a congenial environment and also awarded me a postdoctoral fellowship that allowed me to rewrite most of the dissertation manuscript for publication. In the summer of 1998 the Centre for History and Economics at King's College, Cambridge offered me access to their facilities to complete the necessary archival work. My new employer, the Economics Department at Universitat Pompeu

Fabra in Barcelona, permitted me to work at Nuffield College as a visiting fellow in the spring of 1999, where the finishing touches were put to the manuscript.

I also wish to thank Liam Brunt, Paul A. David, Jay Gershuny, Tim Leunig, Jim Oeppen, Wolfgang Reinhard, Jean-Laurent Rosenthal, and John Styles for generously sharing their ideas with me. Parts of the thesis were presented at the Cliometrics Conference in Kansas, the Social History Conference in Glasgow, the Economic History Society Conference in Lancaster, the Economic History Association meetings at Berkeley, the European Historical Economics Society Conference in Lisbon, at All Souls College and Nuffield College (Oxford), at Corpus Christi College (Cambridge), the Cambridge Group for the History of Population and Social Structure, at the Max-Planck-Institut für Geschichtswissenschaft (Göttingen), at EUI (Florence), Valencia, Stanford University, Pompeu Fabra, the University of California at Berkeley, and Northwestern University.

H.-J.V.
Barcelona and Cambridge
January 2000

TABLE OF CONTENTS

viii   *Contents*

I

Time and the Industrial Revolution

Did the Industrial Revolution mark a watershed in terms of time-use? Many scholars have argued that Britain experienced not only rapid structural change in the period 1750–1850, but that the rhythm of labour and leisure also changed profoundly. Marx assumed that the length of the working day was a direct indicator of the extent of capitalist exploitation.[1] The supposed transition from a merry old England where time was plentiful, play common, and work short and irregular, to the iron discipline of the cotton mills has long fascinated social and economic historians. Not only was the new production technology voracious in its appetite for ever longer working days of men in the prime of life, but its profitable adoption also appeared to rely on the use of women and child labour: 'The fact is that . . . young persons and children were worked all night, all day, or both *ad libitum*.'[2] The image of sheer endless toil, stretching the limits of physical endurance, is powerfully linked in public consciousness with the process of industrialization. At the same time, research in the last two decades has emphasized just how small, compared to the rest of the economy, the 'revolutionizing' sectors (such as cotton) were. Also, we have very little direct information on patterns of labour and leisure before the onset of the Industrial Revolution. As a result, we know surprisingly little about the way in which time-use changed between the middle of the eighteenth and the nineteenth centuries.

The significance of time-use for the Industrial Revolution is discussed in the following section. I argue that the potential usefulness of improved labour input estimates for our understanding of economic change and the course of living standards is particularly large. The second section reviews the range of accessible sources. It also clarifies why the importance of time-use for our understanding of industrializing Britain is only matched by the degree of our ignorance.

---

[1] Karl Marx, *Das Kapital*, i, sect. 1, p. 4 (Berlin, 1983 [1867]).
[2] Reports of the factory inspectors, cit. ibid., sect. 6, p. 24.

Labour and Leisure in England, 1750–1850

Time-use during the Industrial Revolution matters because it connects with two fundamental questions. First, working time is an integral part of economic production. In most production processes, labour is responsible for 50 to 70 per cent of total output.[3] The productivity of nations is often assessed on the basis of figures about GDP per capita or per employee. In economic history, emphasis on GDP per capita is also widespread. This practice ignores variations in the number of hours worked per member of the labour force—no account is taken of leisure lost in efforts to boost output. Crafts has recently shown how this practice can produce misleading results in the case of East Asia, where impressive output per capita was partly achieved via exceptionally long hours of work.[4] Intensive use of both time and capital—and not high productivity—was behind an important part of the Asian miracle.[5] This is why Krugman has recently referred to the rise of the Asian tigers as a case of 'Stalinist growth'.[6] Arguably a better measure of productivity is output per hour worked, instead of per capita. To construct more appropriate measures of economic output per unit of input can potentially add substantially to our understanding of the First Industrial Revolution.

Second, time is central to our notions of well-being. Becker's seminal article 'A Theory of the Allocation of Time' in 1965 described time as a necessary intermediate input.[7] In his perspective, utility is not directly derived from consumer goods. Rather, it is the combination of leisure and commodities that produces satisfaction.[8] Households become equivalent to small factories, combining intermediate goods (leisure, consumer durables, food, etc.) to produce the final product—the satisfaction of wants.[9] Time, in a fundamental sense, is all we have to spend. It can be converted either into purchasing power, by selling it in the labour market, or into leisure, when it needs to be combined with other goods to generate satisfaction.

---

[3] See N. F. R. Crafts, *British Economic Growth during the Industrial Revolution* (Oxford, 1985).

[4] Id., 'The East Asian Escape from Economic Backwardness', in Paul David and Mark Thomas (eds.), *Economic Challenges of the 21st Century* (London, forthcoming).

[5] Cf. also Alwyn Young, 'The Tyranny of Numbers: Confronting the Statistical Realities of the East Asian Growth Experience', *Quarterly Journal of Economics*, 110 (1995).

[6] Paul Krugman, 'The Myth of Asia's Miracle', *Foreign Affairs*, 73 (1994).

[7] Gary S. Becker, 'A Theory of the Allocation of Time', *Economic Journal*, 75 (1965).

[8] Ibid.; id., *The Economic Approach to Human Behavior* (Chicago, 1976).

[9] A simple application, together with the appropriate literature, is presented in Ch. 4.

Working time is a simple disamenity in this perspective—an assumption, however, that is often contradicted by modern-day surveys.[10]

In the context of industrializing Britain, both aspects are relevant. Labour as an input in the production process has not attracted much attention in recent years. In striking contrast, considerable efforts have been made during the past thirty years to find new data and compile improved measures of capital inputs and total output. Deane and Cole were among the first to use the newly developed method of national accounting, and to apply it to the case of Britain, 1750–1850. They succeeded in measuring economic production more accurately than had long been thought possible.[11] Following their path-breaking work, Crafts and Harley significantly altered our understanding of the First Industrial Revolution by reweighting the growth rates in the revolutionizing and non-revolutionizing sectors. The emerging picture of relatively slow output and productivity growth, accompanied by a rapid structural transformation, has become the new orthodoxy in the historiography of the Industrial Revolution.[12]

Rapid increases in capital input were long seen as almost synonymous with industrialization itself. Landes's *Prometheus Unbound* strongly suggested that the development and adoption of new techniques was central to the process of sustained economic expansion that began in the eighteenth century. Rostow's concept of 'take-off' was premised on the idea that investment ratios had to double rapidly, over a brief period, before growth could accelerate.[13] It was not before Feinstein's work on capital inputs that new estimates of capital formation finally became available.[14] Instead of the doubling over a brief period assumed by Rostow, he found more gradual change, with gross domestic investment rising by half over half a century.

---

[10] See F. Thomas Juster, 'Conceptual and Methodological Issues Involved in the Measurement of Time Use', in id. and Frank Stafford (eds.), *Time, Goods, and Well-Being* (Ann Arbor, Mich., 1985), table 13.1, p. 336.

[11] Phyllis Deane and W. A. Cole, *British Economic Growth, 1688–1959*, 2nd edn. (Cambridge, 1969).

[12] This is true despite some challenges: Maxine Berg and Pat Hudson, 'Rehabilitating the Industrial Revolution', *Economic History Review*, 45 (1992). Cf. the response by N. F. R. Crafts and Knick Harley, 'Output Growth and the British Industrial Revolution: A Restatement of the Crafts-Harley View', ibid.

[13] Walt Rostow, *The Stages of Economic Growth: A Non-Communist Manifesto* (Cambridge, 1960).

[14] Charles H. Feinstein, 'Capital Formation in Great Britain', in Peter Mathias and M. M. Postan (eds.), *The Cambridge Economic History of Europe, vii, The Industrial Economies: Capital, Labour, and Enterprise*, pt. 1 (Cambridge, 1978).

Compared to the massive effort directed at improving capital input and total output estimates, the issue of labour has been neglected. The main step forward was Wrigley and Schofield's *Population History of England*.[15] Based on much improved population figures, and combined with reasonable estimates of labour force participation, the size of the labour force can be inferred. However, changes in the size of the labour force will only proxy changes in labour input if working hours per worker remain constant. For the period 1750–1850 this has always been a questionable assumption. Crafts was quick to point out that changes in labour input could have very considerable implications both for the history of living standards as well as for productivity estimates.[16] Also, variations in standard working hours often have an impact on the running time of equipment. Therefore, even in more capital-intensive industries, the total amount of working time per employee and its organization remains of crucial importance.

It is part of conventional wisdom about the Industrial Revolution that workers toiled for longer hours in 1830 than in 1760.[17] Tranter suggests that annual hours may have gone up from 2,500 to 3,000.[18] Freudenberger and Cummins argued for change on a similar scale, with annual hours rising from 3,000 to 4,000 between the middle of the eighteenth and the middle of the nineteenth centuries. As the range of estimates makes clear, there is currently no reliable basis to infer working hours before the 1850s.[19] The verdict in the profession is unanimous. Mokyr observed that 'we simply do not know with any precision how many hours were worked in Britain before the Industrial Revolution, in either agricultural or non-agricultural occu-

---

[15] Edward Anthony Wrigley and Roger Schofield, *Population History of England, 1541–1871* (London, 1981).

[16] Crafts, *British Economic Growth*, 82, 110–11.

[17] Douglas Reid, 'The Decline of St. Monday, 1776–1876', *Past and Present*, 71 (1976); Asa Briggs, 'Work and Leisure in Industrial Society', *Past and Present*, 30 (1965), 98; Hermann Freudenberger, 'Das Arbeitsjahr', in I. Bog *et al.* (eds.), *Wirtschaftliche und soziale Strukturen im sækularen Wandel. Festschrift für Wilhelm Abel zum 70. Geburtstag, ii, The vorindustrielle Zeit: Außeragrarische Probleme* (Hanover, 1974), 314 ff.; Eric Jones, *Agriculture and the Industrial Revolution* (Oxford, 1974), 116–17; Sidney Pollard, 'Labour in Great Britain', in Mathias and Postan (eds.), *Cambridge Economic History of Europe, vii.* 162.

[18] Nick Tranter, 'The Labour Supply, 1780–1860', in R. Floud and D. McCloskey (eds.), *The Economic History of Britain since 1700* (Cambridge, 1981).

[19] Robin Matthews, Charles Feinstein, and John Odling-Smee, *British Economic Growth, 1856–1973* (Oxford, 1982); Angus Maddison, *Dynamic Forces in Capitalist Development* (Oxford, 1991).

pations.'[20] Crafts, referring to the Freudenberger and Cummins hypothesis that working hours increased sharply, observed that '[m]easurement of this supposition has never been adequately accomplished.'[21] Hatcher argued that '[i]t may never prove possible to measure with any pretence of accuracy the total amount of labour supplied in seventeenth- and eighteenth-century England, or to monitor precisely how it changed over time.'[22] The next section surveys the state of historical research, and explores the reasons why no reliable estimates currently exist.

The State of Historical Research

For the period after 1850, wage books and industrial censuses are the main sources used to estimate annual hours worked. In the postwar period, large-scale household and occupational surveys have also become available. For pre-industrial times, equivalent data that directly record either the number of hours worked per day or the number of days worked per year are scarce. The problem is also that information from one place or period has been portrayed as typical of 'pre-industrial work', when actual practices varied widely over time, between areas, and between individual occupations.

Some of the longest time-series on working hours are available for builders on selected sites. Using builders' account books, Thorold Rogers argued that the number of holidays on which all work effectively ceased in late medieval England was quite small, and that the eight-hour working day was common in fifteenth-century England.[23] With his calculation of total labour input, he takes the middle ground on the topic. Some estimates assume that as many as 115 days (including Sundays) were devoted to religious observance in some areas of medieval Europe—even if some of these were only half-holidays on which work stopped for a number of hours. Others have come to the conclusion that the total number of holidays impinging on the

---

[20] Joel Mokyr, 'The Industrial Revolution and the New Economic History', in id. (ed.), *The Economics of the Industrial Revolution* (London, 1985), 32.

[21] Crafts, *British Economic Growth*, 82.

[22] John Hatcher, 'Labour, Leisure and Economic Thought before the Nineteenth Century', *Past and Present*, 160 (1998), 85.

[23] Thorold Rogers, *A History of Prices and Wages* (London, 1884), 256.

working year was closer to zero.[24] E. H. Phelps-Brown and M. H. Brown add to these dissonant voices by claiming that in an average year labourers toiled for 10.5 hours per day, six days a week, while enjoying a total of 90 to 100 days off.[25] Simons found considerable regional differences: while a master of the works at Vale Royal Abbey in 1279–81 rested on only four feast days, builders at Eton college celebrated 42 holy days.[26] Woodward's analysis of builders in Northern England during the early modern period also uses a wide range of information on wage rates as well as employment records. Despite the very extensive use of his archival sources, his study only contains observations on the length of the working year for three carpenters. No evidence on the hours of work per day and per week is available.[27]

Hatcher's work on the coal industry has provided us with much valuable data on the number of days worked in the 1680s.[28] Unfortunately, little comparable evidence is available for other industries. One exception is agriculture, where some scattered records have been found. Recently, Clark and van der Werf have unearthed records on agricultural labourers in Derbyshire, Bedford, and Northampton.[29]

Because direct evidence is scarce and often unrepresentative, historians have often relied on literary material, regulations and government reports, occasional employment records, and demographic data. The amount of information they furnish about patterns of time-use in Britain during the eighteenth and early nineteenth centuries is, however, limited.

We owe the most prominent statement about time and work in industrializing Britain to E. P. Thompson, and it is convenient to take

---

[24] Sebastian de Grazia, *Of Time, Work and Leisure* (New York, 1962). Freudenberger ('Arbeitsjahr', 309 ff.) argues that holy days were not an important constraint themselves, and only mirrored the general scarcity of food which limited the number of hours which could be worked.

[25] Ernest Henry Phelps-Brown et al., 'Labour Hours: Hours of Work', *Encyclopedia of the Social Sciences*, 7 (New York, 1968), 487 ff. Wilhelm Abel, *Der Pauperismus in Deutschland* (Hanover, 1970) found that builders in Xanten, Germany, worked 250 days in 1356.

[26] T. S. Simons, 'Working-Days, Holidays, and Vacations in England in the Fourteenth and Fifteenth Centuries', unpub. Ph.D. thesis, University of Boulder at Colorado (1936), 62–9.

[27] Donald Woodward, *Men at Work: Labourers and Building Craftsmen in the Towns of Northern England, 1450–1750* (Cambridge, 1995), 131.

[28] Hatcher, 'Labour, Leisure and Economic Thought'.

[29] Gregory Clark and Y. van der Werf, 'Work in Progress? The Industrious Revolution', *Journal of Economic History*, 58 (1998).

his contribution as a starting-point. In his seminal article 'Time, Work-discipline, and Industrial Capitalism' he assembles evidence from bio-graphical and literary sources. The cornerstone of traditional work practices before the industrial revolution was 'St Monday', the habit of taking the first day of the week off to recover from the weekend. Thompson cites satirical rhymes describing the practice as well as the glaring indictments by moralists and producers.[30] The latter were par-ticularly scornful of the heavy drinking that often took place on 'St Monday'.[31] The slack often continued until Tuesday; it was during the later half of the week that hours (and intensity) of work mounted so that the agreed amount of produce could be handed over to the employer or customer. The weekly cycle was less pronounced for chil-dren and women, who pursued their tasks already at the beginning of the week, but who none the less shared in the rush towards its end.

Stark contrasts between idleness and grinding toil, according to Thompson, also characterized the working year. Agricultural employ-ment was strongly seasonal, and the long hours during the harvest or the ploughing season alternated with periods of low pressure at other times of the year. Further, cottagers and small farmers often exhibited a strong preference for structuring workloads in their own fashion. Production of agricultural goods or the collection of fuel for their own consumption often took up a substantial part of their time, to the annoyance of large landholders and agricultural improvers.[32] The essence of 'preindustrial' working patterns,[33] according to Thompson, was the ability of men and women to set their own pace; hence work was irregular, varied, and often interrupted by socializing and play.[34]

In this perspective, discipline and regularity were the result of a need to co-ordinate the schedules of workers.[35] Where one-handed

---

[30] E. P. Thompson, 'Time, Work-discipline, and Industrial Capitalism', *Past and Present*, 38 (1967), 74–6.

[31] Ibid., 76.

[32] Ibid., 77; Jane Humphries, 'Enclosures, Common Rights, and Women: The Proletarianization of Families in the Late Eighteenth and Early Nineteenth Centuries', *Journal of Economic History*, 50 (1990), 29.

[33] Thompson himself is sceptical about the use of the term, cf. Thompson, 'Time, Work-discipline, and Industrial Capitalism', 79–80.

[34] A similar view is advanced by Hans Medick, Peter Kriedte, and Jürgen Schlumbohm, *Industrialization before Industrialization: Rural Industry in the Genesis of Capitalism* (Cambridge, 1981), 44 ff.

[35] Thompson, 'Time, Work-discipline, and Industrial Capitalism', 70. The most impor-tant statement on time and social co-ordination of activities is by Norbert Elias, *Über die Zeit* (Frankfurt am Main, 1984).

clocks had once sufficed, watches with minute and second hands became widespread.[36] What transformed the self-determined and leisurely pace into the stringency of later schedules were the division of labour and the growing capital-intensity of manufacturing in the 'dark satanic mills'. These, according to Thompson, were necessary corollaries; but they do not explain why working hours per day in nineteenth-century cotton mills reached fourteen or even sixteen hours.[37] In the final analysis, exploitation by capital owners is the driving force for these excesses. Thompson describes the employers' attempts to regulate and exploit the workforce through the use of time as a disciplinary device. Watches were taken from workers when they entered the factory so that manipulations of 'official' clocks went unnoticed and the capitalist's time could rule.[38]

Thompson's views are subject to debate at two levels. First, there are doubts about the accuracy and reliability of his interpretations. Second, the empirical evidence itself is not fully convincing. The view that factory discipline was an alien regime imposed on unwilling workers is contentious. Hobsbawm had earlier opined that workers, whether preindustrial or not, 'did not dislike work'.[39] On a more substantial level, Clark has recently argued that factory workers preferred discipline and higher pay over alternative modes of employment. If one accepts the basic tenets of economic theory about individual decision-making, then, according to Clark, it can be argued that factory workers effectively hired capital owners to overcome their own bounded rationality—externally imposed discipline ensured that myopic time-preferences could not be exercised.[40] The image of preindustrial work presented by Thompson is also subject to debate. McKendrick has criticized the view that workers before the factory age worked short hours at a leisurely pace and without strict discipline as a 'prelapsarian myth of the golden past'. From his point of view,

---

[36] Thompson, 'Time, Work-discipline, and Industrial Capitalism', 56, 89; David Landes (*Revolution in Time. Clocks and the Making of the Modern World* (Cambridge, Mass., 1983), 97) argues that, depending on labour conditions, the spread of clocks could also have a liberating effect, separating workers' own time from that of their employers.

[37] Thompson, 'Time, Work-discipline, and Industrial Capitalism', 81–2.

[38] Ibid. Karl Marx also discussed the question at some length: Marx, *Kapital*, i. 249 ff.

[39] Eric Hobsbawm, 'Comment on Asa Briggs, "Work and Leisure in Industrial Society"', *Past and Present*, 30 (1965).

[40] Gregory Clark, 'Factory Discipline', *Journal of Economic History*, 54 (1994).

premodern labour schedules were as exacting as factory work, but not as well paid.[41]

More fundamentally, the factual foundation of Thompson's description appears to be very thin. Literary sources and the writings of Protestant moralists provide colourful images, to be sure. Yet it is difficult to assess how accurate they are. First, it is important to note that Thompson does not seem to describe practices from a clearly defined period in history. His latest source dates from 1903,[42] while the earliest example of premodern attitudes to work and time comes from Chaucer's *Canterbury Tales*.[43] Thompson himself seems to circumscribe the era in question when he argues that 'the years between 1300 and 1650 saw ... important changes in the apprehension of time', yet then goes on to cite some complaints about that pillar of 'pre-industrial' labour practices, 'St Monday', from as late as the 1870s.[44] Second, Thompson's reliance on literature and moral tracts means that he adduces very little direct evidence on labour practices.

Contemporary descriptions of rules, regulations, and practices contain numerous observations on working time. Rule, for example, provides a wealth of information on labour practices outside the mechanized factories. His results do not lead either to an outright rejection of Thompson's hypotheses or to their full corroboration. Rule finds little evidence of short hours before industrialization; for breeches makers, carpet weavers, coopers, saddlers, woolcombers, and shoemakers, fourteen-hour days (including mealtimes) were often prescribed. Even longer working days prevailed among pin makers, calico printers, bookbinders and glovers, with sixteen-hour days being the maximum recorded.[45] Rule's source for this information is, however, not the actual number of hours worked, but the labour regulations documented in Campbell's *London Tradesman*. The reliability of this information is questionable; as was argued above, to know that certain hours of work were prescribed is not the same as demonstrating that people actually worked. When the tailors argued for a reduction of their regular hours, they claimed that in 'most handicraft

---

[41] Neil McKendrick, 'Home Demand and Economic Growth: A New View of the Role of Women and Children in the Industrial Revolution', in id. (ed.), *Historical Perspectives: Essays in English Thought and Society* (London, 1974), 163.

[42] Thompson, 'Time, Work-discipline, and Industrial Capitalism', 75.   [43] Ibid., 56.

[44] Ibid., 74.

[45] John Rule, *The Experience of Labour in Eighteenth Century Industry* (London, 1981), 58 ff.

trades', twelve hours were common.[46] This is appreciably shorter than the median of fourteen hours recorded by Campbell.[47] If 1 to 1.5 hours for meals in each case are taken into account, the difference amounts to approximately 20 per cent—not exactly eloquent testimony to the reliability of either contemporary comments or prescriptive sources. In the case of tailors, administrative sources used by Rule show a trend towards shorter hours.

Both the length of the working day and its tendency to shorten in some cases seem to contradict Thompson; yet there is also some corroborating evidence. Hatcher found that workers at the Gatherick colliery toiled for 3.9 to 6.1 days per week in 1683–4.[48] Miners worked around six to eight hours a day on five to six days of the week during the later half of the eighteenth century. During the following fifty years, this gave way to twelve-hour shifts.[49] The driving force behind the intensification of work practices was, according to Rule, 'the demands of capitalising industry'.[50] Higher capital–labour ratios meant that the gains from longer working hours (through reduced capital costs per unit of output) increased sharply.[51] Rule also sides with Thompson when he describes the prevalent practice of 'St Monday' as well as the numerous holidays observed by workmen before the factory age. He does so on the basis of the same literary sources as well as biographical material.[52] The discussion of holy days also treats a longer period than the entire eighteenth century as a monolithic entity, juxtaposing complaints about the cost of absenteeism in 1802 with work practices of Cornish miners during the early decades of the eighteenth century.[53] By 1817, however, according to a contemporary observer, a turn towards a more diligent schedule in Cornwall could be observed:[54] 'Desperate wrestling matches, inhuman cockfights, pitched battles and riotous revellings are happily now of much rarer occurrence than heretofore; the spirit of sport has

---

[46] Id., *The Labouring Classes in Early Industrial England, 1750–1850* (London and New York, 1986), 132.

[47] R. Campbell, *The London Tradesman* (London, 1747), 331 ff. N = 182, mode = 14, mean = 13.86.

[48] Hatcher, 'Labour, Leisure and Economic Thought', 89. He also finds that the number of days worked by miners at Gatherick varied inversely with their skill level and wage per day.   [49] Rule, *Experience of Labour*, 59.

[50] Ibid. Interestingly, there is no positive association between capital requirements and working hours for the trades listed by Campbell. Regression analysis suggests a weakly negative relationship.

[51] For a more detailed discussion, see Ch. 4.   [52] Rule, *Experience of Labour*, 56.
[53] Ibid., 56–7; id., *Labouring Classes*, 217.   [54] Cit. id., *Labouring Classes*, 217–18.

evaporated, and that of industry has supplied its place . . . the constant pursuits of steady labour have nearly banished the traditional seasons of vulgar riot and dissipation.'

That individual areas experienced different patterns of labour and leisure is borne out by Hopkins' and Reid's work.[55] Reid shows on the basis of parliamentary papers and the child employment commissions' (CEC) reports that 'St Monday' prevailed in Birmingham until the 1860s. The evidence of contemporaries is, however, contradictory, as Reid himself notes. In parliamentary papers, information on the matter is scarce and scattered, and the CEC reports hardly relate to a representative sample of industry. The reason why the custom prevailed longer in Birmingham than appears to have been the case elsewhere is the late arrival of steam power—lower capital–labour ratios allowed for the persistence of premodern customs. Only during the 1860s, when large-scale manufacturing appeared and the Saturday half-holiday became popular, did 'St Monday' disappear. This is also the conclusion of Hopkins, who examined the Black Country and Birmingham.[56] In the Black Country, neither mines nor ironworks seem to have extended working hours during the first half of the nineteenth century. Also, the building trades in general show little tendency towards longer hours.[57]

In addition to these works using more traditional sources, there are four kinds of indirect evidence that have been used to infer hours worked. First, information on nutrient availability has been harnessed. Second, changes in wages and the wealth recorded in probate inventories have been combined to establish the direction of change. Third, comparisons between daily and annual wages have been used to calculate the length of the working year. Fourth, demographic data have been used as a source.

Freudenberger and Cummins suggest that the supply of nutrients before the 1750s was so severely constrained that workers could not have toiled for a large number of days in the year. Therefore, effort-saving customs like old holidays and 'St Monday' persisted. When the nutritional constraint was lifted, additional hours could be supplied.[58]

[55] Eric Hopkins, 'Working Hours and Conditions during the Industrial Revolution: A Re-Appraisal', *Economic History Review*, 35 (1982); Reid, 'Decline of St. Monday'.
[56] Hopkins, 'Working Hours', 62.
[57] Malcolm Thomis, *The Town Labourer and the Industrial Revolution* (n.p., 1974).
[58] Hermann Freudenberger and Gaylord Cummins, 'Health, Work and Leisure before the Industrial Revolution', *Explorations in Economic History*, 13 (1976), 8 ff.

Fogel has more recently presented estimates suggesting that the bottom 10 per cent of the population only had enough energy for six hours of light work per day.[59] Their work is, however, not without critics since precise, direct evidence on nutrients consumed is scarce.[60] Further, since a large part of digested calories is required for basal metabolism, small changes in estimates of mean calorie intake yield very different results for the amount of energy available for work. The evidence will be examined in more detail below. At this point, it is important to note that information on nutrient availability appears not much more precise than more direct forms of evidence on time-use.

DeVries has recently used evidence from probate inventories to argue that there is strong indirect evidence of a rise in hours worked over the early modern period. He finds that measures of individual wealth derived from probate inventories and real wage trends are largely contradictory during the early modern period—while the value of material goods that are passed on from one generation to the next rises rapidly, hourly pay shows no similar signs of improvement.[61] This puzzle can be solved if the growing number of hours worked more than offset the adverse effect of stagnant or falling wages, leading to the accumulation of ever greater material wealth.[62] DeVries's argument is of considerable elegance. What is lacking is a more direct confirmation that would allow us to accept the underlying assumptions of: (i) no major change in the durability of household goods, (ii) consistency and accuracy of recording practices, (iii) constant labour force participation, especially amongst women and children.

Clark and Van Der Werf compare the annual full employment income of male agricultural labourers with daily wage rates. Dividing the former by the latter yields an implied length of the annual working year. Their data suggest some intensification of the working year,

---

[59] Robert Fogel, 'New Sources and New Techniques for the Study of Secular Trends in Nutritional Status, Mortality, and the Process of Aging', *Historical Methods*, 26 (1993), 11–12.

[60] James C. Riley, 'Nutrition in Western Europe, 1750–1985: Melioration and Deterioration', Indiana University Population Institute for Research and Training, 92–7 (1991).

[61] Jan DeVries, 'Between Purchasing Power and the World of Goods: Understanding the Household Economy in Early Modern Europe', in Roy Porter and John Brewer (eds.), *Consumption and the World of Goods* (London, 1993). Jan DeVries, 'The Industrial Revolution and the Industrious Revolution', *Journal of Economic History*, 54 (1994).

[62] Id., 'Between Purchasing Power and the World of Goods', 107 ff.

with an increase in the total number of days worked from 257 before 1600 to around 300 by the nineteenth century.[63] However, more direct evidence from wage-books does not appear to support this conclusion.

Clark is also one of the few to have tackled the issue of work intensity, again using indirect evidence. Comparing day and piece rates, he derives estimates of how much work was actually performed per day. In the case of sawing, Clark argues that increases in hours per day worked or in work intensity are not apparent.[64] The same is true for threshing, where results vary by the type of grain. Finally, Clark and van der Werf also compare the wages of those paid with food provided by the employer with wage rates of those without food. At any given wage rate, food consumption appears high in the Middle Ages, which they interpret to suggest that the length of the annual working year must have been considerable.

For all the ingenuity of the methods used, some points need to be made. The underlying assumption is that (nearly identical) workers were compensated at wage rates reflecting their marginal productivities. This appears unlikely—even in a relatively developed early modern economy such as England. The most important reason why comparisons of day rates and annual wages are problematic concerns the nature of the Poor Law. Poor Law provisions were intended to keep a sizeable part of the labour force on the land, even if it was not needed throughout the year, so that it could be used for the harvest and other periods of peak labour demand.[65] With this form of welfare provision paid out of tax revenue, farmers could afford to offer temporary workers less than their marginal product during the harvest season. Consequently, some of the assumptions underlying the indirect approach of Clark and van der Werf may not hold, potentially undermining their results. This may be especially true after 1750. A similar argument appears to apply to their comparisons of wages with and without food. Clearly, the budget share of food varies with relative prices.[66] The dramatic fall in the price of many commodities should

---

[63] Clark and van der Werf, 'Work in Progress?', 837.

[64] Ibid., 836. Note that the midpoint estimate does suggest a prolonged and gradual rise in output per day, from about 70 feet sawed in 1275 to 110 in 1825 (fig. 3). It is because of the considerable standard errors that Clark and van der Werf reject the notion of a rise in work intensity. Yet to demonstrate that there was substantial variation around a rising mean is not necessarily the same as rejecting changes in average levels.

[65] George Boyer, *An Economic History of the English Poor Law* (Cambridge, 1990).

[66] Sara Horrell, 'Home Demand and British Industrialization', *Journal of Economic History*, 56 (1996).

have caused a shift in consumption behaviour away from food and towards other goods.[67] Consequently, the relatively high implied food consumption in the middle ages may not necessarily contradict the notion of an industrious revolution—it may simply reflect changes in relative prices.

Data from demographic sources have also been used to examine changes in time-use. Some authors have used the seasonality of conceptions to assess the extent to which holy days continued to be observed after the Reformation.[68] The results show a high degree of variation at the local level, but appear to suggest that most of the old festivals ceased to be observed from the seventeenth century onwards. The main limitation of this approach is the need to aggregate data over considerable periods (or areas) to reach acceptable numbers of observations, so that the precision of estimates based on this method is necessarily limited.

From a methodological point of view, recent work by Harrison is closely related. Harrison uses the timing of 'crowd events' to examine the length of the working week. The underlying assumption is that, if any one day of the week or the year shows a particularly high frequency of riots and other forms of crowd events, it was less likely to have been a day of regular work.[69] An imaginative attempt was also recently made by Reid, who examined the timing of weddings in urban England between 1791 and 1911.[70] Since the law stipulated that weddings had to take place between 8:00 and noon, he assumes that a weekday wedding involved time away from work for those concerned.[71] In Birmingham, for example, he finds that Monday weddings constituted a full 30–40 per cent in every decade between the 1790s and 1880s. He therefore concludes that 'St Monday' cannot have vanished before the last quarter of the nineteenth century. Reid

[67] John Komlos, *Nutrition and Economic Development in the Eighteenth Century Habsburg Monarchy* (Princeton, NJ, 1989).

[68] Peter Kitson, 'Festivity and Fertility in English Parish Life, 1558–1713', BA thesis, Cambridge (1999); Evelyn Lord, 'Fairs, Festivals and Fertility in Alkmaar, North Holland, 1650–1810', *Local Population Studies*, 42 (1989); Hans-Joachim Voth, 'Seasonality of Baptisms as a Source for Historical Time-Budget Analysis: Tracing the Disappearance of Holy Days in Early Modern England', *Historical Methods*, 27 (1994).

[69] Mark Harrison, 'The Ordering of the Urban Environment', *Past and Present*, 110 (1986).

[70] Douglas Reid, 'Weddings, Weekdays, Work and Leisure in Urban England, 1791–1911', *Past and Present*, 153 (1996). The method was first used by Jeremy Boulton, 'Economy of Time? Wedding Days and the Working Week in the Past', *Local Population Studies*, 43 (1989).   [71] Reid, 'Weddings, Weekdays, Work and Leisure', 141.

concedes that only the better-paid could afford to take a day off at the beginning of the week.[72] He then goes on to show that, none the less, large numbers visited Edgbaston Botanical Gardens on Mondays.[73]

The pattern of weddings seems to vary considerably by location—in Blackburn, for example, the timing of weddings in the 1850s already begins to suggest that Monday may have been a day of regular work. Also, the timing of other events such as funerals and baptisms lends only limited support to the notion that weddings are a consistent indicator of work practices.[74] The underlying assumption, that weddings would be much more likely to occur on days of regular rest, is also questionable. Weddings are sufficiently rare an event for people to make special arrangements. Also, it is not clear to what extent parishioners were free to choose, and how much of the variation is simply a reflection of chaplains' preferences.[75] The credibility of the method is further undermined by a large and sudden increase in the number of weddings taking place on Thursdays (after 1850)—there is no reason to think that workers were suddenly beginning to take a day off in the middle of the week.

Since E. P. Thompson's pathbreaking study, numerous historians have tried to fill in the details in his broad panorama of changes in the use of time over the last 400 years. Much effort has been directed at collecting more reliable evidence of actual patterns of work and leisure, and a wide range of ingenious methods have been devised to compensate for lacunae in the more traditional sources.

What emerges from the historical studies surveyed in this section is a high degree of divergence both at the local level and for different occupations. Evidence on trends over time, using the same source for the same location, is rare. Also, occasional comments in reports of the child employment commission are anything but a reliable indicator of actual time-use in most professions. The same is true of the minute fraction of the population visiting pleasure gardens or satirical rhymes examined by Thompson.[76] Owing to the limitations of the sources, the evidence is partial, skewed, perhaps even misleading. Lack of

[72] Reid, 'Decline of St. Monday', 78 ff.
[73] We do not know how many of the up to 41,639 visitors per year (or 801 on an average Monday, less than 1 per cent of the population) came from the working classes.
[74] Cf. Reid, 'Weddings, Weekdays, Work and Leisure', figs. 2 and 3, pp. 148–9.
[75] Note that the obvious alternative to a Monday wedding is on Sunday, when clerics will be busy for a variety of other reasons.
[76] Thompson, 'Time, Work-discipline, and Industrial Capitalism', 81.

representativeness is only matched by the difficulty with which these sources can be interpreted. Just as there was no single 'industrial work pattern', constructing typical preindustrial labour practices from a handful of sources is not possible. This is not say, however, that aggregate measures cannot be compiled. What is needed is a new method that yields direct evidence on patterns of labour and leisure among the population at large, and on a broad empirical basis. This data should be available on a consistent basis, from the same source, and should be collected for more than one location.

2
Method

Did England work any harder during the Industrial Revolution? Marx said so, and so did E. P. Thompson, but we had no way of knowing. Literary sources are difficult to interpret, wage books are few and hardly representative, and clergymen writing about the sloth of their flock did little to validate their complaints. Instead of using these problematic sources, more than 2,800 men and women from eighteenth- and early nineteenth-century England give evidence in this study. They come from all strata of society and all age groups, and appear as witnesses before the Old Bailey to answer a simple question: 'What were you doing at the time of the crime?' These testimonies provide snapshots of everyday life—preserved by the scribes in the Old Bailey courtroom who took down verbatim reports of the proceedings in shorthand, and in the depositions taken before the Justices of the Peace in the North of England.

Uncovering Time-use in the Past

Before the courtroom material can be used, we need to establish how time-budget data should be collected under ideal circumstances. I first describe how modern-day sociologists collect information on time-use, and argue that courtroom material can be used as a substitute where more direct information is not available. Next, the time-use evidence available in the *Old Bailey Sessions Papers* and in the *Northern Assize Depositions* is described along with the judicial process which generated these sources. Finally, a systematic comparison of witnesses' accounts and sociological surveys is made.

Modern Time-budget Studies

How is time spent? Ideally, we would want to observe directly the activities of every member of the group we are interested in (say, the population of the United States) for twenty-four hours a day, on all days of the year. For a number of reasons, this is neither practical nor economical. First of all, the physical presence of an observer would hardly leave the timing and duration of all activities unchanged—some ways of spending time may well be avoided altogether. Second, the costs would very soon reach prohibitive levels—both because all days of the year and all members of the group under consideration are included in the study. Time-budget projects have therefore used a variety of different techniques that avoid these two pitfalls.

The most common form of data collection used today involves diaries. These are either left with the respondent, to be filled in at certain times of the day, or interviewers visit the study subjects, asking them to recall the whole sequence of events on the previous day.[1] Often, both primary and secondary activities, occurring at the same time, are recorded. Validity is generally high with the exception of short telephone calls, which tend to be underreported. The study design can also be differentiated according to the format in which the data are collected. Free-form diaries allow the collection of time-use information in natural language. Different forms of time-use are allocated to specific categories by the researchers themselves. Alternatively, booklets listing activities and their respective codes are used. The disadvantage is that respondents are constrained in the activities they can record by what their lists contain—there will be a bias in favour of excessive uniformity.

An alternative way of collecting time-use data is the use of electronic pagers.[2] These are programmed to sound a beep at random hours, thirty to forty times per day. The study subject is asked to record his or her primary and secondary activity at this time. The advantage of this technique is that there is virtually no delay between the activity and the act of recording—the weaknesses of human memory have the smallest possible consequence. Unfortunately, respondents are often reluctant to carry the beeping device when they leave their homes. Some outdoor activities are therefore systematically underrecorded, such as shopping and social visits.

A third technique combines some of the features of the diary and the electronic pager method.[3] An interviewer will visit the household,

[1] F. Thomas Juster, 'The Validity and Quality of Time Use Estimates Obtained from Recall Diaries', in id. and Frank Stafford (eds.), *Time, Goods, and Well-Being* (Ann Arbor, Mich., 1985), 28 ff.

[2] James Robinson, 'The Validity and Reliability of Diaries versus Alternative Time Use Measures', in Juster and Stafford, *Time, Goods, and Well-Being*, 34–5.

[3] Ibid., 38 ff.

but instead of trying to reconstruct the entire day, one activity after another, he will enquire about the respondents' activities at random hours of the previous day. Random hour recall studies have the advantage that none of the (often enervating) work has to be performed by study subjects, which may lead to inaccuracies in the case of self-reporting diaries. Response rates tend to be high because of face-to-face contact with the interviewer. Also, because there is a time-lag between the activity reported and the question of the interviewer, daily schedules are not as easily upset as with the paging device—outdoor activities and telephone calls, for example, will be reported with greater accuracy.

Anthropologists often use a modified version of the random hour recall method.[4] Since their study subjects rarely carry watches, interviews are not feasible. They therefore visit individuals at random hours during the day and record their activities. The obvious problem is, of course, that the observer's presence may interfere with normal schedules. Also, random visits are more often successful (in encountering the respondent) if he or she is at home, rather than engaged in outdoor activities.

Finally, there have been experiments in which individuals were invited to report their estimates of how many hours they spend in certain activities. These 'stylized' answers are typically the result of a question along the lines of 'How many hours do you normally spend on activity x?'. The period for which these estimates have to be made can vary from the previous day to the whole year. Typically, respondents come from small and fairly homogenous groups—e.g., course participants at a particular college. The main problem is that a large fraction of total waking time is spent on very short activities which can hardly be recalled. This difficulty is most acute if the task performed is neither repeated on a daily basis nor part of market-based transactions (i.e., paid work).

It is not easy to assess the relative efficacy of the different models. Some theoretical and practical limitations have already been described. Which method should be trusted when we are faced with sharply different results? In the case of 'stylized' estimates, a simple check of consistency can be performed by adding all the duration

---

[4] Typical studies are Allen Johnson, 'Time Allocation in a Machiguenga Community', *Ethnology*, 14 (1975); Charles Erasmus, 'Work Patterns in a Mayo Village', *American Anthropologist*, 57 (1955).

estimates of all activities. If the sum differs from twenty-four, there is direct evidence against this method. In most studies, many more than twenty-four hours of activity are claimed per day, casting strong doubt on this study design. The length of the recall period appears to be the main cause of these disappointing results. If time-use during the last week is examined, regular activities will dominate. These tend to be overreported since remembering them is relatively simple. Over the course of a year, however, irregular events such as house repairs, etc. will be remembered, but underestimated in length.[5] Working hours are frequently reported quite accurately.[6]

In most cases, validity tests are more complicated. Since there is no objective standard with which results can be compared, the largest possible number of study designs is administered to the same group, ideally on the same day. All the methods are then compared with each other. The 'stylized' time-use approach normally leads to answers that differ very substantially from all the other techniques. It is therefore commonly regarded as one of the least reliable.[7] For the diary, pager, and random hour recall method, the estimates normally agree quite closely. Such divergences as exist are often matched against those that might be expected from a certain technique (e.g., the underreporting of outdoor activities with the pager). The absence of such differences is regarded as a sign of high-quality data. The detailed experiments conducted as part of the 1975–6 US time-use study cannot be reviewed here in full. The final result, however, is unambiguous:

> The overall conclusion is that the diary method dominates, with the only serious bias being an underreporting of telephone conversation time. The pager will underreport activities taking place outside the home, the stylized method will overreport virtually everything, although differentially, and the random hour is just as good as the diary—probably better—but is much more costly. *With an unlimited budget, one would pick the random-hour method; budget limitations argue for the diary.*[8]

Recently, it has been suggested that the number of activities reported for any given day is also a good indicator of response quality—all else being equal, the respondent was able to provide more information.[9]

---

[5] Juster and Stafford, 'The Allocation of Time: Empirical Findings, Behavioral Models, and Problems of Measurement', *Journal of Economic Literature*, 29 (1991), 484.

[6] Juster and Stafford go as far as to claim that labour time estimates derived from diaries are more accurate than those in the US Current Population Survey, etc. (ibid., 486).

[7] Ibid., 484 ff.   [8] Ibid., 484 (my italics).

[9] Robinson, 'Validity and Reliability of Diaries'.

The general conclusion reported above is reinforced if such experiments are undertaken—the random hour recall and the diary method are superior to the other alternatives.[10]

On a purely theoretical level, it might be expected that the social desirability of certain activities will influence responses—individuals normally seek to portray themselves as upright and virtuous citizens. Empirical studies found that voting behaviour and voluntary work are often overreported; television viewing, however, which may be seen as a socially undesirable activity, is not underreported.[11] No systematic bias therefore exists, but some activities (e.g., sex) are excluded from questionnaires to avoid embarrassment.

Studies using any one of these techniques are typically administered to a random sample of the population. Very often, it is impossible to select a probability sample of days during the year since meeting an interviewer on the next day is rarely convenient for respondents. In the United States, where mobility is high, such a study has not been undertaken;[12] in other countries, markedly lower response rates had to be countenanced. An alternative to a non-random day approach and low response rates is longer recall periods. Consequently, extensive experiments have been conducted to assess how the quality of replies is associated with the time elapsing between event and interview. Patterns for events on weekdays and on the weekend differ sharply. During the week, between twenty-four and forty-eight hours after the day under consideration, there is a marked decline in response quality, with between 10 and 20 per cent fewer activities being reported. Thereafter, there is no clear evidence of further deterioration; surprisingly, the data show a weak recovery after four to seven days (Fig. 2.1). For Friday, Saturday, and Sunday, there is no association between the length of recall period and the number of activities reported.[13] An interesting experiment concerns memory

[10] Juster ('Conceptual and Methodological Issues Involved in the Measurement of Time Use', in id. and Stafford, *Time, Goods, and Well-Being*) uses the number of activities reported as an indicator of response quality.

[11] C. Weiss, 'Validity of Welfare Mothers' Interview Responses', *Public Opinion Quarterly*, 32 (1968); C. Allen, 'Photographing the TV Audience', *Journal of Advertising Research*, 8 (1968).

[12] Juster, 'Response Errors in the Measurement of Time Use', *Journal of the American Statistical Association*, 81 (1986), 390. On the probable consequences of using 'convenience' samples of days see G. Kalton, 'Sample Design Issues in Time Diary Studies', in Juster and Stafford, *Time, Goods, and Well-Being*, 93 ff.

[13] Juster, 'Response Errors in the Measurement of Time Use', table 1, pp. 394–5. Some earlier authors are more sceptical. Cf. Kalton, 'Sample Design Issues', 95.

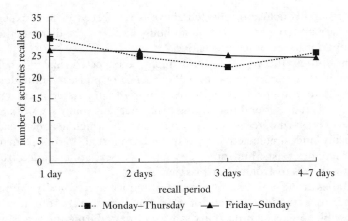

FIGURE 2.1. *Response quality and recall period*

decay and the context of events. Juster uses data on the activity patterns of couples. Each partner was asked to report at various times of the day if the other partner was present. Obviously, with perfect memory, the two reports should be identical. This is only the case for about 80 per cent of all activities. On average, data from later hours of the day are more reliable. His interpretation is as follows:

> match rates would be expected to be relatively low early in the day, and to improve throughout the day as the cumulative probability of a salient event increased. Thus the match rate data are consistent with two propositions: that recall diaries get to be pretty reliable once a salient event has occurred that provides a stimulus to respondents' memory; and second, that if there are enough salient events in a day there will not be very much diary time characterized by unacceptably large memory errors.[14]

This brief review of sociological techniques suggests a few key factors that are essential in collecting reliable time-use data:

1. Of all the methods reviewed, random hour recall has the most advantageous characteristics, but it is also more costly.
2. A probability sample of the entire population should be collected.
3. Response rates ought to be as high as possible.
4. A salient event during the day will slow memory decay, leading to much improved data quality.

[14] Juster, 'Validity and Quality of Time Use Estimates', 82.

5. Ideally, the interviewer should not be present at the time when activities are carried out. Self-reporting by individuals that are conscious of the time of the day (alone or with an interviewer) is to be preferred to direct observation.
6. The days of the year included in the study ought to be chosen on a random basis.
7. On weekdays, the delay between event and interview should be either shorter than 24 hours or longer than 4 days. The length of the interval between an event and the interview has no appreciable effect on the weekend.
8. A crucial determinant of data quality is the use of 'intensive and obtrusive methods'.[15]

Witnesses' Accounts—A Substitute

It is easy to see why none of the methods described above is suitable for historical studies. The individuals that we are interested in cannot be interviewed or asked to complete detailed time-use diaries—they happen to be dead.[16] We could alternatively use the few conventional diaries that have survived. During the eighteenth century, for example, the famous diaries of James Boswell would recommend themselves. By the standards of modern studies, such documents would hardly be adequate. First of all, those that kept a diary are likely to have been a very small section of the population. There is also no reason to suppose that this small group even vaguely resembles a random sample—there will be a strong bias in favour of the upper strata of society. There are few papers from the lower classes—12 of the 303 autobiographical works of the working classes indexed by Burnett *et al.* refer to the period before 1800, and the majority of papers contain little information about time use.[17] Most narrative accounts by observers are also of limited value; their interest in time-use is often selective and marred by a strong moralistic undertone.

What is needed are a data source and a reliable technique that give an impression of everyday patterns of time-use amongst all classes. Ideally, all the criteria enumerated above should be fulfilled. Witnesses' accounts, while less than ideal, are remarkably similar to the information gathered by sociologists and anthropologists. In the course of a trial, witnesses are called for different reasons. They are

[15] Robinson, 'Validity and Reliability of Diaries', 44.
[16] The only exception is contemporary history, where survivors could be interviewed. They would have to recall rather distant events.
[17] John Burnett, David Vincent, and David Mayall, *The Autobiography of the Working Class: An Annotated, Critical Bibliography* (Brighton, 1989).

often asked to testify to the character of a suspect. Witnesses also describe details of the crime, identify perpetrators, or testify to the place and time where it occurred. In these latter cases, they are normally asked to recall their observations on a particular day and at a particular time in the past. For testimonials to be credible, witnesses' accounts have to fulfil a number of criteria. First, they are normally expected to be 'of good character'—although fellow criminals occasionally come forward as well. Second, the testimonial should be consistent. Cross-examinations are often conducted to establish if a witness begins to contradict earlier statements. Third, witnesses often establish credibility by giving details about their activities at the time of the crime. In a typical example, the witness, Martha Eaton, sells candles to a murderess, who enters her shop sullied with blood.[18] The information on her activity is not exactly pertinent to the accusation ('did Susannah Broom murder her husband?'). For the judicial process, the relevant detail is that the shopkeeper saw Susannah Broom, 'her arms and face ... all over blood'. Yet to convince the judge and the jury that she saw this important detail, the witness furnishes extensive descriptions of the context. She explains how she came to have contact with the murderess at a particular time and place—the witness was in her shop, waiting for customers. One of them was Susannah Broom, who asked for a candle at 3:00. Often, other incidental information ('we are normally very busy at this time') will also be provided to enrich the context—the more detailed the recollection of a witness, the more credible the statement. Thus, the criterion that sociologists use to compare the effectiveness of modern techniques—the number of activities that can be remembered—was also likely to impress a jury.

We are interested in the incidental information on time-use provided by witnesses. How does this source compare with modern techniques? There is some similarity with the diary method. Since extensive details enhance a witness's credibility, sequences of events are occasionally described. As is the case with the diary method, the 'interview' is conducted *post factum*. However, the time between the event and its recording is often considerably longer than in modern studies. Also, sequences are almost never reported for an entire day. In the rare cases where two or three consecutive activities are described, they seldom span more than a few hours. The pager method is more

---

[18] Old Bailey Sessions Papers, Case No. 2, 1739.

similar to the information provided in witnesses' accounts. Both the pager and crime are likely to interrupt the respondent's schedule at unforeseen times of the day—even if the incidence of crime is not entirely random. In modern time-budget studies, the activity one was engaged in will be written down immediately (a pad is often attached to the beeping device itself).[19] This is obviously not true in the case of crime. Quite substantial periods of time may pass between an activity and its recording in court. Further, the pager is carried by one person, whose time-use can be examined at thirty to forty different times of the day. Witnesses almost never report on more than one crime on a single day. 'Stylized' time-budgets also bear some similarity to some of the information in court records. Bystanders and others giving testimony occasionally give estimates of the duration of their activities before or after the crime. The parallel is at best a loose one since they, in contrast to present-day study subjects, make no attempt to describe a 'typical day'. Combined with the fact that even modern studies based on 'stylized' time-use are highly inaccurate, this information is the least interesting for historical time-budget analysis.

Random hour recall is the modern technique that resembles witnesses' accounts most—respondents are asked to remember their activities at a certain hour on the day of the experiment.[20] Witnesses are also asked about what they were doing at a specific time—the time of the crime. Just as the random hour chosen by the interviewer, crime occurs at all times of the day. Should certain times of the day be overrepresented, this can easily be remedied by reweighting. The great similarity of the random hour recall method and testimonials in court is particularly fortunate since it is this method that is clearly preferred in modern studies. Witnesses' accounts also have one advantage over present-day studies: all the days of the year are likely to be included. Further, criminals may be biased samples of a population, but the same is less obvious in the case of witnesses, who just happen to be passing by the scene of a crime.[21]

---

[19] Robinson, 'Validity and Reliability of Diaries', 34–5.

[20] The similarity to the anthropologists' method of random spot visits is also great. However, with this technique, it is an outsider who observes activities, and does so without any time lag between the event and its recording. The method is described in Johnson, 'Time Allocation'.

[21] There are, of course, also cases where neighbours act as witnesses, or where the criminal visits a place afterwards and is observed there (e.g., Susannah Bloom). Distinguishing between witnesses and victims in the Old Bailey Sessions Papers is not always a simple matter.

Testimony in court also fulfils one of the criteria for successful modern time-budget studies: the questions in court—particularly during cross-examinations—are likely to be an 'intensive and obtrusive method'[22] for gathering data. Witnesses' accounts may also be superior in another way. Response rates in even the most sophisticated studies today are often disappointing (60–75 per cent).[23] In a 1966 time-budget study of forty-four American cities, for example, more than 25 per cent of all individuals in the study failed to return their diaries.[24] This is owing to the onerous task of completing diaries, to high mobility, and to lack of incentives. None of these constraining factors affects witnesses' accounts. While coming to court may be time-consuming, there are normally strong penalties for witnesses who are summoned but fail to appear. The method of enquiry during the judicial hearing provides incentives not to remain silent.

Those who do not come forward, either as witnesses or as respondents in modern studies, may pose a serious threat to the validity of time-budget data—there are good *a priori* reasons to believe that the section of the population that fails to participate has patterns of time-use that differ from the rest of the population. Busy people, for example, may be significantly less likely to fill in their questionnaires.[25] The few witnessing a crime, but not willing to come forward to testify what they have seen, may do so for a variety of reasons. The most obvious one— and the one most detrimental to the efficacy of our technique—is (active or passive) participation in the crime. Criminals come from a subgroup of the population that cannot be assumed to have an average pattern of time-use. In historical as in contemporary time-budget studies, it will therefore be likely that non-respondents have markedly different activity patterns from the responding part of the population. The crucial question then is whether the remaining part of the population that is willing to speak in court is a biased sample owing to the 'selection procedure'. Note, however, that patterns of time-use are coded together with the occupation of the witness. It is therefore not

---

[22] Johnson, 'Time Allocation', 44.
[23] Cf., for example, the rates for Belgium, West Germany, and the US: Alexander Szalai (ed.), *The Use of Time* (The Hague, 1972), 514, 518, 525.
[24] Ibid., statistical app., 525.
[25] Experimentation with less onerous forms of data-collection, however, seems to suggest that the overall deviation between true population mean and sample result is—at least for most activities—rather limited. Jay Gershuny, 'The Time Economy or the Economy of Time: An Essay on the Interdependence of Living and Working Conditions', unpub. ms, Nuffield College, Oxford (1991), ch. 5.

necessary that the average time-use of all witnesses closely resembles the time-budget for society as a whole. For the purposes of the study presented here, it suffices if we can assume that within each profession, those being called before the judges do not have widely different activity patterns. Of course, those trying to evade the duties and burden of a witness may—as in the case of sociological studies—be the more active part of the population.

The issue of social desirability is more difficult. As witnesses are naturally inclined to surround themselves with an aura of respectability, they may lie. The empirical section discusses some of the evidence for and against such a presumption. Outright lies are also to be expected if they fear—rightly or wrongly—that they might be charged with complicity. Cross-examinations can be relied on to identify the most blatant distortions of the truth.

Possibly the biggest single shortcoming of our source is that the age of a witness is rarely recorded in the Old Bailey Sessions Papers and in the Northern Assize Depositions. The scribe only noted a person's age in those cases where either the very young or the very old were called upon to give evidence. Since all modern studies clearly show that activity patterns vary with age, the whole data set lacks one important component. Information on the age of witnesses becomes more easily available after 1800, but it is impossible to differentiate between actual changes in time-use and changes arising from shifts in the age distribution of the sample. The very old and very young are almost always identified, since their age is an important factor in assessing their reliability as witnesses. Elderly persons were often asked about their age and place of birth, whereas youngsters had to answer questions like: 'Do you know what will become of you if you swear that which is not true?'.[26] The correct answer to such a question is, 'I shall go to the naughty man.' It is therefore likely that other witnesses were regarded as being of normal working age. The occupation of witnesses often gives at least a rough guide to their age—it is inherently unlikely that apprentices are fifty years old. Hence, much of the variation that one would wish to capture through the use of age as an explanatory variable can actually be explained through the 'profession' category. Only large-scale shifts in the age composition within one profession are likely to influence the results significantly.

[26] A variant of this is the common question 'What is the nature of an oath?' (not to tell any lies is the expected answer). See Old Bailey Sessions Papers, Case No. 777, 1801.

Another key factor of success established by experiments with modern data is that the recall period should be either shorter than one day or longer than four days for events that occurred during the week. Lags of less than a week are not rare when judicial records are used, but they do not constitute the majority of cases. Witnesses may be questioned immediately after the crime, but since most of the evidence is normally generated in the courtroom, the delay may be quite long. It is, however, not clear how serious this problem is. First, the rapid decline noted in Figure 2.1 cannot persist for long. Even if the average decay of recall quality between the first and the seventh day (for weekday events) is used, all memories would fade in two months.[27] This is clearly an overestimate—as the recovery of scores after four to seven days demonstrates, these results should not be used for linear extrapolations. Second, human psychology also suggests that a respondent's activities at the time of the crime may be more easily remembered than those that are unconnected with any spectacular event. People are known to economize on cognitive effort. In experiments, it is common to find that the frequency of events is often inferred by the ease with which we can recall them. Suicides in New York are more frequent than murders, but because the latter are much more 'sensational' events, which can be recalled more easily, their frequency will be grossly overestimated.[28] People are notoriously inaccurate when it comes to remembering small and menial activities. Also, the reduction in data quality is normally much more rapid for weekdays, where routine prevails.[29] Temporal proximity of 'unimportant activities' to an important occurrence is very likely to change this, as the data on match rates demonstrate. There are therefore good reasons to think that the decay in data quality will slow down for longer intervals, and that witnesses' accounts may be less affected because of the spectacular context in which the activities have become relevant. The empirical section of this book will discuss the actual length of the recall period, and the likely effects on data quality.

On the basis of these considerations, witnesses' accounts recommend themselves as a source that is remarkably similar to modern ones. Judicial records may not be perfect substitutes, but for every shortcoming there is one aspect that should be more accessible

[27] On the basis of the weekend results, this would occur after 100 days.
[28] Amos Tversky and Daniel Kahneman, 'Judgement under Uncertainty: Heuristics and Biases', *Science*, 185 (1974).
[29] See also Juster, 'Validity and Quality of Time Use Estimates', 24.

through witnesses' accounts than through any of the modern methods. The type of time-use information that can be inferred is, however, markedly different.

In most time-use studies, estimates of duration are of central importance. We want to know how many hours the average Englishman works, or if women enjoy more leisure than men. Diaries, pagers, 'stylized estimates', and random hour recall all readily provide such results. In the case of witnesses' accounts, however, this would only be true if the hours of the day, the days of the year, and the witnesses before the court were all 'randomly selected' by the incidence of crime. Where they are not, we need to reweight observations according to the degree of over- or undersampling in our dataset. An alternative route measures the timing of events. If the average starting and stopping of work can be ascertained, the duration of work can be inferred. In this case, the oversampling of certain hours would be irrelevant. Similarly, we may want to know if a certain day of the year was generally used for leisure. This day will then not have to register as many observations as all the other days—we can answer our question if a high proportion of people testifying to their activities on a certain day claim to have been engaged in recreational activities. If such analyses are carried out, only one of the three possible sources of bias is still relevant—the one relating to the witnesses themselves. In the empirical section, all these methods will be used.

Crime and the Courts

Few crimes during the eighteenth century left any trace in historical records. It has been estimated that less than one in ten offences led to any court action; there are therefore strict limits to what can and cannot be said about the pattern of crime.[30] The vast majority of crimes during the eighteenth century was committed against property.[31] Violent crime was less frequent, and few cases of murder or assault

[30] William Cornish and Geoffrey Clark, *Law and Society in England, 1750–1950* (London, 1989), 548. A similar conclusion is presented by Joanna Innes and John Styles, 'The Crime Wave: Crime and Criminal Justice in Eighteenth-Century England', in Adrian Wilson (ed.), *Rethinking Social History. English Society and its Interpretation* (Manchester, 1993), 212.

[31] George Rudé, *Crime and Victim. Crime and Society in Early Nineteenth-century England* (Oxford, 1985), 79; John Maurice Beattie, 'The Pattern of Crime in England, 1660–1800', *Past and Present*, 62 (1974), 73 ff. Local variation was pronounced. Sussex showed a much larger proportion of property crime than Surrey, and urban Surrey in particular. See Beattie, 'Pattern of Crime in England, 1660–1800', graph 1, pp. 68–9, graphs 2–4, pp. 75–7.

were associated with property crimes.[32] Public disturbances, ranging from unlawful gathering to riots, were even less frequent. Instead of distinguishing between crimes against property and people, crime can be classified as either (a) acquisitive, (b) social, or (c) protest crime.[33] In London in the early nineteenth century, according to Rudé, the bulk of crime fell into the 'survival' category.[34]

Contemporaries clearly felt that there were large variations, often over very short periods of time, in unlawfulness. The early 1750s, for example, saw a panic because of the increase in the number of crimes.[35] Around 1800 many Londoners again felt that they were faced with a crime wave.[36] This brings us to the relationship between economic conditions and the level of crime. Over the past decades, a number of researchers have used time-series on the number of indictments, and have tried to link them to social and economic change. Beattie summed up the results of his investigation of crime in Sussex and Surrey as follows: 'The evidence of the indictments seems to point clearly to this conclusion: that crimes against property in the eighteenth century arose primarily from problems of employment, wages and prices.'[37] In particular, he finds some striking correlations between the number of crimes and the Schumpeter-Gilboy price index.[38] Hay has argued a similar case for Staffordshire. There, the effect of price movements was often amplified by the prime factor influencing crime levels—the effect of war on employment levels. Since in England, as Chalmers put it, the 'sword had not been put into *useful* hands',[39] wars emptied the streets and highways of Britain of the most dangerous elements. The return to peace, and the discharge of these individuals, led to a wave of crime, hysteria, and judicial harshness.[40]

Such analysis of the incidence of indictments is not without critics. Because few crimes were prosecuted, even small changes in the ratio of committed to indicted crimes may lead to large changes in absolute numbers. Innes and Styles, in particular, have pointed out that the small number of indictments during wartime may be a statistical illu-

---

[32] Cornish and Clark, *Law and Society in England, 1750–1950*, 548.
[33] Rudé, *Crime and Victim*, 78.   [34] Ibid., table 2.3, pp. 29, 80.
[35] Cornish and Clark, *Law and Society in England, 1750–1950*, 549.
[36] Beattie, 'Pattern of Crime in England, 1660–1800', 47.
[37] Ibid., 95.   [38] Ibid., graphs 6, 7, 8, pp. 89–91.
[39] Cit. T. S. Ashton, *Economic Fluctuations in England, 1700–1800* (Oxford, 1959), 52 (his italics).
[40] Douglas Hay, 'War, Dearth and Theft in the Eighteenth Century', *Past and Present*, 95 (1982), 124 ff.; Cornish and Clark, *Law and Society in England, 1750–1950*, 549.

sion.[41] They demonstrate that, in wartime, magistrates often offered apprehended suspects the possibility of joining the armed forces. Such a case would then not lead to an indictment. The demands of war may well have reduced the number of indictments, but the underlying cause might have been very different from the one proposed by Hay and Beattie. Similarly, the buying-off of prosecutors seems to have been common. Years of high prices would then only have led to a lower ability of some suspects to appease their prosecutors; instead of removing restraint, lean years reduced the barriers to justice running its course.[42]

Policing and Prosecution

Before the establishment of metropolitan police forces after 1829,[43] the tasks of detection and policing were discharged in a number of ways. England had no equivalent to the French system of career officials, employed by the state and charged with law enforcement. In general, parishes had to bear responsibility for policing by electing a parish constable. He was supervised by the local Justices of the Peace.[44] In theory, therefore, constables should have been the first contact of victims and the principal agent enforcing the law at a local level. By the eighteenth century, however, this was clearly no longer the case.[45] In urban areas, where the duties of public office were particularly demanding, many parishioners preferred to pay a fine. In the larger cities, the system was complemented by parish beadles and night watchmen. Beadles were paid employees who had to carry out a whole range of duties—acting as a town crier, ensuring orderly church services, helping in the administration of the poor law, and supporting the parish constable.[46] During the eighteenth century, this system was supplemented by parish watchmen. Theoretically, these should have been inhabitants of a parish. Yet actual duty had become a rarity by this time. It became customary for watchmen to be hired by the beadle or constable with money paid by parishioners in lieu of watch

---

[41] Innes and Styles, 'Crime Wave', 213.   [42] Ibid., 214.

[43] Douglas Hay and Francis Snyder (eds.), *Policing and Prosecution in Britain, 1750–1850* (Oxford, 1989), 9.

[44] Cornish and Clark, *Law and Society in England, 1750–1950*, 551.

[45] Cf. the examples of neglect given by Leon Radzinowicz, *History of English Criminal Law and its Administration from 1750*, ii (London, 1956), 160 ff.

[46] John Tobias, *Crime and Police in England, 1700–1900* (Dublin, 1979), 32–3.

duties. A new system came into existence by local initiative. In the parish of St George's, Westminster, the vestry decided in 1735 that a system of local taxation was to be introduced to pay for regular night watchmen. Although many historians are sceptical about the effectiveness of this system, there is some indication that it improved the level of safety.[47] In 1737 the new approach was adopted by the City of London and extended to provide a day watch.[48]

In the metropolis surrounding the City, some parishes copied St George's system as well. Since the days of Thomas de Veil at least, the Bow Street office was even more important. De Veil, one of the few incorruptible judges of his day, acted as the Court Justice, a magistrate funded by the Crown.[49] His successors, Henry Fielding and his brother John, continued to organize a highly successful police body, funded directly by the government and known as the 'Bow Street Runners'. By the end of the eighteenth century the old system of 'trading justices' in Middlesex and Westminster was regarded as anachronistic. An Act of Parliament in 1792 introduced a number of Bow Street style police offices throughout the metropolitan area;[50] stipendiary magistrates became common.[51]

Prior to Peel's reform, prosecution was most often left to the victims of the crime or other private individuals. In most cases, they had to bring a crime to the attention of the constable or beadle, secure an indictment from the court clerks, ensure the attendance of witnesses, and present their case at the trial.[52] Often they had to publicize the theft of goods or find some of the witnesses, again at their own expense.[53] Important witnesses, however, would normally be bound by recognizances to attend the trial.[54] The costs of prosecution could be considerable, particularly when a solicitor was hired. This had three consequences. First, many prosecutions were not brought at all—as Henry Fielding put it, 'prosecutors ... are often ... avaricious, and will not undergo the expence [sic] of it'.[55] Second, many men of prop-

[47] John Tobias, *Crime and Police in England, 1700–1900* (Dublin, 1979), 36–40.

[48] Cornish and Clark, *Law and Society in England, 1750–1950*, 554; Tobias, *Crime and Police in England, 1700–1900*, 42.

[49] Tobias, *Crime and Police in England, 1700–1900*, 44.   [50] Ibid., 45.

[51] John Maurice Beattie, *Crime and the Courts in England, 1660–1800* (Oxford, 1986), 619.

[52] The hiring of lawyers became increasingly common in the later part of the eighteenth century: ibid., 276 ff.   [53] See examples, ibid., 38.

[54] Hay and Snyder, *Policing and Prosecution in Britain, 1750–1850*, 26.

[55] Henry Fielding, *Enquiry into the Causes of the Late Increase in Robbers* (London, 1751), 164. Among the other reasons he lists are fear of reprisals, indolence, and tenderheartedness.

erty sought to insure themselves against the crippling cost of prose-cution by joining associations. These would pay for the expenses out of members' contributions.[56] Third, there existed a whole system of inducements—ranging from 'Parliamentary rewards' in the case of felonies to payments by the Home Office—that sought to make pros-ecution less of a financial hazard. The possibilities for abuse were vast.[57] Many scandals involved wrongful convictions, engineered by those who merely sought the 'blood money', as the Parliamentary rewards were known.[58] Inducements were financially attractive in the case of felonies, but even for lesser crimes, prosecutors could hope to be given a share of any imposed fine.[59]

Generally, defendants were not allowed counsel to present their case.[60] It is only after the 1730s that, in the case of felonies, prisoners were more often allowed legal support, at the discretion of the judge. There was no legal right to ask for a defence counsel before 1836. Defendants could use sworn witnesses from the beginning of the eighteenth century, but they had no right to force their attendance through recognizances.[61]

Trial and Conviction

A number of steps were required between a crime being brought to the attention of a magistrate and the conviction of a criminal. First, a justice would examine the merit of the case against the suspect, ques-tioning the prosecutor and his or her witnesses.[62] If the evidence was sufficient, the defendant (if he had been arrested) would be sent to the county gaol. The trial would take place at the next quarter session or assize.

Formal indictments had to be drawn up by clerks of the court, which were circulated among the grand jury. It would decide, having heard

---

[56] Hay and Snyder, *Policing and Prosecution in Britain, 1750–1850*, 26.

[57] Beattie, *Crime and the Courts in England, 1660–1800*, 374; Cornish and Clark, *Law and Society in England, 1750–1950*, 552.

[58] Radzinowicz, *History of English Criminal Law*, ii, 327 ff. Cf. some of the examples in R. Paley, 'Thief-takers in London in the Age of the McDaniel Gang, *c*.1745–1754', in Hay and Snyder (eds.), *Policing and Prosecution in Britain, 1750–1850*, 310 ff.

[59] Cornish and Clark, *Law and Society in England, 1750–1950*, 553.

[60] The only exception was when, on the point of indictment, there was a point of law aris-ing: see John Hamilton Baker, *An Introduction to English Legal History* (London, 1990), 582.

[61] Ibid.

[62] Cornish and Clark, *Law and Society in England, 1750–1950*, 561.

the witnesses for the prosecution, whether a trial should be held. The
jury would almost invariably consist of members of the 'middling
classes'.[63] The proceedings would normally begin with a charge by a
senior judge or the recorder, giving a summary of recent developments in unlawfulness and some general observations on the evil of
crime.[64] The defendant would then be brought before the jury, and
the indictment would be read out in court. The accused could then
plead guilty or not guilty. After these preliminary steps, the prosecution could present its case, supported by evidence from its witnesses.
The accused, his counsel, or the judge could question these witnesses; the defence could also present additional ones.[65] Finally, the
defendant would give his view of the matter. Old Bailey sessions in
particular were noted for their considerable speed. Even in the case
of felonies, trials rarely took longer than half an hour.[66] As late as
the early nineteenth century, the average trial only lasted a few
minutes.

The judge then instructed the jury, often leaving them in little
doubt about his own opinion. He was not required to sum up the evidence just heard. The jurors not only had to decide the question of
guilt, but also the nature of the offence. Before the early nineteenth-
century reforms, there were over 200 capital crimes, the so-called
'Bloody Code'.[67] The list extended from murder, rape, abduction to
forgery, arson, the stealing of livestock, and the cutting down of cherry
trees in an orchard. Lesser offences were punishable by transportation
to a colony (the American ones at first, later Australia).[68] In the case of
theft, the punishment depended on the value of stolen goods.[69] For
particularly grave cases of larceny, the punishment was equivalent to
that for felonies. Grand larceny (to the value of more than 1 shilling)
carried transportation to the colonies as a punishment; if the jury
decided that only a petty larceny had been committed, the judge could

---

[63] Beattie, *Crime and the Courts in England, 1660–1800*, 318 ff.   [64] Ibid., 331 ff.

[65] The use of counsel was becoming more frequent after 1730, but it remained anything
but the norm. Cf. Cornish and Clark, *Law and Society in England, 1750–1950*, 562–3.

[66] Baker, *Introduction to English Legal History*, 582.

[67] Rudé, *Crime and Victim*, 102. The term 'Bloody Code' in its strict sense should only be
applied to non-clergyable crimes. For the latter, cf. Cornish and Clark, *Law and Society in
England, 1750–1950*, 558; Beattie, *Crime and the Courts in England, 1660–1800*, 141.

[68] Beattie has argued that the introduction of transportation constituted the most dramatic change in penal practice prior to Peel's reforms because juries now had a choice apart
from either hanging or 'light' punishment such as whipping and branding.

[69] Beattie, *Crime and the Courts in England, 1660–1800*, 406 ff.

decide whether the accused would be sent to the colonies or publicly whipped.[70]

Historians have often noted that, in practice, punishments were rarely related to the gravity of a crime. Class prejudice, a defendant's appearance in court, and the mood of the wider public often seem to have had a larger influence on the punishment than the merits of the case.[71] Discretion could be exercised to a much larger extent than the brief sketch above suggests.[72] Juries could lower the value of the goods stolen in order to convict for a petty larceny where a felony had been committed. Also, judges often instructed the jury of the legal position in such a way as to almost determine the verdict.[73]

Concluding Remarks

For our method, a few features of the criminal justice system are particularly relevant. First, the proportion of all crimes ever tried was very low. The reliability of our method rests on the assumption that, simply because a crime was unusual since it led to trial, the same was not true of those testifying. The representativeness of witnesses will be examined in more detail in Chapter 3, but it is important to clarify this precondition at this point. Second, the examination of witnesses before the court would either be conducted by the prosecutor, the defendant, their respective counsels, or the judge himself. Third, the majority of witnesses would attend the trial at the behest of the prosecutor. Since a witness's status could be as important as his statement, the prosecutor would have a clear interest for them to be respectable members of society.

In one of the following sections, we compare in some detail the conditions during the three periods represented in our datasets, 1749–63, 1799–1803, and 1829–32. In passing, we may note that all three periods for which data have been collected contain years of heightened anxiety—owing to crime waves—and relative calm. Also, because the link between socio-economic conditions and the number of crimes is probably not as direct as some have argued, we need not be too concerned about the fact that real wages (according to some indices) and unemployment rates varied considerably between these three periods.

[70] Cornish and Clark, *Law and Society in England, 1750–1950*, 545–6; Rudé, *Crime and Victim*, 102. [71] Rudé, *Crime and Victim*, 103–6.
[72] Beattie, *Crime and the Courts in England, 1660–1800*, 623.
[73] Cornish and Clark, *Law and Society in England, 1750–1950*, 564.

Since there is no conclusive evidence to suggest that this influenced
the types of crime tried, there is even less reason to expect any influence on those testifying before the court.

The Old Bailey Sessions Papers and
the Northern Assize Depositions

Demand for news about sex and crime has always been buoyant. It was
in the second half of the seventeenth century that entrepreneurs
began to print reports about the proceedings at the Old Bailey in order
to satisfy this demand. The 'Proceedings of the Sessions of the Peace,
and Oyer and Terminer for the City of London and County of
Middlesex' came into existence as a precursor of the modern 'yellow
press'. From the 1680s onwards, the city of London established some
oversight over this publication, which received the Lord Mayor's
imprimatur.[74] After 1729 the newspaper format was dropped, and the
proceedings began to appear in quarto format. While the publication
as a whole became much more respectable, it still contained advertisements for anything from cough pills to cures for syphilis. During the
1720s verbatim reporting was introduced.[75] For our purposes, the
reports from the Old Bailey become truly useful after 1748. It was in
this year that Thomas Gurney began to take down the proceedings in
shorthand. He and his son acted as scribes for the next thirty-five
years. While the publisher changed with considerable frequency,[76] the
reports from the courtroom maintained a high degree of consistency,
accuracy, and detail. Incidentally, one other detail also suggests
increased respectability: advertisements were limited to those for
Gurney's own book on shorthand.

The Northern Assize depositions are a less colourful source.
'The assizes' refer to a set of judicial procedures performed from the
thirteenth century onwards by riding Justices of the Peace. They
amalgamated four distinct functions: hearing of *nisi prius* cases, gaol
delivery, conducting assizes, and use of their commissions of general
oyer and terminer.[77] *Nisi prius* cases were in principle to be tried at one
of the king's benches, unless one of the king's justices happened to
visit the county in question beforehand. In these—relatively rare—

---

[74] Mark Harris, 'Introduction', in *The Old Bailey Proceedings. Pts. 1 and 2. A Listing and Guide to the Harvester Microfilm Collection, 1714–1834* (Brighton, 1984), 9.

[75] Ibid., 10–11.   [76] Ibid., 11–12.

[77] Baker, *Introduction to English Legal History*, 25.

cases, the judges had no immediate jurisdiction, but served as local substitutes for the king's courts. Assizes allowed them to hear cases concerning accused persons held in gaol. When they received commissions of general oyer and terminer, the Justices of the Peace could try anyone accused, whether in gaol or not. The cases heard before the judges of the Northern circuit were relatively similar to those heard at the Old Bailey, ranging from petty larceny to felonies. Written depositions of witnesses formed the most important part of the evidence heard before the riding judges. The country was organized first into four (later six) circuits during the middle ages. The Northern Circuit contained the counties of Westmorland, Durham, Northumberland, Cumberland, Derbyshire, the city of York, and the North, East, and West Ridings of Yorkshire. In each county town, the Justices of the Peace appeared twice a year to deliver the gaol, take the assizes, and try the *nisi prius* cases.[78] Witnesses' statements were not taken down verbatim, but are referred to in the third person and paraphrased.

A typical example of time-use information from the Old Bailey provided by witnesses reads like this:

> WITNESS. I am a baker, I had been making my dough, on the 19th of April, about twelve at night, I heard a noise of breaking, I looked to the prosecutor's cellar door, and saw one half of the door broke, soon after I saw the prisoner come up out of the cellar, on which I asked him what business he had there ... [79]

We can infer from this case that a baker was working on 19 April 1753. He was labouring in his own profession, making bread at around midnight. The case is consequently coded as 'paid work'—the baker's bread is intended for sale, not domestic consumption.

In some cases, we are informed about the activities of more than one person at a time. The following is part of a representative verbatim report:

> WITNESS. I am a wheelwright. On Saturday was sen'night [*sic*] at night, my partner and I had left off work, and were going to the Crown in Chick-Lane to make our bill in order for the receiving our money. We hear the cry murder! murder! I am robbed; I went up to the prosecution and said, are you actually robbed?[80]

The decision to record this as either one or two observations should not be taken lightly. If we code it as only one individual leaving work,

---

[78] Ibid., 25.   [79] Old Bailey Sessions Papers, Case No. 221, 1753.
[80] Old Bailey Sessions Papers, Case No. 485, 1753.

we would disregard the experience of one individual in the past. In the alternative case, if we record this as two instances of wheel-wrights leaving work, we would trust this single witness to report accurately not only his, but also his partner's activities. Because of practical considerations, it seemed best to favour the first alternative, and to use this case as if we only had information of one person's time-use. If the second approach had been adopted, many categories of time-use would have been dominated by the occasional case where, say, a foreman remunerates twenty-seven of his workers after the end of work. The dataset would have lost much of its representativeness.[81]

Cross-examinations often yield very detailed accounts, enabling us to assess even more accurately the quality of information provided. The precision of these accounts is so great that it is possible, for example, to ascertain a shopkeeper's activities (specializing in tea) on 20 November 1776, and to do so on an hourly basis:

PROSECUTION. You had been at home from nine to ten?
WITNESS: Yes.
PROSECUTION. You had not been out of the shop?
WITNESS: No ...
PROSECUTION. Had you been stopped by any body that afternoon with a bundle?
WITNESS: I brought home this parcel of tea in the afternoon, from Holborn, between seven and eight o'clock ...
PROSECUTION. You came home then between seven and eight o'clock, and was never out afterwards?
WITNESS. I do not recollect that I was.[82]

In the depositions taken for the Northern Assizes, the kind of information collected is very similar. Some of the statements contain elaborate descriptions of the location and the persons taking the evidence, but the way in which the timing of activities is described is broadly comparable:

The information ... of John M. Lee of Gateshead in the county of Durham, labourer, taken on oath the tenth day of August one thousand eighthundred and twenty nine before us, two of his Majesty's Justices of the Peace, in and for the town and county of Newcastle upon Tyne, at the guildhall, in the said town. Who

---

[81] For explicit tests of this property see pp. 131–7.
[82] Old Bailey Sessions Papers, Case No. 19, 1779. Of course, if information is collected (roughly) on an hourly basis, some activities will be virtually excluded, since they normally take much less time.

saith, that on Friday, the 24th day of July last about eleven o'clock or a little
after at night he was returning home from work and was passing along Tyne
Bridge ...[83]

Of course, we do not know how long ago John Lee had stopped working when he was going home, and it would be inaccurate to consider
23:00 as anything but an upper bound on the time at which he stopped
working. What we do know, however, is that he worked on Friday, 24
July 1829.

Some witnesses' accounts are reported in the first person singular,
adding to the sense of immediacy that is similar to the Old Bailey
sessions papers.

James Denley of Shipley Comber being sworn says that about half past four
o'clock on Wednesday morning the eighteenth of June I was going to my work,
and saw the deceased and William Mitchell together in the high road in Shipley,
they were standing together ... [84]

The reliability of witnesses' accounts appears to be high. Witnesses
could be cross-examined if their statements seemed implausible. All
cases in which witnesses contradicted themselves or appeared
untrustworthy were excluded. This solves the problem of lies before
the court that were recognized at the time. Inaccuracies and more
blatant forms of being economical with the truth that went unnoticed
present a larger problem. There is no empirically sound way of estimating the proportion of uncaught liars in our sample. Yet the very
fact that the lie went unnoticed means that this should not concern us
unduly. Witnesses at least produced an image of themselves and of
their activity pattern that was convincing for their contemporaries.
They may have described typical or expected forms of behaviour,
thereby being able to conceal their actual activities. If there is a large
proportion of such cases in our sample, then we would underestimate
the extent to which individuals departed from the average patterns of
time-utilization.

Dishonesty could arise from three sources: witnesses have some-
thing to hide—possibly because they were implicated in the crime;
they may simply conform to the pressures exerted by the existence of
certain norms and codes of conduct; or they may be what contemporaries called 'thief-catchers', professionals who used their skills and

[83] Northern Assize Depositions, 1829 (case tried 10 Aug. 1829).
[84] Northern Assize Depositions, 1829 (case tried 5 Aug. 1829).

knowledge of the law to secure a conviction.[85] Logic suggests that the first source of witnesses' dishonesty was not likely to go unrecorded in every case. If someone testifying before the court brought evidence against the defendant, and was actually a fellow perpetrator of the crime, this fact would often be used to undermine the witness's reputation. From the 1750s judges often directed juries to acquit if the only evidence against the defendant came from his ex-accomplice.[86] In the reverse case, of course, it is perfectly possible that someone implicated in the crime gave untruthful evidence that supported his fellow criminal. The second possible objection—overreporting of socially desirable activities—can be tested indirectly. When we examine witnesses' accounts, there is little evidence to suggest that witnesses attempted to create an ideal image of social respectability before the court. While the language of the court is often of an elevated nature (sexual intercourse is normally referred to as 'carnal intimacy'), those called to give evidence have few inhibitions, talking about 'blowing brains out'[87] or drinking themselves 'insensible'.[88] As regards 'thief-catchers', there is little direct or indirect evidence that can be used to assess the extent of the problem. Historians of eighteenth-century crime have always maintained, however, that such instances were very rare.[89]

The Datasets in Context

Data collection was carried out for three periods, 1749–63, 1799–1803, and 1829–30.[90] A total of 10,800 court cases was evaluated, leading to 2,827 observations.[91] These witnesses' accounts were organized into six datasets—two main ones, with 1,002–1,005 observations each, and four auxiliary ones. The two largest datasets were extracted from London's Old Bailey Sessions Papers in the 1750s and 1800s, and contain witnesses' accounts of their activities at the time of

---

[85] Hay and Snyder, *Policing and Prosecution in Britain, 1750–1850*, 47–9. Henry Fielding thought that the evidence of a turncoat alone was never sufficient for a conviction. See Fielding, *Enquiry*, 172.

[86] Cornish and Clark, *Law and Society in England, 1750–1950*, 563.

[87] Old Bailey Sessions Papers, Case No. 255, 1800.

[88] Old Bailey Sessions Papers, Case No. 208, 1758. Note that similar language is used much more rarely in the Northern Assize Depositions, where scribes were not producing verbatim reports.

[89] Hay and Snyder, *Policing and Prosecution in Britain, 1750–1850*, 48.

[90] When a trial was held in 1800 for a crime committed in 1799, these observations were also entered. The same applies to 1749–50.

[91] The number of occasions when a single trial led to more than one entry was small.

the crime. An additional dataset for London in the 1830s was col-lected. To broaden the geographical coverage, I also collected wit-nesses' testimonies from the Northern Assize Depositions from the 1750s, 1800s, and 1830s.

In a majority of cases, a lack of information either on the time of the crime or the witness led to the exclusion of a case from the dataset. The scarcity of sufficient information was more pronounced for the earlier periods, when data collection had to be carried out on records from fourteen years to collect a dataset of sufficient size. In sixty-two cases, witnesses' accounts were ruled not to be admissible evidence before the court, and were consequently excluded—even if the lie did not pertain to time-use information.[92] It is likely that some inaccu-racies, even gross misrepresentations, went unnoticed before the court. Insofar as they relate to time-use, this is not necessarily a grave problem: the witness was obviously able to invent a probable, possibly even a typical, activity pattern.

Of the 2,827 observations, 84.7 per cent pertain to men. In nine cases, the gender of the witness could not be ascertained. In another case, a witness referred to the activity of a large number of children, containing both boys and girls. The skewed distribution of observa-tions indicates that witnesses are not a completely random sample of the population. Many pressures may have played a role in shaping the peculiar asymmetry: men may have been present more often in public places, where the majority of crime occurred. Also, it is likely that men were—rightly or wrongly—seen as better witnesses, being less likely than women to succumb to the pressures of cross-examination. Sir John Hawkins, a Middlesex magistrate, believed that many prose-cutions were abandoned because of the danger that witnesses 'may be entangled or made to contradict themselves, or each other, in a cross examination, by the prisoner's council.'[93]

The dates suggested themselves because 1760, 1801, and 1831 are regularly used as points of reference. They are also broadly com-parable in terms of prevailing economic conditions. Two kinds of events dominated short-term fluctuations: wars and the weather. Urbanites such as Londoners were further removed from the

---

[92] A typical example reads like this: 'The jury declared they believed but very little of what Tindal had sworn; and not a word that Woolf, Trueman, and Pretyman had sworn: And desiring that the three last might be committed for perjury, they were committed accordingly.' Old Bailey Sessions Papers, Case No. 73, 1756.

[93] Beattie, *Crime and the Courts in England, 1660–1800*, 375.

vicissitudes of nature than, say, farmers. Yet the impact of dearth or plenty was none the less pronounced. The link between London life and the effects of the weather operated through two mechanisms. First, adverse weather and the harvest failures it caused could increase the cost of provisions in the capital. The price of bread rose, and the brewing of gin and beer was curtailed either by government intervention or supply shortages.[94] In particularly unfortunate circumstances, when rivers froze, the supply of fuel would also suffer. Further, output in other parts of the economy almost always declined when the harvest fell short of the norm. Ashton identified the diversion of demand as the main cause of the wider downturns in economic activity associated with crop failures. What delighted farmers, the increase in their total income in years of dearth, weakened other sectors because less could be spent on their produce.[95]

During the earlier period, between 1749 and 1763, there was only one time of real shortage: 1756–8.[96] The price of bread in London increased by 50 per cent, from 5d. to 7½d. per quartern loaf.[97] Remarkably, the bad harvest does not seem to have been associated with any reduction in other output. The much less severe shortfall of the harvest in 1753, which sent bread prices up to 6½d. per quartern loaf,[98] coincided with a mild depression.

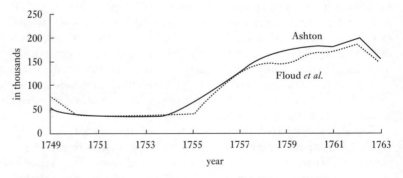

FIGURE 2.2. *Number of men in the armed forces, 1749–63*

[94] Ashton, *Economic Fluctuations in England, 1700–1800*, 36–7.
[95] Hans-Ulrich Wehler, *Deutsche Gesellschaftsgeschichte*, i (Munich, 1987), 78–9; Ashton, *Economic Fluctuations in England, 1700–1800*, 41–2.
[96] Ashton, *Economic Fluctuations in England, 1700–1800*, 36.
[97] Ibid., app., table 1, p. 181.   [98] Ibid.

Military conflict left a more pronounced impression during these years. Of the fifteen years between 1749 and 1763, Britain found itself at war for seven. With the end of fighting after the Peace of Aix-la-Chapelle in 1748, exports began to soar, and the years 1749–51 were characterized by a boom. Easy access to external finance encouraged heavy investment in port facilities and food processing.[99] The following five years saw a moderate decline of foreign trade compared to these heady years. The economy at large was hit by recession after the poor harvest of 1753, and remained in this state until 1754.[100] 1755 saw a minor recession in exports and imports and a revival of the economy at large. Ashton attributes these changes to the combined effects of the Lisbon earthquake, which inflicted heavy losses on British traders, and the outbreak of hostilities between Britain and France.[101] The beginning of the Seven Years War had a benign effect on economic activity. Output improved, and between 1756 and 1758, exports continued to grow at a moderate rate. With the armed forces growing rapidly (see Figure 2.2), unemployment was sharply reduced.[102] The hefty increases in military expenditure abroad were probably responsible for the rapid rise of exports in 1759–61, but the capture of French market share may also have played a role.[103] The economy at large benefited from good harvests and the stimulating effects of deficit spending.[104] Investment in buildings, particularly public ones, continued at a high rate.[105] 1762 saw a recession, triggered by the financial crisis of the previous year and the widening of the war.[106] Imports recovered in 1763, but the same is not true of exports—the sharp reduction in the British government's expenditure and the slump in Amsterdam and Hamburg were largely responsible for their disappointing performance. For the period 1749–63, Ashton classifies two years as peaks of the economic cycle—1751 and 1761. Depressions affected five years: 1752–5 and 1762. This is not to say that economic conditions were more often bad than good—the peaks were preceded by longer periods of healthy expansion. Hoppit classified the years 1750–3 and 1759–66 as 'prosperity', and 1753–9 as

---

[99] Ibid., 148.   [100] Ibid., 149.   [101] Ibid., 60.

[102] Data come from Roderick Floud, Kenneth Wachter, and Annabel Gregory, *Height, Health and History. Nutritional Status in the United Kingdom, 1750–1980* (Cambridge, 1990), table 2.1, p. 45, table 2.6, p. 68; Ashton, *Economic Fluctuations in England, 1700–1800*, app., table 8, p. 187.

[103] Ashton, *Economic Fluctuations in England, 1700–1800*, 60.   [104] Ibid., 148.

[105] Ibid., 150.   [106] Ibid., 61.

depression.[107] Overall, the Crafts–Harley figures suggest that industrial production expanded at an average rate of 0.5 per cent over the period.[108] Feinstein has recently constructed annual estimates of unemployment, using non-quantitative descriptions of business conditions. His figures suggest an average unemployment rate of 5.25 per cent.[109]

If war was an important influence during the first period for which data were gathered, the same is even more true for 1799–1803. Britain was at war for virtually the entire period. The one exception was the brief lull of fighting between the Peace of Amiens in March 1802 and the resumption of war in May 1803.[110] Peace lasted for a little more than a year. Throughout the period, the government was running a deficit.[111] Exports were buoyant in 1798, and government expenditure led to high levels of general economic activity. What cast a shadow over the period was the depression of the following year. A bad harvest in 1799 and a serious financial crisis in Hamburg brought the slump about. The following harvest was even worse, and Ashton classified 1800 as a year of 'depression'.[112] Not all sectors suffered. There was a sharp rise in shipping activity in 1799 and 1800, boosting the fortunes of London's port.[113] Capital spending to expand London's port facilities accelerated, and improvements were also made to ports in most parts of the country.[114] Shipbuilding accelerated as well during these two years, rising by 9.7 per cent and 36.8 per cent per annum 1801 saw a mild downturn, with a reduction in tonnage built by 8.7 per cent.[115] By 1802 building and textile production expanded again. The general upward movement culminated in the boom of 1802.[116] The second period therefore also contains more than a full cycle in economic activity. Years 1799 and 1802 experienced booms, while 1800 and 1803 saw downturns. Hoppit sees a 'setback' in 1796–7, and

---

[107] Julian Hoppit, *Risk and Failure in English Business, 1700–1800* (Cambridge, 1987), table 14, p. 107.

[108] N. F. R. Crafts and Knick Harley, 'Output Growth and the British Industrial Revolution: A Restatement of the Crafts–Harley View', *Economic History Review*, 45 (1992), 726 (revised best guess).   [109] Charles Feinstein, private communication.

[110] Rodney Castleden, *British History. Chronological Dictionary of Dates* (London, 1994), 199–200.

[111] Arthur D. Gayer, Walt Rostow, and Anna Schwartz, *The Growth and Fluctuations of the British Economy, 1790–1850* (Oxford, 1953), 44.

[112] Ashton, *Economic Fluctuations in England, 1700–1800*, 172–3.   [113] Ibid., 69.

[114] Gayer, Rostow, and Schwartz, *Growth and Fluctuations*, 35.

[115] Ashton, *Economic Fluctuations in England, 1700–1800*, 73, n. 64.   [116] Ibid., 172–3.

prosperity in 1797–1800.[117] Growth in industrial production was more vigorous, averaging 1.8 per cent per annum over the period.[118] Unemployment compared to the first period was virtually unchanged, at 5 per cent of the labour force. The strong bargaining position of labour is reflected in the Combination Acts of 1799 and 1800—in part, some authors argue, a reaction to the increasing demands for higher wages and shorter hours.[119] Estimating changes in real wages over the period is difficult since Feinstein's new index only extends back to 1770.[120] If it is spliced onto earlier data, this suggests a reduction in real wages by approximately 6 per cent between the middle and the end of the eighteenth century.[121]

Ashton often credits the onset or widening of hostilities with both positive and negative economic consequences. In the case of London, the overall effects were likely to be shifted towards the positive end of the scale. The city's port was of vital importance to the Royal Navy, and troops would often be concentrated in areas close to the city.[122] Some of the trades benefited from the interruptions that war brought for foreign competitors. These advantages have to be weighed against the increased dangers for shipping, particularly along coastal routes, and the 'crowding out' of building activities by government borrowing.[123] On balance, the result may well have been advantageous rather than detrimental, but in each case the relative magnitude of effects has to be considered.

During the third period, 1829–32, Britain was not at war. An average of 144,000 men served in the army, navy, and royal marines—approximately half of the levels seen during the Napoleonic period, and marginally more than during the middle of the eighteenth century.[124] Unemployment, which stood at around 5 per cent during the

[117] Hoppit, *Risk and Failure*, table 14, p. 107.

[118] Crafts and Harley, 'Output Growth', 726.

[119] Gayer, Rostow, and Schwartz, *Growth and Fluctuations*, 57.

[120] Charles H. Feinstein, 'Pessimism Perpetuated. Real Wages and the Standard of Living in Britain during and after the Industrial Revolution', *Journal of Economic History*, 58 (1998).

[121] Using the series by Peter Lindert and Jeffrey Williamson ('English Workers' Living Standards during the Industrial Revolution: A New Look', *Economic History Review*, 36 (1983)).

[122] L. D. Schwarz, *London in the Age of Industrialization: Entrepreneurs, Labour Force, and Living Conditions, 1700–1850* (Cambridge, 1992), 95.

[123] John Landers, *Death and the Metropolis: Studies in the Demographic History of London, 1670–1830* (Cambridge, 1993), 80.

[124] Relative to the size of the population, the armed forces were much smaller than they had been during the two earlier periods. Floud, Wachter, and Gregory, *Height, Health and History*, table 2.1, p. 47, table 2.6, p. 70.

two earlier periods, doubled to 10 per cent. Industrial output was none the less growing at an average annual rate of 1.4 per cent, very similar to the 1.8 per cent seen some thirty years earlier. Exports rose sharply in 1830, and then declined somewhat.[125] Brick production was lower than it had been in the early 1820s. At the same time, the railway network was expanding rapidly, with twelve new lines being completed between 1827 and 1832.[126] The cost of living was generally a little lower in 1829–32 than it had been at the turn of the century. Feinstein's new cost of living index suggests that prices had fallen by some 14 per cent compared to the turn of the century. Full-employment money earnings were virtually identical, having declined by a little more than 2 per cent. Consequently, real wages were a little higher than they had been thirty years earlier.

Economic and political circumstances were therefore largely similar for the first two periods, 1749–63 and 1799–1803. Harvest failures affected the English during both the earlier and the later periods, and each period also had some years of moderate plenty. More than a full cycle of economic activity from boom to bust left a mark on employment and prosperity in each set of years. Perhaps even more importantly for the situation in London, both periods saw times of war and peace. To be sure, the respite afforded by the Peace of Amiens in 1802 was a brief one, but as Figure 2.3 demonstrates, the economy none the less experienced a major demobilization shock. Both Ashton's and Floud *et al.*'s series show a marked decline in the size of the armed

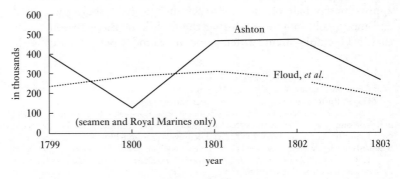

FIGURE 2.3. *Number of men in the armed forces, 1799–1803*

---

[125] Gayer, Rostow, and Schwartz, *Growth and Fluctuations*, 213. [126] Ibid., 216.

forces between 1802 and 1803.[127] If there is a difference in the general economic climate, it is in favour of the second period—wartime 'deficit-spending' kept unemployment low and the economy growing. Consequently, in tracing secular changes in working patterns, it should be borne in mind that sharp increases between the two first periods may to a limited extent be a reflection of differences in the stage of the economic cycle. The third dataset, collected for a standard reference date, comes from a period that is markedly less dynamic than the first two. With unemployment almost double the levels seen some thirty years earlier, it would be difficult to argue that the labour market was in a similar situation.

Watch-ownership and Time-consciousness

Telling the time is not trivial. A large number of witnesses in 1750–63, 1799–1803, and 1828–32 in both London and the northern counties were able to give the timing of their activities. Access to such information cannot be taken for granted. How did our witnesses know when they had finished work, drunk a pint of 'hot', or sold handkerchiefs? It is important to know how common were watch-ownership and a clear appreciation of the time of day. If only a small and elevated group could furnish such information, then our method would be fundamentally flawed.

Landes observes of the English that, as early as 1700, 'no nation was so time-bound in its activities and consciousness'.[128] The unusual size of the middle class as well as the very high proportion of the population living in cities both contributed to this.[129] The 'precocious, rapidly growing, and socially diversified demand' for watches and clocks underpinned Britain's role as a manufacturer of timepieces.[130] The English were a nation of timekeepers partly because, in Napoleon's words, they were a nation of shopkeepers. The spread of time-measurement is one of the defining characteristics of the age. As an anonymous journalist recently described the eighteenth century: 'Clocks had taken time from the skies and put it in houses and pockets, while Newton had turned the skies themselves into clockwork ...'[131] E. P. Thompson argued that the number of

---

[127] Ashton seems to use planned figures ('establishment') rather than actual ones. Floud, Wachter, and Gregory, *Height, Health and History*, table 2.1, p. 45, table 2.6, p. 68; Ashton, *Economic Fluctuations in England, 1700–1800*, app., table 8, p. 187.

[128] David Landes, *Revolution in Time. Clocks and the Making of the Modern World* (Cambridge, Mass., 1983), 227. [129] Ibid.

[130] Ibid., 230. [131] *The Economist*, 5 Mar. 1994.

timekeeping instruments increased sharply during the second half of the eighteenth century.[132]

That the production of clocks and watches increased greatly in itself tells us little about time-awareness in Hanoverian London.[133] How widespread was watch-ownership? I shall first estimate the total stock of operational clocks and watches in Britain. As a second step, I examine access to time-use information more directly, using witnesses' accounts as a source.

If we accept that watch-ownership is a useful indicator of time-awareness, production figures are a potentially useful source. To be sure, output estimates are a distorted indicator not only because contemporary statistics are less accurate than might be hoped. We also know too little about exports. Landes argues, however, that (considerable) exports were roughly offset by the influx of smuggled watches, largely from Switzerland.[134] It has been estimated that England produced approximately half of Europe's total output during the second half of the eighteenth century—between 150,000 and 200,000 pieces per year by the last quarter of the century.[135] We can use these estimates of annual production to calculate the stock of watches in England between 1750 and 1830.

First, we have to extrapolate from Landes's figures for the last quarter of the century to the periods that are of interest to us. Landes is not very specific as to the time when the stated output range was achieved. For convenience, I have assumed that 'the last quarter' of the eighteenth century is equivalent to 1775. Settling on a later date would have reduced the estimates for 1800 somewhat, but the impact is not large.[136] I assume that watch production grew in line with industrial output, as calculated by Crafts and Harley.[137] Of course, we can-

---

[132] 'the situation was changing in the last decades of the century... There were a lot of timepieces about in the 1790s... Indeed, a general diffusion of clocks and watches is occurring ... at the exact moment when the Industrial Revolution demanded a greater synchronisation of labour': E. P. Thompson, 'Time, Work-discipline, and Industrial Capitalism', *Past and Present*, 38 (1967).

[133] From here on, I shall use the term 'watch' as it was understood by contemporaries—as a clock with a dial. See Landes, *Revolution in Time*, 95.   [134] Ibid., 230.

[135] Ibid., 231.

[136] The range of the nine different estimates given below is barely affected if, say, 1787 is used.

[137] Crafts and Harley, 'Output Growth and the British Industrial Revolution', table 4, p. 715. For the years 1775–1800, I used their growth rate for the years 1780–1801; for the period 1750–1775, I used their figures for 1760–1780, and for the years 1738–1750, I used Crafts's (*British Economic Growth*, 32) figures for 1700–60.

not be certain that the average growth rate in industry and commerce is a good indicator of output change in the watch industry. The purpose of our exercise is to arrive at a lower-bound estimate of watch-ownership. Overall growth rates may understate the true increase in watch output since this industry is normally thought to be part of the 'revolutionizing' sector. We therefore bias our results against finding a high degree of watch ownership.

If our assumption about growth rates is correct, annual production more than doubled between 1750 and 1800. By 1831 output would have reached more than half a million timepieces per year. In order to convert annual output into the total number of watches available for timekeeping, we have to make assumptions about the average useful 'life' of a watch. Exact evidence is conspicuous by its absence, but we can make some educated guesses. It seems unlikely that such a prized item would last for less than five to seven years. If a consumer durable is relatively valuable, repairs are more likely to be economical than the purchase of a replacement. A (conservative) upper bound might be set at twelve years; it is also unlikely that repairs would have been uneconomical before a watch was at least five years old. Table 2.2 presents twelve estimates of the total stock of watches in England in 1750 and 1800. The range of our calculations is not small—the total number of watches in 1750 is estimated at between 1,162,000 and 2,959,000. The single most important factor determining the stock is average useful life to obsolescence. In comparison, output figures play a much smaller role.[138] If we are to gain some indication of how widespread watch-ownership was, these stock estimates have to be compared with the number of individuals who might have had use for such an item. In Table 2.2 I have expressed the number of watches in circulation as a percentage of the population over the age of 14. Based on the most pessimistic production figures in Table 2.1, and an average 'life' of only five years, 16 per cent of the total population in 1750 would have been able to own a watch.[139] Amongst males of prime age, the percentage would have been much higher, and even moderately conservative assumptions lead to the conclusion that up to one-third could have owned a watch. More optimistic assumptions suggest figures of up to

---

[138] When Pitt attempted to introduce a tax on watches and clocks in 1797–8, various estimates of prospective revenue were made. These imply a total of approximately 2,600,000 timepieces in England by the end of the century. This is in line with our estimates in col. (4). Cf. Thompson, 'Time, Work-discipline, and Industrial Capitalism', 68.

[139] The underlying assumption is that only very few possessed more than one watch.

TABLE 2.1. *Annual production of watches, 1750–1831, in thousands*

	1750	1775	1801	1831
Upper bound	145	200	302	760
Midpoint estimate	127	175	264	665
Lower bound	109	150	226	570

Note: The production figures (upper bound and lower bound) for 1775 are from David Landes, *Revolution in Time*, 230. The 'midpoint estimate' is the arithmetic mean of both figures. Production in 1750 and 1800 was estimated on the basis of output growth in industry, using N. F. R. Crafts and Knick Harley ('Output Growth and the British Industrial Revolution: A Restatement of the Crafts–Harley View', *Economic History Review*, 45 (1992), table 4, p. 715). Figures rounded to the nearest thousand.

40 per cent in 1750, over 60 per cent in 1800, and close to 100 per cent in 1830. Even if we conclude that the last estimates are too high, the labourers, privates, and coachmen reporting in court that they lost their watches may not have been the exception but the rule. Given that recent estimates put the number of clocks and watches in England in 1700 at 200,000, this suggests a sharp rise in the diffusion of time-pieces during the first half of the century.[140] Another important conclusion that emerges from Table 2.2 is that, despite relatively rapid output growth, watch-ownership grew at much more modest rates—the effect of the rise in annual production was partly checked by fast population growth.[141]

Corroborating evidence comes from the Essex pauper inventories collected by King.[142] In this socially disadvantaged group, 20 per cent owned watches or clocks before 1769. The inventories produced between 1770 and 1812 show watch or clock ownership among 38 per cent of paupers.[143] This is broadly similar to the lower bound estimates given in Table 2.2, assuming a useful life of twelve years, but higher than even the most optimistic production figures suggest when we assume five years. In terms of the change between the earlier and the later period, we may well have been too cautious. While King's

[140] Paul Glennie and Nigel Thrift, 'The Spaces of Times', mimeo, University of Bristol (1999).

[141] The number of adults did not grow as fast as the total population—the proportion under the age of 15 was rising rapidly. Without this effect, relative change between 1750 and 1800 would have been even slower.

[142] Peter King, 'Pauper Inventories and the Material Lives of the Poor in the Eighteenth and Early Nineteenth Centuries', in T. Hitchcock, P. King, and P. Sharpe, *Chronicling Poverty: The Voices and Strategies of the English Poor* (Basingstoke, 1997).

[143] Ibid., table 3.

TABLE 2.2. *Watch ownership, 1750–1831*

	Mean life of watch	1751		1801		1831	
		12 years	5 years	12 years	5 years	12 years	5 years
Stock (in thousands)	Upper bound	1,674	855	3,512	1,563	7,881	3,601
	Midpoint	1,466	749	3,073	1,368	6,896	3,151
	Lower bound	1,258	643	2,634	1,172	5,911	2,701
Adult population (in thousands)	Total	5,922		8,671		13,254	
	% 0–14	32.4		36.4		38.8	
	% adult	67.6		63.6		61.2	
	Total adult	4,006		5,515		8,117	
Adult ownership rates	Upper bound	42%	21%	64%	28%	97%	44%
	Midpoint	37%	19%	56%	25%	85%	39%
	Lower bound	31%	16%	48%	21%	73%	33%

Note: The stock was calculated by extrapolating production backwards from the benchmark years in Table 2.1, using the output growth figures in N. F. R. Crafts, *British Economic Growth*, 32. The proportion of the adult population was calculated on the basis of population figures and age composition for 1751, 1801, and 1831 (Wrigley et al., *English Population History*, table A9.1, p. 614). Figures rounded to the nearest thousand.

data suggest an increase by 90 per cent, the changes between the middle and the end of the eighteenth century calculated in Table 2.2 rarely exceed 30 per cent. If correct, this implies that watch or clock ownership became much less of a sign of social distinction.

How did this growing access to timekeeping instruments affect time-consciousness in our group of witnesses? Since timepieces represented objects of value, they ranked high on thieves' lists.[144] None the less, we find numerous individuals of modest social standing appearing before the court because their watches have been stolen. In 1760, indeed, we encounter an individual who is too poor to afford a bed of his own, but who none the less owns a watch.[145] At about the same time two bricklayers' labourers lose their watches.[146] In 1802 a coachman and a private in the Life Guards have their watches stolen.[147] In 1829 we find an agricultural labourer at a farm in Greensfield, two miles from Alnwick, going to bed (in the same room as another labourer). The next morning, his silver watch is gone.[148] That there was brisk demand for watches amongst thieves thus does not imply that they were above the means of average workers. As early as 1750 we find a metal watch in London valued at a mere 10s.[149] According to the wage data compiled by Schwarz for the London building trades, bricklayers would have had to work little more than three days for such a watch; bricklayers' labourers a little less than five.[150] The price of timepieces therefore hardly acted as a constraint on watch-ownership. Indeed, we already find high degrees of time-awareness and punctuality in witnesses' statements during the 1750s:

Q. What time do you frequently dine?
A. We always dine exactly at two; we never are ten minutes under or over.[151]

This suggests that 'exact' time-use information was available to within no more than ten minutes. Answers that indicate the 'norm' rather than time-use on a particular day, such as this one,[152] have to be treated

[144] See for example, Old Bailey Sessions Papers, Case No. 57, 1800.

[145] Old Bailey Sessions Papers, Case No. 165, 1760.

[146] Old Bailey Sessions Papers, Case No. 75, 1759 and Case No. 68, 1758.

[147] Old Bailey Sessions Papers, Case No. 242, 1802 and Case No. 300, 1802.

[148] Northern Assize Depositions, 1829 (no case number assigned).

[149] Old Bailey Sessions Papers, Case No. 3, 1749. There is no information on the quality of the watch.

[150] See L. D. Schwarz, 'The Standard of Living in the Long Run: London, 1700–1860', *Economic History Review*, 38 (1985), app. I, p. 37.

[151] Old Bailey Sessions Papers, Case No. 50, 1754.

[152] For another interesting example cf. Old Bailey Sessions Papers, Case No. 354, 1756.

with special caution. On the one hand, they contain information not just on an isolated event, but of regular and repeated patterns of time-use. On the other hand, they are possibly not too accurate about the day of the crime itself—someone who resorts to custom rather than precise knowledge of activity and timing on a specific day may more easily give inaccurate information. Another example of an almost pedantic awareness of time comes from a bookkeeper to a Mr Thomas Gilbert, who was running a coach company out of a pub named the Old Bell in Holborn. The bookkeeper introduces his testimonial thus: 'On Saturday, the 9th of November, about three minutes past seven, I went into the office to settle with the Egham coachman . . .'[153]

The bookkeeper clearly had direct access to a reasonably accurate timepiece. This was possibly a source of considerable pride for him, given that the great precision—'three minutes past seven'—had little relevance for the trial. However, the precision of a witness's account may have been important in establishing his or her trustworthiness. Yet watches and clocks were not the only means that provided witnesses in our samples with an awareness of time. Clocks on churches or public buildings were common. Also, many inns had clocks in the taproom.[154] In 1772 a visitor to Bristol remarked on the importance of quarter-hour bells in providing 'a constant monitor of time to all the inhabitants of the four quarters of the city.'[155] In 1759 the great accuracy of a witness's statement based on such information aroused the suspicion of the prosecution:

Q. How come you to be so exact as to the time?
A. I can look out at the clock, and see what a clock it is at any time.
Q. Can you take upon you to say you looked at the clock that time?
A. I looked at the clock at six o'clock at night.
Q. Did you see the clock at seven?
A. No, I could not, then it was candle-light, I heard it strike seven; he was then coming from the Hay-market.[156]

This case is curious since the witness invokes both optic and acoustic information. The latter (either church bells or watchmen shouting the hour) is often mentioned.[157] A typical example reads like this:

---

[153] Old Bailey Sessions Papers, Case No. 51, 1799.
[154] Glennie and Thrift, 'Spaces of Times'.   [155] Cited ibid.
[156] Old Bailey Sessions Papers, Case No. 154, 1759.
[157] Old Bailey Sessions Papers, Case No. 367, 1751 and Case No. 27, 1758.

A. On the fifteenth or sixteenth of December, I know it was Monday night, between five and six, I left work, and went in at the Gentleman and Porter; there was the prisoner: when I went home about a quarter after nine, I left him there . . .

Q. How do you recollect the time of the night?

A. We were talking what it was o'clock; and we heard Spittle-fields bell ring eight; the prisoner sat near me, and he never went out of the house while I was there.[158]

Particularly during the earlier period, reasonably accurate time awareness coexisted side by side with traditional forms of timekeeping. In 1760 a shopkeeper reports that someone entered the shop 'about the dusk of the evening'.[159] Imprecise information is, of course, inappropriate for our purposes, and cases containing such statements are not used. Sometimes, cross-examinations help in identifying a poor appreciation of the time of day:

A. I am a pawnbroker, and live in Stanhope-street. The prisoner Mason was at our house on the twenty-second of September, and had left some things for a guinea. I know it was about two or three hours after we had lighted candles, but will not pretend to be exact to an hour.

Q. What time did you light the candles then?

A. I believe about five, and look upon it to be about eight when he came.

Q. At that time the sun does not go down till about six; do you light candles before the sun goes down?

A. I cannot be exact as to the time.[160]

Such cases are rare (and excluded from our analysis); in most cases, whenever the timing of a crime emerged as important during the court proceedings, witnesses could tell the time with reasonable accuracy. By 1800, even in the Northern counties, rather exact statements about the timing of activities aroused no apparent suspicion. This is true even in cases when no source of time-information was apparently mentioned to the examining judge:

The information of William Hogson of Sandhill, in the parish of Bongate and county of Westmorland, weaver, taken upon oath before me . . . Who saith that on Wednesday the fifth day of August instant he was weaving in the weaving house of John Jon of Sand Hill in the Parish of Bongate in the said county, weaver, which said weaving house adjoins to the dwelling house of the said John Jon, that

---

[158] Old Bailey Sessions Papers, Case No. 88, 1752. The court later ascertained the exact date.   [159] Old Bailey Sessions Papers, Case No. 55, 1760.

[160] Old Bailey Sessions Papers, Case No. 27, 1753.

about ten minutes past twelve o'clock at noon of the said day he left his work to go to his dinner ...'[161]

When reporting the time at which they engaged in a specific activity, our witnesses normally do not do so with perfect accuracy. During the data-collection process, cases were coded according to the precision of the witnesses' statements about timing. 'Between five and six o'clock', for example, would be coded as accurate to within one hour. The time for the reported activity would be entered as 5:30. The potential error is then 30 minutes either side. Witnesses that do not qualify their statements in this fashion fall into two categories. Some give times that suggest 'rounding'—an activity that actually took place at 7:07 is reported as having occurred at 7:00. In such cases, we can only hazard a guess as to the true margin of error. Somewhat arbitrarily, I assumed that these statements were accurate to within 30 minutes. In other cases, such as the bookkeeper mentioned before, even greater accuracy could be attained. An average error of 5 minutes was assumed.[162]

Between 1760 and 1830 the accuracy of time-reporting did not change much in our samples.[163] In the London sample, the proportion of witnesses giving the time to within 60 minutes fell over the 70 intervening years, and the proportion reporting to within half an hour rose sharply from 3 to 55 per cent. At the same time, those that were coded as reporting to within 15 minutes fell from over 64 to 21 per cent. One possible interpretation of this surprising decline is that being able to tell the time accurately became less of a distinguishing feature; witnesses might have been less proud of watch ownership by 1830 than they had been in 1750. Those stating the time of their main activity when the crime occurred with greatest accuracy constituted a very small proportion—approximately 1 per cent in London during the 1750s and 1760s. Over the next 70 years, this proportion was to double, giving a total of 2 per cent. In the North, there are no witnesses in the 1750s and early 1760s that reported their activities to within 15 minutes, let alone with the accuracy of the bookkeeper. Using the mean expected accuracy, we can calculate the average 'error'. It increased slightly in the case of London witnesses, from 30

---

[161] Northern Assize Depositions, 1801 (no case number assigned).

[162] Note that none of the results reported here or in other parts of the text is affected if we use different assumptions about the likely mean error.

[163] In a subsample of 60 cases collected from the London data in 1800, 70 per cent of witnesses were accurate to within 30 minutes. In the North, the respective figure is 66 per cent.

TABLE 2.3. *Precision of time-reporting (percentage of all witnesses)*

Accuracy in minutes	London		North	
	1760	1830	1760	1830
5	1.1	2.0	0	0
15	64.4	20.8	0	19.9
30	3.3	55.0	64.7	60.3
60	30.6	21.3	34.1	19.1
120	0.8	1.0	1.2	0.7

minutes to 33 minutes.[164] In the Northern counties examined in this study, it fell slightly from 41 minutes to 33 minutes. If the degree of precision appears low, it should be borne in mind that the error it can introduce into estimates of the timing of any one activity are small compared to the variability in the underlying data.

Take the time of rising in the morning in London during the 1750s, for example. Given the limited sample size and the less than perfect nature of information provided, the mean of 6:10 can only be calculated with a limited degree of precision. There are two factors that drive this lack of accuracy. They affect all the activities examined in this study, and therefore require some further discussion. The statistical properties of our dataset alone produce a wide margin of error. With a standard error of the mean of 15 minutes, we can, however, be 95 per cent certain that the true mean is between 5:41 and 6:39. This confidence interval would apply if we had been able to measure the time of leaving bed to the nearest minute. Obviously, this was not the case. As discussed above, some witnesses made rather general statements, claiming to have engaged in a particular activity between, say, 5:00 and 6:00. In such a case, 5:30 would have been entered into the database in the hope that errors would cancel each other out. Yet this may not necessarily have been the case. How sensitive is our estimate to inaccuracies of this kind? The vast majority of observations is precise to within less than 15 minutes (75 per cent). Only 25 per cent (15 out of 59) of all cases contain statements that are precise to one hour. The mean for these observations is 6:38. Without these observations, the overall mean would have been 6:00. Let us assume that all these individuals had been much closer to the lower bound of the range than

---

[164] The difference is not statistically significant.

to the upper bound: every time a witnesse claimed to have risen between 3:00 and 4:00, he or she would have left bed at 3:10 (instead of the 3:30 that we assigned). Every single one of our observations in this category would then have introduced an error of 20 minutes into the calculation of the mean. It seems inherently unlikely that they would have all erred on the same side. Even if this had been the case, the effect on our estimate of the overall mean is none the less small. If the less accurate statements were all 'off' by 20 minutes in the same direction, then a maximum bias of 5 minutes would have been introduced ($0.25*20$). If such a systematic form of imprecision existed, we would have to revise the average to 6:05. Similarly, if every single witness in this category had erred on the high side, the upper bound would be 6:15. The overall confidence interval therefore has to be widened by 5 minutes on either side. Compared to the error bands arising from the statistical properties of our data, the maximum inaccuracy introduced by using midpoint estimates is small.

There is one sense in which time-consciousness—if we want to use the term—did shift significantly and dramatically during the period. The proportion of cases containing information on time-use increased sharply between 1760 and 1800. Table 2.4 gives the proportion of cases containing accurate and useful information on the timing of witnesses' activities as a proportion of the total number of cases examined.

For the period 1749–63, fourteen annual volumes of Sessions papers with a total of 5,025 cases had to be scrutinized to arrive at 1,005 observations. An approximately equal number of observations was extracted in 1799–1803 from 3.3 annual volumes with a total of 2,863 cases. In the earlier sample, 20.3 per cent of all cases contain sufficiently accurate information. For 1800, this figure grows to 34.7 per cent. The availability of adequate information per number of cases examined therefore increased by 71 per cent; the shortening of the

TABLE 2.4. *Proportion of usable cases*

	North			London		
	1750	1800	1830	1750	1800	1830
Cases examined	1,250	952	667	5,025	2,863	685
Used	150	200	200	1,005	1,002	281
Proportion	12%	21%	30%	20%	35%	41%

sample period was also facilitated by the 141.5 per cent growth in the number of cases tried per year. Unfortunately, time-use information was not the only constraint; many cases were rejected because activities were not described sufficiently, or because the timing of actions was of no interest to the court. The proportion of useful cases therefore constitutes a lower bound on the availability of accurate time-use information. One in five cases or less from our mid-eighteenth-century material could be entered into the database. In both the North and in London, the proportion of usable material rises sharply between the 1750s–early 1760s and the turn of the century. The pace of improvement then slows down somewhat in London, doubling the usable proportion overall between 1760 and 1830. The rate of progress is very similar in the North, where ultimately almost one in three cases contains the relevant information.

Verbatim reports from the Old Bailey, and the depositions made by witnesses in the counties of the Northern circuit, demonstrate eloquently that access to timekeeping instruments was not the privilege of the wealthy few, and that, in London at least, even those without watches could easily tell the time to within one hour.

3

Patterns of Time-use, 1750–1830

According to George Stigler, the plural of anecdote is data.[1] The Old Bailey Sessions Papers and Northern Assize Depositions are filled with the colourful tales of witnesses appearing before the court. The previous chapter discussed how these anecdotes can be used as a dataset on time-use in eighteenth- and early nineteenth-century England. This chapter presents the results of analysing this kaleidoscope of snapshots in a systematic manner. There are two principal types of time-use information in the Old Bailey Sessions Papers. We can use witnesses' accounts either to analyse the frequency of certain activities, or we can examine their timing. This chapter uses both kinds of information in turn.

First, basic regularities are established, using overall averages. As a first step, we examine the extent to which the number of observations varies systematically over the course of the day, the week, and the year. No attempt is made to take gender, class, and occupational differences into account. The units of analysis are periods of time. I then explore the timing of basic, everyday activities such as work and sleep—the daily rhythm of life. This set of necessary and recurring activities largely lends the perception of time-use a coherent structure. Next, the timing and incidence of labour and leisure, sleep and rest are traced over the 'seven-day cycle' of the week.[2] Having discussed variations during the week, it would not be sensible to proceed mechanically to an examination of patterns within each month—there are neither *a priori* reasons nor is there empirical support for striking differences between, say, the first and the last weeks of each month. The annual cycle is a more appropriate point of reference; amongst the questions discussed is the extent to which the seasons and holy days influenced activity patterns.

Second, time-use is analysed according to the characteristics of study subjects. I examine the relationship of domestic work, paid

[1] Cit. Ernst Berndt, *The Practice of Econometrics* (Reading, Mass., 1991).
[2] The term is borrowed from Eviatar Zerubavel, *The Seven Day Cycle. The History and Meaning of the Week* (New York, 1985).

work, etc. and gender, class, and occupation. Again, the object is to identify contrasts and similarities between categories. Whereas the first section largely disregards the sample composition as it relates to study subjects, this part makes little attempt to control for temporal characteristics (e.g., the number of Mondays in a given sample). There is a simple reason for this. Ideally, we would want to examine both aspects simultaneously: by, for example, asking how the timing of women's domestic work changed between weekdays and weekends. Unfortunately, such multiple subdivisions rapidly reduce the amount of information available—even in a study with more than 2,800 observations. It is only in rare circumstances that we can control for all available criteria simultaneously.[3]

Third, I attempt to construct estimates of annual time-budgets, using the information on the timing of certain activities as well as the frequency with which witnesses are observed. The estimates of the length of the working year that we derive for the periods 1749–63, 1799–1803, and 1829–31 form the basis for estimates of change over time. Finally, I present some tests to examine the robustness of our findings.

The Temporal Pattern of Crime

Crime did not occur at random hours of the day, or on random days of the year. Our dataset shows clearly that some periods witnessed a markedly higher incidence of crime than others.[4] The busiest time of the day for offenders appears to have been in the late afternoon, between 17:00 and 19:00.[5] The daily pattern of crime is highly variable. The most crime-ridden periods of the day record four to six times more incidents than the periods of minimal criminal activity.[6] Overall, the degree of similarity is not small. The averages for the North and the London data are significantly correlated.[7] Both datasets

---

[3] The one instance where this was attempted is holy days. See below.

[4] The underlying assumption is that the timing of crimes observed by our witnesses is representative of crimes at large. Since only a small percentage of offences was actually brought to trial (of which we observe only a subsection), this is difficult to examine empirically.

[5] There is some evidence to suggest that this peak is associated with the onset of darkness. The question is examined in more detail below, in the section on seasonality.

[6] For London on average, the multiple of maximum to minimum period is six; in the North, it is four. For individual subsets, the difference is even larger.

[7] The coefficient is 0.47, significant at the 2 per cent level.

show similar troughs in the 'small hours' between midnight and 4:00, a sharp increase around 5:00, a marked decline at around 11:00 in the morning, and then a pronounced rise to the peak in the late afternoon between 17:00 and 19:00. The similarity between data from the same area is higher than similarities between different locations at any one point in time. The number of crimes per hour in London in the 1750s and early 1760s is significantly correlated with the London figures for 1800 and 1830 (Table 3.1).[8] The same is not true for the data from the North of England. There, the hourly pattern from the 1750s is

TABLE 3.1. *Crime per hour, percentage of all observations*

Hour		London			North		
from	to	1760	1800	1830	1760	1800	1830
0	1	4.6	2.3	4.2	5.7	4.6	2.7
1	2	1.6	1.0	2.4	2.3	3.1	1.6
2	3	1.7	1.6	0.9	2.3	5.4	3.3
3	4	2.3	1.6	0.5	2.3	1.5	3.8
4	5	3.0	2.0	0.5	0.0	1.5	3.8
5	6	4.6	2.5	2.8	6.8	3.1	6.0
6	7	4.3	4.2	3.3	1.1	4.6	6.0
7	8	4.1	4.4	4.7	5.7	4.6	6.0
8	9	4.0	3.7	3.8	0.0	3.1	6.0
9	10	3.4	4.0	3.3	2.3	4.6	4.9
10	11	3.7	4.0	2.8	2.3	1.5	2.7
11	12	1.9	4.1	0.9	2.3	6.9	3.3
12	13	2.7	3.5	1.9	9.1	6.9	2.7
13	14	2.6	4.4	5.2	1.1	3.1	1.6
14	15	3.2	4.5	4.2	3.4	2.3	0.5
15	16	3.1	4.5	6.1	8.0	3.8	0.5
16	17	3.4	5.1	7.5	12.5	5.4	3.3
17	18	4.3	7.2	7.5	3.4	5.4	5.4
18	19	7.0	9.4	7.1	9.1	6.2	6.5
19	20	7.5	6.4	12.7	5.7	1.5	4.3
20	21	6.6	7.0	4.2	4.5	5.4	3.8
21	22	6.6	4.8	5.2	3.4	6.2	6.0
22	23	6.7	4.2	2.8	3.4	6.9	7.6
23	24	7.1	3.6	5.2	3.4	2.3	7.6

[8] The correlation coefficient is 0.61 and 0.59, significant at the 1 per cent level. Evidence from London for 1800 and 1830 is also significantly correlated (0.68).

TABLE 3.2. *Crime by day of the week, percentage of all observations*

	London			North		
	1760	1800	1830	1760	1800	1830
Sunday	9.1	9.0	9.8	11.9	8.9	15.0
Monday	17.0	15.8	19.3	15.1	14.3	17.0
Tuesday	13.3	15.3	10.5	13.5	10.7	12.2
Wednesday	16.2	14.7	12.0	11.1	22.0	12.2
Thursday	14.9	14.8	12.0	15.9	13.7	19.0
Friday	15.3	13.6	18.9	15.9	14.9	17.7
Saturday	14.3	16.7	17.5	16.7	15.5	6.8

similar to the one from 1800, but not similar to the one from 1830.[9] Between the two geographical areas, there appears to be a limited degree of similarity. The hourly pattern from the North in the 1750s is significantly correlated with London data from 1800 and 1830, and London data from the 1750s correlates with the pattern in the Northern data from the 1830s.

Variation during the week was less pronounced than during the day (Table 3.2). In the North in 1760, Saturday, the day with the highest number of witnesses' reports, shows merely a 40 per cent greater incidence of crime than Sunday, the day of lowest activity. In London the difference is larger, with a peak-to-trough difference of 97 per cent. There, Sunday also recorded an unusually low incidence of crime, but the peak activity occurred on Mondays.

The pattern of crime during the day appears more similar between the different datasets than the pattern during the week. The averages of the London and Northern datasets show a correlation coefficient of 0.6, which is not large enough to reject the null of no significant correlation at the customary 10 per cent level of significance.[10] Despite the low number of degrees of freedom, there are some significant similarities. The weekly patterns of London crime from the 1760s and 1800s are highly correlated, and so is the London data from the 1760s with Northern data from 1800 and London data from 1830 with

[9] Correlation coefficients are 0.35 and − 0.07. Only the former is significant (at the 10 per cent level).

[10] The coefficient is significant at the 15 per cent level. The order of magnitude is not altogether different from the ones found in the hourly pattern of crime. Since there are fewer observations and, consequently, fewer degrees of freedom, statistical significance requires higher observed degrees of correlation.

TABLE 3.3. *Number of observations per month (London)*

	1760		1800		
	Number of observations	Deviation from average	Number of observations	Adjusted number of observations	Deviation from average
January	93	11.25	114	86	13.58
February	98	16.25	87	65	−7.42
March	93	11.25	72	54	−18.42
April	76	−5.75	66	66	−6.42
May	79	−2.75	63	63	−9.42
June	58	−23.75	55	55	−17.42
July	69	−12.75	80	80	7.58
August	64	−17.75	51	51	−21.42
September	56	−25.75	92	92	19.58
October	77	−4.75	109	109	36.58
November	94	12.25	107	80	7.58
December	124	42.25	90	68	−4.42

Northern data from 1760.[11] Table 3.3 presents the number of observations per month. If the probability of a crime being reported and tried is itself independent of the month, this should be an indicator of the temporal incidence of crime. During the 1750s and 1760s there is a pronounced peak in the winter, with December registering almost 50 per cent more cases than average. In no month was crime more rare than in September, with June being almost as favourable. Monthly differences are large—a crime (with a witness talking about time) is more than 2.2 times more likely to occur in December than in September.[12] The pattern in 1800 is similar. In general, summer months seem to record fewer crimes than winter months. However, this is partly caused by the fact that data collection started with cases tried at the Old Bailey in January 1800 and stopped in April 1803. Because of the lag between the time when the crime was committed and the time

[11] The correlation coefficients are 0.79, 0.72, and 0.68, significant at the 5, 10, and 10 per cent levels, respectively.

[12] The coefficient of variation is 23.96 per cent, indicating a higher variability relative to the mean than during the week. We can easily reject the hypothesis that this pattern of variation is random; with a χ^2–statistic of 51.62 and 11 degrees of freedom, there is less than a 0.001 per cent chance of observing such differences in a sample drawn from an evenly distributed population.

TABLE 3.4. *Number of observations and daylight—London*

	Daylight			1760			1800		
	Hours	Minutes	Total in minutes	Number of observations	Daylight (January = 100)	Number of observations (January = 100)	Number of observations	Daylight (January = 100)	Number of observations (January = 100)
January	8	4	484	93	100.00	100.00	86	100.00	100.00
February	9	20	560	98	115.70	105.38	65	115.70	75.60
March	11	4	664	93	137.19	100.00	54	137.19	62.80
April	13	56	776	76	160.33	81.72	66	160.33	76.70
May	15	7	907	79	187.40	84.95	63	187.40	73.30
June	16	22	982	58	202.89	62.37	55	202.89	64.00
July	17	34	994	69	205.37	74.19	80	205.37	93.00
August	15	13	913	64	188.64	68.82	51	188.64	59.30
September	14	32	812	56	167.77	60.22	92	167.77	107.00
October	11	16	676	77	139.67	82.80	109	139.67	126.70
November	10	30	570	94	117.77	101.08	80	117.77	93.00
December	8	10	490	124	101.24	133.33	68	101.24	79.10

when it was tried, this means that the dataset contains a disproportionate number of cases from November, December, January, February, and March. The penultimate column in Table 3.3 contains a revised set of figures. In order to correct for this bias, the numbers for the months in question were multiplied by 0.75. Note that, as we require data from a number of years to establish the seasonality-pattern, the dataset from 1830 was not analysed in this way.[13]

The number of witnesses testifying (and giving sufficient evidence about their use of time) rises and falls with the number of hours of darkness (Table 3.4).[14] The correlation coefficient in 1760 is high (−0.83), and a regression of the number of observations per month on the hours of daylight explains a large fraction of the variation (Table 3.5).[15] An explanation of this phenomenon could be that longer hours of darkness during the winter months were conducive to crime. With only a minimum of public lighting, the difficulty of recognizing faces and clothes must have proved a formidable obstacle for the prosecution. Two elements would have added to the large variance in Table 3.4. First, the changing proportion of cases actually brought before the court—owing to the changing quality of evidence at different times of the year—may have accounted for a large part of the pronounced differences. Second, if thieves acted rationally, the lower chances of being brought to justice during the winter should have boosted crime rates.[16]

TABLE 3.5. *Daylight and number of observations*

	B	t-statistic	adj. R^2	F-test	Correlation coefficient
1760	−0.0869**	−4.73	0.66	22.41	−0.83
1800 (*uncorrected*)	−0.082**	−3.30	0.47	10.99	−0.72
1800 (*adjusted*)	−0.025	−0.088	0.02	0.78	−0.26

Note: ** indicates significance at the 95 per cent level of confidence.

[13] Also, the much smaller sample sizes in the datasets derived from the Northern Assize Depositions do not allow us to subdivide the data by month in a meaningful way.

[14] The difference between sunrise and sunset on the first Saturday of any given month was calculated from modern data. This may not present the exact average for any one month; it none the less gives an unbiased estimate of relative movements over the annual cycle. *Oxford Almanack* 1954.

[15] It should be noted that a regression with merely 12 observations can only serve an illustrative purpose.

[16] Alternatively, it could be argued that winter unemployment increased 'subsistence' crime.

The very high correlation observed in the 1750s is no longer present when either the uncorrected or the adjusted series is used as a dependent variable. The unadjusted number of observations shows a similar coefficient, but a lower t-statistic, R^2 and correlation coefficient. The change is even more marked if the adjusted series is used. July, for example, registers one of the highest numbers of offences, the number being on a par with the value for November. The coefficient on daylight in the regression falls to less than one-third of its original size, and the t-statistic becomes insignificant. For all its imperfections, the last series arguably provides a more accurate description of the number of crimes occurring.

If we conclude that the inverse relationship between daylight and crime weakened during the second half of the eighteenth century it is logical to ask what might have caused such a change. One obvious candidate is improved street-lighting. At the beginning of the eighteenth century, London was notorious for its badly illuminated streets full of refuse. According to Maitland, it had the reputation of being the worst lit of the great cities of Europe.[17] Lighting Acts in 1736 and 1738 led to some improvement, but it was not before the Paving Acts in the 1760s and 1770s that the situation changed fundamentally. New oil-lamps replaced the old candlelights, and their number was increased.[18] When Archenholtz visited London in the 1780s he remarked: 'In Oxford Road alone there are more lamps than in all the city of Paris. Even the great roads, for seven or eight miles round, are crowded with them, which makes the effect exceedingly grand'.[19] It is easy to see why crime and hours of darkness were no longer correlated to the same extent: improved public lighting meant that the veil of darkness shielding thieves from arrest and recognition was wearing thin by the end of the eighteenth century. Whereas a rational, utility-maximizing thief of the 1750s and early 1760s had every incentive to perpetrate his crimes after sunset, the benefits of such a strategy had largely vanished for his successors some fifty years later.

---

[17] Cit. George Rudé, *Hanoverian London, 1714–1808* (London, 1971), 135.

[18] William D. Nordhaus, 'Do Real Output and Real Wage Measures Capture Reality? The History of Lighting Suggests Not', in Tim Bresnahan and Robert Gordon (eds.), *The Economics of New Goods* (Chicago and London, 1997), table 1.9, p. 61, calculates a very considerable increase in total lighting per household (from 28 kilolumenhours to 117), but the data are too crude to be taken as more than a general indication of an upward trend.

[19] Rudé, *Hanoverian London*, 137.

The Structure of Daily Life

If one would live the life of that statistical construct, the average witness that we encounter in the court records from London and the North of England, what would one's day look like? There are four basic activities that lend everyday life a good deal of its structure: rising in the morning, going to bed, starting work, and stopping work. Once their timing has been established, we can calculate important components of time-budgets such as hours of sleep and hours of work. Individuals would rise early, at around 6:00 in the morning.[20] Within the next half-hour or so, people would start work. Breakfast would be taken later, at around 9:00 and afterwards. The morning's work would finish with 'dinner'—probably taken between 12:30 and 14:00. Work continued until late. For some, there was tea in the late afternoon, between 17:00 and 18:00. It would be common not to leave one's work before 19:00. After the evening meal, people would go to bed at around 22:00.

Table 3.6 gives the timing of main activities in London and the North of England, 1750–1830. The basic pattern of daily life is remarkably uniform across time and space—our average witness would rise at around 6 o'clock in the morning, and start work shortly afterwards. Typically, a period of twelve hours would separate the time of starting and of stopping work. There is some evidence of a

TABLE 3.6. *Timing of main activities during the day, London and North of England*

	1750		1800		1830	
	London	North	London	North	London	North
Rising in the morning	06:10	06:00	05:56	06:00	07:08	05:49
Going to bed	22:50	22:40	23:21	22:04	22:46	22:33
Starting work	06:50	06:10	06:33	06:45	07:50	06:03
Stopping work	18:48	19:00	19:06	n/a	19:05	20:00

[20] In later parts of this section, I shall use the precise point estimate (to the nearest minute) of the timing of certain activities. This is not to suggest a false sense of accuracy; rather—as in the case of work on historical national accounts, for example—it is useful to provide the point estimates for subsequent calculations despite the fact that these variables are observed with an error.

somewhat shorter working day in London in the 1830s developing, when the average difference falls to 11 hours 15 minutes. The change compared to 1750 is statistically significant. The apparent lengthening of the working day in the North, however, is not due to limited sample size.

Sleep

The earliest riser in our dataset is a publican who gets up at 2:00 on 4 July 1756 to go 'a mowing'.[21] No individual rose later than a domestic servant, who, on Sunday, 14 March 1759 was lying in bed until 10:30.[22] These extremes were highly unusual. To see that the vast majority of Londoners rose at a time much closer to our estimate of the mean, consider the cumulative frequency plot in Figure 3.1. In 1760 there is a slow and continuous rise in the proportion of our witnesses who have left their beds between 3:00 and 8:00. Thereafter, the rate of increase tails off. The mean of 6:10 suggests a rather early start to the day. In 1800 the overall pattern is similar. There are major increases in the distributions at 5:00 and 7:00. By 7:00 almost 90 per cent of the witnesses have risen to their daily labours. The remaining latecomers, however, take another three hours to leave their beds.

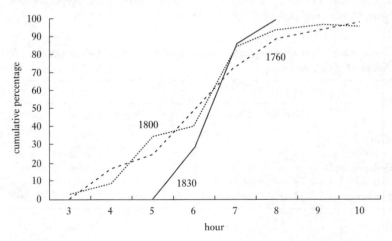

FIGURE 3.1. *Rising in the morning, 1760–1830 (London)*

[21] Old Bailey Sessions Papers, Case No. 300, 1756.
[22] Old Bailey Sessions Papers, Case No. 173, 1759.

The pattern in 1830 is somewhat different. Nobody appears to wake up before 5:00. Thereafter, the rate of increase is high, with a particularly sharp rise in the cumulative distribution between 6:00 and 7:00. By 8:00 all of our witnesses have left their beds. The trend towards slightly longer hours of sleep in 1830 is not statistically significant. It does, however, tally with a tendency to start work slightly later.

There is not sufficient evidence from the North of England to examine cumulative distributions in the same way. Overall, the differences between the North and London are rather small—10 minutes in the 1760s and 5 minutes in the 1800s. The sharp divergence in 1830 is not statistically significant.

Not only did our witnesses rise early, they also went to bed rather late. Figure 3.2 gives the cumulative distributions for London witnesses. Some 10 to 15 per cent of witnesses were in bed by 21:00. One of the earliest bedtimes recorded in our sample stems from a milkwoman, who went to bed at 21:00.[23] The percentage then rises slowly, to reach 50 per cent between 22:00 and 23:00 for all three distributions. Narrative accounts lend further credibility to our finding that the average time of going to bed was substantially after 22:00. When a witness was giving evidence before the court in 1779, he mentioned

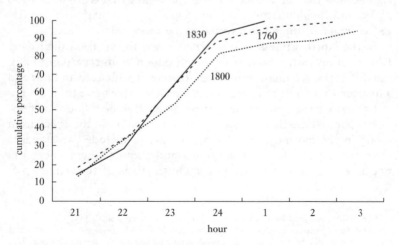

FIGURE 3.2. *Going to bed, 1760–1830 (London)*

[23] Old Bailey Sessions Papers, Case No. 597, 1802.

not only that his neighbour, a leatherseller, regularly went to bed at 22:00, but also notes that this is quite unusual:

As I was going up Borough High-Street ... , I observed ... Mr. Edward Lloyd before me with a parcel; ... yet I was going home, and living just at the foot of the said bridge on the Surrey side, at a Mr. George Beck's, a leatherseller, who is very particular with regard to the time of going to bed, seldom sitting up later than ten o'clock, I should not have concerned myself about it at the time ... [24]

Only approximately one-third of the observed population was in bed by 22:00. George Beck may have belonged to a minority, but it was a substantial one. By midnight, between 80 and 90 per cent of our witnesses have gone to bed. The remaining few, however, find the way to their beds at a rather slow (if constant) pace over the next four hours. The latest bedtimes seem to have been the result of important social events: on 24 December 1800 a journeyman tailor is being entertained and is dancing at his master's house, until he finally goes home at 4:00.[25] Also, social duties could result in unusually late bedtimes. On 19 September 1802, for example, we find a mother staying up until 3:00 because her child is ill with smallpox.[26]

London witnesses in 1800 go to bed a little later than those examined at the Old Bailey in 1760. The difference is not statistically significant—the confidence interval for 1760 extends from 22:25 to 23:15, and thus overlaps with the 1800 one from 22:47 to 23:55. By 1830 average bedtime has reverted to the 1760s value.[27]

In the North witnesses consistently begin to rest from their daily labours at an earlier hour than their London counterparts. Initially, the difference is a mere 10 minutes. In 1800 it widens to an hour and a quarter, only to be reduced to less than a quarter by 1830.

Basing our estimate on the means, an average of 7 hours 20 minutes separated the time of going to bed in London in the 1760s from rising in the morning. Given that we have to include two standard errors in the calculation of an upper and a lower bound, these will not be very close to the best guess. On the basis of the activity pat-

---

[24] Old Bailey Sessions Papers, Case No. 19, 1779 [not used in calculations].

[25] Old Bailey Sessions Papers, Case No. 117, 1800. It would be perilous to claim that this was a 'normal' day of the year, and that behaviour reflected everyday regularities. This observation was consequently discarded in the subsequent calculation of the average as well as of upper and lower bounds.   [26] Old Bailey Sessions Papers, Case No. 852, 1802.

[27] Again, the shift is not significant, as the confidence interval extends from 22:06 to 23:26.

terns observed in the sample from the 1750s and early 1760s (comparing means), we can be certain that hours in bed were not likely to be longer than 7 hours and 54 minutes and not shorter than 6 hours and 46 minutes.[28]

By 1800 the difference in the London data between going to bed and rising in the morning had been reduced to 6 hours and 17 minutes of sleep on average. We can therefore infer that the true mean was between 7 hours and 5 hours 34 minutes. The change between 1800 and 1830 is also strong and statistically significant. Witnesses slept an average of 8 hours 22 minutes by the later date, and the 90 per cent confidence intervals do not overlap.

Estimates of sleep duration are derived indirectly by comparing the beginning and end of sleep of a large number of individuals. Is there any reason to assume that those going to bed come from the same group as those rising in the morning? We can examine this proposition using two sources of information in our dataset. The first one constitutes a very direct test—in the London data in 1760, 13 witnesses commented on both their times of going to bed and of rising in the morning. For example, on 26 March 1760 a surgeon comes home at midnight and goes to bed. The next morning he rises between 7:00 and 8:00, his usual time.[29] On average, these witnesses were in bed for 8 hours and 10 minutes. This figure constitutes an upper bound on the hours of sleep since, in three cases, only one time is given for the activity immediately preceding the witness's going to bed and retiring to bed itself.[30] Evidence from sequences of going to bed and rising in the morning therefore suggest a total duration of sleep that is not very different from the one calculated above—the upper bound was 7 hours and 54 minutes.

The second way in which we can compare the two groups of witnesses is by their other characteristics. I have allocated witnesses to one of five broad occupational categories—agriculture, services, trade, manufacturing, and public service. If those going to bed come from a very different group from those getting up, we would expect that this should leave a trace in occupational compositions. Standard

---

[28] Both the 95 per cent confidence intervals and the inaccuracies of witnesses have been taken into account.

[29] Old Bailey Sessions Papers, Case No. 137, 1760.

[30] See Old Bailey Sessions Papers, Case No. 112, 1758 (visiting a prostitute), Case No. 155, 1760 (coming home), Case No. 137, 1760 (coming home).

statistical tests fail to find evidence of this.[31] It must be stressed that this test does not provide conclusive evidence that the people observed at the beginning and at the end of these activities stem from a homogenous group. Rather, we are unable to find a systematic difference between the two subgroups, using occupation as a proxy for sample composition. Note that the same is also true of the later London samples and the material gathered from the North of England.[32]

Work

In our London data from 1760, there are 44 observations on the time of starting work in our dataset. Nine concern women, 35 refer to men. The average start of work was at 6:50.[33] The short interval—a mere forty minutes—between rising in the morning and starting work suggests that workplaces were close to people's homes. Further, there was not very much time for basic hygiene between getting out of bed and starting work. Breakfast was taken later, at around 8:00.[34] Figure 3.3 shows how the number of people starting work increases slowly from 3:00 to 4:00, followed by a large increase between 4:00 and 5:00. More than a quarter of the population is at work by 5:00. Over the next three hours the proportion of those already at their desks and workbenches, on the fields, and in the stables increases at an almost constant speed. By 8:00 almost 90 per cent of all people had begun their

[31] I conducted a simple two-sample χ^2–test. With a Pearson statistic of 2.6 and 5 degrees of freedom (those not allocated to an occupational category were assigned to a separate group), there is a 62.4 per cent probability of the two groups coming from the same background. It must be stressed that 5 cells registered expected frequencies of less than 5. This is sometimes believed to undermine the efficiency of the test. The same procedure can be applied to the gender composition of the two samples—in almost every case the sex of the witness could be ascertained. The result was a test statistic of 2.92, which does not allow us to reject the null hypothesis (no difference) even at the 80 per cent level of confidence.

[32] The χ^2–statistics for the London data were 0.27 in 1800 and 0.21 in 1830. For the North, the results were 0.15, 0.2, and 0.11.

[33] The confidence interval is rather large—from 6:08 to 7:31. With 15 (out of 44, or 34 per cent) of observations based on statements that work was started within one hour, the imprecision of witnesses' statements compounds the problem. The average time of starting for those giving imprecise information was 6:10; without these observations, the sample mean would have been 7:11. The lower and upper bounds consequently have to be adjusted by an additional 7 minutes (0.34*20) if we assume that it is unlikely for all 15 witnesses to have erred simultaneously on the high or low side by more than 20 minutes.

[34] Results are not very different if we use bootstrapping to estimate standard errors.

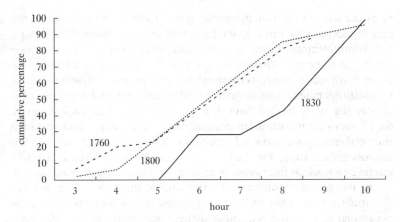

FIGURE 3.3. *Starting work, 1760–1830 (London)*

daily labours. Those starting even later were the privileged few, such as a stockbroker, who begins to work at 10:00 on 30 May 1759.[35]

Campbell's *London Tradesman* from 1747 contains a long list of London trades including their 'hours of working'.[36] The average starting time for the 182 professions contained in his work is 6:08. This does not agree perfectly with our estimate; it is none the less easily within the 95 per cent confidence interval. The slight difference between our witnesses and Campbell's trades is probably due to sample composition—Campbell restricts himself to artisans, whereas our sample also contains occasional labourers and others who were more likely to start work later in the day.

The start to the working day in 1800 is remarkably similar. On average, people in our sample from 1799–1803 began work at 6:33, a quarter of an hour earlier than witnesses some forty years earlier. The cumulative distribution rises slowly between 3:00 and 4:00, and then becomes virtually identical with the one from 1760. Again, few individuals start work as late the plasterer who began to work on Tuesday, 11 February 1801 at 10:30.[37]

By 1830 the pattern has shifted markedly. In earlier periods, approximately forty minutes had separated the time of rising in the

---

[35] Old Bailey Sessions Papers, Case No. 317, 1759.
[36] R. Campbell, *The London Tradesman* (London, 1747), 330 ff.
[37] Old Bailey Sessions Papers, Case No. 224, 1801.

morning and the start of the working day. In line with the shift in the end of sleep, our witnesses start to work at a later time. On average, their daily labours begin at 7:50. Just as there were no witnesses reporting to be up before 5:00, there is also none that started work at such an early hour. Witnesses' reports in the Northern Assize Depositions paint a similar picture. Between 1750 and 1830 the time of starting work moved from 6:10 to 6:33, and then back again to 6:03.[38] Agriculture, for all its reputation for long hours, also provided the opportunity for some relatively late starts to the working day. On 12 November 1800, for example, we find an agricultural labourer starting to work in the potato field of a Mr Denison at 10:00.[39]

On average, work finished at 18:50 during the 1750s. This average also includes the many unskilled labourers who were employed on an occasional basis and often finished their daily work during the early afternoon.[40] Skilled craftsmen, apprentices, and masters worked until 19:00 or 20:00. This finding is in line with eighteenth-century regulations: Campbell records an average of almost precisely 20:00.[41] During no interval do more individuals stop work than between 18:00 and 19:00, when the cumulative frequency plot shows a sharp rise from 27 to 53 per cent. Thereafter, quite a few individuals carry on working, like the smith who, giving evidence in 1751, said that he 'was coming home from work . . .' on 6 May at 22:15,[42] or the chairman who finished working at 23:00.[43] In London in 1799–1803, there are 44 observations on the time at which work ended. Three female and 41 male witnesses provided information of sufficient accuracy. The average time was 19:07.[44] Half of all witnesses stopped working during the one-and-a-half-hour interval between 18:15 and 19:45. The earliest time of finishing work is reported by a day labourer who had been

---

[38] The change is not statistically significant.

[39] Northern Assize Depositions, Case No. 129, 1800.

[40] The estimate of the mean is not very precise: the 95 per cent confidence interval extends from 17:44 to 19:57. To this, we have to add 7 minutes on either side because of the 35 per cent of all observations which were only accurate to within one hour. This yields an estimate of 17:37 to 20:04—clearly a more than narrow range. Yet this is only partly due to the small number of observations. As described above, large differences existed between occupational groups, thereby widening the confidence interval further.

[41] Campbell, *London Tradesman*, 330 ff.

[42] Old Bailey Sessions Papers, Case No. 367, 1750. We cannot rule out the possibility that he spent quite some time on his way back: e.g., by going to a public house. Yet he very clearly felt that the interval was not large enough not to define his coming back as a return from work.   [43] Old Bailey Sessions Papers, Case No. 436, 1754.

[44] The 95 per cent confidence interval extends from 18:30 to 19:44.

employed by a warehouse-man.[45] Of course, very late hours prevailed for shopkeepers, coach drivers, and the like. In the calculation of the 'normal' time for stopping work, we have excluded all those labouring in professions that regularly required work at night. The latest time of finishing work in a trade that is normally conducted during daytime was 23:30, when a tailor was delivering a suit to a customer's house.[46] In London, thirty years later, the average end of work had moved little—the mean is now 19:05, with more witnesses stopping at 20:00 than at any other hour. Initially the time of stopping work in the North of England was virtually indistinguishable from London patterns. It also appears to move back slightly between 1760 and 1830 (Figure 3.4). While witnesses from the Northern counties finished work at 19:00 in the middle of the eighteenth century, the average for 1830 is 20:00. Long hours were not always the result of employers' pressure. We find a female servant from the West Riding of Yorkshire working late on Saturday night. Her master suggests that she retires

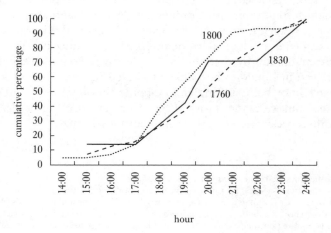

FIGURE 3.4. *Finishing work, 1760–1830 (London)*

[45] Short-term and irregular employment was a sign of the times. It is very possible that the same man found other employment for the rest of the day. Yet since the only information we have indicates that he stopped work, it seems defensible to subsume his case under the category 'end of work'. Old Bailey Sessions Papers, Case No. 811, 1800.

[46] The tailor declared that it was unusually late. See Old Bailey Sessions Papers, Case No. 676, 1800.

to bed, while she insists that her work has to be finished first.[47] There are no observations for 1800 of individuals finishing work.

Before we can use information on starting and stopping times to calculate the length of the working day, we need to be sure that we are comparing like with like. Were those starting and stopping work sufficiently similar to compare the means? Using the control variables introduced earlier—occupation and gender—we are again unable to detect systematic differences.[48] Note that, in the case of sleep, the witnesses' characteristics used to test sample composition were not necessarily systematically related to the activity under examination. Since it may be supposed that occupation and working hours are not independent of each other, we have also performed a much more direct test of the hypothesis that those starting and stopping work came from very different groups.

Having established that the two groups are comparable, we can now calculate the duration of work. The difference between starting and stopping work in 1760 and 1800 suggests a working day of almost exactly 12 hours' length.[49] Given that we have taken irregular employment into account, this also corroborates the less quantitative historical literature on the subject.[50] Initially in London the working day appears to lengthen by half an hour, only to be reduced to 11 hours and fifteen minutes by 1830. In the North, where hours were initially longer than in London, they appear to have lengthened even further by 1830. Since both starting and stopping times are only observed with an error, we cannot prove at the customary rejection levels that such differences between periods and locations existed.[51]

---

[47] Northern Assize Depositions, Case No. 160, 1800.

[48] For the London data in 1760, using the sectoral composition as a control, the χ^2–Pearson statistic is 5.19, which suggests that we cannot reject the null hypothesis (no significant difference) at confidence levels as low as 65 per cent. This result is reinforced if the exercise is repeated on the basis of gender. Of the 44 witnesses beginning work, 36 were male. For those stopping work, the proportion is somewhat larger—32 out of 36. The absolute difference is small. It is also statistically insignificant. A χ^2–test yields a statistic of 2.1, which leaves a probability of 35 per cent that both groups are identical with regard to gender composition. In 1800 and 1830 the results are broadly similar, yielding χ^2–statistics of 3.7 and 2.3 for sectors and 1.7 and 1.9 for gender.

[49] The difference amounts to 13 hours if we compare medians.

[50] Daily working hours for fully employed artisans ranged from 12 to 14 hours. See, e.g., Mary Dorothy George, *English Social Life in the Eighteenth Century* (London, 1925), 205 ff.

[51] A systematic calculation of the length of the working day, taking into account mealtimes, is performed below.

Discretionary activities

Sleep is a physical necessity, and for those without a large inheritance or other means of support, work is imperative as well. Having discussed these two forms of necessary time-use, we now turn to what has been called 'discretionary time'. Despite the long working hours and the demands of sleep, a substantial part of the day can still be put to other uses. Most of them are not leisure pursuits, but necessary as well. Domestic work such as washing, cleaning, and shopping has to be carried out if social norms are to be respected, and even seemingly 'free' forms of time-use such as social visits are not entirely at the liberty of the persons concerned. If the term 'discretionary' is appropriate, it is because the timing and duration of the act (rather than the act itself) can be influenced by the actors themselves. The activities subsumed under this heading do not all share this characteristic to the same extent. Eating is a physical necessity, and meals taken at the workplace may be subject to strict rules. Supper, on the other hand, is much less influenced by the discipline of the workplace. Timing and duration can largely be determined by individuals; in this regard, it is more similar to domestic work, etc. At the far end of the spectrum, we find leisure activities such as drinking, gambling, visits to the theatre, and social interaction with one's friends and acquaintances. Let us begin by examining the more 'restricted' activities.

Breakfast was taken after the start of work, thereby interrupting work during the early morning. In 1760 the nine witnesses in our sample who reported this activity ate their early morning meal at 8.50. Four ate at 8:00, two at 9:00, two more at 9:30, and the last one was having breakfast at 10:30. Information about the last witness is incomplete—we only know that he was male, and that he enjoyed breakfast at such a leisurely time on a Monday.[52] By 1800 six individuals witnessed a crime during or just after breakfast. In line with the earlier start to the working day and an earlier time of leaving bed, we find a shift in the timing of breakfast. By 1830 breakfast was being taken at almost exactly the same time as seventy years earlier—an average of 8:45. The last witness to report having breakfast is a gentleman, who eats at 10:00 on Thursday, 17 January 1833.[53]

Breakfast in the Northern counties occurs at a similar hour, but the evidence is more patchy. There are no observations for 1760. In 1800

---

[52] Old Bailey Sessions Papers, Case No. 151, 1753. The 95 per cent confidence interval extends from 8:08 to 9:32.   [53] Old Bailey Sessions Papers, Case No. 228, 1833.

we find a miller having breakfast with his family on Saturday, 28 December 1799 at 9:00, which is the most common time to have breakfast in the sample.[54] The average is 8:24, as some witnesses are having breakfast before 8:00. In 1829 the average is only marginally later, at 8:30. There are only two observations—the wife of a blacksmith having breakfast at 8:00 on 27 July 1829, and a clothdresser eating his morning meal at 9:00 on a Saturday.[55]

Lunch can be analysed along the same lines. In our London data from the 1760s, fourteen individuals reported having lunch (leading to twelve observations);[56] more than half did so between 13:00 and 14:00. The earliest occasion is reported on 25 May 1753 by a couple keeping a haberdasher's shop, who go out for lunch at 11:30.[57] Nobody has 'dinner' later than the workman on board a ship, who eats some time between 15:00 and 16:00 on 3 March 1760.[58] The average time for lunch was 13:43.[59] The dataset from 1799/1803 contains 25 observations on the taking of 'dinner' (= lunch). The average time for this activity was 13:30.[60] There was some indication that members of the upper classes had lunch at later hours, but this has not emerged as a significant trend.[61] By 1830 lunch appears to have been taken slightly earlier. The average is now 12:45, with most witnesses interrupting their work at 13:00.

Patterns in the North are more difficult to reconstruct, but show no major divergences. Between 1800 and 1829 the average time for the midday meal changes from 13:13 to 12:15. Owing to the limited sample size, this is not a significant shift.[62]

---

[54] Northern Assize Depositions, Case No. 47, 1800. We also find a butcher and a servant in husbandry in the North Riding having breakfast at this hour.

[55] The second witness had breakfast on 27 May 1829. Northern Assize Depositions 1829 [no case no. assigned].

[56] Whenever the activity of more than one person could be inferred from the statement of a single witness, this was counted as one observation. The rationale for this procedure is simple—it would be nonsensical if one of our estimates was dominated by a single statement simply because the witness mentions the presence of a large number of other people.

[57] Old Bailey Sessions Papers, Case No. 285, 1753.

[58] Old Bailey Sessions Papers, Case No. 116, 1760.

[59] The confidence interval for the mean extends from 12:39 to 14:06—a little less than one and a half hours.

[60] With a standard error of 14.6 minutes, this implies upper and lower bounds of 13:54 and 13:06, respectively.

[61] Such a finding would constitute a precise parallel to the Austrian case, where the timing of the lunch break indicated precisely a man's position in society. Robert Rotenberg, *Time and Order in Metropolitan Vienna: A Seizure of Schedule* (Washington, DC, 1992), 20.

[62] Note that there are no observations on lunchtimes in our dataset from the North in 1750.

In London during the 1750s and 1760s supper was clearly taken after work had ended, at 21:00 on average.[63] Fifteen of our witnesses reported on the time of their evening meal. The restricted sample size obviously cautions against any far-reaching conclusions. Nevertheless, it is interesting to observe that only one-third of respondents had started eating by 20:00. One of these was a farmer who started to have supper between 19:00 and 20:00. The largest single increase in the cumulative distribution occurs between 20:30 and 21:00, when an additional one-third of the sample is observed having supper. The subsequent rise is reasonably rapid only until 22:00. During these hours we find the servant having bread and cheese plus a pint of beer for supper,[64] as well as the customer at an inn who is being served by the owner between 21:00 and 22:00 on 5 July 1754.[65]

By 1800 supper was being taken marginally earlier in the evening, at 20:50. There was considerable diversity in the underlying population—while almost half of the witnesses reported taking supper at 22:00, the earliest time was 17:30. Our data therefore do not indicate a significant shift during the second half of the eighteenth century. As in the earlier dataset, we can be assured that supper was definitely taken considerably later than the end of work.[66]

Tea was taken around 18:00 in London during the middle of the eighteenth century. With only six observations, the precision of this estimate is low; the time of taking tea is not significantly different from the time of stopping work. For some, tea as a short meal (and distinct in character and timing from supper) may have signalled the end of the working day—our estimate of the timing of both activities gives overlapping confidence intervals.[67]

[63] The 95 per cent confidence intervals of the two activities do not overlap, with the lower and upper bound estimates for supper being 8:21 to 21:42. Only four of the total of 15 observations were 'precise' to within one hour; on the basis of the assumptions discussed above, this widens the confidence interval to 8:16 to 21:47. (0.26 × 20 = 5.3).

[64] This occurred on 13 March 1759; Old Bailey Sessions Papers, Case No. 158, 1759.

[65] Old Bailey Sessions Papers, Case No. 370, 1754.

[66] There is only one observation on supper times in our last dataset—a baker is dining in a pub at 23:10 on Wednesday, 19 December 1832 (Old Bailey Sessions Papers, Case No. 333, 1832). From the North, we only have two observations, in 1800, on the timing of supper—both give a time of 20:00: Northern Assize Depositions, Case No. 158, 1800 and Case No. 160, 1800.

[67] We cannot prove that our witnesses did not refer to the evening meal as 'tea', yet the large interval compared to the average time for supper makes it unlikely that such a confusion could have arisen.

In 1799–1803 sixteen of the individuals giving evidence before the Old Bailey claim to have been taking tea at the time of the crime.[68] They report an average time of 18:08. Of all the activities analysed so far, tea time displayed the greatest degree of homogeneity— Londoners around 1800 differed more in the timing of all other activities than they did with respect to the time when they took tea.[69] No one in the sample had tea before 17:00 or after 19:00. By 18:00 more than 60 per cent of witnesses had had 'time for tea'. Shopkeepers seem to have retired to a back room to enjoy a little rest and have tea. For other professions, this activity may have marked the end of the working day.[70] Tea moved to an earlier time by 1830, when the average is 17:17.[71]

Our data also afford us a glimpse of the drinking habits of Englishmen between 1750 and 1830 (Figure 3.5). It was one of the more popular activities mentioned by witnesses—with thirty-five observations from London in the 1750s alone, sample sizes are not small. The average time for drinking was shortly before 18:00. The first quarter of witnesses stops for a pint before 17:00—this is occasional drinking that comes with travelling and outdoor work. A coachman, for example, tell us that, on Monday, 29 December 1762, he 'pulled [his] coach out into the street, at 10 o'clock in the morning. I went into the house, to get a pint of beer . . .'.[72]

The mid-eighteenth century's 'happy hour' begins at 18:00. It is after this time that the steepest increase in the cumulative distribution occurs. More than 40 per cent of the total drinking we observe takes place between 17:30 and 21:00—shortly after the end of work, and

---

[68] Two prostitutes who also claimed to have had tea were excluded from the sample.

[69] The standard error of the mean was equal to 7 minutes, the smallest of all those examined in this study.

[70] I conducted an ANOVA test, pooling the times for stopping work and taking tea. With an F-ratio of 4.35, there is only a 4 per cent probability of the two times being equal. To establish the length of the interval, a t-test was used. Levene's test for equality of variances ($F = 9.975$, $P = 0.003$) strongly rejects the null hypothesis of equal variances. On the basis of this result, a t-test for unequal variances yields a value of 4.22, which is significant at the 99.8 per cent level. The 95 per cent confidence interval consequently indicates a difference of at least 26 minutes. The possible maximum difference amounts to 1 hour 52 minutes. While I find a statistically significant result, it seems improbable that work started for as short a time as 26 minutes. Given the nature of our historical data, it seems best to conclude that the time for tea and the stopping of work coincided for at least some individuals.

[71] Evidence from the North is scarce. In 1800 we find one couple keeping a public house having tea 'in the afternoon', and in 1829, we find a dealer in old rags and his wife in York having tea at 16:00. Northern Assize Depositions.

[72] Old Bailey Sessions Papers, Case No. 101, 1763.

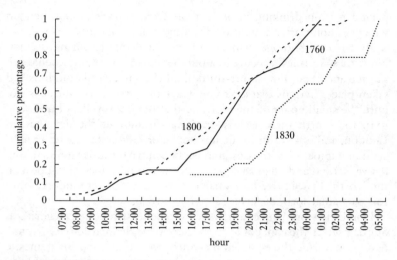

FIGURE 3.5. *Drinking, 1760–1830 (London)*

before supper. The rate of increase of the cumulative distribution slows somewhat after 21:00. Compared to the earlier hours of the day, quite substantial drinking is still carried out between 22:00 and 1:00. As many witnesses report drinking during these three hours as between 9:00 and 3:00—an interval of six hours. Around midnight, a recruiting sergeant is drinking with one of his recruits on 22 November 1758,[73] and a leather-dresser drinks with a prostitute on 24 April 1756.[74] The overall pattern is confirmed by the timing of work in pubs and inns.

In London in the 1800s we find the earliest case at 7:30 in the morning—a gardener who visits an inn on 7 May 1800.[75] Until 15:00 the cumulative frequency curve rises slowly. Most of the drinking is then concentrated in the later afternoon and evening, with this particular form of merriment continuing into the early hours. The last

---

[73] With the war in North America attaining a high intensity (the British took Louisburg in Nova Scotia in the same year), the army's need for new recruits was strong. The size of the Royal Navy had jumped from 12,000 in 1755 to 45,155 in 1758. See Roderick Floud, Kenneth Wachter and Annabel Gregory, *Height, Health and History. Nutritional Status in the United Kingdom, 1750–1980* (Cambridge, 1990), table 2.6, pp. 68–9.

[74] Old Bailey Sessions Papers, Case No. 27, 1758; Case No. 226, 1757. Arguably, the recruiting sergeant was working.   [75] Old Bailey Sessions Papers, Case No. 427, 1800.

person to stop drinking in our sample from 1800 is a hoop-bender, who goes home after a night of drinking at 2:45 on 9 June 1801.[76]

By 1830 we find less evidence of regular drinking during the day. No witness testifies to being in a pub before 16:00, a time when, both in 1760 and 1800, almost one-third of all visits to taverns and inns had taken place. Serious drinking now takes off after 21:00 and it is not until the small hours of the morning that the last revellers leave.[77]

In the North there is less drinking throughout the day than in London, and in 1830 and 1760 it is not before 18:00 that we find a substantial number of witnesses in inns. The move towards later drinking between 1800 and 1830 that we found in London does not appear in the North. Instead, we find a particularly late start (around 21:00) to this particular form of leisure activity in 1800.

Domestic work is necessarily one of the least precise categories in our dataset. If the concept of work as a clearly defined activity is a difficult one during the eighteenth century, then this is true of domestic work to an even greater extent. It is a heterogeneous category at best. Domestic work, as defined for this project, comprises all unremunerated activities necessary to preserve a socially defined minimum standard of living, such as the buying and preparation of food and provisions for a clean, warm, and safe home, as well as child care.[78]

For most of the activities discussed above it was sensible to ascertain both arithmetic averages and the degree of certainty with which this mean could be inferred from the data. In the case of domestic work this is not the case. This is an activity that took place throughout the day—but the relative frequencies clearly differed. If the overall range extends from 9:00 to midnight, calculations of the mean attain a degree of artificiality much larger than if the range extends from 17:00 to 19:00. The 'average' timing of an activity is always an artefact; in the case of activities like domestic work, it would not be a very useful one. One should also expect that unremunerated activities of this kind occur throughout the day, being much less constrained by the necessities of the workplace, availability of daylight, and the interaction with fellow workers. In London in the 1750s and 1760s domestic work took place throughout the day. The probability of finding witnesses engaged in domestic work is virtually constant between 8:00

---

[76] Old Bailey Sessions Papers, Case No. 637, 1801.
[77] Old Bailey Sessions Papers, Case No. 233, 1832.
[78] To be sure, it is not easy to separate the socially necessary from the indulgent and superfluous.

and 18:00. The largest part of these activities is performed by house-wives such as the woman who hangs up two gowns in a garret at noon on 21 March 1755[79] or the wife warming some broth for her husband on 2 September 1757 at 14:30.[80] The acceleration of domestic activities after 18:00 is probably due to the end of work. While the work of housewives continues, many menial duties are performed on the way back from work. On 19 June 1751 a baker comes home, bringing back some wood he bought on the way.[81] Also, as the hours of sleep and darkness approached, considerable care was taken to make houses safe during the night.[82] In November 1749 a widow who takes in washing is fastening her windows between 18:00 and 19:00. Three years later, on Christmas Day 1752, we find a spinster locking her doors at 22:00.[83] These precautions are considered so important that considerable care is devoted to checking if doors and windows have been properly secured—such as the haberdasher who, after coming home at 23:00 on 27 November 1749, checks locks, etc.[84]

The same uniform distribution can be found in London in 1800. Only between 18:00 and 20:00 is there a slight increase in the observed frequency of domestic work. In 1829 most of the domestic work is performed between 16:00 and 18:00, but the small sample size cautions against reading any deeper meaning into this shift. The Northern data do not contain enough observations to merit an extended discussion, but they share one important characteristic with the London data. As might be expected, there is a disproportionate number of women and children engaged in domestic work—an observation all the more striking given the generally low number of females and children in our sample.

Another activity which should be considered under the heading of 'discretionary time-use' is visits to prostitutes. Quite a few crimes tried before the Old Bailey occurred in the *demi-monde* of London's brothels and taverns. Consequently, there is no shortage of information on the business hours of 'mankind's oldest profession'. Clearly, for the prostitute, her services are a form of work, not leisure. Yet her

---

[79] Old Bailey Sessions Papers, Case No. 160, 1755.
[80] Old Bailey Sessions Papers, Case No. 319, 1757.
[81] Old Bailey Sessions Papers, Case No. 421, 1751.
[82] Of course, shops, etc. took at least comparable care. If the putting up of shutters etc. was an integral part of the workday, it was counted under that heading. Because of the context in which our witnesses testify, the locking of doors, etc. is recorded quite often.
[83] Old Bailey Sessions Papers, Case No. 59, 1750 and Case No. 218, 1753.
[84] Old Bailey Sessions Papers, Case No. 22, 1750.

customers—and there are only female prostitutes in our sample—are engaging in what they consider enjoyment. In London in 1760 we have a total of twenty-seven observations on the timing of prostitution. The earliest services of this kind are provided at 16:00, after a man had been drinking with prostitutes on Monday, 24 January 1756.[85] Business picks up after the time for supper, around 21:00. For example, the son of a pawnbroker who is still living with his mother visits a prostitute at 22:00 on Saturday, 28 March 1761.[86] Amongst the other customers satisfying their desires in the back alleys of London we find a sailor, an enameller, and a brewer's servant.[87] Demand continues to be brisk until 1:00. The last customer is being served at 4:00.

The pattern in 1800 was very similar. From the eleven cases in which either prostitutes or their customers gave evidence, it emerges that demand was probably most buoyant between 21:00 and 22:00, when almost half of all reported visits to prostitutes or brothels took place ($N = 5$). This does not mean that 'opening hours' were short: those who sought sexual adventures could satisfy their desires as early as 14:00 or as late 2:00.[88] Compared with the earlier period, the number of visits to prostitutes recorded in our court cases declined from 27 to 11. The reduction in so small a sample should be interpreted with care. It is none the less interesting to note that this may contradict Stone's claim that '[t]he eighteenth century … saw a rise in prostitution …'.[89] If our data are a good indicator, the rise must have occurred during the earlier half of the eighteenth century. By 1830 there are no visits to prostitutes during the day or early afternoon. Instead, we find witnesses 'enjoying' this particular form of diversion late at night until the early hours of the morning. Class distinctions mattered little—we find a solicitor inside a brothel at 5:00 on 27 October 1832, and a servant out of a place picking up a prostitute at 8:00 on 3 December 1832.[90] In the Northern dataset we find only one witness visiting a prostitute—a drover who is drinking in a Northumberland public house, and then picks up a whore at 22:00 on 4 February 1801.[91]

---

[85] Old Bailey Sessions Papers, Case No. 152, 1756.

[86] Old Bailey Sessions Papers, Case No. 135, 1761.

[87] Old Bailey Sessions Papers, Case No. 457, 1754; Case No. 180, 1756; Case No. 356, 1751.

[88] Old Bailey Sessions Papers, Case No. 232, 1800, and Case No. 283, 1801, respectively.

[89] Lawrence Stone, *Family, Sex and Marriage in England, 1500–1800* (New York, 1977), 645.   [90] Old Bailey Sessions Papers, Cases No. 233 and 269, 1832.

[91] Northern Assize Depositions, 1801 [no case assigned, case tried on 5 Feb. 1801].

Weekly and Annual Patterns

A substantial literature has argued that pre-modern work schedules differed from present-day ones in two regards: the annual and the weekly patterns of labour and leisure. Sections below discuss the incidence of labour during the year. Here, weekly variations are analysed. During data collection, all cases were coded according to the primary activity that individuals were performing at the time. Initially three different codes were used in order to classify whether the witness was engaged in paid work, unpaid work, or leisure. This information can now be used to establish if the English were less likely to work on a specific day of the week.[92] First, the proportion of people observed in paid work is grouped by the day of the week. Table 3.7 gives the percentage of individuals working by day of the week.

Three different definitions of work were employed. W1 denotes all those cases where witnesses engaged in normal work activities during the day;[93] w2 also includes those cases where witnesses started or stopped work on a specific day. W3 is the most comprehensive of the definitions employed—it includes all cases in w2 plus work in shops, which has been excluded in w1 and w2 because there is some evidence that shopkeepers kept different hours. On weekdays around 21 per cent of the individuals observed were engaged in paid work in 1760, according to the most narrow definition of work. Wednesday, Thursday, Friday, and Saturday registered a slightly higher ratio;

TABLE 3.7. *Percentage of witnesses at work by day of the week, London (w1)*

Day of the week	1760	1800	1830
Monday	16.2	23.1	23.2
Tuesday	21.4	29.8	19.9
Wednesday	23.9	25.5	23.3
Thursday	24.0	21.9	26.8
Friday	24.0	26.9	28.1
Saturday	25.7	27.9	33.7
Sunday	12.4	14.6	14.2

[92] Even an insignificant result for the whole sample would not rule out the possibility that certain subgroups never worked on, say, Wednesdays.

[93] Differences are more pronounced if the more encompassing definitions of work are used.

TABLE 3.8. *Logistic regressions, London (dependent variable: individuals engaged in work (w3))*

Weekday	B	Wald	Δ Odds Ratio	Significance
1750				
Sunday	−0.40	3.02	0.67*	0.08
Monday	−0.41	5.52	0.66**	0.019
Tuesday	0.14	0.54	1.15	0.46
Wednesday	0.08	0.22	1.08	0.64
Thursday	0.11	0.36	1.11	0.55
Friday	0.18	1.00	1.19	0.32
Saturday	0.23	1.63	1.26	0.20
1800				
Sunday	−1.12	4.25	0.30**	0.01
Monday	−0.085	0.24	0.92	0.62
Tuesday	0.18	1.04	1.20	0.31
Wednesday	0.56	9.10	1.70**	0.03
Thursday	−0.15	0.67	0.86	0.41
Friday	0.37	3.91	1.45**	0.047
Saturday	0.52	8.68	1.67**	0.003
1830				
Sunday	−1.25	8.89	0.28**	0.029
Monday	−0.21	0.46	0.81	0.49
Tuesday	−0.39	1.90	0.67	0.19
Wednesday	−0.18	0.24	0.83	0.62
Thursday	0.27	0.45	1.31	0.50
Friday	0.49	2.10	1.63	0.15
Saturday	1.50	11.50	4.70**	0.007

Note: * and ** indicate significance at the 90 and 95 per cent levels, respectively, according to the Wald-test. (Walter Hauck and Allan Donner, 'Wald's Test as Applied to Hypotheses in Logit Analysis', 851 ff.)

Mondays and Sundays both show less than 20 per cent of those observed as working. The patterns in 1800 and 1830 are similar, except for an overall rise in the proportion of individuals found in work, and a rise in the proportion observed in work on Mondays.

The variation in the numbers of those recorded as working by weekday is not random.[94] This, however, is not sufficient to conclude that, for example, Monday was different from all the other days of the

[94] χ^2–tests give results of 19.7, 29.9, and 24.9, which in each case is sufficient to reject the null hypothesis of random variation at the 99 per cent level of confidence.

week. To clarify this question, it is convenient to use logit regressions.[95] For each case, we construct a simple dichotomous variable equal to one if the witness was engaged in work, and zero otherwise. This is then regressed on a set of other characteristics, including the day of the week.[96] Table 3.8 gives the results of a number of such regressions that compare the probability of finding witnesses at work on any given day with all other days of the week.[97]

In the 1750s and 1760s Sunday, Monday, and Tuesday show a negative divergence from the average. For Mondays and Sundays the difference is statistically significant. In both cases the odds of observing individuals in work are almost halved. Wednesdays, Thursdays, and Fridays again show small increases, but the significance levels are very low. This finding is not affected by the definition of work used. Figure 3.6 gives the relative size of coefficients under the three alternative definitions of work, using Saturday as a reference point.

Sundays and Wednesdays show almost identical relative sizes. The same is not true for Tuesday, Thursday, and Friday, where divergences are large. Monday is almost identical in relative size under definitions

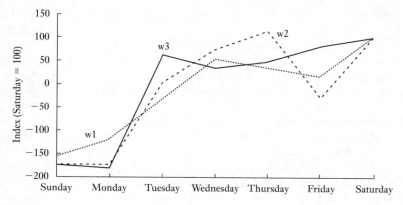

FIGURE 3.6. *Work during the week, 1760 (London)*

---

[95] For the methodological background see Melissa Hardy, *Regression with Dummy Variables* (Newbury Park, 1993), 9.

[96] Amongst the additional variables included are gender, time of the day, and sector of occupation. The weekday effects are not influenced markedly by the inclusion of such variables. Table 3.8 therefore reports the results of simply regressing the dependent variable on the day dummies.

[97] Cf. Walter Hauck and Allan Donner, 'Wald's Test as Applied to Hypotheses in Logit Analysis', *Journal of the American Statistical Association*, 72 (1977), 851 ff.

w2 and w3. The reduction in the probability of work vis-à-vis Saturday is less pronounced for w1. Since Sundays and Mondays are still remarkably similar, there is no reason to doubt that both should be counted as days 'off'.[98]

Traditional interpretations receive some support from the results in Table 3.8. The later days of the week, when workloads are supposed to have mounted so that the previously agreed number of products could be finished, register large odds ratios in all specifications.[99] Interestingly, Saturday ranks amongst the three most intense working days of the week. The odds ratio is substantially larger than unity, and is significant under definition w3.

In London in 1800 the gradual intensification of work over the course of the week is still a feature of our data. Interestingly, we no longer observe a change in the probability of observing witnesses on Mondays. While the odds ratios for Monday are among the smallest for all the working days in the week, they are never statistically significant.[100] Sunday continues to show a sharp reduction in the number of witnesses engaged in work. Wednesday, Friday, and Saturday show higher than average work probabilities. It therefore seems sensible to assume that the practice of 'St Monday' vanished some time between 1760 and 1800.

The London data from 1830 display the familiar pattern of a sharp fall on Sundays, and then a gradual rise in the intensity of work throughout the week. The large coefficient for Saturday appears to suggest that the intensification during the week became more acute over time, but the relatively limited sample size for 1830 cautions against putting too much emphasis on this finding.

The sample from the North shows no evidence of 'St Monday' being observed, either before or after 1800. Sunday registers the familiar reduction in the percentage of people engaged in work. Also, the gradual increase in work frequency towards the end of the week observed in London does not occur in our sample in the same way. Fridays in 1800 and 1830 register higher than average frequencies of work, but the result is only significant at the turn of the century.

[98] To check for robustness, I also tested the significance of the Monday effect using a non-parametric technique. The Mann-Whitney U-tests reported in the Appendix (Tables A2 and A4) yield almost identical results.

[99] E. P. Thompson, 'Time, Work-discipline, and Industrial Capitalism', *Past and Present*, 38 (1967), 65 ff.

[100] This is true under all the possible definitions of work. See Appendix, Table A4, and Figure A1.

TABLE 3.9. *Logistic regressions, North of England (dependent variable: individuals engaged in work (w3))*

Weekday	B	Wald	Δ Odds Ratio	Significance
1760				
Sunday	−0.90	2.72	0.41*	0.099
Monday	0.84	2.14	2.30	0.14
Tuesday	−0.46	0.74	0.63	0.39
Wednesday	0.53	0.88	1.70	0.35
Thursday	0.69	1.99	1.99	0.16
Friday	−0.24	0.25	0.78	0.62
Saturday	−0.11	0.05	0.90	0.82
1800				
Sunday	−0.99	2.57	0.37*	0.08
Monday	−0.06	0.02	0.94	0.88
Tuesday	0.51	0.98	1.67	0.32
Wednesday	−0.47	1.60	0.60	0.21
Thursday	0.05	0.01	1.05	0.92
Friday	1.60	7.90	4.90*	0.01
Saturday	−0.43	1.05	0.65	0.31
1830				
Sunday	−0.75	3.01	0.47*	0.08
Monday	0.38	0.59	1.46	0.44
Tuesday	0.63	1.60	1.87	0.21
Wednesday	0.16	0.14	1.17	0.71
Thursday	−0.97	3.48	0.38*	0.06
Friday	0.17	0.07	1.19	0.79
Saturday	−0.46	0.83	0.63	0.36

Note: * indicates significance at the 90 per cent level.

Leisure is another activity reported by our witnesses. I subsumed under this category all forms of social interaction which are clearly not aimed at an immediate advantage, such as visits to friends, going to the theatre, drinking in a pub, or gambling. The number of witnesses reporting any one of these pastimes was not large. On average, only between 7 and 10 per cent claimed to be engaged in leisure activities. There appears to be some bias in favour of outdoor activities, which may have facilitated the observation of crimes. Table 3.10 gives an overview by day of the week.

In London in the 1760s, Monday shows the largest proportion of people enjoying leisure. Since we concluded that work ceased on this

TABLE 3.10. _Leisure activities by day of the week—London (percentage of all witnesses observed, unweighted average)_

	1760	1800	1830
Monday	12.00	14.10	9.40
Tuesday	3.80	10.60	6.90
Wednesday	8.80	7.60	9.10
Thursday	4.80	8.90	3.00
Friday	4.70	8.20	5.80
Saturday	9.30	6.70	2.10
Sunday	8.90	15.70	22.20

day, this is not particularly surprising.[101] The later days of the week, Thursday and Friday, show less time for pleasure. Tuesday marks the week's low point, while Wednesday, Friday, and Saturday—the traditional payday—report slightly above average levels of _divertimento_. Surprisingly, the percentage of witnesses claiming to have been engaged in leisure on a Sunday is approximately of the same magnitude as on these weekdays.

By 1800 the weekly pattern has become more volatile, and the proportion of witnesses engaged in labour has actually increased. Interestingly, despite finding no evidence of a disproportionate number of witnesses taking time off on Mondays, we still find the second-highest proportion of witnesses engaged in leisure activities. Saturday goes from being the second most active day to the one registering the lowest proportion of witnesses engaged in leisure pursuits. Sunday now becomes the day when most recreational activity is concentrated. This position becomes even more pronounced by 1830. Monday again shows a relatively high number of witnesses drinking or visiting relatives.

Logit regressions demonstrate that not all elements of the weekly pattern were statistically significant (Table 3.11). Our results on leisure and labour during the average week in 1760 are largely in line with expectations. The only exceptions are Monday and Saturday. I present evidence that Monday was a day of rest, almost on a par with Sunday. Leisure activities were more frequent, and our witnesses were less likely to be observed at work on a Monday. Saturdays, however,

---

[101] In the section on the 1800 dataset, I will show that Monday continued to be a day for leisure pursuits even after it became a regular working day.

TABLE 3.11. *Logistic regressions (dependent variable: individuals engaged in leisure)*

Weekday	B	Wald	Δ Odds Ratio	Significance
1760				
Monday	0.69	6.30	2.01*	0.012
Tuesday	−0.76	2.58	0.46	0.09
Wednesday	0.25	0.63	1.28	0.43
Thursday	−0.51	1.55	0.60	0.21
Friday	−0.54	1.76	0.58	0.19
Saturday	0.31	0.94	1.36	0.32
Sunday	0.28	0.82	1.27	0.35
1800				
Monday	0.52	3.98	1.67*	0.046
Tuesday	0.12	0.16	1.12	0.688
Wednesday	−0.31	0.855	0.74	0.355
Thursday	−0.11	0.123	0.89	0.726
Friday	−0.21	0.39	0.81	0.53
Saturday	−0.47	2.03	0.62	0.15
Sunday	0.618	3.93	1.86*	0.047
1830				
Monday	0.54	0.98	1.70	0.30
Tuesday	0.09	0.01	1.09	0.91
Wednesday	0.44	0.44	1.55	0.51
Thursday	−2.56	0.15	0.0013	0.70
Friday	−0.14	0.04	0.87*	0.04
Saturday	−1.31	1.58	0.27	0.21
Sunday	1.10	3.20	2.90*	0.07

Note: * indicates significance at the 90 per cent level.

were clearly normal working days.[102] By 1800, we only find Sunday and Monday showing significant divergence from the remaining days of the week. Both register large increases in the proportion of witnesses engaged in recreational activities. We can therefore conclude that only two days in the week differed markedly from all others in terms of leisure activities—Monday and Sunday. Both registered a far

[102] Mann-Whitney U-tests (Appendix, Table A2) show that only Monday differed from all other days. The Z-scores are too low to reject the null hypothesis (no difference) in all other cases by quite a margin. The one exception is Tuesday, which shows less leisure. Here the null hypothesis is rejected with 89 per cent confidence, just below the customary level.

above average probability of witnesses being engaged in forms of leisure. The similarity of Monday and Sunday can be interpreted as qualifying the 'St Monday' hypothesis. It is important to remember that our evidence is possibly biased towards leisure activities enjoyed outside the home. Since heavy drinking at night can easily be enjoyed after a day's work, this is not necessarily an inconsistency in our data. From the evidence assembled in this section it appears that Monday was the occasion of more outdoor leisure, rather than a day of no work. The literature has always regarded work and outdoor leisure as mutually exclusive.[103] Our results suggest otherwise, with Monday showing a marked increase in outdoor leisure, yet no significant reduction in work activities.

Sunday remains a day of high activity in 1830. Monday and Wednesday continue to register relatively high frequencies. Friday shows a relatively small, but significant reduction in the odds of encountering witnesses engaged in leisure activities. Patterns in the North show a limited degree of similarity with London ones (Table 3.12). Saturday in the 1750s and 1760s is a popular day for a drink or a chat, but shows below-average activity in 1800 and 1830. Sunday is unremarkable in 1760, but then becomes much more popular in the later samples. The weekly pattern in 1760 in the North and in London are not correlated, but the one from 1800 is.[104] By 1830 the correlation is lower than in 1800, but is still relatively high.[105] I refrained from using logit analysis on the Northern data—even in the case of large

TABLE 3.12. *Leisure activities by day of the week—North*

	1760	1800	1830
Monday	6.30	13.30	4.30
Tuesday	5.00	16.70	8.00
Wednesday	11.80	5.60	5.30
Thursday	7.10	5.40	5.30
Friday	15.00	8.70	10.70
Saturday	20.00	3.80	3.80
Sunday	4.80	11.50	10.00

[103] Thompson, 'Time, Work-discipline, and Industrial Capitalism'.

[104] Correlation coefficient 0.08 and 0.675, respectively. The latter result is significant at the 10 per cent level.

[105] With a coefficient of 0.49, the significance level is 25 per cent—too low by most standards.

coefficients, the limited sample size results in insignificant test statistics. What emerges from the comparison with the London data is that witnesses in the North of England did not engage in a systematically different pattern of leisure activities.

The Year and the Seasons

Our image of the past has many facets. In addition to the importance of religious holy days, wakes, and 'St Monday', sharp seasonal differences are also central to our view of traditional time-use.[106] How large was the impact of the seasons on time use during the 1750s, early 1760s, and at the turn of the century?

Let us begin by assessing the seasonality of work. At the most general level, the argument about the importance of the seasons is centred on the alleged importance of natural light for work. I examine the impact of shorter hours by testing how the probability of observing witnesses in work is reduced during the darker months (October–March). Aggregation of this kind is not intuitive; our findings are, however, insensitive to finer differentiations.

Table 3.13 reports Mann-Whitney U-tests for the three definitions of work introduced above.[107] There are no significant differences between the winter months and the rest of year; this finding is independent of the definitions of work we employ. In the dataset from 1749–63, shopkeeping activities showed some sensitivity to the seasons. For the earlier years, the higher probability of finding people at work in shops reflects the incidence of crime, and not of work itself. The lower risk of being identified or caught during the periods of

[106] See Stanley Engerman, and Claudia Goldin, 'Seasonality in Nineteenth Century Labor Markets', *NBER Historical Working Papers Series*, 20 (1991); Robert Gallman, 'The Agricultural Sector and the Pace of Economic Growth', in David Klingaman and Richard Vedder (eds.), *Essays in Nineteenth Century Economic History: The Old North-West* (Athens, 1975).

[107] The Mann-Whitney U-statistic is calculated as follows: first, the data from both samples are combined, and then ranked from smallest to largest. The first test-statistic is then calculated by examining each A value (from sample A) and counting the number of B values which precede it. The second test statistic, the number of times a B value precedes an A value, is then given by the formula: $U_2 = (n_1 * n_2) - U_1$ [$U_{1,2}$ first and second test statistic, $n_{1,2}$ sample sizes]. The *smaller* of the two values becomes the Mann-Whitney test statistic U. On the basis of this non-parametric technique, we are able to establish if the overall pattern is random, and if individual days diverge significantly. See Marija Norusis, *SPSS-X Introductory Statistics Guide for SPSS-X Release 3* (Chicago, 1988), 137 ff. Alternatively, we could have run the logit regressions used before, but results are essentially unchanged.

TABLE 3.13. Mann–Whitney U-Tests for Work During 'Winter'—
London

	W1	W2	W3	Shop
1760				
U	121982	122618	117332	116742
Z	−0.41	−0.20	−1.53	−2.49
Probability	0.68	0.84	0.13	0.01
Mean Rank	−5.50	−2.90	24.40	26.80**
1800				
U	106401	104027	104767	108384
Z	−0.85	−1.45	−1.16	−0.25
Probability	0.40	0.14	0.25	0.81
Mean Rank	−12.99	−24.30	−20.78	−3.54

Note: ** indicates significance at the 95 per cent level.

short daylight hours would then have been responsible for the disproportionate number of shopkeepers mentioning that they were working. As Table 3.13 shows, this increased likelihood of thefts occurring
under the cover of darkness seems to have vanished by 1800. We can
interpret this as a further consequence of the improvement and
spread of street-lighting during the second half of the eighteenth
century.

At the broadest level of aggregation, there is therefore no proof
that the seasons influenced time-use strongly. The same is not true
when we turn to more specific activities. When we outlined the basic
features of daily life, particular attention was devoted to the timing of
work and sleep. Did these activities differ over the annual cycle?

It would be desirable to subdivide our dataset into four groups—
activities during spring, summer, autumn, and winter. Limited sample
size rules out such an approach. If, however, the year is divided into
two six-month periods (October–March and April–September), some
conspicuous contrasts can be established.[108]

Let us begin with the hours of sleep. One of the strongest reasons
why we expect large contrasts between summer and winter involves
hours of daylight—in the absence of efficient artificial lighting, many
activities will be uneconomic or even outright impossible. The exis-

[108] There were not enough observations in the dataset from the North to replicate the
analysis conducted for the London data.

tence of improved public lighting tells us little about conditions within houses. We should therefore expect witnesses to report earlier hours of rising in the summer period than in the six months from October. Figures 3.7 and 3.8 demonstrate that this was the case. During both periods the cumulative frequency curve for summer is consistently above the one for the winter. Divergence is small before 5:00. Thereafter, the gap widens. The first 50 per cent of witnesses during the summer have left bed before 5:30. The same ratio is reached almost an hour later in winter in 1800, two hours in 1760.

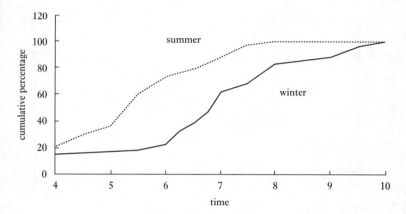

FIGURE 3.7. *Rising in the morning—seasonal differences in 1760*

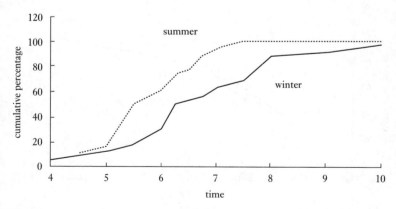

FIGURE 3.8. *Rising in the morning—seasonal differences in 1800*

During the winter, 40 per cent are still in bed at 7:00, when almost 95 per cent of individuals during the warmer months have already risen. It is only after 7:30 that the gap narrows, with the last witnesses rising in the autumn and winter at 10:00. It should be borne in mind, however, that subdividing our sample greatly reduces the number of observations.

No similar pattern is visible in the case of study subjects going to bed (Figures 3.9 and 3.10). With twenty observations for October–March and eighteen for April–September, conclusions can again only be tentative. It appears, however, that bedtimes were remarkably similar. The

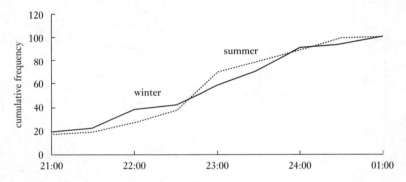

FIGURE 3.9. *Going to bed—seasonal differences in 1760*

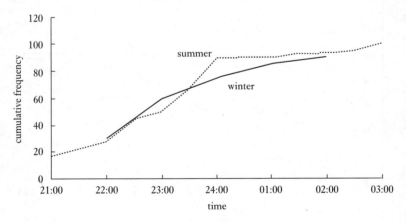

FIGURE 3.10. *Going to bed—seasonal differences in 1800*

largest difference in 1800 between the two cumulative frequency distributions occurs at midnight, when a slightly higher proportion of individuals during the summer are already in bed. In the 1760 maximum divergence was reached at 23:00. If we are to believe that this is not due to an unsatisfactory sample, then it may be rationalized as a response to the need to rise earlier during the warmer period. The lack of a divergence is not too surprising. Even from May to September, respondents stayed up much longer than daylight hours would have permitted. Consequently, seasonal differences were minute.

There was therefore a difference in the hours of sleep at different times of the year—rising earlier in the summer implies less sleep. On the basis of means, sleep lasted for approximately six hours during the summer and for almost seven hours in the winter.[109] If we focus on differences in the medians, then hours in bed increased from a little less than seven during the summer to seven and a half in the winter.

The issue of seasonality has even greater interest in the context of working hours. Implicit in our argument that daylight hours influenced the time of rising was the assumption that daylight was indispensable for a large number of occupations. We should therefore find a similar pattern for the time of starting work. This hypothesis is confirmed by Figures 3.11 and 3.12. The summer months saw earlier times of starting work. By 5:30 approximately half of the witnesses reporting on their time-use during the summer had started their daily

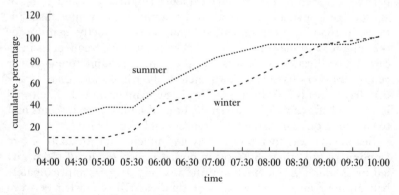

Figure 3.11. *Starting work—seasonal differences in 1760*

[109] The overall mean differs from the average of the two figures since one sample is larger than the other.

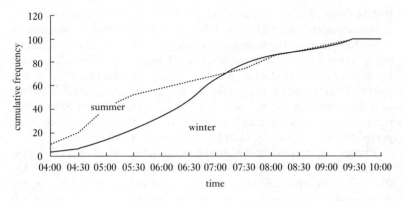

FIGURE 3.12. *Starting work—seasonal differences in 1800*

labours. At the same time during the winter months less than one-quarter had done so. Not before 6:30 had the first half begun to work. The gap between both cumulative distributions disappears around 7:00 in 1800, when 70 per cent of the total report they have started work.[110] In the sample from 1760, it takes until 9:00 for the differential to narrow substantially.

Our hypothesis regarding daylight would predict that longer working hours during the summer should also be driven by the opportunity to work late during the warmer months of the year. This is only partly supported by the available evidence (Figures 3.13 and 3.14). In 1760 there is a small gap between the summer and winter distributions. In 1800 the mean time of stopping work is exactly identical for the summer and the winter—19:06. The cumulative frequencies indicate minor divergences at best. In the winter, around 19:00, 50 per cent of workers have laid down their tools, while more than 65 per cent have already left during the April–September period. The trend is reversed after 20:30, but given the limited sample size, it seems best to conclude that no marked differences can be discerned.

Seasonality was therefore clearly an influence on the daily life of Londoners and other witnesses in both samples. Hours of sleep varied by as much as one hour, and the working day was approximately half an hour longer. Seasonality of time-use fell somewhat between the middle and the end of the eighteenth century. This is especially

---

[110] Sample size was again less than optimal—19 for the summer and 29 for the winter half-year.

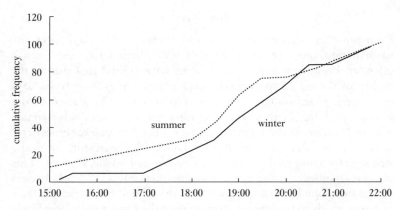

FIGURE 3.13. *Stopping work—seasonal differences in 1750*

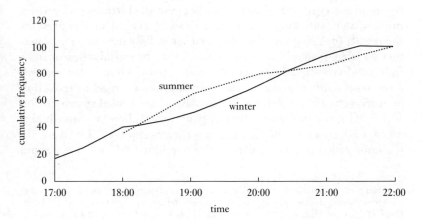

FIGURE 3.14. *Stopping work—seasonal differences in 1800*

true of the time of rising in the morning, and of starting work. In assessing the magnitude of the seasonality effect, it should also be remembered that our procedure tends to dilute contrasts somewhat. Differences between, say, December and June were probably much larger than the winter–summer dichotomy would suggest. The presence of observations from months such as May and March is likely to have diminished the overall effect of seasonality.

Holy days

Even after the disappearance of old Catholic holy days after the Reformation, there was no shortage of festive occasions in the English calendar. Freudenberger and Cummins have argued that during the middle of the eighteenth century work ceased on up to forty-six days in the year, plus Sundays, Easter, and Whitsun.[111] Our datasets from London and the North of England allow a direct test of this hypothesis. In London in the 1750s and 1760s work was markedly less frequent on holy days. Using all holy days as the regressor, we find a striking reduction in the odds of observing individuals in work. This effect is significant at the 95 per cent confidence level.[112] Yet holy days do not form one large, homogenous group. The most obvious distinction that needs to be drawn is between political and non-political holy days. The former were much less frequent than the latter—in Millan's list from 1749 there are fifteen political holy days (like 5th November, the anniversary of the Gunpowder Plot, and the birthdays of various princes) alongside thirty religious festivals.[113] Table 3.14 also presents the results for using the disaggregated set of holy days as an explanatory variable. It should be borne in mind that the introduction of multiple subdivisions reduces sample sizes rapidly. Despite limited cell sizes, both political and religious holy days show a marked reduction in work activities.[114] Religious holy days show a weaker association with a reduction in the incidence of paid work. Where statistically significant effects exist, they are also large in magnitude. The change in the odds ratios is very similar to the one observed on Sundays and

[111] Hermann Freudenberger and Gaylord Cummins, 'Health, Work and Leisure before the Industrial Revolution', *Explorations in Economic History*, 13 (1976), based on J. Millan, *Coins, Weights and Measure of all Nations Reduced into English* (London, 1749), 15.

[112] Table 3.14 reports results for w1, the most narrow definition of work. Table A6 in the Appendix shows that this is also true of w2-normal work activity plus starting and stopping of work. If, however, shopkeeping is included also, the result is reversed. Work is more frequent now, but the difference is not significant. Clearly, this suggests that shopkeeping did not follow the same temporal pattern as, say, making watches or driving sheep. A number of regressions was run to test for omitted variable bias, including a vector of control variables such as the day of the week, the hour of the day, gender, and sector. See Hans-Joachim Voth, 'Time and Work in Eighteenth-Century London', *Journal of Economic History*, 58 (1998), for the results in detail. Our findings were not materially affected.

[113] The total is actually 46, since 2 September, the day of the commemoration of the Great Fire in London, is probably best categorized as neither a religious nor political festival.

[114] In the case of church festivals, this finding is robust even if starting and stopping is included, but the same cannot be said of work (w2) on political holy days.

TABLE 3.14. *Logistic regressions—work on holy days*

Dependent variable (w1)	Holy days				Political 'holy days'				Religious holy days			
	B	Wald	Probability	Change in odds ratio	B	Wald	Probability	Change in odds ratio	B	Wald	Probability	Change in odds ratio
London												
1760	−0.63	5.60**	0.018	0.53	−1.18	2.70*	0.09	0.31	−0.52	3.50*	0.06	0.59
1800	0.29	2.26	0.13	1.34	−0.01	0.00003	0.99	0.99	0.23	0.93	0.33	1.30
1830	0.08	1.40	0.63	1.08	0.03	0.70	0.87	1.03	0.11	0.92	0.71	1.12
North												
1760	−0.56	3.60*	0.09	0.57	−0.31	2.70	0.14	0.73	−0.74	4.40**	0.046	0.49
1800	−0.21	1.90	0.21	0.81	0.13	2.20	0.17	1.14	−0.46	3.40*	0.095	0.63
1830	−0.10	1.20	0.32	0.91	0.07	0.30	0.49	1.07	0.18	0.90	0.23	1.20

Note: * and ** indicate significance at the 90 and 95 per cent levels, respectively.

'St Mondays'. This strongly suggests that, in London in 1749–63, neither 'St Monday' nor Millan's holy days were 'normal working days'.

Freudenberger and Cummins argued not only that holy days reduced the length of the working year during the middle of the century, but also that their effect gradually waned during the later decades. If we find evidence that a large proportion of Londoners engaged in work on these days, then Freudenberger's and Cummins's hypothesis is partly corroborated. On the whole, the results in Table 3.14 suggest that in London in 1800 holy days differed little from other days of the year in terms of working behaviour. The coefficients on the feastday dummy are insignificant for all political 'holy days'.[115] In both 1800 and 1830 we do not find a significant and large coefficient for the traditional holy days. This is true in London of both the religious and the political festivals.[116]

In the Northern counties we find a marginally weaker holy day effect for the 1750s than in London. Disaggregation shows that it is only the religious holy days that register a reduction in the likelihood of observing witnesses. Political festivals are associated with lower work frequency, but it is not significant at the customary rejection levels. In contrast to our London data, the influence of religious festivals continues until 1800. At the same time, the size of the coefficient falls, signalling a smaller reduction in the odds ratio than in 1760. Political festivals, which showed a small but insignificant reduction in 1760, now cause a small and insignificant increase in the odds of finding witnesses at work. By 1830 neither religious nor political holy days appear to have any effect.

If our conclusion is correct, then we should be able to test it in two ways. First, we should observe similar reductions in the likelihood of witnesses being engaged in work during Christmas and Easter. Second, we should also be able to observe a strong increase in leisure activities on holy days. I have reconstructed the time of Easter for the fifteen years in the first London dataset.[117] The impact of holy days was again analysed using a dummy variable which takes the value of

---

[115] When religious holy days are used as a regressor, only definitions w2 and w3 give a statistically significant, positive coefficient. See Appendix, Table A7.

[116] Some of the days given by Millan (admittedly, only a few) are birthdays of princes, etc. Some fifty years later there is little reason to assume that these days were still celebrated. The insignificance of the aggregate variable is not driven by this, as Table A7 demonstrates.

[117] This was established using the tables in Christopher Robert Cheney (ed.), *Handbook of Dates for Students of English History* (London, 1945), 83 ff.

one if an observation is on a holy day, zero otherwise. In Table 3.15, I give results from estimating the relationship using Christmas and Easter as a single exogenous variable with w1, w2, and w3 as the dependent variable.[118]

The results indicate marked reductions in work activities at Easter and Christmas. The size of the effect is not firmly established, ranging from a reduction of the odds to one-third (w3) to 70 per cent of their previous level (w1). Significance is assured at the 90 per cent level in all cases, with an even higher confidence level being attained if shopkeepers are included. Compared to the results for Millan's holy days, the average magnitude of the reduction in the odds ratio is similar. These results lend further credibility to our argument that the traditional festivals enumerated by Millan were still observed during the 1750s and early 1760s. We have strong *a priori* reasons for thinking that Easter and Christmas were observed. Because we find effects of similar magnitude for the other holy days, there is an indication that both types of festivals impinged in approximately equal measure on everyday patterns of time-use. One difference is conspicuous: whereas the inclusion of shopkeepers lead to insignificant results in table A.6, we now find the strongest 'holy day' effect if they are included.

It would now be useful to repeat the exercise for 1800 and 1830. The increased incidence of work on holy days might be the result of other, unobserved developments; if we could demonstrate that Easter and Christmas registered markedly less work, the credibility of our

TABLE 3.15. *Work at Christmas and Easter, London 1749/63*

Dependent variable	Christmas + Easter			
	B	Wald	Probability	Change in odds ratio
w1	−0.36	2.40*	0.100	0.70
w2	−0.42	3.30*	0.080	0.65
w3	−1.02	6.30**	0.011	0.36

Note: * and ** indicate significance at the 90 and 95 per cent levels, respectively.

[118] I experimented with disaggregating the exogenous variable into Christmas and Easter. In the case of w3, for example, the probability of finding individuals in work fell from 44 per cent during the year to 23 per cent at Christmas and to 20 per cent during Easter. Small sample sizes, however, lead to significance levels that are marginally below the customary rejection levels.

new method could be enhanced. Unfortunately, there are only nine observations from Easter or Christmas for the years 1799–1803. Two of the nine witnesses engage in some form of work, and seven do not.[119] There is exactly the same number of individuals observed on these days per year for which data was collected;[120] but since there are three times as many years in the earlier dataset, we are left with an insufficient sample. In the London data from 1830 there are only two observations.[121] The evidence on the incidence of work at Christmas and Easter lends qualified support to our general finding. At the time when the influence of holy days matters most for our estimates of the length of the working year, we find clear and unambiguous evidence that work activities during religious and political festivals were curtailed to a similar extent as on generally observed holidays.

Holy days have traditionally been scorned as occasions of much licence and revelry. If our finding of a reduction in work activities on holy days is correct, it should also be the case that we find a marked increase in recreational activities. On an anecdotal level, the Old Bailey Sessions Papers lend support to this hypothesis. Recall also the case of the servant who dances in his master's house until late on Christmas Eve. On Shrove Tuesday, March 1753 a large party of weavers and others, men and women, met to eat, drink, and make merry.[122] A little more than five years later, on a Thursday during Easter week, we find a man drinking himself 'insensible'.[123]

On a more rigorous level, the type of analysis applied to paid work can also be extended to less onerous activities. Leisure for our purposes is defined as all non-work activities that are not physical necessities, such as visiting relatives, drinking with friends, or walking in the park. In 1760 religious holy days did indeed cause a large increase in leisure. The odds of observing recreational activities on a feast day are 1.7 times those on an average day.[124] The suggested increase in the

---

[119] Under definition w1 and w2.   [120] There were 26 observations in 1749–63.

[121] The Northern datasets, suffering from an even more acute shortage of cases, also do not contain a large enough number of observations to repeat the analysis.

[122] Old Bailey Sessions Papers, Case No. 217, 1753. The presence of women is telling. Alan Dyer ('Seasonality of Baptisms: An Urban Approach', *Local Population Studies*, 27 (1981), 26–34) showed that Shrove Tuesday often registered a large rise in the number of conceptions.

[123] The event occurred on 30 March 1758. Old Bailey Sessions Papers, Case No. 208, 1758.

[124] This suggests a 63 per cent likelihood of observing someone resting or making merry. From the Wald statistic, we can infer that the effect is statistically significant at the 90 per cent level.

probability of leisure is very similar to the reduction of work activities; if confidence intervals are taken into account, there is no significant difference in magnitude between the relative rise in leisure and the fall in work activities. Political holidays do not show the same effect.[125] Since there were only a few political holidays, this can either indicate an absence of the expected activity pattern or small sample size. Combining both sets of holy days (row (1)) again gives a significant and strong effect (Table 3.16).

The results from the North of England lend a limited degree of support to our conclusions about the observance of holy days (Table 3.17). The only period for which we find significant results is the middle of the eighteenth century. Using the full list of holy days shows a strong and significant effect, indicating that witnesses were more likely to engage in leisure activities on holy days. The effect is particularly pronounced during political festivals; on religious ones, the change only attains marginal significance. There is still a mild effect, significant at the 17 per cent level, in 1800. Again, political festivals are more likely to cause a rise in revelry than religious holy days, which now show a negative (and insignificant) divergence. By 1830 there is no obvious relationship between leisure activities and holy days.

TABLE 3.16. *Holy days and leisure—London*

	B	Wald	Probability	Change in odds ratio
1760				
Millan's holy days	0.55	4.400*	0.08	1.73
Religious holy days	0.58	3.700*	0.09	1.78
Political 'holy days'	0.18	0.300	0.86	1.20
1800				
Millan's holy days	−0.32	0.210	0.64	0.72
Religious holy days	−0.27	0.930	0.33	0.76
Political 'holy days'	−0.34	0.130	0.72	0.71
1830				
Millan's holy days	−0.17	0.002	0.99	0.84
Religious holy days	0.07	0.004	0.99	1.07
Political 'holy days'	−0.20	0.001	0.99	0.98

Note: * indicates significance at the 90 per cent level.

[125] The Wald statistic is too low to attach any significance to the coefficient.

TABLE 3.17. *Holy days and leisure—North*

	B	Wald	Probability	Change in odds ratio
1760				
Millan's holy days	0.42	3.70*	0.087	1.49
Religious holy days	0.32	3.20	0.130	1.37
Political 'holy days'	0.50	4.40**	0.460	1.64
1800				
Millan's holy days	0.17	2.10	0.170	1.18
Religious holy days	−0.09	0.70	0.230	0.91
Political 'holy days'	0.28	2.60	0.140	1.32
1830				
Millan's holy days	−0.02	0.20	0.490	0.98
Religious holy days	0.38	0.90	0.230	1.46
Political 'holy days'	−0.45	1.20	0.320	0.64

Note: * and ** indicate significance at the 90 and 95 per cent levels, respectively.

Class and Gender Differences

In the first section, the focus of analysis was on different time periods. In this section, I reverse the procedure. Instead of asking how the incidence and timing of activities varied by day, month, or hour, I attempt to identify some contrasts and similarities in time-use according to the characteristics of individual witnesses. Ideally, we would want to reconstruct the exact pattern of time-use for all male shopkeepers aged 45–50, etc. With a small sample, a much more limited degree of disaggregation can be achieved. The following pages are an attempt to break down time-use as much as possible. Categories to be employed are gender, class, and occupation. The age of witnesses is very likely to have been important; unfortunately, this information is almost never recorded in the Old Bailey Sessions Papers.

One of the standard categories used by sociologists in the analysis of present-day data is gender. Differences in time-use between the sexes regularly receive media attention, and the value of household production is a topic of heated discussion. How did gender influence the timing and frequency of certain activities in England, 1750–1800? (Tables 3.18, 3.19, and 3.20.)

The first notable feature is the difference in sample size. In 1749–63 there are 766 males (76.5 per cent) and 236 females in our dataset. Out

TABLE 3.18. *Gender differentiation of time-use—London*

	Paid work (w3)	Unpaid work	Leisure	Total number of observations
1760				
Men	367 (47.70%)	30 (3.90%)	77 (10.00%)	769
Women	71 (30.10%)	39 (16.50%)	22 (9.30%)	236
1800				
Men	553 (66.90%)	32 (4.00%)	95 (11.50%)	826
Women	55 (26.60%)	54 (26.10%)	6 (3.00%)	207
1830				
Men	166 (70.60%)	7 (2.97%)	26 (11.06%)	235
Women	16 (50.00%)	4 (12.50%)	4 (12.50%)	32

Note: Percentages refer to the proportion of the total for each sex.

TABLE 3.19. *Gender differentiation of time-use—North*

	Paid work (w3)	Unpaid work	Leisure	Total number of observations
1760				
Men	58 (47.20%)	17 (13.80%)	21 (17.10%)	123
Women	9 (39.10%)	6 (26.10%)	4 (17.30%)	23
1800				
Men	87 (54.70%)	6 (3.70%)	19 (11.90%)	159
Women	24 (58.50%)	5 (12.20%)	1 (2.40%)	41
1830				
Men	68 (41.20%)	19 (11.50%)	21 (12.70%)	165
Women	6 (17.20%)	6 (17.20%)	2 (5.70%)	35

Note: Percentages refer to the proportion of the total for each sex.

of a total of 1,005 cases from 1800, 826 (82.1 per cent) refer to males. By 1830 this has risen to 88 per cent (32 women vs. 235 men). This casts doubt on the notion that our witnesses are a representative sample of the population. There is a reporting bias in favour of outdoor activities. If it were the case (and the possibility cannot be ruled out) that women were more likely, for example, to engage in work inside the home, then the nature of our source would lead us to underestimate the number of females engaging in paid work. As discussed

TABLE 3.20. *Gender differences in timing of main activities*

	Rising in the morning	Starting work	Leaving work	Going to bed
London				
1760	−13 minutes	−6 minutes	1 hour 40 minutes	−5 minutes
1800	−7 minutes	−1 hour 48 minutes	21 minutes	−2 hours 44 minutes
1830	45 minutes	n/a	n/a	45 minutes
North				
1760	n/a	n/a	n/a	n/a
1800	n/a	3 hours 14 minutes	n/a	1 hour 46 minutes
1830	1 hour	n/a	n/a	1 hour 3 minutes

Note: A negative value indicates that the average for women was lower.

before, there is also good reason to believe that the conduct of trials was not conducive to women being used as witnesses.

All cases were coded according to the witness's gender. Table 3.18 shows the results when we use activity frequencies for broad aggregates of time use. More men than women are engaged in paid work; this is independent of the definition of work used.[126] When unpaid work is considered, the pattern is reversed—in relative terms, many more women than men are engaged in unremunerated activities. Leisure activities involved both sexes in roughly equal measure in London in 1750 and 1830—between 9 and 10 per cent of the individuals observed were engaged in the pursuit of pleasure. In 1800 there is a larger asymmetry. The broad categories used to classify activities capture time-use in roughly equal measure for both sexes. While between 55 and 75 per cent of the female witnesses reported activities that fit our scheme, the same is true of 62 to 83 per cent of all men.

Just as in London, we find men predominantly engaged in paid work. In only one of our samples a higher percentage of women than of men is performing paid work. All of our samples from the Northern assize depositions are beset by small-sample problems, and we cannot rule out the possibility that any of the shifts and differ-

---

[126] The widest possible definition was used to minimize small-sample problems.

ences reported in Table 3.19 are driven by them. Women un-ambiguously seem to dominate unpaid activities. They also are less likely to report that they were engaged in leisure activities at the time of the crime than men. Over time, there appears to be a sharp upturn in the percentage engaged in paid work between 1760 and 1800, and a reduction thereafter.

Interpretation of these results has to proceed with care. The technique applied is a poor substitute for the construction of full time budgets for both sexes. On the basis of activity frequencies, it appears that men did more paid work and enjoyed more leisure, whereas women devoted more of their time to unpaid work. This finding is broadly in line with expectations, and should thus be interpreted as giving further credibility to the general method.

Did the strong gender differentiation of time-use suggested by our earlier analysis influence the hour at which people engaged in certain activities (Table 3.20)? Absolute differences are small throughout—the timing of main activities did not diverge by more than fifteen minutes. The one exception is the stopping of work, which recorded more than one and a half hours between the average for men and that for women. Clearly, small sample sizes present a problem—especially in the Northern dataset, where we sometimes lack observations on women completely.[127]

Any analysis of the influence of class on patterns of time-use is fraught with difficulties. First, if dividing our sample into two groups (male and female) already resulted in perilously small sample sizes, then any classification by class, using a much larger group of categories, will present even greater difficulties. Second, any classification scheme applied will be subject to criticism—there is an almost inevitable element of arbitrariness in assigning witnesses to specific classes.

---

[127] A simple way to test for contrasts is to use ANOVA tests. This statistical technique uses the variability in the population. Two measures of dispersion are calculated: the sum of squares between groups and within groups. If the two groups are not significantly different from each other, then the ratio of the two should be close to unity. This hypothesis is examined using the standard F-test. Should the F-test reject the equality of variances within and between groups, we interpret this as a sign of significant differences in timing. Throughout, the ANOVA-technique does not allow us to reject the null of no difference. There is only one significant result—the F-test for starting work in London in 1800. Variances between and within the groups defined by the gender of witnesses differed strongly; yet, with only five observations, it seems perilous to base any historical conclusion on this. For a summary of the ANOVA-method see J. Edward Jackson, *A User's Guide to Principal Components* (New York, 1991), 302 ff.

Schwarz distinguishes a number of groups in London society during the eighteenth century. At the upper end of the scale, there is what he terms the 'upper income group', consisting of the aristocracy and the most prosperous merchants and bankers. The opposite end of the scale is marked by the semi- and unskilled. Between these two extremes he finds three groups. Employed artisans are considered somewhere between the semi- and unskilled and the middle classes. The latter Schwarz subdivides into shopkeepers, self-employed artisans, and others. I have been able to assign the majority of witnesses to one of these broad categories. Self-employed artisans could be distinguished, but I had to combine shopkeepers and other members of the 'middling classes'. There are therefore five categories in total (Table 3.21).

The least useful category is 'upper income', in Schwartz's classification scheme. In the 1750s the one case of somebody working from the upper income group concerns the director of the Bank of England, who is attending a meeting in London on 3 October 1758.[128] In the London data from the 1750s it is not easy to distinguish a clearcut pattern for other occupational groups. Semi- and unskilled labourers seem more likely to be working at the time of a crime. This is a persistent feature, with two exceptions. Under definition w2

TABLE 3.21. *Paid work by class—London*

	Semi- and unskilled	Artisans	Shopkeepers and middle class	Self-employed	Upper classes
1760					
Paid work (w3)	220	69	78	14	1
Total	393	104	201	20	10
Percentage	56.00	33.70	38.80	70.00	10.00
1800					
Paid work (w3)	254	94	88	16	1
Total	419	164	159	38	13
Percentage	60.60	57.30	55.30	42.10	15.40
1830					
Paid work (w3)	92	23	40	11	1
Total	126	42	51	15	1
Percentage	73.00%	54.80%	78.40%	73.30%	100%

[128] Old Bailey Sessions Papers, Case No. 199, 1759.

employed artisans show a higher incidence of work, and under definition w3 self-employed artisans are even more likely to be encountered while at work. The overall impression, then, is one of an inverse relationship between class and the incidence of work. Yet sample sizes, especially for the self-employed and the upper classes, make any such statement perilous.

By 1800, compared with 1750/63, there is an almost universal increase in the percentage of each subgroup observed in work activities, however defined.[129] This is particularly true of classes with large sample sizes (semi- and unskilled, artisans). The increase in the incidence of work is only to be expected if, as I have argued above, the working year included many more days in 1800 than 1760. Differences between individual classes seem to be relatively constant over time. As in 1760, the semi- and unskilled as well as employed artisans registered some of the highest probabilities of being seen in work; the reverse applies to the upper classes. The London data from 1830 also suggest a certain degree of further intensification across occupational categories, with the possible exception of artisans.[130]

As the results from logistic regressions show, most of the patterns examined in Table 3.22 are also statistically significant. There is, however, one important caveat. Because we are often able to identify individuals and assign them to a specific class on the basis of their working activity, it shouldn't surprise us too much that the vast majority of classes register large increases in the odds of being engaged in paid

TABLE 3.22. *Paid work (w3) by class—logistic regressions—change of odds ratio*

	Semi- and unskilled	Artisans	Shopkeepers and middle class	Self-employed	Upper classes
1760	5.01**	7.70**	2.10*	9.20**	0.44**
1800	2.60**	2.30**	1.90*	1.20	0.36
1830	2.01*	0.62	2.30**	1.55	n/a

Note: * and ** indicate significance at the 90 and 95 per cent levels, respectively.

[129] Note that we are not controlling for the over- or undersampling of certain hours of the day, which tends to accentuate shifts in the distributions. We leave the exercise to a later section.

[130] Note that, in a pooled sample, the shift from 1760 to 1800 is significant, but from 1800 to 1830 it is not.

work. The relative magnitude of effects is of more interest. The semi-
and unskilled as well as employed artisans throughout register some of
the largest coefficients. Shopkeepers and the middle classes follow,
and the upper ranks actually register a reduction in the odds ratio
throughout (Table 3.23).

We have already noted that the number of people observed in
leisure was relatively small. Again, limited sample sizes in most cases
strongly suggest that these results should be interpreted with caution.
Leisure activities seem to have similar importance among the semi-
and unskilled, employed artisans and shopkeepers, and the middle
class. The percentage of semi- and unskilled witnesses engaged in
leisure activities increases sharply between 1760 and 1800, and then
returns to its former level. In contrast, the proportion of artisans
found in the public houses of London, visiting relatives, or resting at
home, shows relatively little variation between 1760 and 1830. The
same is true of shopkeepers and the middle classes between 1760 and
1800. It is difficult to attribute much significance to the shift in 1830,
as it is based on a much smaller sample (Table 3.24). For the self-
employed and the upper-income group, it would also require heroic
assumptions to infer much from period-to-period variations.

Not many of the changes in probability are statistically significant.
The semi- and unskilled as well as shopkeepers and the middle classes
seem to do markedly less unpaid work in the London of the 1750s and

TABLE 3.23. *Leisure by class—London*

	Semi- and unskilled	Artisans	Shopkeepers and middle class	Self-employed	Upper classes
1760					
Leisure	26	10	13	1	3
Total	393	104	201	20	10
Percentage	6.60	9.60	6.50	5.0	33.30
1800					
Leisure	44	22	12	7	3
Total	419	164	159	38	13
Percentage	10.50	13.40	7.50	18.40	23.10
1830					
Leisure	8	5	1	2	0
Total	126	42	51	15	1
Percentage	6.30	11.90	1.96	13.33	0

TABLE 3.24. *Leisure by class, change in odds ratio, London*

	Semi- and unskilled	Artisans	Shopkeepers and middle class	Self-employed	Upper classes
1760	0.55**	0.77	0.90	0.48	3.96*
1800	2.12**	2.80**	1.40	4.10**	5.40**
1830	0.98	2.30	0.25	2.40	n/a

Note: * and ** indicate significance at the 90 and 95 per cent levels, respectively.

1760s. The upper classes enjoy more leisure while there is definitely less for the semi- and unskilled. The advantage of the upper classes is retained in 1800, and the results for artisans and the self-employed now suggest a significant shift. In 1830, due to limited sample sizes, not one of the coefficients in our logit regressions is significant. Independent of the statistical significance of these findings, historical judgement cautions against assigning too much importance to results based on very restricted samples.

How did the timing of activities change with the witnesses' class? I use the familiar ANOVA procedure to establish differences. Table 3.25 summarizes the results. In the London sample from the 1750s and 1760s none of the differences in the timing of principal activities is statistically significant. Consequently, there is not much scope for interpreting the sometimes large differences. On an impressionistic level, the upper classes seem to sleep longer; artisans sleep less, and shopkeepers and the middle classes appear to have shorter working hours. By 1800 some statistically significant differences become apparent. The semi- and unskilled rise earlier in the morning, just as the self-employed definitely enjoy a later start to the day. Shopkeepers and the middle class continue to start work later than the average witness, just like the upper classes and the self-employed. By 1830 we find the self-employed starting work unusually late, as well as going to bed more than an hour after the average witness has retired for the day. Overall, the semi- and unskilled show the smallest average deviation from overall patterns.[131]

The preceding section tried to group witnesses according to their social status. The classification was carried out on the basis of Schwarz's categories. It is of course possible to group witnesses according to other criteria. One such alternative is to use broad

[131] The one exception to this rule appears to be the time of stopping work in 1800.

TABLE 3.25. *Timing of principal activities—differentiation by class*

	Rising in the morning	Starting work	Leaving work	Going to bed
Semi- and unskilled				
1760	−1 minute	−39 minutes	−50 minutes	−2 minutes
1800	−46 minutes*	+20 minutes	−2 hours 2 minutes	+3 minutes
1830	−5 minutes	−46 minutes	+6 minutes	+4 minutes
Artisans				
1760	−1 hour 10 minutes	−1 hour 12 minutes	+40 minutes	−20 minutes
1800	+10 minutes	+27 minutes	+7 minutes	n/a
1830	+45 minutes	n/a	n/a	−26 minutes
Shopkeepers and middle class				
1760	+20 minutes	+1 hour 25 minutes	−2 hours 10 minutes	+25 minutes
1800	−11 minutes	+20 minutes	−3 hours 19 minutes	+18 minutes
1830	n/a	n/a	n/a	+14 minutes
Self-employed				
1760	+1 minute	n/a	+1 hour 40 minutes	n/a
1800	+1 hour 19 minutes*	+1 hour 22 minutes	+1 hour 6 minutes	+2 hours 1 minute
1830	n/a	+1 hour 55 minutes	−5 minutes	+1 hour 14 minutes
Upper classes				
1760	+1 hour 5 minutes	n/a	n/a	+10 minutes
1800	+1 hour 19 minutes	+1 hour 22 minutes	+1 hour 6 minutes	+2 hours 1 minute
1830	n/a	n/a	n/a	n/a

Note: Entries refer to the difference between an individual group and the mean. A negative value implies that the average for a class was lower. * indicates significance at the 90 per cent level.

occupational categories, such as agriculture, manufacturing, or services (Table 3.26). In virtually all sectors—public employees in 1760 and 1800 being the exception—work is the activity reported by more than half of all witnesses (using definition w3). The percentage of witnesses in agriculture reporting to be at work rises strongly between 1760 and 1830. The same is true of services and trade.[132]

In the case of leisure also, there are some pronounced differences between individual sectors (Table 3.27). Agriculture consistently records few or no leisure activities, whereas manufacturing and services show significant percentages engaged in recreation. The unusually high percentage recorded for the public sector in 1800 is probably driven by limited sample size.

There are some significant results when logistic regressions are used (Table 3.28). Agriculture shows a large increase in the likelihood of paid work; the same is true of trade. Only in the latter case is the shift consistently statistically significant. Change in agriculture may partly be driven by higher proportions of agricultural labourers—instead of farmers—reporting. Public sector workers also show relatively constant reductions in their probability of being found at work. In the case of leisure, significant coefficients are few and far between.

TABLE 3.26. *Paid work by sector—London*

	Agriculture	Manufacturing	Services	Trade	Public
1760					
Paid work (w3)	14	60	120	93	6
Total	29	92	278	142	27
Percentage	48.30	65.20	43.20	65.50	22.20
1800					
Paid work (w3)	25	113	120	127	7
Total	33	204	222	171	37
Percentage	75.80	55.40	54.10	74.30	18.90
1830					
Paid work (w3)	7	46	71	44	2
Total	8	69	97	52	3
Percentage	87.50	66.70	73.20	84.60	66.70

[132] Note that we are not correcting for the uneven incidence of crime, but are using uncorrected percentages. The correction is performed in a later section. Sample size in the case of public employees is too small to interpret in a meaningful way.

TABLE 3.27. *Leisure activities by sector, London sample*

	Agriculture	Manufacturing	Services	Trade	Public
1760					
Leisure	0	5	4	1	1
Total	29	92	278	142	27
Percentage	0	5.43	1.44	0.70	3.70
1800					
Leisure	1	28	17	9	8
Total	33	204	222	171	37
Percentage	3.00	13.70	7.70	5.30	21.60
1830					
Leisure	0	7	7	0	0
Total	8	69	97	52	3
Percentage	0	10.10	7.20	0	0

TABLE 3.28. *Paid work by sector—logistic regressions (odds ratios)*

	Agriculture	Manufacturing	Services	Trade	Public
Work (w3)					
1760	1.22	2.67**	0.98	2.87**	0.36*
1800	4.46**	1.77**	1.68**	4.10**	0.30*
1830	3.97	1.14	1.83*	3.69**	0.27
Leisure					
1760	0.008	1.75	0.33*	0.17*	1.10
1800	0.28	1.40	0.70	0.50*	2.40**
1830	0.039	2.06	1.22	0.004	0.01

Note: * and ** indicate significance at the 90 and 95 per cent levels, respectively.

The only exceptions are services and trade in 1760, which show marked reductions, and trade and public services in 1800—the former shows a marked reduction, whereas the latter registers significantly more recreational activities.

Sample sizes are too small to assemble data for individual occupations and to compare them with one another. What can be ascertained, however, is that there are some significant differences if individuals are grouped into broader occupational categories. To the present day, agriculture is famous not only for long hours but also for an early start of the day. Using the standard techniques introduced above, we can now test if individuals who worked the land started their working day

TABLE 3.29. *Rising in the morning—occupational differences*

	Agriculture	Manufacturing	Public	Trade	Services
Rising in the morning					
1760	−2 hours 10 minutes	+5 minutes	n/a	+1 hour 5 minutes	−4 minutes
1800	−11 minutes	−5 minutes	+4 minutes	+49 minutes	−17minutes
1830	n/a	+22 minutes	n/a	n/a	−8 minutes
Starting work					
1760	−1 hour 50 minutes	+6 minutes	n/a	+25 minutes	−1 hour 14 minutes
1800	−1 hour 31 minutes*	+1 hour 26 minutes	n/a	−5 minutes	+19 minutes
1830	n/a	+56 minutes	n/a	n/a	n/a
Stopping work					
1760	n/a	+25 minutes	n/a	+57 minutes	−6 minutes
1800	+54 minutes	−18 minutes	+1 hour 9 minutes	−1 hour 50 minutes*	+1 minute
1830	−1 hour 50 minutes	−1 hour 20 minutes	n/a	−5 minutes	+4 hours 17 minutes
Going to bed					
1760	−20 minutes	+10 minutes	n/a	+12 minutes	+5 minutes
1800	+39 minutes	+1 hour 20 minutes	+3 hours 9 minutes	+28 minutes	−21 minutes
1830	n/a	+14 minutes	n/a	+29 minutes	+4 minutes

Note: * indicates significance at the 90 per cent level.

at an earlier hour than those in other sectors. In both 1760 and 1800 the average witness working in agriculture started work one and a half hours before the average person in the full sample.[133] As might be expected, those in the primary sector also rose earlier (Table 3.29). The difference is particularly striking in 1760, and then narrows by 1800.[134] There is also some evidence of those working the land going to bed earlier in 1760, but this is reversed by 1800.

Changes in Time-use

The preceding sections presented data on time-use for three periods, 1750–63, 1799–1803, and 1829–32. How did patterns of labour and leisure change over time? First, I shall give a short overview of shifts in time allocation during the period 1760–1830. Second, the distinctive characteristics that emerge for the 1750s and 1800s are placed in a long-term perspective.

The basic structure of life remained largely unchanged during the three-quarters of a century under consideration. The timing of main activities during the day shows barely any differences. Hours of work during the day were also largely static. While people in the Old Bailey Sessions Papers on average started work at 6:45 during the 1750s and early 1760s, the respective figure for 1800–3 is 6:33. The difference is equally small between the times of stopping work. Work activities ended at 19:48 in the middle of the eighteenth century; fifty years later the average working day extended to 19:06. Again, these differences are not statistically significant. The best-guess estimate for daily working hours for both periods is eleven hours. By 1830 the average time of starting work had moved to 7:50, while stopping times had barely changed at all (19:05). There is therefore some evidence to suggest that average daily hours in London may have been reduced to as few as ten per day, by the 1830s. On balance, the early start to the day is also confirmed by other sources. In Chester in 1725 the normal working hours for journeymen were fixed as 6:00 to 20:00.[135]

---

[133] The difference is statistically significant, with the ANOVA procedure giving a 0.085 per cent probability of the two groups having the same starting time at work.

[134] Confidence intervals are too large to claim statistical significance. Hence, even though the means imply that agriculturists started work before they got up in the morning in 1800, there is no basis for such a claim if the error bands are taken into account.

[135] See Donald Woodward, *Men at Work: Labourers and Building Craftsmen in the Towns of Northern England, 1450–1750* (Cambridge, 1995), 125. Hull labourers and workmen in Liverpool also appear to have started their daily labours at around 6:00.

Hours of sleep in London were shorter towards the beginning of the nineteenth century than in the middle of the eighteenth century, but the difference is also not large. While sleep averaged 7 hours and 27 minutes for 1750–63, this figure had fallen to 6 hours and 35 minutes in 1800–3. It must be stressed that the difference is not statistically significant at the customary 90 per cent and 95 per cent levels. Of the 52-minute difference between the averages, 24 were caused by people rising earlier, while 28 minutes of rest were lost owing to later bedtimes. By 1830, however, hours of sleep on average had lengthened to 8 hours 22 minutes. Again, the difference is not statistically significant. Most of the change is the result of a later time of leaving bed.

Evidence from the North is more patchy. During the middle of the eighteenth century time-use patterns in London and the North were almost identical. By 1800 we still find only minute differences in terms of rising in the morning and starting work. The time of stopping work is unobserved, and bedtimes are not markedly earlier than in the London sample. By 1830 there is significant divergence in terms of starting times and the time of rising in the morning. If our data are to be taken at face value, then average daily hours in the North lengthened between 1800 and 1830.[136]

In marked contrast to the largely unchanging pattern of daily life, time allocation both during the week and during the year exhibits radical change. E. P. Thompson argued that 'St Monday' was universally observed until the beginning of the nineteenth century.[137] As discussed above, in London in the 1750s, the probability of finding an individual at work was lower on Mondays than on other days of the week. Indeed, Monday was virtually identical with Sunday in this regard. This strongly suggests that, in London during the middle of the eighteenth century, Monday was a day off. In the North of England, however, there was no evidence of 'St Monday' curtailing the length of the working year. The probability of observing witnesses in paid work differed little by day of the week, and there was no clear shift of the weekly pattern between the middle of the eighteenth and the nineteenth centuries.

By the turn of the century witnesses' time-use in London had changed markedly. While the probability of observing individuals

---

[136] Note that our estimate of meal times also changes in the Northern sample, reducing the magnitude of the upward shift.

[137] Thompson, 'Time, Work-discipline, and Industrial Capitalism'.

engaged in work activities on a Monday is again smaller than on average, logistic regressions demonstrate that this effect is not statistically
significant.[138] With respect to patterns of paid work Monday does not
differ from other days of the week. Using the probability of observing
individuals at work as a yardstick, there is no conclusive evidence to
suggest that workers still enjoyed an extended weekend through the
custom of 'St Monday' as late as 1800–3. This impression receives
further support from our finding that Monday appears to have been a
normal working day in London in 1830 as well. It therefore seems sensible to conclude that 'St Monday' declined rapidly during the second
half of the eighteenth century, and that it had all but disappeared by
the turn of the century.[139]

A similarly large change occurred on public and religious holidays.
The importance of holy days in England before and during the
Industrial Revolution has been a matter of discussion for some time.
The most influential statement on the topic is Freudenberger's and
Cummins's.[140] Freudenberger and Cummins assume that a large part of
this extra work was carried out on days formerly devoted to festivities.
The basis of their contention is a list of holy days contained in a handbook published by J. Millan in 1749.[141] He gives forty-six fixed days on
which work at the Exchequer and other government offices ceased.
Later, during the second half of the century, the observation of these
holy days is said to have slowly vanished. Consequently, Freudenberger
and Cummins argue, annual labour input possibly increased from
less than 3,000 to more than 4,000 hours per adult male between 1750
and 1800.[142]

As the preceding sections demonstrated, the holidays registered by
Millan exercised a strongly negative effect on the probability of
observing people in paid employment during the 1750s. The effect is
clearly evident in both the Northern and London samples. The
impact was large, suggesting that work was as rare on a holy day as on
a Sunday (or on 'St Monday'). By 1800–3 London and Northern samples show strong divergence. In London the old holy days seem to
have vanished almost completely, whereas religious holidays appear to
exert a continuing influence in the Northern counties.

---

[138] This is true despite the fact sample size was respectable.
[139] Reid ('Decline'), using wedding days as a source, comes to different conclusions. The
limitations of this approach are discussed in Ch. 2.
[140] Freudenberger and Cummins, 'Health, Work and Leisure'. See above, Ch. 2.
[141] Millan, *Coins, Weights and Measure*, 15.
[142] Freudenberger and Cummins, 'Health, Work and Leisure', 6.

How long, then, was the working year during the eighteenth century? There are two ways to establish the overall length of the working year from our data. First, we construct an annual time budget from the timing of individual activities. To this end the length of the working day is calculated by taking the difference of starting and stopping times, and adjusting the result for mealtimes, etc. Next, we need to decide how many days of work were performed per week. Finally, the number of holidays that curtailed the length of the working years needs to be taken into account. The second approach employs a simple short-cut. Everybody's day has twenty-four hours. If people were asked what activities they were engaged in during randomly chosen hours of the day, and one-third answered that they were sleeping, we could infer that respondents slept an average of eight hours per day. The witnesses' accounts can be used in this fashion, but certain peculiarities need to be taken into account. These will be discussed below. First, I shall use the timing method to estimate the length of the annual working year, 1760–1830.

I estimated that in London the average working day was 11 hours long, and that in the 1750s Sundays and Mondays as well as the 53 holy days (46 listed by Millan plus 7 during Christmas, Easter, and Whitsun) were days off. [143] This leaves 208 working days per year. If our conclusions about changing time budgets during the second half of the eighteenth century are correct, this implies 2,288 hours of work per year. [144] For 1800–3, the calculation is more straightforward. There is little evidence to suggest that 'St Monday' was still the occasion of much absenteeism. Holy days no longer influenced work activities.

---

[143] Allowing two days for Christmas and four days for Easter. Anecdotal evidence on working patterns during the eighteenth century has always stressed the importance of fluctuating short-term employment (e.g., on the docks). Cf. L. D. Schwarz, *London in the Age of Industrialization: Entrepreneurs, Labour Force, and Living Conditions, 1700–1850* (Cambridge, 1992), 108 ff. Since those employed short-term are included in my estimates of the time when work started and stopped, this factor has been taken into consideration. The underlying assumption is that occasional labourers were as likely to appear as witnesses (given their share in the total labour force) as members of other professions.

[144] This result represents a lower bound. We assume that, since the probability of observing individuals on Mondays, Sundays, and holy days is sharply reduced, these are not 'normal working days'. Yet the changes in the odds ratio only show a reduction by roughly half on these days compared with all the others. These 'other days', however, contain (if we are interested in Mondays, say), Sundays and weekdays which were holy days. Consequently, the relative reduction in the probability is understated. Compared to the average working day, it is more accurate to assume that Mondays, Sundays, and holy days registered a 70 per cent lower probability of observing individuals in paid work. It seems likely that the remaining 30 per cent simply point to individuals who are not employed in professions keeping 'normal hours', such as inn keepers, coach drivers, or chairmen.

Work ceased on 52 Sundays in the year, plus 7 days at Christmas, Easter, and Whitsun. This implies a working year of 306 days; combined with the 11-hour working day, this suggests 3,366 hours of work per year. The estimate for 1830 is identical.

In the North the starting level of annual labour input in 1760 is higher than in London, owing to the absence of a 'St Monday' effect. This suggests an annual working year of 260 days.[145] Assuming, as we did in the case of London, 11 hours of work per day, this implies an annual workload of 2,860 hours. By 1800 the political festivals cease to be observed. Therefore, the length of the working year rises to 3,036 hours. Finally, by 1830, the religious holidays as well appear to have fallen into disuse. The annual total thus rises to the same level as the one attained in London from 1800 onwards, 3,366 hours per year. Our timing-based estimates therefore suggest an increase of annual working hours by 47 per cent in London, and by 18 per cent in the North (Table 3.30).[146]

The assumption of a constant working day cannot be rejected on the basis of our data. Yet this is not necessarily the most intuitive assumption—'there is no reason to regard zero as a closer approximation to the truth than a reasonable guess'.[147] The alternative is to let both the length of the working day and the amount of time taken up by meals vary from one sample to the next. Table 3.30 contains the estimates. In the case of London this suggests an even sharper increase in working hours, albeit from a lower level. The reverse is true of the Northern samples, where the assumption of varying daily hours and varying mealtimes leads to a higher starting level in 1760, as well as a more rapid rise in annual labour input.[148]

---

[145] Note that Hatcher ('Labour') finds an average of 232.5 days amongst 11 hewers, putters and watermen working in Gatherick Colliery in 1683–4. This is not significantly different from the 260 days that I find for 1760. Alternatively, it may indicate that the process of labour intensification had begun earlier, and that an average of 27.5 days of leisure had already been lost by the middle of the eighteenth century.

[146] We do not know when the change in time use occurred between the benchmark years in question.

[147] Robinson, cit. in Charles H. Feinstein and Mark Thomas, 'A Plea for Errors', unpub. MS, All Souls College, Oxford (1999), 9.

[148] Note that, to derive mealtimes, we need to use frequency-based estimates—thus potentially partially undermining the independence of our two methods. Since individuals rarely comment on the starting and stopping time of individual meals, there is, however, no methodological alternative. I used the estimates of the length of time taken up by breakfast, lunch, and tea, taking the uneven distribution of crimes into account. The procedure counteracted the increase in hours, especially in the North—while the difference of starting and stopping times suggests a workday of close to fourteen hours, our method suggests that 147 minutes were spent on meals, thereby reducing the length of the working day to 11 hours and 30 minutes.

TABLE 3.30. *Annual labour input, timing-based estimates*

	London			North		
	1760	1800	1830	1760	1800	1830
Days/year	365	365	365	365	365	365
Days						
Festivals	−46			−46	−30	
'St Monday'	−52					
Easter, Christmas, Whitsun	−7	−7	−7	−7	−7	−7
Sundays	−52	−52	−52	−52	−52	−52
Days	208	306	306	260	276	306
Hours/day (constant = 11 h)						
Varying hours/day, varying mealtimes	10.50	10.30	10.70	11.20	10.80	11.50
Annual total						
Constant hours/day	2,288	3,366	3,366	2,860	3,036	3,366
Varying hours/day, varying mealtimes	2,184	3,152	3,274	2,912	2,981	3,519
Index						
Constant hours/day	100	147	147	100	106	118
Varying hours/day, varying mealtimes	100	144	150	100	102	121

How do these trends compare with the results of the frequency-based estimates? Of course, witnesses could not observe a crime while sleeping. The witnesses who do give information about being asleep at a certain hour were either describing a longer sequence of events, or were woken up by noise resulting from the crime. In using the frequency method, it therefore seems best to exclude night-time observations. Second, crimes did not occur with equal frequency throughout the day. This means that certain hours of the day will be over- or undersampled. Our estimate of total hours of work would, for example, be biased upwards if a high incidence of crime coincided with high work frequency. We therefore need to adjust the weight given to each observation by a corrective factor that takes into account the degree of undersampling during the same time-interval. Experimentation with the data suggested that corrections for frequency bias should be undertaken for hours of the day and days of the week. To ensure that each observation has the same influence in the final estimate of total working hours, the corrective weight for each observation is

$$C = [(O^E_D/O_D)(O^E_H/O_H)] \qquad (3.1)$$

where O^E denotes the expected number of observations, O the observed number, D refers to days of the week, and H to hours of the day.[149]

Disregarding the atypical effect of sleep, we should find 4.2 per cent of all observations in each hour. Discarding all observations between midnight and 6:00 in the morning raises this figure to 5.6 per cent for the remaining hours of the day. Each observation is reweighted to remove the effect of the uneven distribution of crime. This is carried out for times of the day and days of the week. The corrective weights for days of the week are adjusted for any effect of certain days of the week having higher proportions of observations dating from specific times of the day. In the corrected dataset, the proportion of witnesses found at work (using the widest possible definition, w3) is used to derive estimates of annual labour input. The percentage of witnesses found at work is first multiplied with the relevant time period per day (18 hours in our case, as we excluded the hours from midnight to 5:59).[150] The estimate of the number of hours per day is then multiplied with 365—since we include all days of the year in the analysis, and not only days of work. Table 3.31 gives the results.

The results of the two methods are not identical. In the case of London the frequency-based calculation consistently yields a higher point estimate than the timing-based one. In the North the reverse is

TABLE 3.31. *Frequency estimates*

	London		North	
	hours/year	index	hours/year	index
1760	2,431	100	2,691	100
1800	3,416	141	3,532	131
1830	3,350	138	3,211	119

[149] Some of the undersampling of certain days is driven by the hours for which witnesses' accounts are available. Therefore, the correction factor for days of the week only incorporates differences between observed and expected number of reports that cannot be explained by the composition of our sample being skewed towards certain hours of the day.

[150] Since many witnesses rise before 6, and some start to work, I also experimented with using 4:59 as a cut-off. The results were very similar.

true, thus diminishing the difference in levels between the two regions. The London trends over time are very similar—plus 47 per cent in timing-based estimate, and plus 41 per cent in the frequency-based one between 1760 and 1800.[151] The slight downward trend between 1800 and 1830 suggested by the frequency method in the London sample is not present in our timing-based estimate.

The frequency and the timing method both suggest that working hours in the North were longer around the middle of the eighteenth century than they were in London. The increase between the 1750s–1760s and 1800 is less dramatic—plus 6 to plus 31 per cent, instead of a rise of 41 to 47 per cent in London. In contrast to the timing method, the frequency method suggests a clear reduction in working hours in the North between 1800 and 1830.

How can we derive national estimates from these figures? There are two main ways in which we can use the calculations carried out so far to arrive at guesses of the length of the annual working year. First, we can focus on the contrast between London and the rest of England. England was urbanizing rapidly during the period under investigation, with a significant share of the total increase going to London. This change of location for many workers also entailed a shift in working patterns. Second, urbanization was part of a larger process of structural change, with employment in the primary sector contracting rapidly. Alternatively, we can use the data available to construct estimates based on the change in the percentage of the labour force employed in agriculture.

Table 3.32 gives the best-guess estimates of national totals. First, the London data are used as representative of only London itself, and the Northern data as representative of the rest of England (method A).[152] The national aggregates reflect the increase in totals in each subsample. However, as population moves from the more labour-intensive sector (outside London or the towns) into urban centres, the overall increase is mitigated. The same effect is visible using the second approach, which treats our London data as representative of the urban population as a whole (method B).[153]

[151] Using the timing-based estimates under the assumption of no change in the length of the working day.

[152] Population figures for London are from Schwarz, *London in the Age of Industrialization*, table 5.1, p. 126 (based on Wrigley). The figures for England are from Wrigley and Schofield, *Population History*, table A3.1, pp. 528–9 f.

[153] The data on urbanization are from Jan DeVries, *European Urbanization, 1500–1800* (Cambridge, Mass., 1984), table 3.8, p. 44. The value for 1831 was derived by linear interpolation.

TABLE 3.32. *National totals, working hours per annum*

	Hours/year			Index		
	1760	1800	1830	1760	1800	1830
Method A						
Frequency-based	2,661	3,520	3,231	100	132	121
Timing-based, constant hours	2,795	3,070	3,366	100	110	120
Timing-based, varying hours	2,829	2,999	3,483	100	106	123
Method B						
Frequency-based	2,649	3,508	3,256	100	132	123
Timing-based, constant hours	2,768	3,103	3,366	100	112	122
Timing-based, varying hours	2,796	3,016	3,439	100	108	123

The direction and magnitudes of change are not particularly sensitive to the weights used in deriving national aggregates. If London is only regarded as representative of itself, and the Northern sample as reflecting trends elsewhere, the total increase in annual hours between 1760 and 1830 amounts to 20 to 23 per cent relative to the starting level. If London is seen as representative of all urbanized centres, the range is 22 to 23 per cent.

The use of different methods in deriving the length of the annual working year has few consequences. The contrast between 1760 and 1800 is more uncertain. The weighting procedure does not have a large impact, but the difference between the frequency- and the timing-based estimates is considerable. Under method A the range of the percentage increase is 6 to 32 per cent; under method B it is 8 to 32 per cent. That there was a rise in annual labour input is clear, but we can be more certain of the direction of change between 1760 and 1800 than of the magnitude of the shift. Overall levels are even more uncertain. The uncertainty surrounding our estimates for 1800 imply that, while the direction of change between 1760 and 1800 (and between 1760 and 1830) is unambiguous, the same cannot be claimed for the period 1800 to 1830. The timing-based estimates suggest a further increase in annual working hours, while the frequency-based ones indicate that hours may actually have fallen somewhat. The frequency-based estimates differ conceptually from the timing-based ones. The latter are estimates of hours for those members of the labour force engaged in full-time work. Changes in the unemployment rate or in the labour force participation rate will not influence the estimates of annual hours. Frequency-based estimates, however, are affected by changes in the number of people working. They are thus more comprehensive, but also not free from the influence of employment variations.[154]

Which estimates are we to believe? Where timing- and frequency-based results broadly agree, there is no problem of interpretation. In those cases when they are at odds, we need to recall that the timing-based estimates are by construction based on many more a priori assumptions than the frequency-based results. The frequency-based method, after use of corrective weights, provides a relatively direct estimate of the proportion of the population working—and thus, of the length of the working year. In contrast, the timing-based method uses various assumptions about the length of mealtimes, the potential number of holy days curtailing the length of the working year, etc. to make sensible guesses about the length of the working day, the number of normal working days per week, and the observance of festivals in the course of the year. This suggests that the frequency-based estimation, using the whole dataset directly in calculating annual labour input, has some advantages over the timing-based approach.

So far, I have ignored changes in the occupational composition of the labour force, and focused on urbanization instead. Structural change, however, is now widely regarded as one of the defining characteristics of Britain's Industrial Revolution. As outlined above, agricultural employment, while exhibiting the same overall trend, showed markedly higher probabilities of employment on Sundays, Mondays, and holy days. This implies that our estimates of annual totals will be affected by the rapid structural transformation of the British economy.[155] The first question therefore has to be if it is credible that the working year in agriculture was even longer than in the other professions. If our answer is yes, then we will have to adjust the change in annual labour input downwards. The percentage of the labour force employed in agriculture declined quickly during the second half of the eighteenth century and the early nineteenth century. Therefore,

---

[154] It is therefore no surprise that the estimates from the frequency-based method (except for 1800) return lower figures than the timing approach. We will return to this point when we derive estimates of labour input.

[155] See N. F. R. Crafts, *British Economic Growth during the Industrial Revolution* (Oxford, 1985), for the wider implications of this process.

the shift out of one of the most labour-intensive sectors would have diminished the increase in working hours. If, however, we believe that the working year in agriculture was roughly equivalent to that in other professions, then no further adjustments are needed.

Indirect evidence supports the notion that working hours were particularly long in agriculture. Clark and van der Werf argue that, during the middle ages, the working year in agriculture had almost reached the modern standard of approximately 300 days.[156] During the industrialization process, the reallocation of labour from the primary to the secondary sector is normally accompanied by low productivity in the former. In England, however, output per agriculturist was not very far below the level attained in other sectors. By 1800 the sectoral productivity gap had almost disappeared (Table 3.33).

The comparatively small (and rapidly disappearing) difference in productivity, and the ability of English agriculture to feed a rapidly growing population while employing an almost constant number of men and women, both lend indirect support to the hypothesis that labour input per member of the agricultural workforce was high. In our dataset we are significantly more likely to encounter those in the primary sector at work than the average of all other sectors—using the frequency-based method (with or without corrective weights), the share of witnesses engaged in paid labour is about 20 per cent higher in agriculture than elsewhere.[157]

Crafts' figures suggest a decline of 9.7 per cent in the agricultural share of the labour force between 1760 and 1800, and a further reduc-

TABLE 3.33. *Productivity gap in agriculture*

	1700	1760	1800	1840
Percentage of labour force in primary sector	57.1	49.6	39.9	25.0
Percentage of income in primary sector	37.4	37.5	36.1	24.9
Productivity gap in the primary sector (percentage of average)	−34.5	−24.4	−9.5	−0.004

Source: Crafts, *British Economic Growth*, table 3.6, pp. 62–3.

[156] Gregory Clark and Y. van der Werf, 'Work in Progress? The Industrious Revolution', *Journal of Economic History*, 58 (1998).

[157] Using the uncorrected average, we find (across all samples) that 61 per cent of witnesses in agriculture were engaged in paid work. The corresponding average for all other professions is 49.7 per cent.

tion by 11.2 per cent between 1800 and 1830.[158] In revising the previous estimates, we therefore have to take into account two additional factors: first, agriculture's special work rhythm raises the estimated labour input for 1760. Second, the shift out of the primary sector acts as a countervailing force to the increase in the overall length of the working year.

Table 3.34 uses the frequency-based estimates for the length of the working year in two parts of the economy—agriculture, and all other sectors.[159] The peak in annual labour input is again recorded in 1800, with hours in agriculture particularly high.[160] We now obtain an increase in annual hours by 30 per cent between 1760 and 1800, and a small reduction between 1800 and 1830. Note how closely the pattern of change agrees with the results using the timing-based approach—despite the large change in weights on individual observations, the overall trend between 1760 and 1830 is almost identical. Between 1760 and 1800 the sector-based estimates agree closely with the timing-based ones.

TABLE 3.34. *Structural change and national totals for labour input*

		1760	1800	1830
Hours/year	agriculture	2,867	4,171	3,716
	other sectors	2,547	3,092	3,071
	percentage of labour force in agriculture	49.6	39.9	28.7
Total	hours/year	2,706	3,523	3,256
	index	100	130	120

[158] The value for 1830 was inferred from linear interpolation between 1800 and 1840.

[159] The use of timing-based estimates was not feasible, as the sample sizes were too small to construct precise estimates of the timing of all activities in our six samples. It could be argued that a more detailed assessment of sectoral change would have benefited the analysis. Since estimates of the length of the annual working year did not differ markedly between sectors in the rest of economy, this would have been of little consequence to our final estimates.

[160] It is tempting to argue that the high prices and peak demand associated with the Napoleonic wars are responsible for the extreme length of the working year. Given the limited sample size, however, this would be stretching the reliability of our evidence too far.

Earlier work had used a relatively wide range of estimates for changes in labour input between the middle of the eighteenth and the middle of the nineteenth centuries. Crafts used Tranter's guess of an increase from 2,500 to 3,000 hours, whereas Freudenberger and Cummins argued for a possible change from 3,000 to 4,000 hours p. a. The total increase of between 20 and 33 per cent can be determined with greater confidence. Table 3.35 summarizes the results of this study. We compare the national totals derived from the two main methods of establishing the length of the working year, and the two main approaches to derive national totals. The range of estimates in 1760 and 1830 is relatively small—the highest value in the earlier period is 6.9 per cent above the lowest one. In 1830 the range is 7.8 per cent. Perhaps unsurprisingly our estimates are firmly within the range suggested by Freudenberger–Cummins and Tranter. Our estimates agree that, by 1830, the length of the annual working year had increased by approximately 20 to 23 per cent. This is virtually identical with the figure used by Crafts, building on Tranter's work. It is also markedly below the increase of one-third suggested by Freudenberger and Cummins.[161] Note, however, that the years

TABLE 3.35. *Comparison of national totals, annual labour input, 1760–1830*

| | | hours/year | | | index | | |
		1760	1800	1830	1760	1800	1830
Sectoral estimates	frequency-based	2,706	3,523	3,256	100	130	120
Urban/rural	frequency-based	2,661	3,520	3,231	100	132	121
method A	timing-based, constant hours	2,795	3,070	3,366	100	110	120
	timing-based, varying hours	2,829	2,999	3,483	100	106	123
Urban/rural	frequency-based	2,646	3,504	3,267	100	132	123
method B	timing-based, constant hours	2,760	3,115	3,366	100	113	122
	timing-based, varying hours	2,785	3,022	3,421	100	109	123

[161] In line with Robin Matthews, Charles Feinstein and John Oddling-Smee (*British Economic Growth, 1856–1973*) for 1856, we find no evidence to suggest that hours in the aggregate reached a peak of more than 3,600 hours. This is not to say that work schedules in some factories could not have reached such a level.

1829–32 are somewhat less buoyant in economic terms than was the period 1759–63.[162] Such a narrow range suggests a precision that our attempts at reconstructing historical time-budgets do not fully attain. One alternative way of establishing a plausible range of values for the magnitude of the shift between 1760 and 1830 is to compare the highest estimate for 1830 with the lowest one in 1760. The upper bound on the increase in annual hours worked thus calculated is 32 per cent. Comparing the highest value in 1760 with the lowest one in 1830 gives a lower-bound estimate—plus 14 per cent. The true value must have fallen somewhere within this range. What is ruled out is a stagnation of labour input.

How did working time change in the long run? Currently, there are data on the number of working hours in the year for little more than the last century.[163] While it must be stressed again that our estimates are inferior to more recent ones, and that our data are only based on records from London and the Northern counties, we can now provide a rough outline of the course of working hours since the Industrial Revolution. Figure 3.15 gives an overview.

Development in the long run lends empirical support to suggestions in the literature that changes in labour input described an inverse U. The length of the working year in 1760 was similar to that seen during the second half of the nineteenth century. In 1800 the upper-bound estimate is higher than any observed since 1850. Even by 1760 annual labour input appears to have reached levels equivalent to those in the 1850s–70s. The speed of change was also high. If our calculations are approximately correct then the development between 1760 and 1830 was as rapid as the decline of working hours after the First World War. The rise in annual labour input per person (+ 550 to + 654 hours/year) is roughly as large as the reduction in working hours between 1924 and 1989 (− 667). While the changes implied by our results took place over seventy years in the eighteenth century, the

---

[162] See above, pp. 40–7.

[163] Based on Angus Maddison, *Dynamic Forces in Capitalist Development* (Oxford, 1991), table C.9, p. 270. The Maddison series is augmented in 1870 with the figure inferred from M. A. Bienefeld, *Working Hours in British Industry: An Economic History* (London, 1972), 111. MFO is the series in Matthews, Feinstein and Oddling-Smee, *British Economic Growth*, table 3.11, p. 64. Differences are largely due to assumptions about vacations, sick leave, etc., but the empirical basis of the MFO series appears to be more reliable. Michael Huberman and Wayne Lewchuck ('Glory Days? Work Hours, Labor Market Regulations and Convergence in Late Nineteenth Century Europe', paper presented at the All- U.C. Group in Economic History Conference, University of California, Davis, 14–16 November 1997) have recently presented slightly revised rates; trends over time in their series are none the less very similar.

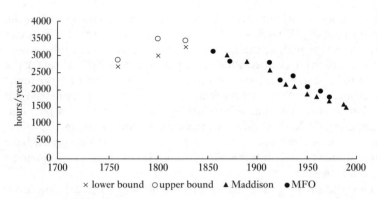

FIGURE 3.15. *Working hours in England, 1750–1989*

decline of working hours by the same order of magnitude required sixty-five years. These findings are more or less independent of the data used for the period after 1850—long-run trends in working hours in the Maddison and the MFO series are broadly similar.

The increase in working hours between 1750 and 1800 is not only remarkable for the length of the working year that it brought about. It is also noteworthy for its context. In his survey of working hours in British industry Bienefeld observed that the reductions in annual labour input since 1850 were not gradual, but concentrated in four relatively short periods.[164] All of them registered marked price increases, a circumstance that, according to Bienefeld, was causally related to the reductions in working hours. Unions sought to negotiate 'lasting' improvements, and in a context of rapid price changes, fewer hours were a more 'durable' good. Our period is also one of rapidly increasing prices—especially between 1760 and 1800—but the movement of working hours is exactly the reverse. This may either indicate that the mechanism pointed out by Bienefeld is spurious—he effectively relies on four observations. Or it may show that the eighteenth-century labour market was fundamentally different from later ones, and that unionization of a sizeable proportion of the labour force during the nineteenth century led to a clear break with the past. One of the following sections will explore the forces underpinning longer hours; the conclusion will indeed be that labour supply decisions were caused by factors unique to our period.

[164] M. A. Bienefeld, *Working Hours in British Industry: An Economic History* (London, 1972), 179 ff. A similar observation is made by Matthews, Feinstein, and Oddling-Smee, *British Economic Growth*, 70–1 f.

In 1985, Crafts, commenting on the substantial body of literature suggesting an increase in the number of working hours per year, wrote that '[m]easurement of this supposition has never been adequately accomplished . . .'.[165] The results that have emerged from studying the Old Bailey Sessions Papers and the Northern Assize Depositions cannot be said to provide wholly accurate measurements of working hours. The merit of the new method is, however, twofold: first, while still being far from precise, the estimates based on court records present an improvement because they are based not on anecdotal evidence, but on the everyday patterns of labour and leisure of more than 2,800 individuals. They thus replace hearsay with attempts at measurement. Second, the method presented can readily be applied to court records from other areas and other periods, ultimately enabling historians to measure historical time-budgets accurately.

Fact or Fiction? Testing the New Method

We have now derived detailed estimates of time-use in 1760, 1800, and 1830, and calculated rates of change between these three benchmark periods. The method of inferring time-use information from witnesses' accounts provides us with a wealth of new data. Yet how reliable are these results? The purpose of this subsection is to examine a number of possible objections to our method. In addition to checks on the internal consistency of the data, I examine additional evidence from the wage books of a canal company.

The Representativeness of Witnesses and Changes in Sample Composition

Sample selection bias in the case of witnesses could take two possible forms. Either our witnesses are not a representative sample of the population as a whole—then the usefulness of our results would be in serious doubt—or the sample composition between individual periods changed in such a way as to favour a particular type of results.[166] I shall discuss these possibilities in turn.

How representative of the population at large are our witnesses? Since we cannot test this aspect directly, I shall follow the standard

---

[165] Crafts, *British Economic Growth*, 82.
[166] If the sample is representative, the estimates of changes in aggregate hours would still be correct—but different factors would have caused them.

procedure of choosing an additional characteristic which is recorded for witnesses and also known for the population overall.[167] Two statistics suggest themselves—sectoral composition and social stratification. For both, there is some evidence at the county level, and our data on witnesses contains information on these categories.

Table 3.36 gives an overview of sectoral composition in our six datasets. We can compare these with the relatively exact breakdown of labour force by county from the 1841 census. For London in 1841, for example, the census suggests that 2.95 per cent of the labour force are employed in agriculture. Amongst the witnesses appearing before the Old Bailey in 1831, 3.5 per cent worked in agriculture.[168] The gap is small. Also, the fact that the census records a lower figure at a later date suggests that the true gap might be even smaller—employment in agriculture as a percentage of the labour force was probably falling in London over time (just as in the rest of England). The discrepancy is somewhat wider when we compare the manufacturing share of employment. In the Old Bailey data from 1830, we found 30.1 per cent

TABLE 3.36. *Sectoral origin of witnesses*

	1760	1800	1830
London			
Agriculture	5.1%	4.9%	3.5%
Manufacturing	16.1%	30.1%	30.1%
Public	4.7%	5.5%	1.3%
Services	48.7%	32.8%	42.4%
Trade	25.4%	26.7%	22.7%
North			
Agriculture	34.0%	23.3%	22.4%
Manufacturing	23.6%	26.2%	34.2%
Public	4.7%	2.3%	0.6%
Services	22.6%	31.4%	25.5%
Trade	15.1%	16.8%	17.3%

[167] A good example of this technique can be found in Paul Johnson and Steve Nicholas, 'Health and Welfare of Women in the United Kingdom, 1785–1920', paper presented to the NBER conference on health and welfare during industrialization, Cambridge, Mass., 21–2 April 1995, 10 ff.

[168] Clive H. Lee, *British Regional Employment Statistics, 1841–1971* (Cambridge 1979), pt. II. In table 3.36 unclassified cases have been excluded. I therefore also excluded Lee's 'N.C.' category from calculations.

employed in this sector. This contrasts with 36.9 per cent of total (classified) employment in 1841, according to the census. Again, the difference in time periods may go some way towards reducing the discrepancy. If the proportion of witnesses employed in manufacturing had grown at the same rate after 1841 as it did between 1760 and 1830, then the predicted value for 1841 (in our dataset) would have been 32.7, only 4.2 percentage points below the observed value from the census. Similarly, what we classified as service sector employment represented 42.4 per cent of all witnesses. In London in 1841 there were 45.2 per cent of the labour force employed in these sectors, a difference of 2.8 percentage points.[169] Also, the share taken by the public sector is broadly comparable. While 1.3 per cent of our witnesses were employed there, the 1841 proportion is 2.1 per cent. In the case of London, some differences between the sectoral composition of our witnesses and the labour force exist. In almost all cases, these discrepancies are small, and there is little reason to question the representativeness of our sample.

Our Northern sample fares equally well when sectoral composition is used as a proxy for representativeness. In 1830 we found an average of 22.4 per cent of witnesses employed in agriculture. This contrasts with a labour force weighted value of 19.2 per cent in the same counties in the 1841 census.[170] Again assuming a linear change in employment shares, the expected value in 1841 in our sample given the observed rates of change would have been 20.3 per cent—a difference of 1.1 per cent. In the case of manufacturing, there appears to be some undersampling. The census gives an average of 44.9 per cent, whereas we find 34.2 per cent in our Northern sample. Adjusting for the difference in dates, we still find a gap of 8.8 per cent. Several reasons may be responsible. It is possible that structural change accelerated between 1830 and 1841. There is some evidence for this in our dataset. If we use the rates of change in the manufacturing share observed between 1800 and 1830 to calculate the implied rate for 1841, the gap falls further to 7.8 per cent. Unless the acceleration after 1830 was even sharper than it was between 1800 and 1830, the residual difference suggests a limited degree of sample selection bias. In the case of services, the discrepancy is smaller. We find 25.5 per cent of our

---

[169] Categories 20, 21, 22, 24, 25, and 26 in the census (ibid.).

[170] The counties were Yorkshire, West Riding, East Riding, North Riding, Cumberland, Northumberland, Westmorland. The weights, derived from the relative size of the respective labour force, are 0.58, 0.1, 0.1, 0.08, 0.12, and 0.02. Cf. ibid.

witnesses employed in the service sector; the average for the Northern counties is 24.8 per cent. Similarly, 0.6 per cent of our witnesses come from the public sector, while the weighted average from the census for the North is 0.71 per cent. Overall, the sectoral composition of the labour force and the occupations of our witnesses do not suggest any major problems of sample selection bias.

The second indicator we can use for assessing the representativeness of our sample is social stratification. Data are not abundant. For London in 1800 Schwarz has estimated shares in the male working population according to socio-economic status.[171] He concludes that only 2–3 per cent of London's adult male population belonged to the upper income group (over £200 p. a.). The middling sort contributed another 16–21 per cent. The remainder he calls 'the working population'. Schwarz also provides a more detailed (and more tentative) breakdown of this residual.[172]

If we can show that witnesses testifying before the Old Bailey came from a similar background, it would be more likely that they are a representative sample of the population as a whole. Definitions of socio-economic class are not always clear-cut, and not all of our witnesses provide sufficient information about themselves to assign them to a particular group. I follow Schwarz's definition that the middling classes consisted of 'anyone below an aristocrat or very rich merchant or banker, but above a journeyman worker or small-scale employer in one of the less prestigious trades.' Small shopkeepers are not included in this group, according to Schwarz; they contribute another 9–10 per cent of the male working population.[173] In the Old Bailey Sessions Papers I was unable to distinguish between the 'middling sort' and shopkeepers in this way. It therefore seemed more appropriate to combine these two categories for purposes of comparison. In 1800, 793 of the male witnesses gave an occupational description that allows us to allocate them to one of Schwarz's groups. The results are summarized

---

[171] We could use the social tables constructed by Peter Lindert and Jeffrey Williamson ('Revising England's Social Tables, 1688–1913', *Explorations in Economic History*, 19 (1982)) to compare the Northern Assize data with national totals. However, there is little reason to expect that regional variation in terms of social composition should be any less than in the case of economic sectors; comparisons of the national average with essentially regional figures would only be of limited value. I therefore refrain from such an exercise.

[172] Schwarz, *London*, 57.

[173] Schwarz also analyses the female working population. Since proportions cannot be derived from his description, the analysis is not extended to women.

in Table 3.37, where I also give upper and lower bounds from Schwarz.[174]

The distributions are remarkably similar. For the upper income group as well as for the self-employed and artisans, the figures are almost identical. The estimate from the Old Bailey Sessions Papers for the combined 'middle income and shopkeeper' group is below even the lower bound given by Schwarz, and there seem to be too many witnesses in the 'semi- and unskilled' group. How do we assess the importance of the similarities and differences? Chi-squared tests fail to reject the null hypothesis of no significant difference. Another technique commonly used to explore the relationship between observed sample characteristics and the control group is simple correlation analysis.[175] Table 3.38 reports results for the Pearson and Spearman test. The correlation between the population shares from Schwarz and the witnesses in the Old Bailey Sessions Papers is always 0.9 or above. In the context of historical studies this is a high degree of similarity. We can therefore conclude that, if we use social class as our standard of comparison, no significant difference between our sample and the population can be found. However, this should not be confused with positive proof that witnesses are representative of the (male working) population at large.

Ideally, we would want to apply the same tests to the sample from the 1750s–60s and from 1830. Unfortunately, there are no sufficiently detailed and reliable estimates of labour force composition for these

TABLE 3.37. *Composition of the male labour force*

	Schwarz		Old Bailey—1800
	Lower bound	Upper bound	
Upper income	2	3	1.64
Middle income+shopkeepers	25	29	20.05
Self-employed	5	6	4.79
Artisans	23.8	21.7	20.68
Semi- and unskilled	(44.2)	(40.3)	52.84
Sum	100	100	100

[174] I used the upper and lower bound estimates described in Schwarz, *London*, 57. The semi- and unskilled category was then derived as a residual.

[175] Johnson and Nicholas, 'Health and Welfare of Women', 10.

TABLE 3.38. *Correlations—Percentage of Male Labour Force*

	Lower bound	Upper bound	Old Bailey—1800
Pearson			
Lower bound	1		
Upper bound	0.99	1	
Old Bailey—1800	0.98	0.94	1
Spearman			
Lower bound	1		
Upper bound	1	1	
Old Bailey—1800	0.90	0.90	1

periods.[176] Instead, we can examine the proposition that shifts in sample composition between the two benchmark years might bias our results. The most striking finding in our empirical section was the increase in the number of working days per year. As emerged quite clearly for both periods, the likelihood of observing individuals in work is inversely related to their social status. It could now be argued that the longer working year is not due to any changes in actual working practices in each socio-economic group. Rather, it could reflect changes in the number of witnesses coming from individual groups. If, say, the semi- and unskilled worked appreciably longer than the rest of the population, and their share in the total number of witnesses rose between 1750 and 1800, then one of our main findings might have been caused by a statistical illusion.[177] Such a shift in selection bias could even be expected as watch ownership spread from the top of the social hierarchy to the lower ranks. Table 3.39 compares sample composition between the middle of the eighteenth and the nineteenth centuries.

The share of the semi- and unskilled remained virtually unchanged between the middle and the end of the eighteenth century, slipping by a little more than 1 per cent. The proportion from the upper income group declined, but is most affected by issues of small sample size. By

---

[176] Comparisons with the (revised) social tables for England, compiled by Lindert and Williamson ('Social Tables, 1688–1913', tables 3 and 4, pp. 396–7 and 400–1) are difficult because they use a different stratification scheme.

[177] Strictly speaking, this would only be true if witnesses are not a representative sample of the population. If they are, then the rise in labour input would be due to shifts in labour force composition—society's 'great day' would still have changed.

TABLE 3.39. *Sample composition in 1760–1830, London*

	Old Bailey—1760	Old Bailey—1800	Old Bailey—1830
Upper income	1.4	1.6	0.4
Middle income+ shopkeepers	27.6	20.1	21.7
Self-employed	2.8	4.8	6.4
Artisans	14.3	20.7	17.9
Semi-and unskilled	54.0	52.8	53.6
Sum	100	100	100

1830 it has almost returned to its initial level. This is eloquent testimony against the idea that a 'trickling down' of watch ownership biased our results.[178]

The proportion of artisans (not self-employed) rises from 14 to 20 per cent, only to slip to 18 per cent by 1830. During the second half of the eighteenth century, the share of shopkeepers (plus those from the middle income group) declined from 27 to 20 per cent before rebounding to 22 per cent in 1830. Is the magnitude of these differences sufficient to offer an alternative explanation of the dramatic change in time allocation found above? Let us examine the case of artisans, so as to gain a sense of how plausible such an interpretation would be. By examining a group that undergoes one of the largest proportional changes of all between 1760 and 1800, we are biasing our result in favour of a significant link. The assumption then has to be that employed artisans worked longer than the population at large, and that the increase in labour input by more than 30 per cent can be attributed to their increased share. How much longer than the average witness would they have to work to influence the aggregate to this extent? The average length of the working year (D) is equivalent to

$$D = \sum_{i=1}^{m} p_n d_n \qquad (3.2)$$

where p_n is the share of the nth group in the total (working) population, m is the number of different occupational groups, and d_n is the length of the working year for the nth group. D^{1800} in London was

[178] How little social stratification in our sample changes is documented by the fact that columns 1 to 3 are significantly correlated at the 1 per cent level (coefficients 0.97 to 0.99).

(at least) 30 per cent longer than D^{1760}. Using the labour input of the remaining population as a numeraire as well as the shifts in sample composition from Table 3.39, we can now calculate relative efficiencies that would explain the observed rise in labour input.[179] We have to solve

$$\frac{p_r^{1800} + d_a p_a^{1800}}{p_r^{1760} + d_a p_a^{1760}} \geq 1.3$$

$$\Leftrightarrow d_a \geq \frac{1.3 p_r^{1760} - p_r^{1800}}{p_a^{1800} - 1.3 p_a^{1760}}$$

(3.3)

[p_r is the share of non-artisans in the population, p_a is the artisans' share, and d_a is the relative length of the artisans' working year, compared to the rest, with the length of the normal working year (for the rest of the population) normalized to unity].

If the increase in the artisans' share boosted annual labour input by 30 per cent, then they would have had to work at least 15.4 times longer than the average of the remaining population. This is unlikely.[180] It appears safe to conclude that shifts in sample composition were not decisive for the changes observed in the data analysis sections.

The same logic can be applied to sectoral shifts among our witnesses. Some trades were more famous for long working hours than others, and it is theoretically possible that an increase in the share of respondents in particularly labour-intensive professions boosted the probability of finding people at work.[181] A brief calculation can easily demonstrate that these shifts cannot have been responsible for the increase in the number of working hours observed. The largest shift in sectoral composition occurred in London between 1760 and 1800—the share of witnesses employed in manufacturing rose from 16.1 to 30.1 per cent. How much harder would those employed in the manufacturing sector have had to work to effect a 30 per cent rise in total

[179] There is no particular reason why d_a, the relative length of the working year of artisans compared to the rest of the population, should be constant over time. If we allow it to vary, there will be no unique solution to our problem.

[180] Note also that the proportion found in work is bounded from above at 100 per cent. Since the rest of the population did not work as little as at 6.5 per cent of the time, the shift in the share of artisans cannot be driving our results.

[181] See the long working hours for those in trading and the service sector given by Campbell (*London Tradesman*). Note that our result would still stand, if the change in composition reflected a change in the population at large, rather than being the result of a change in selection bias.

labour input? Using equation (3.3), the numerical answer is—at least 4.3 times longer than the rest of the population. Again, this is implausible, given the range of normal physiological possibilities. Changes in the sectoral composition of our sample were not responsible for the increase in labour input.

Memory Decay and Recall Period

How long was the interval between the crime and the court trial? Both dates are given in the Old Bailey Sessions Papers and the Northern Assize Depositions. We can therefore easily reconstruct the time period over which witnesses had to recall their activities. The number of sessions at the Old Bailey varied from year to year, but six to eight were common between the middle and the end of the eighteenth century. Since approximately 50 days had passed since the last session, we would expect that the average witness's memory had to bridge 25 days. This is the minimum we would expect if the timing of court sessions was the only constraining factor. If the average figure was appreciably longer, this could be interpreted as indicative of either longer legal procedures (establishing evidence, etc.) or of a substantial backlog of cases before the court.

The average lag between crime and trial in London in 1749–63 was 45.6 days (Figure 3.16). This statistic is influenced strongly by outliers. The extreme is marked by one case in which someone was tried six and a half years after he had allegedly committed a crime.[182] The most frequent delay was between 10 and 20 days—as it is for all London samples.[183] Variability was not large—a lag of only 31 days separates the top from the bottom 25 per cent of the distribution. By 1800 in London the mean lag has fallen to 39.2 days (Figure 3.17). The maximum delay was 521 days; this observation alone raised the arithmetic average by 0.5. In this case, a better measure of central tendency may in this case be the median, which is 25. This is exactly the figure we expected if there were no delays in the judicial procedure except those caused by the Old Bailey's intermittent schedule. Figure 3.17 gives the overall distribution—cases in the last interval also include any values higher than 100. In London in 1830 a mean lag of 38.2 days indicates a small additional reduction (Figure 3.18).

[182] Old Bailey Sessions Papers, Case No. 268, 2 July 1755 (crime committed on 11 Jan. 1749).   [183] As inferred from the mode.

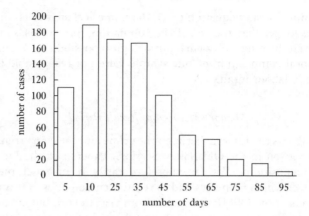

FIGURE 3.16. *Lag between crime and trial, Old Bailey, 1760*

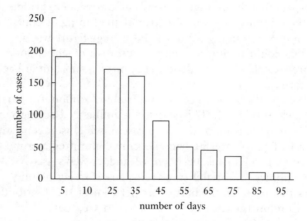

FIGURE 3.17. *Lag between crime and trial, Old Bailey, 1800*

In the Northern Assize Depositions we find a similar pattern (Figures 3.19, 3.20, and 3.21). The mean length of the lag between crime and trial varies from 10 to 49 days, and is thus broadly similar to the range found in the Old Bailey Sessions Papers. The mode is in the interval 0–10 for all samples.

Did the quality of witnesses' accounts vary with the length of the recall period? Modern-day experiments suggest that, if we are concerned with time-use on a weekday, 1.6 per cent of all activities are

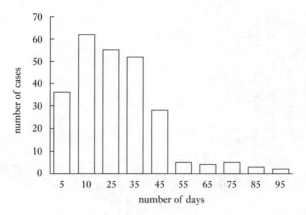

FIGURE 3.18. *Lag between crime and trial, Old Bailey, 1830*

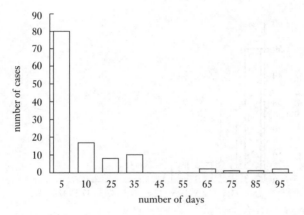

FIGURE 3.19. *Lag between crime and trial, Northern Assize Depositions, 1760*

forgotten per additional day.[184] There are some objections to applying this rule, both because linear extrapolation from this figure is problematic and because we are not dealing with ordinary events—even common, everyday activities were probably remembered better because of the unusual context of crime. But let us assume for a

---

[184] F. Thomas Juster, 'The Validity and Quality of Time Use Estimates Obtained from Recall Diaries', in id. and Frank Stafford (eds.), *Time, Goods, and Well-Being* (Ann Arbor, Mich., 1985).

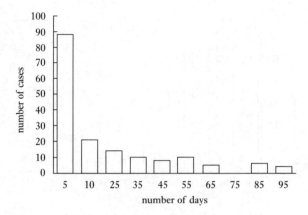

FIGURE 3.20. *Lag between crime and trial, Northern Assize Depositions, 1800*

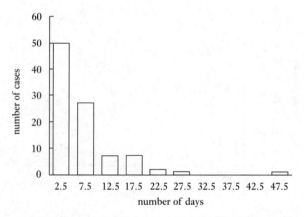

FIGURE 3.21. *Lag between crime and trial, Northern Assize Depositions, 1830*

moment that our witnesses are no better at remembering events than modern respondents (for weekdays). Then 42 per cent of all activities on a day would have been forgotten after 25 days. This clearly does not rule out the possibility of the average witnesses still remembering the handful of activities they engaged in immediately before the crime.

We can strengthen this argument further by examining if recall period and data quality are in any way related. There is one immediate indication of faulty reporting in the verbatim reports—if the day of the week mentioned by the witness and the date (which implies a certain weekday) do not agree.[185] This was true in a number of cases. If we can now show that the lag between crime and trial has no appreciable influence on the quality of recollection in this regard, then there is even less reason for concern about the length of the recall period. To test this possibility I assigned the value 0 whenever there was agreement between the two days (in the sense defined in the data section), and 1 otherwise. We would now expect the probability of this new variable being equal to 1 to vary with the lag between trial and crime if witnesses' reports in general become less accurate over time. The results from logit regressions are seen in Table 3.40. For all samples, the coefficient on the mean lag is insignificant.[186] The only exception is the Northern dataset in 1760. There, the odds of a witness making a mistake increased somewhat the longer the recall period. The magnitude of the effect, however, is not large enough to question the validity of the method—an increase of the mean lag by 10 days raises the probability of an error by 3 per cent.

The results for both 1800 and 1760 clearly suggest that the delay between crime and the statement before the court was comparatively small—even if it is much longer than in modern time-use studies. Further, there is no conclusive evidence that would link the recall period to data quality. For a variety of reasons, witnesses were sometimes unable to give all the details we would want to know, but forgetfulness was probably not one of them.

TABLE 3.40. *Delay of trial and memory decay*

		Lag	Wald	ΔOdds ratio
London	1760	0.0044	1.60	1.0044
	1800	−0.0039	0.40	0.9961
	1830	−0.0036	0.75	0.9964
North	1760	0.0121	5.60*	1.012
	1800	−0.0005	0.06	0.9995
	1830	n/a		

Note: * indicates significance at the 95 per cent level of confidence

[185] Implicit in this method is that witnesses (and not scribes at the court, etc.) are responsible for errors. This approach would be invalidated if the errors of witnesses varied inversely with the scribes' errors, depending on lag length. Such a possibility is, however, purely speculative.

[186] In 1830 there were not enough erroneous statements before the court for which the mean lag between crime and trial could also be observed.

'Waves' and the Gradual Extension of our Datasets

Modern time-use studies use a further instrument to control for data quality. Most of them are organized in consecutive 'waves', each of which administers the same test to a subsample of the total group of respondents. In the multinational study from the 1960s, for example, a single town in both West Germany and the United States was examined before the national tests were conducted. The two separate estimates from the two countries could then be used to test the reliability of the data.

The data from the Old Bailey were also collected gradually. At various stages I interrupted the data collection process to calculate some preliminary results. If our method yields robust results, the use of smaller subsamples should not lead to vastly different point estimates. We have to bear in mind that our datasets (even in their final state) are not very large, and that some of the error bands are consequently quite wide. Table 3.41 compares descriptive statistics for an inter-

TABLE 3.41. *Descriptive statistics—main activities*

	Number of operations	Mean	Standard deviation
1800–3—430 cases			
Rising	20	6:12	22
Going to bed	22	23:04	39
Start of work	23	6:40	24
End of work	21	18:48	20
1800–3—1005 cases			
Rising	34	5:56	15
Going to bed	38	23:21	17
Start of work	48	6:33	15
End of work	44	19:07	19
1749–63—230 cases			
Rising	11	7:22	31
Going to bed	17	22:26	14
Start of work	9	6:13	32
End of work	3	16:20	1.10
1749–63—1033 cases			
Rising	59	6:10	15
Going to bed	79	22:50	9.7
Start of work	44	6:50	33
End of work	36	18:50	30

mediary and the final stage of data collection. The point estimates for successive 'waves' in the historical data rarely agree. What concerns us is the extent of disagreement. There would be clear evidence of inconsistency if the confidence interval around an earlier point estimate does not overlap with the confidence interval for the final calculation. This is never the case—none of the eight combinations shows any signs of inconsistency. The largest absolute difference is between the two observations on the end of work in 1749–63. Yet because the standard error on the estimate from the smaller sample is large, the two are not different in terms of statistical significance.

A more sophisticated form of successive sampling administers the same test to the same group of people, but on different days. We are unable to replicate such a procedure with our historical data.

Unobserved Shifts in the Age Distribution

One of the most important shortcomings in the verbatim reports from the Old Bailey is the absence of information on the age of witnesses. Unless a person seemed far too young, we have no indication of age at all. Could unobserved shifts in the age composition of those testifying before the Old Bailey be responsible for the growth in working hours? Because we have no direct indication of the age of witnesses, I examine trends in age composition in the population at large. Since our witnesses appear to be a representative sample of London's population, this seems appropriate. None the less, we must note at the outset that there is no way of establishing if the witnesses' age structure changed in a way that differed from the aggregate.

The main demographic force between 1750 and 1850 was rapid population growth, triggered by a fall in the mean age of marriage and a fall in the percentage of those that never married.[187] Also, a decline in stillbirths may have been responsible for approximately one-fifth of the overall acceleration.[188] The consequences of this growth for the age distribution are summarized in Table 3.42.

---

[187] Edward Anthony Wrigley, 'The Growth of Population in Eighteenth-Century England: A Conundrum Resolved', *Past and Present*, 98 (1983), 223 ff. Note that Wrigley, R. S. Davies, Jim Oeppen, and Roger Schofield (*English Population History from Family Reconstitution, 1580–1837* (Cambridge, 1997)) have recently qualified this conclusion; the relative contribution of improvements in life expectancy appears slightly more important than previously assumed. The main thrust of the argument is likely to remain unaffected.

[188] Wrigley, 'Explaining the Rise in Marital Fertility in England in the "Long" Eighteenth Century', *Economic History Review*, 51 (1998), 461.

TABLE 3.42. *Age distribution in England and Wales, 1756, 1801, and 1831*

Age group	1756	1801	1831
60+	8.37	7.26	6.54
24–59	40.02	37.6	35.7
15–24	18.48	17.73	18.89
5–14	20.09	23.08	24.41
0–4	13.04	14.32	14.39

Source: Wrigley and Schofield, *Population History of England*, table A3.1, p. 529.
Note: Owing to rounding errors, column (3) does not total 100.

The broad aggregates taken from Wrigley and Schofield show that the proportion of over-60-year-olds and of those in the age group 15–24 was largely unaffected. What did change markedly was the percentage of the total population under the age of 15, which increased by more than 4 per cent. Those in the group of 25–59-year-olds comprised a little more than 40 per cent in 1760, dropping to 37.6 per cent in 1800.

How could these changes have influenced working behaviour? As I discussed in the section on labour input during the Industrial Revolution, demographic trends imply that the labour force participation ratio fell between 1760 and 1800. This would also suggest less labour input, not more. Alternatively, we could argue that younger individuals were willing to supply longer hours, even on traditional feast days and on 'St Monday'. The concept has some intuitive appeal. If we define those aged 15–59 as the potential labour force, then this group became younger, on average, as population grew. The proportion aged between 15 and 24 remained almost constant while the older age group contracted in relative terms. The average age of those in the labour force should therefore initially have fallen. The effect, however, is probably quite small—while 31.6 per cent of those in the 'potential labour force' were part of the younger group in 1760, their share had only risen to 32 per cent by 1800. Of course, those within the age groups 15–24 and 25–59 also must have become younger, but the magnitude of the effect is hardly sufficient to explain a 20 per cent rise in labour input.

The same conclusion emerges if we examine shifts in the age structure in London. Estimates of the age distribution in London come

TABLE 3.43. *Age distribution in London, 1750–1829*

Age (in years)		Per 1000				
from	to	1750–69	1790–1809	1810–29	Δ(1)	Δ(2)
0	1	47	47	46	0	−1
2	4	63	83	79	20	16
5	9	69	83	88	14	19
10	19	119	119	136	0	17
20	29	197	171	172	−26	−25
30	39	198	193	185	−5	−13
40	49	160	158	149	−2	−11
50	59	95	98	94	3	−1
60	69	39	37	38	−2	−1
70	79	15	13	15	−2	0
mean age		30.01	29.15	28.8		
mean age (10–59)		33.48	33.85	33.14		

Note: Δ(1) refers to the change between 1750–69 and 1790–1809, Δ(2) refers to the change between 1750–69 and 1810–29.

from Landers.[189] As Table 3.43 unambiguously demonstrates, changes in average age were small as well. If we focus on those comprising the potential labour force, we find that average age actually increased between 1750–69 and 1790–1809.[190] Between 1790–1809 and 1810–29 it fell slightly. In either case, the change in the average appears far too small to account for the dramatic rise in labour input.

Randomisation of Time-Use

Theoretically, there exists another alternative interpretation of the test results presented above. There, we had found that, for Mondays and old holy days, logistic regressions on the 1800 sample no longer showed the reductions in the probability of observing people in work that were conspicuous fifty years earlier. Put simply, I argued that this indicated an increase in labour input. Alternatively, we could assume

[189] John Landers, *Death and the Metropolis. Studies in the Demographic History of London, 1670–1830* (Cambridge, 1993), 180.

[190] The reason is the above-average reduction in the group of those aged 20–9. It should be noted that the method of calculating averages from classified data is necessarily less than perfect.

that patterns of time-use became more randomized as the eighteenth century wore on. If everyone still took two days per week off in 1800, but the second day in addition to Sunday could be any day of the week, our econometric techniques would not indicate such a shift. The same argument can be applied to traditional holy days.

There is one simple way of examining the likelihood of such a development. Not all the cases used in our logistic regressions conformed to the overall pattern—there was a certain amount of 'background noise'. If the objection described above is correct, then the number of incorrect predictions (on the basis of the regression coefficients) should have increased dramatically. Table 3.44 gives an overview.[191]

Independent of the definition adopted, there is some evidence—especially in London—of an increase in the number of 'misclassified' cases. In the North we find increases and reductions in about equal measure. While the London pattern between 1760 and 1800 gives some support to the objection raised above, we also have to note that the reduction in the percentage of cases classified correctly is very small throughout. It appears unlikely that increases of less than 4 per cent in the number of cases that do not conform to the patterns we have identified could have led to insignificant coefficients on the holy day and the Monday variables.

It is possible, however, to argue that the correctly predicted cases are of a different character in 1750 and in 1800. In the extreme, one

TABLE 3.44. *Percentage of cases classified correctly*

	Holy Days W1	Holy Days W2	Holy Days W3	Monday W1	Monday W2	Monday W3
London						
1760	78.01	70.10	56.10	77.70	69.80	56.40
1800	76.40	67.60	52.50	76.20	67.60	52.70
1830	75.20	68.20	53.20	75.90	62.50	52.60
North						
1760	63.20	57.20	55.10	60.20	59.90	55.30
1800	61.30	58.20	56.80	61.20	59.40	55.80
1830	62.20	58.70	57.10	60.10	59.10	55.10

[191] I report the results for 'naive' logistic regressions, using only the feastday dummy as a predictor variable.

could assume that all 'misclassified' cases in 1750 represent sampling error, while in 1800, they contain all those who take a day off as a result of randomization. It is straightforward to infer the maximum impact that such an interpretation could have. The effects of randomization were probably restricted to the semi- and unskilled. From Schwarz's estimates we know that this group represented 40 to 44 per cent of the male labour force in 1800. This suggests that no more than 9.9 per cent of the total labour force could have been affected by more 'randomized' time use. Our estimates of changes in labour input would therefore have to be adjusted downward by no more than this figure.

Even such a small correction would be more or less arbitrary. Consider the case of Mondays. If, through the effects of randomization, other working days of the week now had to fulfil the role of an additional day of respite, we would expect the percentage of people observed in work to decline. This was not the case—the (unadjusted) number of witnesses at work grew from 40.5 per cent in 1750 (using the widest definition, w3) to 53.6 per cent approximately fifty years later, an increase by almost 30 per cent in relative terms.[192] Alternative definitions of work yield very similar results, and the same is true in the case of holy days. It therefore appears unlikely that declining co-ordination of leisure time was responsible for the main results reported above. The empirical basis for such a claim is weak, and even if its legitimacy could be demonstrated, the consequences for our estimates would be small.

Comparing Bedtimes of Witnesses and Victims

An obvious difficulty in our dataset is that, in order to act as witnesses, our respondents have to be awake. This causes obvious difficulties when we analyse bedtimes. For example, it could be argued that the surprisingly short hours of sleep found in our sample are the result of a bias towards witnesses that go to bed late and rise early.

The same kind of sample selection bias does not exist for victims of crime. They will often note that they went to bed at a certain hour, rose in the morning, and that they were robbed at some unknown time during the night. Comparing their bedtimes with those of witnesses in our sample allows us to test for a skewing towards early risers and

---

[192] Tables 3.31 and 3.32 above.

those staying up late at night. For each of the sleep-related activities (rising in the morning, going to bed) in the London dataset from both 1760 and 1800, I collected thirty additional observations on the activities of victims of crime.

Figure 3.22 shows the time of rising in the morning for witnesses and victims in 1760. Victims left their beds a little later than witnesses, but since the 95 per cent confidence intervals overlap, we cannot be certain of this. The same is true of the time of going to bed. As Figure 3.23 demonstrates, victims of crime appear to have gone to bed a little ear-

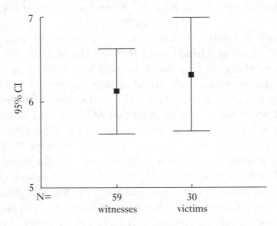

FIGURE 3.22. *Rising in the morning, witnesses and victims (London, 1760)*

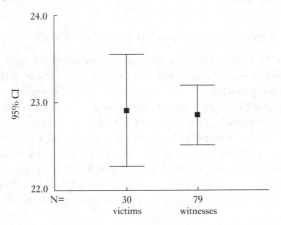

FIGURE 3.23. *Going to bed, victims and witnesses (London, 1760)*

lier than the witnesses in our sample. The absolute difference is small—both groups go to bed before 23:00. Despite the reasonable number of observations, however, the difference is also not statistically significant.

The validity of the a priori objection described above is also borne out by Figure 3.24, showing data on the time of going to bed from 1799–1803. Just as with the earlier dataset, witnesses were rising earlier in the morning than victims, although the differences are small and insignificant. Results for victims and witnesses going to bed in 1800 (Figure 3.25) confirm the impression given by the data

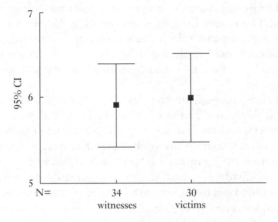

FIGURE 3.24. *Rising in the morning, victims and witnesses (London, 1800)*

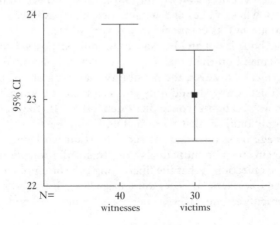

FIGURE 3.25. *Going to bed, victims and witnesses (London, 1800)*

previously examined. Victims retire to bed a little later than our witnesses, but the sampling errors do not allow us to draw wider conclusions from this.

Work on a Cheshire Canal

So far, I have largely examined issues of internal consistency—I have
tested the possibility of witnesses' accounts contradicting themselves,
at least on the issue of time-use, of unobserved shifts influencing our
results, and of inconsistencies between time-use reported by witnesses
and victims. The results have been encouraging. Yet what is really at
issue is how representative the judicial evidence is. Are shifts in time-
use found among those testifying before the Old Bailey indicative of
patterns elsewhere? I use new data from an additional source to examine this question.

The evidence comes from the day wage book (repairs) from the
Burnton and Western Canal in Cheshire in 1801.[193] Payments to carpenters, sawyers, and yard labourers are documented. Their work was
classified as 'extra labour'. This implies that they were not regarded as
a regular part of the company's labour force. During the year 1801,
however, the individuals named in the wage book do not change very
much. What fluctuates in the course of the year is the number of them
that the company employed. Consequently, there was a more or less
stable group of men available for work on the canal. The company
employed their services as it saw fit, but it rarely turned to outsiders.
The workers whose wages are documented may have been a reserve
army of labour, but its composition was very stable.

The wage book is not an ideal source for our purposes. Peculiarities
of labour demand on the canal may have made employment patterns
highly untypical. However, the possibility that work on the canal was
timed in an unsual way should only concern us if the wage book data
and witnesses' accounts contradict each other. If they do not, it
appears highly unlikely that both the Old Bailey Sessions Papers and
the canal wage book recorded the same aberrant work patterns—the
former pertains to 1000 individuals in virtually all professions. A second possible objection is that the fluctuating type of employment may
have induced workers to seek work elsewhere, leaving us with an
understatement of annual working days. Since we find a strong

---

[193] PRO (Kew) Rail 883–189.

upward movement of labour input and a very long working year in absolute terms, this would only be a problem if the number of hours worked on the canal is much lower than implied by the Old Bailey witnesses. Finally, there is no information on the number of hours worked per day. Occasionally, labourers receive more than a day's wage, which implies that they worked longer than normal, but there is no indication either of these regular hours nor the exact amount of overtime. For our purposes the absence of information on hours of work is not as unfortunate as may be supposed—the main finding in the preceding sections concerned weekly and annual patterns of labour and leisure. There was little change in daily time-allocation.

During 1801 a total of 5,924 man-days were worked on the canal. The maximum number of workers employed on any one day was 42; the smallest observed value is zero. On average, 16 men are employed for repair work and the like. Work on the Burnton and Western Canal in 1801 was strongly seasonal. Figure 3.26 shows a seven-day moving average of the number of men employed during the year. The first and fourth quarter of the year register fluctuating, but fairly average levels of labour input. The second quarter shows less work than during

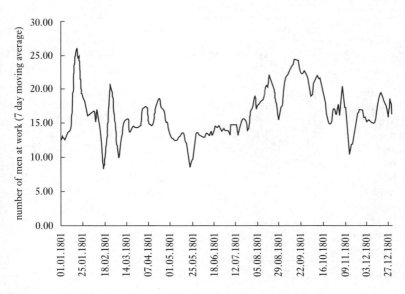

FIGURE 3.26. *Number of men employed on the Burnton and Western Canal, 1801*

the rest of the year. Above average numbers of man-days are worked during the third quarter.

How similar are these patterns to what we observed in the Old Bailey Sessions Papers? Table 3.45 gives absolute numbers per month and percentages. Agreement between the two series is not always perfect; the trough during the summer months, for example, seems to be more acute in the Old Bailey data than on the canal. Overall, similarity between the two datasets is not small. While the more sensitive Pearson correlation coefficient only suggests a value of 0.35, the Spearman rank correlation coefficient is 0.96—far higher than values that are generally regarded as acceptable in the literature.[194]

We are also interested in the days when work stopped, and if they coincide with what we would predict based on our results from court records. Are Mondays days off? Are holidays still celebrated? How many men work on Sunday? There are only 25 days on which nobody worked. All of them are Sundays; no other day saw everyone refraining from working. During the rest of the week, the number of men at work is fairly constant. Table 3.46 compares the data from the Old Bailey with the weekly pattern of work on the canal.

TABLE 3.45. *Work on the canal—months*

	Old Bailey—1800		Canal	
	Count	Percentage of total	Count	Percentage of total
	(1)	(2)	(3)	(4)
January	67	11.6	537	9.1
February	57	9.8	415	7.0
March	45	7.8	433	7.3
April	38	6.6	501	8.5
May	39	6.7	362	6.1
June	29	5.0	412	7.0
July	37	6.4	450	7.6
August	29	5.0	580	9.8
September	58	10.0	665	11.2
October	63	10.9	588	9.9
November	64	11.1	465	7.8
December	53	9.2	516	8.7

Note: Owing to rounding errors, column (2) totals 100.1 per cent.

[194] Johnson and Nicholas, 'Health and Welfare', 10 ff.

TABLE 3.46. *Work on the canal—days*

| | Old Bailey—1800 | | Canal | |
	Count (1)	Percentage of total (2)	Count (3)	Percentage of total (4)
Sunday	35	6.2	199	3.4
Monday	79	13.4	974	16.4
Tuesday	85	14.7	976	16.5
Wednesday	99	17.1	945	16.0
Thursday	85	14.7	910	15.4
Friday	90	15.5	958	16.2
Saturday	106	18.4	962	16.2

In 1800 there are slightly more observations on Sunday, but the difference is small. On the canal, the days of the working week register almost identical manning levels. The variation is somewhat higher in the witnesses' accounts—as is only to be expected since there is more than one profession in the sample. In both datasets Sunday appears to be a day of rest, and Monday shows no significant divergence from other working days. The (Pearson) correlation coefficient between the two relative frequencies (columns (2) and (4)) is 0.91, and the Spearman rank correlation coefficient has a value of 0.93. As regards the weekly cycle of work and rest, the evidence from the Burnton and Western Canal in 1801 does not contradict the data from the Old Bailey (and the Northern Assizes material) in 1799/1803.

We have thus demonstrated that one source of growing labour input that we inferred from the court records, the decline of 'St Monday', was also present on the canal. Is this also true for the second cause of the lengthening working year, the disappearance of holy days? In deciding whether a day was normally used for work or not, it will be convenient to define a certain number of men in employment that clearly marks a working day. Of course, there is a certain element of arbitrariness in deciding which days should be treated as 'days off'. Figure 3.27 gives the frequency of manning levels on the canal. The distribution is skewed to the left. The most common number of men at work was 13–15. To the right of the mode, the number of days observed with a given manning level tails off slowly; to the left, the frequency falls sharply. If we assume that days with up to 13 people in employment should be counted as days off, there would be 57 days of leisure in the year. Almost 79 per cent of these (45 in total) are

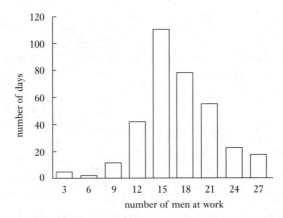

FIGURE 3.27. *Frequency distribution of the number of men employed on the Burnton and Western Canal, 1801*

Sundays. There would consequently be 7 Sundays which we cannot count as days of rest.

This approach cannot be satisfactory because we do not adjust for the seasonality of the working schedule on the canal. The same number of men at work may have been high during the summer and very low in the autumn (cf. the strong seasonal pattern explored above). I will consequently focus on the relative difference between the number of men at work on a specific day and the seven-day moving average. If we decide that 50 per cent of the moving average is a reasonable cut-off point, then 44 days were used for rest. All but three of these are Sundays. The result is not very sensitive to the cut-off point we use. At 30 per cent, it is 41; at 70 per cent, it is 48. This implies that not even every Sunday was a day off. The consequence of moving to a higher threshold is simply to add additional Sundays; there are still only three other non-Sundays. Their dates are 20 and 21 February, and 5 March. None of these coincides with a feast day, even if the first two are close to Shrove Tuesday.[195]

Clearly, none of the traditional holidays persisted, at least on the canal in Cheshire.[196] While the courtroom material allows us to

[195] Christopher Robert Cheney (ed.), *Handbook of Dates for Students of English History*, (London, 1945) 113.

[196] The same can be demonstrated by using a Probit model. Since the other evidence is so overwhelmingly in favour of our interpretation, I refrain from presenting the results.

observe a large number of individuals, but each only over a very short period, the nature of the data in the wage book is exactly the reverse: the number of individuals is comparatively small (about one-sixtieth of the number in the Old Bailey reports), but we are able to track each one over the course of an entire year. Also, the two datasets come from different geographical areas. This lends some support to our procedure of treating London and Northern developments as representative of England as a whole. Both methods agree on the main points—'St Monday' and old holy days held no importance any more in 1800, and the weekly and annual cycles of work and rest are remarkably similar. Unfortunately, we cannot repeat the experiment for 1760. Our conclusions would be fully corroborated if there were evidence from another independent source of traditional practices still persisting in 1760.

In this chapter, a number of tests have been carried out. The main result derived from the timing of activities was compared with frequency-based estimates. Any divergence would have indicated that either some days of the year or certain hours of the day were systematically under- or overreported. While the fit was less than perfect, the overall result was encouraging. The magnitude of estimates was very similar, and change over time was virtually identical. Second, I tested for sample selection bias among witnesses. It emerged that they are reasonably representative of the working population. Changes in the socio-economic status of witnesses were also too small to account for the observed changes in time-use. Third, I tested the possibility of a link between memory decay and the recall period. No such link emerged. Fourth, estimates from initial sub-samples were confronted with those derived from the final dataset. The differences were small and insignificant. Fifth, I explored the hypothesis that unobserved changes in the age-distribution might have been responsible for our results. This alternative explanation was also rejected. Sixth, I discussed the possibility that declining co-ordination of leisure time, and not an increase in work, caused the shifts in the probability of observing witnesses at work on Mondays and holy days. This alternative interpretation is difficult to reconcile with the historical evidence. Seventh, I tested if victims of crime had different bedtimes than witnesses. While a small bias could be observed, I showed that it was very small compared to the standard error of our estimates. Finally, I examined if our new estimates disagree with other elements of the historical record. Information on days of work from a Cheshire canal showed that our main findings hold elsewhere.

None of these tests provides a final proof that we can reliably construct patterns of time-use from witnesses' accounts. Yet the probability of misconstruing the past is diminished by showing that there are no obvious flaws in our method or the group it is applied to, and that no clear inconsistency with other parts of the historical record exists.

4

Causes and Consequences

This study has called thousands of witnesses to the bar of history. To a remarkable extent, they attest to the unchanging nature of time-use during the Industrial Revolution. In one area, however, there appears to be rapid change—between the middle and the end of the eighteenth century the working year lengthened considerably. This chapter is concerned with placing this result in a wider context. It seems that such long hours of toil are incompatible with recent work by Fogel on the nutrition of early modern populations. The first section consequently discusses the literature relating to nutrition, work–capacity, and inequality of nutrient-availability, and offers a solution to the puzzle. The second section attempts to explain why time-use changed in the particular way described in earlier sections. It presents five alternative interpretations, and gives reasons for rejecting two of them completely. My own interpretation of the main changes is given. Finally, implications for the question of growth and productivity during the Industrial Revolution are discussed.

Work, Nutrition, and Inequality

According to the estimates presented above, the working year in 1800–30 was long compared with earlier and later periods of English history. Extensive hours of toil are found for the lower classes as well as the middling sort. These results appear to be incompatible with Fogel's finding that food was so scarce in England during the second half of the eighteenth century that the 'bottom 3 per cent of its labour force lacked the energy for any work, but the balance of the bottom 20 per cent had enough energy for about 6 hours of light work'.[1] Because nutrition was scarce, up to 30 per cent of English growth in per capita income over the past 200 years can be explained by the rise in energy available

[1] Robert Fogel, 'New Sources and New Techniques for the Study of Secular Trends in Nutritional Status, Mortality, and the Process of Aging', *Historical Methods*, 26 (1993), 270.

for work.[2] Shammas strikes a similar chord when she concluded that the diet of the poor could not 'be squared with the supposed sunrise-to-sunset work schedule'.[3] This section will argue that, in contrast to Fogel's and Shammas's findings, we cannot be certain that work effort even of the least favoured groups was constrained by the supply of nutrients.

An individual's calorie intake is used for four purposes. First, the body's basal metabolism has to be maintained. Basal metabolic rates (BMRs) vary between individuals according to height, age, gender, and weight. Typically, rates for adult males vary between 1,350 and 2,000 calories, with 1,240 calories often being regarded as the absolute minimum. Second, even if enough calories are available for basal metabolism, individuals would be unable to survive. The eating and digesting of food as well as basic hygiene increase BMR by approximately 27 per cent.[4] Third, work often makes large demands on energy intake. Heavy manual labour like ploughing may increase BMR by a factor of six during the time period when the task is performed.[5] Fourth, discretionary activities like walking, shopping, preparing food, and social interaction require additional energy. These demands are not unimportant. Walking at a normal pace requires 3.2 times BMR, for example, a rate of increase of basal metabolism that is almost half the rate for the most exacting forms of physical toil.[6] Any residual will be used for storing energy in the form of fat or, in the case of children and adolescents, for growth.

Fogel first observes that the distribution of calories in any population examined today is far more egalitarian than the distribution of income. At the top end, calorie intake is constrained by body builds and the body's ability to digest food. The bottom deciles require a minimum of nutritional energy to survive. Consequently, Gini coefficients have only ranged between 0.22 and 0.11. He then uses other researchers' calculations of calorie production per head based on national food balance sheets to arrive at estimates of mean energy consumption. Toutain's research on France suggests an average of 2,290 calories.[7] Fogel then

---

[2] Robert Fogel, 'The Conquest of High Mortality and Hunger in Europe and America: Timing and Mechanisms', *NBER Historical Working Paper* 16 (1990), 49. On the importance of energy availability for economic activities, especially in agriculture, see Edward Anthony Wrigley, 'Energy Availability and Agricultural Productivity', in Mark Overton and Bruce Campbell (eds.), *Land, Labour and Lifestock* (Manchester, 1991).

[3] Carole Shammas, *The Pre-Industrial Consumer in England and America* (Oxford, 1990), 146.

[4] Fogel, 'Conquest', 15–16.   [5] Id., 'New Sources', table 1, p.8.   [6] Ibid.

[7] Jean-Claude Toutain, 'La Consommation alimentaire en France de 1789 à 1964', *Economies et Sociétés, Cahiers de L'ISEA*, v (1971).

presents three hypothetical distributions of calorie consumption in France around 1785 under the assumptions of high, medium, and low levels of egalitarianism.[8] In the case of a relatively uneven distribution of calories, the poorest 20 per cent of French society would have starved. This seems improbable. Had a high degree of egalitarianism prevailed, then the upper classes would have been left with very low energy rations. Since the known lifestyle and consumption of this group are incompatible with calorie intake on this scale, the case of high egalitarianism is also ruled out. Fogel therefore concludes that medium egalitarianism offers the best description of calorie consumption. Consequently, the bottom 15 per cent of the population lack the energy for any productive activity.

In England, the mean was somewhat higher than in France— 2,700 versus 2,290 calories per day and consuming unit.[9] He again assumes a medium degree of egalitarianism (Table 4.1).[10] Despite the

TABLE 4.1. *Distribution of calorie consumption in England and France (medium egalitarianism)*

Decile	France, medium egalitarianism	Hours of light work/day	or Hours of heavy work	England, medium egalitarianism	Hours of light work/day	or Hours of heavy work
1	3,675.45	59.20	9.87	4,333.50	77.15	12.86
2	2,981.58	40.29	6.71	3,515.40	54.84	9.14
3	2,679.30	32.04	5.34	3,159.00	45.12	7.52
4	2,459.46	26.05	4.34	2,899.80	38.06	6.34
5	2,303.74	21.81	3.63	2,716.20	33.05	5.51
6	2,115.96	16.69	2.78	2,494.80	27.01	4.50
7	1,957.95	12.38	2.06	2,308.50	21.94	3.66
8	1,799.94	8.07	1.34	2,122.20	16.86	2.81
9	1,616.74	3.07	0.51	1,906.20	10.97	1.83
10	1,309.88	NA	NA	1,544.40	1.10	0.18
	(average = 2,290)			(average = 2,700)		

Source: Recalculated from Fogel, 'New Sources and New Techniques', table 3, p.10.

[8] Fogel, 'New Sources', 10.
[9] Fogel calculates on the basis of 'consuming units': i.e., adult males.
[10] Recalculated from ibid., table 3. I used Fogel's estimates of mean calorie consumption and cumulative distributions. Results were slightly different: for the top French decile, Fogel gives 3,672 calories, whereas I find that his assumptions imply 3,675.45. These differences are probably due to rounding.

somewhat higher mean in England, the nutritional situation of most classes is—from Fogel's point of view—precarious. The lowest decile is very close to minimum BMR, with hardly any energy left for work. Even those in the sixth decile would have been incapable of arduous labour for five hours. Only the two highest deciles have access to enough food for more than eight hours of hard work per day.

Fogel's use of the data is ingenious, and his results have potentially large implications.[11] Yet large problems remain, casting doubt on his conclusions about the proportion of the population that is malnourished. Both Fogel's estimates of available calories and his calculations of minimum calorie standards must be qualified. He draws on energy requirements published by the FAO and, in 1951, by Quenouille.[12] Measurements of minimum energy intake are, however, notoriously difficult. A generation of revisionist scholars has argued that it is methodologically invalid to assess the nutritional situation by comparing the calorie intake of an individual population with 'requirements'.[13] The FAO itself notes that:

The figures for recommended intakes may be compared with actual consumption figures determined by food-consumption surveys. Such comparisons, though always useful, *cannot in themselves justify statements that undernutrition, malnutrition or overnutrition is present in a community or group, as such conclusions must always be supported by clinical or bio-chemical evidence.* The recommended intakes are not an adequate yardstick for assessing health because ... each figure represents an average requirement augmented by a factor that takes into account interindividual variability.[14]

If such cautious recommendations go unheeded, improbable conclusions are the result. For the same period (1979–81), for example, the

---

[11] Cf. Fogel's ('Second Thoughts on the European Escape from Hunger: Famines, Chronic Malnutrition, and Mortality Rates', in S. Osmani (ed.), *Nutrition and Poverty* (Oxford, 1992), 271) conjectures about the French revolution.

[12] FAO, *The Fourth World Food Survey* (Rome, 1977); M. Quenouille *et al.*, *Statistical Studies of Recorded Energy Expenditure in Man*, Technical Communication No. 17, Commonwealth Bureau of Animal Nutrition (Aberdeen, 1951).

[13] Colin Clark and Margaret Haswell, *The Economics of Subsistence Agriculture*, 4th edn. (London, 1970), ch. 1; David Seckler, 'Malnutrition: An Intellectual Odyssey', *Western Journal of Agricultural Economics*, 5 (1980); Thirukodikaval Srinivasan, 'Malnutrition: Some Measurement and Policy Issues', *Journal of Development Economics*, 8 (1981); Pandurang Sukhatme (ed.), *Newer Concepts in Nutrition and Their Implications for Policy* (Pune, 1982); P. Payne, 'Public Health and Functional Consequences of Seasonal Hunger and Malnutrition', in D. Sahn (ed.), *Causes and Implications of Seasonal Variability in Household Food Security* (Washington, DC, 1987).

[14] FAO, *Fourth World Food Survey*, 2 (my italics).

World Bank estimates that there were 730 million people in the Third World with insufficient energy for an active working life, while the FAO finds 335 million.[15] Problems of measurement and aggregation of energy requirements are severe.[16] Consequently, it appears doubtful that, on the basis of comparisons with the FAO standards, energy insufficiency can be proved for England's lower classes during the late eighteenth century.

The other side of Fogel's balance sheet, nutritional intake, is equally problematic. One obvious problem is the way Fogel converted national food balance sheets into individual energy availability. Two problems arise. First, there is considerable evidence showing that the estimates of food production are incompatible with observed demand elasticities and the growth of per capita income. If people were inclined to consume extra food to the limited extent implied by some contemporary evidence, then either food production estimates for the late eighteenth century are too low or growth figures of GDP/person too high.[17]

Second, by dividing annual calorie production by the number of individuals and days in the year so as to arrive at daily consumption schedules, Fogel effectively assumes that all days of the week (and the year) were working days. In neither the French nor the British case is this correct. France under the *ancien régime* was known for a large number of holidays, and Britain observed Sundays and a few additional holidays.[18] This suggests that calorie availability per working day has been understated.[19] The extent of the error is not large since only energy for work activities is saved, whereas the much larger amounts for BMR and basic hygiene are still required on days 'off'. Table 4.2 presents revised guesses about the distribution of nutrients in both England and France, again taking Fogel's calculations under the assumption of medium egalitarianism as a starting point.

[15] World Bank, *Poverty and Hunger: Issues and Options for Food Security in Developing Countries* (Washington, DC, 1986); FAO, *The Fifth World Food Survey* (Rome, 1985).

[16] Thirukodikaval Srinivasan, 'Undernutrition: Concepts, Measurements, and Policy Implications', in Osmani (ed.), *Nutrition and Poverty*, 108–16.

[17] Gregory Clark, M. Huberman, and P. Lindert, 'A British Food Puzzle, 1770–1850', *Economic History Review*, 48 (1995). A possible resolution to this 'puzzle' could argue that their assumed elasticities are too high. The end of this section presents some evidence.

[18] George Rudé, 'Prices, Wages and Popular Movements in Paris during the French Revolution', *Economic History Review*, 6 (1953–4), 248; Paul Delsalle, 'Les Loisiers des ouvriers en France XVIᵉ-XVIIIᵉ siècles', paper presented at the XXVI Settimana di Studi, Istituto F. Datini, Prato, 18–23 April 1994, 4.

[19] Cf. Shammas, *Pre-Industrial Consumer*, 146.

TABLE 4.2. *Calorie distributions for days of work*

Decile	France, medium egalitarianism	Hours of light work	Heavy work	England, medium egalitarianism	Hours of light work	Heavy work
1	4,115.26	71.19	11.87	4,704.85	87.27	14.54
2	3,338.36	50.01	8.34	3,816.65	63.05	10.51
3	2,999.91	40.79	6.80	3,429.71	52.50	8.75
4	2,753.76	34.07	5.68	3,148.29	44.83	7.47
5	2,579.41	29.32	4.89	2,948.96	39.40	6.57
6	2,369.16	23.59	3.93	2,708.59	32.84	5.47
7	2,192.24	18.77	3.13	2,506.32	27.33	4.55
8	2,015.32	13.94	2.32	2,304.06	21.81	3.64
9	1,810.20	8.35	1.39	2,069.55	15.42	2.57
10	1,466.62	NA	NA	1,676.75	4.71	0.79
	(average = 2,564)			(average = 2,931)		

Binding energy constraints still apply to the bottom 10 per cent of the English and French populations. From the second-lowest decile upwards, it becomes more difficult to show that lack of nutrients restricted annual labour input. Differences in the case of France are slightly larger than in the English case. This is because I assumed that there were 271 working days in France versus 306 in England.[20]

Other difficulties have larger implications. Fogel's argument in favour of a medium degree of inequality in France is strong. He then applies the same distribution to the English case. The reasons for this are not entirely clear. Fogel ruled out a high degree of egalitarianism in the French case because it implied very low nutritional intakes of the upper classes. Applying the same, medium-egalitarian distribution to England means that the top 10 per cent would have consumed over 600 calories (or 18 per cent) more than their French counterparts, the equivalent of one meal per day. There is no a priori reason (nor any historical evidence) to assume that this was the case. Even in the case of high egalitarianism, the English upper classes could have consistently eaten more food than the French under medium egalitarianism (Tables 4.1 and 4.3).

[20] For the English case see above. The French figure is based on Delsalle, 'Loisiers des ouvriers en France', 4.

TABLE 4.3. *Distribution of calorie consumption in England and France (high egalitarianism)*

Decile	France, high egalitarianism	Hours of light work	Hours of heavy work	England, high egalitarianism	Hours of light work	Hours of heavy work
1	3,196.84	46.15	7.69	3,769.20	61.76	10.29
2	2,775.48	34.67	5.78	3,272.40	48.21	8.04
3	2,580.83	29.36	4.89	3,042.90	41.96	6.99
4	2,436.56	25.43	4.24	2,872.80	37.32	6.22
5	2,214.43	19.37	3.23	2,610.90	30.18	5.03
6	2,200.69	19.00	3.17	2,594.70	29.74	4.96
7	2,090.77	16.00	2.67	2,465.10	26.20	4.37
8	1,973.98	12.81	2.14	2,327.40	22.45	3.74
9	1,836.58	9.07	1.51	2,165.40	18.03	3.01
10	1,593.84	NA	NA	1,879.20	10.23	1.71
	(average = 2,290)			(average = 2,700)		

If we accept that England may have had a higher degree of egalitarianism, then the nutritional situation of the poor and ultra-poor may have been vastly more advantageous. They could easily have performed more than 10 hours of light work or more than 1.5 hours of heavy toil. The differences in relative calorie distribution would have been quite small (Figure 4.1). Fogel himself names some factors such as poor relief under the Speenhamland system that may have caused lower inequality in the English case,[21] but fails to discuss the potential implications.

This brings us to our third objection. There is no a priori reason to assume that the calorie distributions are symmetric around the mean—distributions of wealth or income often show important divergences from symmetry.[22] Systems of poor relief may have caused a skewing of energy distributions as calories are diverted from the higher to the lower classes.[23] Even a small degree of redistribution

[21] Fogel, 'Second Thoughts', 271.

[22] Anthony B. Atkinson, *The Economics of Inequality* (Oxford, 1975), 46.

[23] For example, asymmetry could arise if the calories transferred to the two bottom deciles of the distribution are raised exclusively from the top classes (i.e., by dropping Fogel's assumption that the British upper classes consumed many more calories than their French equivalents).

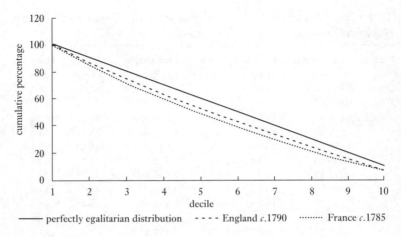

FIGURE 4.1. *Calorie distributions in England and France, end of the eighteenth century (hypothetical)*

would have large implications for the stringency of the lower classes' energy constraint.

Table 4.4 examines the implications of a very small shift in nutritional intake from the upper to the lower classes. We again begin with Fogel's distribution for England under the assumption of medium egalitarianism, giving the top echelons very large advantages over their French equivalents. Let us assume that, possibly as a consequence of poor relief, the top 30 per cent now surrender one-third of the difference between French nutritional intake and their original share, and that these nutrients are transferred to the bottom 20 per cent.[24] As Table 4.4 shows, redistributed calories would give sufficient energy for more than 11 hours of light work even for the bottom 10 per cent.

This thought-experiment established that the impact of any redistribution on the energy constraint of the lower classes is quite high in the English case. Indirect empirical support comes from modern Third World data, which regularly shows a very large impact of inequality on height. Steckel's investigations of this relationship reveal that the effect from a 100 per cent rise in per capita income is

---

[24] In the case of income redistribution, there are normally substantial costs involved in the transfer itself. Since there is little reason to assume that the same is true of nutritional energy, I have assumed no 'wastage'.

TABLE 4.4. *Calorie distribution in England, c. 1795—redistribution of nutrition*

Decile	Original distribution	Hours of light work	Hours of heavy work	Revised distribution	Hours of light work	Hours of heavy work
1	4,333.5	89.49	14.91	4,113.0	82.51	13.75
2	3,515.4	63.61	10.60	3,337.3	57.98	9.66
3	3,159.0	52.34	8.72	2,998.0	47.25	7.88
4	2,899.8	44.15	7.36	2,899.8	44.15	7.36
5	2,716.2	38.34	6.39	2,716.2	38.34	6.39
6	2,494.8	31.34	5.22	2,494.8	31.34	5.22
7	2,308.5	25.44	4.24	2,308.5	25.44	4.24
8	2,122.2	19.55	3.26	2,122.2	19.55	3.26
9	1,906.2	12.72	2.12	2,065.7	17.76	2.96
10	1,544.4	1.28	0.21	1,880.2	11.90	1.98
	(average = 2,700)			(average = 2,700)		

as large as the one resulting from a 6 percentage point change in the Gini coefficient.[25] If height is a good indicator of nutritional intake,[26] then the required accuracy of inequality measurements will be almost impossible to achieve with historical data.[27]

There is also qualitative evidence to suggest that Table 4.4 substantially underestimates the amount of nutrient transfer that actually occurred. Shammas has collected data on poorhouse diets. The average for the period 1794–95 suggests 2,232 calories per inmate, which would allow 19.5 hours of light work or 3.3 hours of heavy work. Since the old and the very young formed a sizeable part of the total workhouse population, nutrient availability per adult male equivalent was higher. Per adult male, there would be enough energy for 46 hours of light work and 7.7 hours of exhausting physical labour.[28] These

[25] Richard Steckel, 'Height and Per Capita Income', *Historical Methods*, 16 (1983), 5.

[26] Recent research suggests that there are clearly defined episodes in history when this was probably not the case. See Hans-Joachim Voth and Timothy Leunig, 'Did Smallpox Reduce Height? Stature and the Standard of Living in London, 1770–1873', *Economic History Review*, 59 (1996).

[27] Fogel gives a possible range of calorie inequality between 0.22 and 0.11 (Gini coefficient). Even if a good guess is only 'off' by 25 per cent between the midpoint and the upper bound (or one-eighth of the total range), the calculated (predicted) height would be as inaccurate as if we had miscalculated income by 138 per cent.

[28] If one clear outlier (Whight Workhouse in 1794 with 1,795 calories) is removed the average rises to 2,305 calories/inmate or 3,293 per consuming unit. These would have been sufficient

figures are probably lower bounds since the accounts scrutinized by Shammas only give purchased items. Vegetables provided important supplements to the diet.[29] It is possible that large parts of the population lived on less food than poorhouse inmates, as Rowntree demonstrated for 14 working families in York in the nineteenth century. Note, however, that the gap between workhouse diets and those of the labouring poor found by Rowntree is appreciably smaller than the one implied by Fogel—27 per cent v. at least 45 per cent.[30]

Recent research into agricultural productivity also fails to show any effect of malnutrition. Using data from Arthur Young's tours of Britain during the late 1760s and early 1770s, Brunt expresses the wages of agricultural labourers in terms of the calories they could have purchased in exchange. Even if a large part of their expenditure was for other items, the variable should capture regional variations in the cost of nutrients. There is no effect of these differences on the efficiency of workers in the primary sector, suggesting that they were not living on the verge of starvation.[31]

The preceding paragraphs argued that even minor changes to Fogel's assumptions lead to a reversal of one of his main findings, namely that a large section of Britain's poorer classes did not consume enough food to engage in more than a very limited amount of work. The striking sensitivity of his estimates for the maximum number of hours of work is the result of two factors. First, BMR and basic hygiene take by far the largest share of all the energy available to the body. Second, his estimates of calorie availability for the lowest deciles are quite close to the biological minimum, which is equivalent to 1.27 BMR. The higher BMR and other basic requirements relative to the estimated energy intake, the larger the sensitivity of the residual to even small changes in assumptions. In Fogel's original distribution for

---

for 3.6 and 8.13 hours of heavy work, respectively. The conversion factor (= 1.42) between male and average calorie consumption was taken from Shammas, *Pre-Industrial Consumer*.

[29] Shammas argues that gains from this source were probably more than offset by the fact that published menus were intended to create the impression of a 'caring institution' (*Pre-Industrial Consumer*, 140).

[30] Otherwise, there would have been few incentives not to enter the poorhouse. It could be argued that factors not relating to nutrition may have still kept large numbers away from indoor relief; yet the importance of such factors in a context of severe energy shortage must be called into doubt.

[31] Liam Brunt, 'Providence or Perseverance? Labour Productivity Growth in the Agricultural Revolution 1750–1800', unpub. M. Phil. thesis, Nuffield College, Oxford (1995), 94, app. III, 107 ff.

England (medium egalitarianism), a 1 per cent increase in average calories (rising from 2,700 to 2,727), leads to a 38 per cent increase in the number of hours of light work that could have been undertaken by the lower classes. An error of 10 per cent more than quintuples energy available for work. A working day of 7.5 hours of light work for 365 days in the year would have been possible if Fogel underestimated the mean by as little as 13 per cent. The even larger sensitivity to changes in assumed inequality has already been demonstrated. Given the nature of the historical evidence, it seems unlikely that it will be possible to establish with great certainty that (1) mean calorie production was definitely not 13 per cent higher than assumed by Fogel, (2) the English upper classes consumed substantially more than did their French counterparts, and (3) that the calorie distribution was symmetric around the mean. If any one of these assumptions is relaxed, there is no reason to believe that working schedules were constrained by food availability.

Can adequate diets even for the poor be reconciled with the history of human stature during the second half of the eighteenth century? Considerable controversy surrounds the question whether heights rose or fell; what is clear, however, is that heights were very low by modern standards.[32] Since genetic potential is generally assumed to be constant in national populations over time, this can be interpreted as direct evidence of malnutrition: height is a function of net nutritional status, the balance between calorie intake and energy expenditure, during childhood and adolescence. The argument presented above, however, is not directly affected. First, the growth of children is not necessarily a good indicator of energy availability for work among the adult population. As is well known from slave populations in North America, very nutritious diets for full-time labourers may coincide with insufficient calorie availability for the young.[33] Second, energy

---

[32] The original contribution is Roderick Floud, Kenneth Wachter, and Annabel Gregory, *Height, Health and History. Nutritional Status in the United Kingdom 1750–1980* (1990). On the debate about trends in average height between Komlos and Floud, cf. John Komlos, 'The Secular Trend in the Biological Standard of Living', *Economic History Review*, 44 (1993); id., 'Further Thoughts on the Nutritional Status of the British Population', *Economic History Review*, 46 (1993); Floud, Wachter, and Gregory, 'Measuring Historical Heights: Short Cuts or the Long Way Round: A Reply to Komlos', *Economic History Review*, 46 (1993); eid., 'Further Thoughts on the Nutritional Status of the British Population', *Economic History Review*, 46 (1993). No consensus has emerged: Katarina Honeyman, 'Review of Periodical Literature, 1700–1850', *Economic History Review*, 48 (1995), 167.

[33] In the case of plantation slaves, 'catch-up' growth was observed as soon as they received labourers' allowances of food. See Richard Steckel, 'A Peculiar Population: The Nutrition, Health, and Mortality of American Slaves from Childhood to Maturity', *Journal of*

requirements for work normally take precedence over those for growth—individuals may have lacked calories for increasing height precisely because they expended much of their energy in the workplace.[34] Third, smaller body size diminishes the amount of nutrients necessary to keep the body alive. Ceteris paribus, of two workers receiving equal amounts of food, the shorter one will have more energy left for productive activities. Consequently, there is no reason to assume that the history of stature provides a good guide to the amount of energy available for work.

Our general conclusion is reinforced by expenditure patterns. If access to nutrients was a serious constraint, we would expect that a large proportion of total income would be devoted to food purchases. Also, any *change* in income should primarily affect food expenditure— the elasticity should be high. This was not the case. Shammas finds that English households from the working class spent only around 60 per cent of their total income on food.[35] This in itself suggests a comfortable cushion between average nutritional intake and minimum requirements. At the same time, however, demand elasticities for food were probably quite high, with estimates suggesting figures between 0.63 and 0.7.[36] A range of 0.7 to 0.9 is often found in the Third World. These high elasticities, however, are insufficient evidence for a general lack of energy. This is for two reasons.

First, the higher of the two estimates does not rule out the possibility that the true elasticity could have been a mere 0.46—the stan-

Economic History, 46 (1986). Opportunities for catch-up can only be exploited if the switch to a rich diet occurs during adolescence, and if it provides sufficient energy for hours of toil and a growth spurt.

[34] Maria De La Paz, 'Child Labor: Its Implications to Nutrition and Health in the Philippines', unpub. Ph.D. dissertation, Columbia University (1990). For an application to the Austrian case see Hans-Joachim Voth, 'Height, Nutrition, and Labor: Recasting the "Austrian Model"', *Journal of Interdisciplinary History*, 25 (1995), 632 ff.

[35] Shammas, 'Food Expenditures and Economic Well-Being in Early Modern England', *Journal of Economic History*, 43 (1983), 126 ff. Komlos ('The Food Budget of English Workers: A Comment on Shammas', *Journal of Economic History*, 48 (1988) criticizes Shammas for calculating budget shares by comparing wages inclusive and exclusive of food, thereby effectively assuming that every day of the year was a working day. Komlos's objection may be correct; the amount of underestimation of food's budget share is a function of the number of working days in the year. If our calculations are correct, Shammas's figures may only have to be revised to 61 per cent instead of the at least 75 per cent found by Komlos on the basis of 275 days of work.

[36] The lower estimate is from Clark, Huberman and Lindert, 'British Food Puzzle', table 3, p. 224, col. 1. The higher estimate is from N. F. R. Crafts, 'Income Elasticities of Demand and the Release of Labour by Agriculture during the British Industrial Revolution', *Journal of European Economic History*, 9 (1980), 156–9.

dard error on the coefficient proves to be quite large. The lower elasticity (0.63) is taken from the Lindert, Clark, and Huberman study. It relates to the rural poor in 1787–96, a period of particularly high prices. What matters for our purposes is not the demand elasticity for food, but for calories—the fact that increases in income lead to more expensive (and possibly unhealthy) food being substituted for cheap nutrients is little proof of calorie insufficiency. Even during this time of unusually dear food, these poor only show a demand elasticity for calories of 0.45. Given that these were times of particular distress, this must constitute an upper bound. At other times, and for more fortunate segments of society, the demand for calories probably varied even less with income. Shammas's study of household budgets also suggests a low elasticity. She does not carry out such a calculation herself, but we can infer an estimate from some of the information she provides. Shammas gives both budget shares and real wages for labourers and master carpenters.[37] On average, these are social groups somewhat above the poor. To construct an index of food expenditure, the percentage of total expenditure that goes on food is multiplied with the real wage index. This is then regressed on the Phelps Brown index. A dummy variable is used to control for the fact that separate observations for labourers and master carpenters are reported:

$$F = P_f^* w$$
$$F = a + bw + cD \tag{4.1}$$

[F = total expenditure on food, P_f = proportion of expenditure devoted to food, w = real wage, c = the Phelps–Brown Hopkins index, D = dummy variable, 1 for master carpenters, 0 otherwise].

The regression gives an elasticity of 0.25, with an upper bound of 0.32 (t-statistic 5.99). Adjusted R^2 is 0.83, and the F-test is significant at the 0.5 per cent level. Small sample size cautions against placing too much emphasis on this result (N = 11). None the less, it suggests that the food expenditure elasticity found by Crafts is on the high side of probable estimates, and that, over time, the true figure may only be half as large. As was demonstrated above, the demand elasticities for calories may even be lower. The conclusion that can be drawn from these different estimates is, again, that margins of error are too high to base firm inferences about the nutritional status of the common man on food elasticities.

[37] Shammas, *Pre-Industrial Consumer*, 128.

Yet even if the estimates are correct, we need not accept Fogel's conclusions. In poorer countries today, high demand elasticities for food do not prove that populations live on the verge of starvation. Recent work has demonstrated that, while elasticities for food expenditure in developing countries are high, the rise in nutrient intake per unit of extra income is normally quite low (around 0.2).[38] As people become better off, they tend to spend on food variety, not extra nutrients.[39] Very much the same appears to have been the case in England. As Adam Smith observed: 'The rich man consumes no more food than his poor neighbour. In quality it may be very different, and to select and prepare it may require more labour and art; but in quantity it is very nearly the same ...'[40]

Contemporary descriptions are also full of condescending remarks about prolific spending by the lower classes.[41] This impression is corroborated by Clark, Huberman, and Lindert's data on expenditure patterns among the rural poor. The income elasticity of demand (η) is commonly defined as the percentage change in expenditure on a commodity if income changes by 1 per cent. Even at a time of particularly high agricultural prices, calories were clearly not a superior good for the poor—η was a mere 0.45. The larger part of any increase in income was spent on goods other than calories. Superior goods normally have elasticities larger than unity.[42] Among the rural poor in 1787–96, only beer was clearly a superior good ($\eta = 3.03$), with dairy products, meat and sugar coming close ($\eta = 0.974, 0.87, 0.866$ respectively).[43] Such a taste for the good life—accompanied by only a small inclination towards nutritional energy itself—is incompatible with Fogel's image of the malnourished poor. It seems unlikely that groups on the verge of starvation spend substantial amounts on luxuries such

---

[38] Barbara Wolfe and Jere Behrman, 'Is Income Overrated in Determining Adequate Nutrition?', *Economic Development and Cultural Change*, 31 (1983).

[39] Jere Behrman, and Anil Deolalikar, 'Is Variety the Spice of Life? Implications for Nutrient Responses to Income', *Harvard Institute of Economic Research Discussion Paper* 1371 (1988), 8 ff. This lends further credibility to the revisionist work on malnutrition: Cf. Seckler, 'Malnutrition: An Intellectual Odyssey'; Srinivasan, 'Malnutrition: Some Measurement and Policy Issues'; Sukhatme, *Newer Concepts in Nutrition*; Payne, 'Public Health'.

[40] Smith, cit. Clark, Huberman, and Lindert, 'British Food Puzzle', 221.

[41] Peter Mathias, 'Leisure and Wages in Theory and Practice', in id. (ed.), *The Transformation of England* (London, 1979), 162. He also holds that this should not be dismissed as part of an ideological discourse.

[42] See, e.g., Robert Frank, *Microeconomics and Behaviour* (New York, 1991),155–6.

[43] Clark, Huberman, and Lindert, 'British Food Puzzle', table 3, p. 224, col. 1.

as coffee, tea, and sugar.[44] Also, the taste of the lower classes for wheaten bread was notorious, particularly in London. Compared to the continent or Ireland, this preference for quality food in itself indicates a high dietary standard.[45] This general conclusion is reinforced by the fact that early modern England's popular culture is unique among European societies in one regard—in English folk tales, references to famine are conspicuous by their absence.[46]

Causes of Longer Toil

Why did the working year lengthen between the middle of the eighteenth and the early nineteenth centuries? According to our data, labour input per member of the labour force increased by 20 to 23 per cent between 1760 and 1831. The two main factors underpinning this upward movement were the disappearance of 'St Monday' and the reduced importance of holy days. As I demonstrated above, this change was both large and swift by historical standards. Yet the causes of this dramatic development have only been hinted at. We do not have sufficient data at the household level on income, relative prices, and all forms of time-use to construct a fully specified model of time-allocation.[47] Instead, we shall first examine if changes in labour input were largely determined by shifts in demand or in labour supply. As will become apparent, it is possible to infer the proximate cause of changes in working hours if labour supply and demand schedules have the conventional form. It emerges that changes in labour supply were probably responsible for the largest part of the increase in labour input. Second, I will examine a number of competing hypotheses seeking to explain changes in labour input.

---

[44] Mathias, 'Leisure and Wages', 162 ff. Eric Jones (*Agriculture and the Industrial Revolution* (Oxford, 1974), 117) argued that in agriculture, high real wages during the first half of the eighteenth century stimulated demand for consumer durables even among simple labourers. As wages fell after 1750, extra work was undertaken so as to maintain the standard of living to which even the lower classes had become accustomed.

[45] Roger Wells, *Wretched Faces. Famine in Wartime England, 1793–1801* (Gloucester, 1988), 14 ff; John Burnett, 'Trends in Bread Consumption', in T. C. Baker, J. C. Mackenzie, and J. Yudkin (eds.), *Our Changing Fare* (n.p., 1966), 61–2.

[46] John Walter, 'The Social Economy of Dearth in Early Modern England', in John Walter and Roger S. Schofield (eds.), *Famine, Disease and the Social Order in Early Modern Society* (Cambridge, 1989), 75.

[47] For the requirements of such an exercise, see M. Hill and F. Thomas Juster, 'Constraints and Complementarities in Time Use', in Juster and Frank Stafford (eds.), *Time, Goods, and Well-Being* (Ann Arbor, Mich., 1985), 440 ff.

The combination of falling wages and longer hours is consistent with a change in labour supply (Figure 4.2). Hours can increase from L_1 to L_2 while wages fall from w_1 to w_2 if the supply schedule shifts upward from S to S'. Figure 4.3 gives the comparative statics for a shift in the demand schedule. With upward-sloping supply curves, a demand shock would increase both hours (from L_1 to L_2) and wages (from w_1 to w_2). As wages were lower in 1800 (and only marginally higher in 1830) than in 1760, a positive demand shift appears unlikely (Figure 4.4).[48] Because the marked rise in labour input coincides with only a small change in wages, this would seem to imply a relatively steep labour demand schedule.

Note that the simple intuition behind our argument in figures 4.2 and 4.3 does not hold if labour supply curves are not upward-sloping. Figure 4.4 develops the comparative statics for a downward shift in the demand schedule. The labour supply curve here is downward-sloping—implying that workers adjust their labour supply downwards when wages increase. A reduction in demand would cause a fall in wages, and hence an increase in labour supply. This would also be in

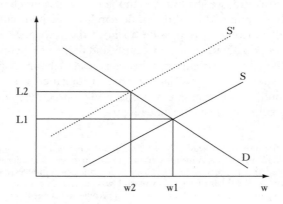

FIGURE 4.2. *Increase in labour supply*

[48] Feinstein ('Pessimism Perpetuated') presents data from 1770 onwards. Splicing his series onto the Lindert and Williamson estimates ('Living Standards') suggests that wages in 1760 were equivalent to 109 (1770 = 100), falling to 103 by 1800 and rising to 114 by 1831.

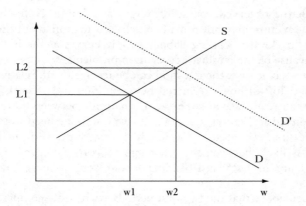

FIGURE 4.3. *Increase in labour demand*

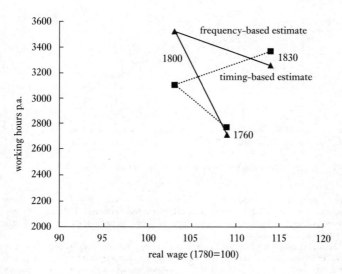

FIGURE 4.4. *Wages and hours in England, 1760–1831*

line with the observed course of wages and hours. Note that the aggregate picture may not provide much information about the existence of 'backward-bending' labour supply curves at the individual level, because of the familiar aggregation problems.[49]

In our specific case, the question can be resolved with relative ease. The main shift in hours occurred between 1760 and 1800. It is this change that we are seeking to explain. To decide between the alternatives depicted in Figures 4.2 and 4.3, two questions need to be considered. First, we need to decide if a downward shift in labour demand is likely between these benchmark years.[50] Second, is there any evidence of backward-bending labour supply curves over the period?

I argued above that the two first periods are broadly comparable in terms of macro-economic conditions—both combined periods of war and peace, of abundant harvests and dearth. According to Ashton's classification, the later period records a slight advantage in the sense that war-related industries, even during the depression of 1800, were working at full capacity. Building activity and public works also

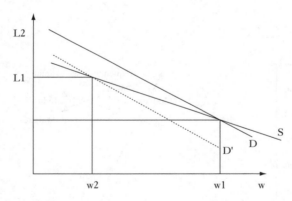

FIGURE 4.5. *Increase in labour demand with downward-sloping labour supply*

---

[49] See Angus Deaton and John Muellbauer, *Economics and Consumer Behaviour* (Cambridge, 1980), 287–8. Hatcher ('Labour, Leisure and Economic Thought', 87–90) provides some evidence of backward-bending labour supply curves in the case of the Gatherick Colliery in Northumberland.

[50] Note that the logic underlying this approach partly depends on the slope of the supply schedule. If labour supply were to fall very strongly when wages increase, it is possible to imagine situations where an outward shift of labour demand can lead to lower wages and greater labour supply.

remained strong. Demand conditions were slightly less favourable during the years 1749–63. The period contains two peaks, according to Ashton's classification, in 1751 and 1761, as well as two full-fledged recessions (in 1752–5 and 1762). Perhaps even more importantly, the armed forces continued to employ approximately 262,500 men in 1799–1802.[51] During the middle of the eighteenth century an average of only 101,500 men served under the flag. If there was a change in labour demand between the benchmark years, then it must have been upwards.

For a long time it has been argued that backward-bending labour supply curves prevailed amongst the lower classes in early industrial Britain. In this model households attempt to attain a certain target income and supply the number of hours necessary to meet this goal. The implication is that higher wages lead to a reduction in the number of hours offered by workers, while low wages induce a significant rise in labour supply. Arthur Young put it succinctly: '[E]veryone but an idiot knows that the lower classes must be kept poor or they will never be industrious.'[52] The phenomenon seems to be universal, having been documented for almost all ages and continents.[53] For the period under consideration, there is some indirect indication that backward-bending labour supply curves may still have had some influence on individuals' behaviour. Complaints of contemporaries abound.[54]

Yet there are two strong reasons to assume that, even if leisure preference was still a factor during the middle of the century, its influence was declining as the eighteenth century wore on. First, Mathias has shown that, at exactly the same time when complaints about high wages and the unwillingness of the lower sort to work abound, the

---

[51] Floud, Wachter, and Gregory, *Height, Health and History*, 69–73. Ashton (*Economic Fluctuations*, table 8, p. 187) suggests that the average number of men changed from approximately 107,000 to 400,000. Ashton's figures for 1800 refer to seamen and marines only. I interpolated the 1800 value instead. Without interpolation, the average for the years 1799–1803 would be 350,000.

[52] T. S. Ashton, *The Industrial Revolution, 1760–1830* (London, 1948), 202.

[53] Mathias, 'Leisure and Wages', 150; M. Miracle and B. Fetter, 'Backward-Sloping Labor Supply Functions and African Economic Behavior', *Economic Development and Cultural Change*, 18 (1970); Christopher Ellis, 'The Backward-Bending Supply Curve of Labor in Africa', *Journal of Developing Areas*, 15 (1981); Maria Martins, 'Labor Supply Behavior of Married Women: Theory and Empirical Evidence for Portugal', *Cahiers Economiques de Bruxelles*, 152 (1996). Hatcher, 'Labour, Leisure and Economic Thought' traces the gradual decline in this belief during the eighteenth century.

[54] Mathias, 'Leisure and Wages'.

latter are also repeatedly scorned for profligate spending and for 'aping their betters'. These two observations are contradictory—if a rise in the hourly wage rate had reduced the number of hours so as to keep weekly (or annual) income constant, there would have been little opportunity for extra spending.[55] On balance, observations such as this one seem more indicative of high labour demand. Mathias also notes in passing that in times of labour scarcity, employers did not reduce wages, which again speaks against the existence of backward-bending labour supply schedules.[56]

Finally, it is easy to see that the magnitudes involved are too large to be accounted for by backward-bending labour supply curves. Killingsworth, in his overview of empirical work on labour supply in modern economies, noted that four out of the twenty studies he surveyed actually showed a positive income elasticity. The average value of the income elasticity in the sixteen studies that did find an inverse relationship between wage level and labour supply was -0.23.[57] Note that this elasticity is broadly similar to the one found by Hatcher, whose data on colliers from the 1680s suggest a coefficient of -0.38.[58] Given the wage trends identified by Feinstein, the average figure from the Killingsworth studies would imply an increase in hours supplied of plus 1.8 per cent between 1760 and 1800, and a reduction between 1760 and 1830 of 1 per cent. Clearly, these implied changes are insufficient to account for the ones we actually observe. Even if we use the highest value ever found in an econometric study of labour supply (-0.72) this suggests only an increase of 5.9 per cent between 1760 and 1800. This is still markedly less than the increase suggested by our preferred method ($+30$ per cent). Perhaps even more importantly, using such an elasticity implies that labour supply should have fallen between 1760 and 1831 by 3.3 per cent, when it was actually rising by at least 20 per cent.

These findings strongly suggest that backward-bending labour supply curves were not the main factor boosting labour input. This is in line with Adam Smith's assessment:

---

[55] Mathias, 'Leisure and Wages', 161. Note that the same contradictory complaints are recorded for the period after the Black Death. Cf. R. H. Britnell, *The Commercialization of English Society, 1000–1500* (Cambridge, 1993), 191.

[56] Note that this could also be explained as a collective action problem.

[57] Mark Killingsworth, *Labor Supply* (Cambridge, 1983), 125.

[58] Calculated on the basis of the data in Hatcher, 'Labour, Leisure and Economic Thought', 89.

Where wages are high, accordingly, we shall always find the workmen more active, diligent, and expeditious than where they are low ... Some workmen, indeed, when they can earn in four days what will maintain them through the week, will be idle the other three. This, however, is by no means the case with the greater part. Workmen, on the contrary, when they are liberally paid by the piece, are very apt to over-work themselves, and to ruin their health and constitution in a few years.[59]

Because backward-bending labour supply curves are unlikely in the aggregate, the basic logic used in Figures 4.2 and 4.3 should hold. This implies that the upward shift in hours was probably the result not of greater labour demand, but of greater supply.

The time-paths of hours and wages suggest that the main determinant of increased labour input must have been a change in labour supply. In this sense, our evidence contradicts the analysis by W. A. Lewis, who argued that 'an unlimited supply of labour [was] available at a subsistence wage.'[60] The question we therefore need to answer is why Englishmen were willing to supply more hours in 1800 and 1830 than they did in 1750. I will examine five competing hypotheses, ultimately favouring two. Before doing so, we should note the limits to this exercise—because we cannot match the observations on working behaviour with demographic and economic parameters at the individual level, the explanation presented will necessarily have to be more suggestive than definitive.

Declining Nutritional Constraints

When Freudenberger and Cummins first put forward their hypothesis, they not only argued that annual labour input grew dramatically during the second half of the eighteenth century. They also suggested that the gradual erosion of nutritional constraints was behind this development. Between the middle and the end of the eighteenth century, Freudenberger and Cummins calculate an increase of more than 30 per cent between 'pre-industrial' and 'industrial' times.[61] The authors find that possibly up to half of the English population in

[59] Adam Smith, *An Inquiry into the Nature and Causes of the Wealth of Nations* (London, 1991 [1776]), i, 72–3.
[60] W. Arthur Lewis, 'Economic Development with Unlimited Supplies of Labour', in A. Agarwally and S. Singh (eds.), *The Economics of Underdevelopment* (London, 1959), 448.
[61] Herman Freudenberger and Gaylord Cummins, 'Health, Work and Leisure before the Industrial Revolution', *Explorations in Economic History*, 13 (1976), 6.

Gregory King's day subsisted on inadequate diets[62]—an argument subsequently extended and refined by Fogel. (see pp. 161–71, above). As agricultural output increased, the nutritional constraint was gradually lifted, allowing people to supply more labour.[63] The continued existence of holy days until the eighteenth century is therefore a sign of cultural adaptation. Social habits had developed to accommodate the generally 'limited productive capacity of the working population';[64] after the middle of the eighteenth century, they withered as agricultural output per capita grew.

Freudenberger and Cummins' interpretation must be rejected for two reasons. First, as I argued above, it is hard to prove that a severe lack of energy curtailed the working year even for the most unfortunate groups of society. Fogel's more cautious conclusions, based on much improved calculations, require a degree of accuracy which historical food balance sheets do not attain. Furthermore, direct evidence from poorhouse diets is incompatible with the concept of large groups in society lacking calories for work.[65] Second, and more importantly, the timing of the rise in labour input argues against Freudenberger and Cummins's interpretation. The period from 1730 to 1760 was one of relative plenty, as they themselves concede.[66] Thereafter, real wages began to fall. Further, all evidence from production statistics suggests that rises in agricultural output did not match the enormous population increase after the middle of the century.[67] While demographic growth averaged 0.58 per cent p.a. between 1760 and 1780, agricultural output grew at 0.13 per cent p.a. Between 1780 and 1801, the population growth rate was 1.05 per cent p.a., whereas Crafts puts output growth in agriculture at 0.75 per cent p.a. (and Deane and Cole at a mere 0.65).[68] Between 1801 and 1831, when population is surging at the unprecedented rate of 1.4 per cent p.a., agricultural output is

[62] Freudenberger and Cummins, 'Health, Work and Leisure', 7 ff.
[63] Ibid., 9.   [64] Ibid., 5.
[65] Shammas, *Pre-Industrial Consumer*, table 5.8, pp. 142–3.
[66] Freudenberger and Cummins, 'Health, Work and Leisure', 9.
[67] This is the accepted view. See Brinley Thomas, 'Food Supply in the United Kingdom during the Industrial Revolution', in Joel Mokyr (ed.), *The Economics of the Industrial Revolution* (London, 1985), 142.
[68] Wrigley and Schofield, *Population History of England*, table A3.3, p. 534; Crafts, *British Economic Growth*, table 2.10, p. 42, Deane and Cole, *British Economic Growth*, table 17, pp. 65–6. Deane and Cole, whose figures refer to corn output, estimate output growth of 0.47 per cent p.a. for 1760–80—again less than what would have been required to check demographic pressure.

only growing at 1.18 per cent p.a.[69] At the very time when our data from court records shows increasing labour input in the economy, there is less food produced per head.[70]

The incompatibility is not as large as implied by the figure above. Because of the changing age composition of the population, the fall in agricultural production per capita is overstated. Wastage may have diminished, giving greater access to digestible calories. Further, as some have argued, urban life is associated with lower energy requirements.[71] At a time of rapid urbanization, this could have freed considerable resources. In practice, the likely effect of both factors is small. Before the new Feinstein earnings series was available, Clark, Huberman, and Lindert argued that food output grew too slowly given the demand elasticities and wage series that they used. Urbanization can, they argued, at best explain up to 4 per cent of their 'food puzzle'.[72] Also, the age distribution does not shift dramatically. While 12.61 per cent of the population are aged 0–4 in 1751, this increases to 14.32 per cent in 1801. The share of those with the highest demands for calories (aged 15–59) falls by a mere 3.5 per cent.[73] In the absence of precise information on spoilage and food adulteration, it seems best to conclude that there is no evidence for a large increase in nutrient availability per capita during the second half of the eighteenth century.[74] Therefore, the Freudenberger and Cummins interpretation of the lengthening working year does not stand up to close scrutiny. Our research confirms the timing and direction of changes in time-use that they argued for. Their explanation, however, of these trends cannot be accepted because there is neither conclusive evidence

[69] Crafts, *British Economic Growth*, 42. According to Deane and Cole, the figure is 1.64—marginally higher than population growth.

[70] Imports were unimportant for the period up to and including the early 1800s. See Wrigley, 'Urban Growth and Agricultural Change: England and the Continent in the Early Modern Period', in id. (ed.), *People, Cities, and Wealth*, 168. Crafts (*British Economic Growth*, 127) suggests that imports in 1800 were equivalent to one-sixth of total food supply; however, since he does not recalculate imports for earlier dates, it is impossible to reassess trends in food availability.

[71] Clark, Huberman, and Lindert, 'British Food Puzzle', 226.   [72] Ibid., 233.

[73] Wrigley and Schofield, *Population History of England*, table A3.1, p. 529. They point out (ibid., 449) that a rising proportion of young people in the population must have increased the demand for agricultural products relative to that for other goods.

[74] One potential argument remains—if the distribution of calories became much more equal between the middle and the end of the eighteenth century, possibly as a result of the Poor Law, then work capacity might have increased very significantly. We find no evidence, however, of the poorest of society being primarily responsible for the short hours observed during the 1750s.

of nutritional constraints before 1750, nor is there any indication of a markedly improved food supply during the subsequent period, when working hours increased.[75]

The Rising Dependency Ratio

The population boom during the second half of the eighteenth century led to a sharp shift in the age distribution of the population. Because it was predominantly induced by changes in fertility, the number of the very young increased disproportionately.[76] Wrigley and Schofield define the dependency ratio as the number under 15 and over 60 per 1,000 people aged 15–59.[77] This figure is highest in 1826, at the end of the accelerating population boom that began in the middle of the eighteenth century. The lowest dependency ratio in England between 1541 and 1871 was recorded in 1671—the result of low fertility during the preceding decades.[78]

Between 1756 and 1831, according to Wrigley and Schofield, the dependency ratio increased from 727 to 836, a rise of 14.9 per cent. We could now argue that the increasing number of mouths that every wage-earner had to feed offered an incentive to work longer hours. Such an argument becomes more convincing when we consider that the change in the dependency ratio is of the same order of magnitude as the increase in hours (+ 20 to 23 per cent). This is a variation on the argument about backward-bending labour supply curves—the worse conditions are, the more people are willing to work in order to preserve their accustomed standard of living. In addition, it could be argued that the accelerated expansion of the labour force called for

[75] The final factor to take into consideration is food imports. Wrigley ('Urban Growth and Agricultural Change', 171) argues that food imports as a whole probably did not have a major impact on aggregate food supply until 1801. Harley and Crafts ('Productivity Growth during the First Industrial Revolution: Inferences from the Pattern of British External Trade', *LSE Working Papers in Economic History*, 42 (1998), 47) show that imports of agricultural commodities from temperate climates increased by 1.2 per cent p.a. between 1770 and 1841, a time when population was rising at exactly the same rate. Food availability per capita was therefore not increasing via this channel either.

[76] Wrigley ('Growth of Population in Eighteenth-Century England') demonstrates that fertility dominated population trends after 1750. Recent work by the Cambridge Group has modified this assessment somewhat: Wrigley, Davies, Oeppen, and Schofield, *English Population History from Family Reconstitution*, 347–52.

[77] A more conventional procedure would have been to use 65 as the top cut-off point. Cf. Wrigley and Schofield, *Population History of England*, 443.

[78] This part contains almost no original research. I simply summarize the research by Wrigley and Schofield, and apply their discussion to the issue of labour input.

additional investment to equip young adults with tools, etc. Before we can address this issue empirically, we need to take one possible criticism into account—the potentially limited impact on consumption.

Wrigley and Schofield do not only calculate dependency ratios, but take their analysis one step further. The young and the old are not simply additional mouths to be fed. They require, for obvious reasons, less food, and their demands for clothing and housing will be lower as well. Further, not all of them will be unable to contribute to the production process. Using model age schedules of production and consumption from the Third World, Wrigley and Schofield gauge the total pressure exerted by the changing age distribution on levels of consumption.[79] Because two offsetting factors operate, the pressure on consumption is much less than what is initially suggested by the rise in the dependency ratio. The authors derive production and consumption levels as implied by the shifting age structure. The ratio of consumption to production levels is then a good indicator of the demographic pressure on living standards. This indicator rises from 948 to 980 between 1756 and 1801 (1826 = 1,000), an increase of 3.4 per cent. By 1831 it stands at 995, an overall increase of 4.95 per cent—or approximately one-third of the increase in the dependency ratio. Therefore, to stabilize household consumption per adult equivalent, the maximum increase in hours necessary was approximately 5 per cent, or one quarter of the total.

Yet pressure on consumption from the shifting composition of households is not the only factor we need to consider. A rising share of young people also alters investment needs and changes average household age. If savings behaviour is not constant over the life-cycle, these factors may also change the labour–leisure trade-off. The connection between savings rates and the dependence ratio has been explored in the development literature. Coale and Hoover first formulated the dependency hypothesis, arguing that a higher proportion of children depressed savings rates.[80] Life-cycle models in the Tobin

---

[79] Wrigley and Schofield, *Population History of England*, tables 10.5 and 10.6, pp. 445 ff. Sara Horrell, Jane Humphries, and Hans-Joachim Voth ('Stature and Relative Deprivation: Fatherless Children in Early Industrial Britain', *Continuity and Change*, 13 (1998)) use slightly different consumption schedules. The results are not materially affected if their adult equivalence values are used. Note also that the minor revisions of the age distribution as presented in Wrigley *et al.*, *English Population History from Family Reconstitution* do not affect our analysis.

[80] Ansley Coale and Edgar M. Hoover, *Population Growth and Economic Development in Low-Income Countries* (Princeton, NJ, 1958).

tradition imply the opposite, with accelerations of population growth leading to a savings rate.[81] Fry and Mason have recently reconciled the two approaches.[82] Empirical evidence from contemporary East Asia and the New World during the 19th century suggests that youth dependency rates had a strong effect on capital flows and savings rates.[83]

Britain's industrialization could not be aided by foreign capital inflows that might compensate for the dual impact of a rising youth dependency burden on savings and the need to equip new workers. In an economy without access to foreign capital, a sudden rise in the percentage of the population below working age would lead to a drop of saving and investment, according to the Coale–Hoover and Fry–Mason approach. In the open economy case, investment increases sharply, but savings fall regardless, leading to large-scale capital inflows.[84] In the case of Britain, investment and the dependency ratio

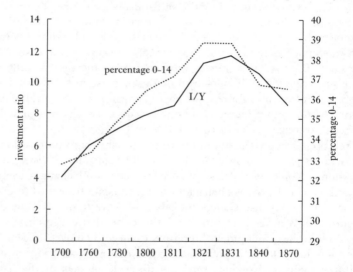

FIGURE 4.6. *Investment ratios and the share of people under 15 in the population, 1700–1870*

[81] James Tobin, 'Life-cycle Savings and Balanced Economic Growth', in William Fellner (ed.), *Ten Essays in the Tradition of Irving Fischer* (New York, 1967).

[82] Maxwell Fry and Andrew Mason, 'The Variable Rate-of-Growth Effect in the Life-Cycle Model', *Economic Inquiry*, 20 (1982).

[83] Alan Taylor and Jeffrey Williamson, 'Capital Flows to the New World as an Intergenerational Transfer', *Journal of Political Economy*, 102 (1994); Matthew Higgins and Jeffrey Williamson, 'Asian Demography and Foreign Capital Dependence', *NBER Working Paper* 5560 (1996).   [84] Higgins and Williamson, 'Asian Demography', 15.

increased in parallel (Figure 4.6).[85] Also, investment ratios were unusually low, given the continental experience.[86]

Before we interpret this as evidence in favour of the Tobin model, we should note that the assumption in both dependency and life-cycle models is that working time is supplied inelastically by those of prime age. Relaxing this assumption yields a richer set of possible responses. Since in the case of Britain, capital imports could not come to the rescue during early development, the (absolute) amounts financed can only rise by either curtailing consumption or increasing income through additional work. Instead of presenting a fully specified model, I examine the connection between the dependency ratio and working hours empirically, estimating a reduced-form equation.

I use Maddison's dataset on hours, population, and labour force in sixteen Western countries. For benchmark years (1870, 1890, 1913, 1929, 1938, 1950, 1960, 1973, and 1989), he gives estimates of annual hours, of the size of the population, as well as of the total labour force.[87] To proxy for changes in the youth dependency ratio, I use the ratio of the labour force to the size of the total population as a proxy. In addition, I add the rate of population growth. In this fashion, we can indirectly distinguish between two alternative reasons why the ratio of the labour force to population size might be falling. If associated with fast population growth, the youth dependency ratio will increase. Alternatively, in the context of slow or negative growth, the ratio will also rise. I estimate the equation

$$H_{t,j} = C_j + b_1 \frac{P_{j,t} - P_{j,t-1}}{P_{j,t-1}} + b_2 \frac{L_{j,t} - L_{j,t-1}}{L_{j,t-1}} + b_3 Z_{j,t} + \varepsilon \qquad (4.2)$$

where H is hours in country j at time t, P is population, L equals LB/P (where LB is the size of the labour force), and Z is a vector of control parameters (in this case, GDP per capita, and population size). The estimation method used is generalized least squares using cross-section weights. In line with other empirical work, I use a fixed-effect model which allows the intercept to vary by country, but constrains coefficients to be equal across countries.[88] Estimation yields estimates of b_1 and b_2 equal to $-2,416.1$ and $11,130.2$.[89] The negative coefficient on

[85] The correlation coefficient for the period 1700–1870 is 0.92.
[86] Crafts, *British Economic Growth*, 64.
[87] Maddison, *Dynamic Forces*.   [88] Higgins and Williamson, 'Asian Demography'.
[89] The t-statistics are – 2.93 and 2.1, significant at the 1 per cent and the 5 per cent levels, respectively.

participation rates suggests that longer hours are associated with a smaller labour force relative to the total population. Faster population growth also pushes up annual labour input. Use of population growth and the participation rate alone explains 60 per cent of the total variation.

How much of the change in hours can be explained if we assume that hours during Britain's industrial revolution responded to demographic pressures in the same way as they did in 16 industrializing countries between 1890 and 1989? We have to note that, if our argument about capital imports and hours being 'substitutes' is correct, the implied change is a lower bound on the effect we should have expected in the case of industrializing Britain. With our estimates of b_1 and b_2, the implied change in working hours p.a. is $+193$. This suggests that, on the basis of our panel estimation procedure, the dependency burden might be sufficient to explain 30 to 35 per cent of the total increase in hours observed between 1760 and 1831.[90] For every per cent of an increase in the dependency ratio, this suggests a rise of 0.47 to 0.48 per cent in the length of working year.

Overall, the evidence presented in this section suggests that approximately one-quarter of the increase in hours between 1760 and 1831 can be plausibly attributed directly to rising pressure of living standards originating from faster population growth. Cross-sectional evidence from a set of OECD countries suggests that at least one-third of the increase overall can be attributed to demographic factors. This already incorporates the consumption-stabilizing effect discussed before, so that the additional investment needs add approximately one-sixth to the total rise.

Morbidity

Annual labour input is not only influenced by 'normal' hours of work and the number of working days in the year. What also determines actual hours worked is the extent to which individuals are able to conform to this norm. One factor that can stand in the way of a regular pattern is morbidity. Recent research in medical history has documented the extent to which illness reduced the amount of work that could be carried out.[91] Records of Union Army recruits show that

---

[90] The total increase in hours is 550 to 654 hours, depending on the method used.

[91] James C. Riley, 'Working Health Time: A Comparison of Preindustrial, Industrial and Postindustrial Experience in Life and Health', *Explorations in Economic History*, 28 (1991), 188 ff.

even short periods of illness in young adulthood may have influenced mortality at later stages of the life-cycle.[92] Conversely, gains in life-expectancy may indicate a reduction in the incidence and severity of disease. Increases in labour input, as described above (pp. 118–26), could therefore also have been the result of fewer days being lost due to illness. If this alternative interpretation is correct, a healthier work-force would have worked for longer, thus boosting the percentage of witnesses observed in paid work.

Such an argument is a priori doubtful—as emerged from the comparisons above (pp. 118–26), the lengthening of the working year was largely the result of the disappearance of 'St Monday' and the reduced observance of old holy days. It is difficult to see why improvements in the disease environment (or the susceptibility of the population) should have been concentrated on these particular 'moments'. There is only one possible way of reconciling the alternative hypothesis described above with the evidence. If there had been a disproportionately large number of holy days in the winter months, and the level of morbidity during the colder half of the year had fallen, this could have increased the level of work-related activity observed in our sample. This is only a theoretical possibility—old feast days were fairly evenly distributed over the annual cycle: there were twenty-seven holy days in the six months from October to March, and nineteen during the summer months.[93] While there are slightly more feasts during the winter half of the year, the magnitude of the difference does not make it likely that this drove the shifts we observe. Also, the seasonality of burials diminished hardly at all during the eighteenth century in England as a whole—the index for the six winter months falls from 104.5 in 1700–49 to 104 in 1750–99.[94] Finally, the same explanation cannot be used in the case of Mondays.

A second argument against a direct link between morbidity and labour input comes from twenty-six parish reconstitution studies.[95] Unfortunately, we cannot observe morbidity levels for the eighteenth century directly. It might, however, be sensibly supposed that mor-

[92] Dora Costa, 'Height, Weight, Wartime Stress, and Older Age Mortality: Evidence from the Union Army Records', *Explorations in Economic History*, 20 (1993).

[93] Millan, *Coins, Weights and Measures*, 15.

[94] A value of 100 would indicate that exactly half of all burials occurred during the winter half-year. Wrigley and Schofield, *Population History of England*, table 8.3, p. 294.

[95] Data were kindly made available by the Cambridge Group for the History of Population and Social Structure.

bidity and mortality generally move in the same direction. The issue is complicated by the fact that morbidity is, in contrast to mortality, culturally defined. Greater interest in one's physical condition may well go hand in hand with increases in living standards. As more health-care facilities become available, recorded morbidity rates often increase.[96] Let us for the moment assume that mortality and morbidity are correlated. Between the middle and the end of the eighteenth century, life expectancy at birth increased from 42.1 years in 1750–9 to 44.8 in 1800–9.[97] A rise by 6 per cent has a similar order of magnitude as the change in labour input we observe. If, say, for every percentage point reduction in mortality, morbidity had fallen by 3 per cent, the rise in workloads could be explained. Disaggregation, however, shows that this is unlikely. Not all gains in life-expectancy can be expected to matter in the context of labour input—only reductions in the mortality rates of those aged 15 or above probably influenced patterns of work.[98] Figure 4.7 gives a breakdown of gains in life-expectancy between the two twenty-five-year periods by age group.[99] Infants profited most from changes in the mortality regime between the middle of the eighteenth and the early nineteenth centuries. Adults on average saw their mortality rates fall at a much slower rate, and those over 60 faced a deterioration.

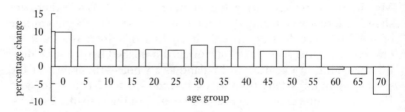

FIGURE 4.7. *Percentage change in life-expectancy, 1750/75–1800/25*

---

[96] There is some evidence that recorded morbidity rates are inversely related to mortality. See Partha Dasgupta, *An Inquiry into Well-Being and Destitution* (Oxford, 1993), 92; James C. Riley, 'Disease Without Death: New Sources for a History of Sickness', *Journal of Interdisciplinary History*, 17 (1987).

[97] Wrigley *et al.*, *English Population History from Family Reconstitution*, 295. The reconstitution data after 1810 cannot be used for deriving life expectancy at birth. The generalized inverse projection (ibid., 514) suggests an increase of 7.2 per cent between 1756 and 1831.

[98] This is true as long as we assume that illness during childhood did not have repercussions for the rest of people's lives.   [99] The data refer to both men and women.

Are the gains in life-expectancy plotted in Figure 4.7 sufficiently large to suggest that reductions in morbidity could have driven the rise in labour input? Let us assume that those aged 25 or above are normally members of the labour force. Life-expectancy at this age rose from 36.6 years in 1750–9 to 37.3 fifty years later. This 2 per cent increase would have to indicate a 20 to 23 per cent increase in the number of working days not affected by disease. For this alternative explanation to have any credibility, we would therefore have to assume a very large elasticity—for every percentage point of change in mortality, morbidity would have to fall by 10 per cent. The available statistical evidence on the long-term relationship between mortality and morbidity suggests that the reverse is true—for every percentage point gain in life expectancy, the number of years spent in health (and therefore, in a physical condition to be fit for work) increases by less than 1 per cent.[100]

Cultural Change

The period from the middle of the eighteenth to the middle of the nineteenth century not only saw rapid structural change, but a major shift in social norms and cultural values as well. Urbanization spread rapidly, with the share of Englishmen living in towns with more than 10,000 inhabitants rising from 16 per cent in 1750 to 33 per cent in 1831.[101] The greater anonymity of towns was not the only way in which the social lives of Englishmen changed. Marriage age fell rapidly as more and more men and women felt able to set up on their own earlier in life. Mean age at first marriage fell from 26.1 years for men and 25 years for women in 1750–9 to 24.9 for men and 23.1 for women. At the same time, England went from having very low rates of illegitimacy (1.35 per cent during the middle of the eighteenth century) to relatively high figures.[102] Between 1750–74 and 1825–37, the illegitimacy ratio rose from 4.64 per cent to 5.27 per cent, having peaked at 6.18 in 1800–24.[103] Could this broad process of social change have been related to the change in working hours?

[100] Indeed, Riley ('Working Health Time') found that gains in life expectancy only resulted in a small increase in the length of the healthy working life.
[101] The data on urbanization are from DeVries, *European Urbanization*, table 3.8, p. 44. The value for 1831 was derived by linear interpolation.
[102] Wrigley *et al.*, *English Population History from Family Reconstitution*.
[103] Ibid., 219.

To link the declining observance of religious and political festivals with the rise of a more secular, 'individualistic', materialistic, and—in the eyes of some—more irresponsible culture appears tempting at first sight. As the power of traditional authority faded, more and more people engaged in work on holy days. Such an argument would however suffer from logical inconsistency. Observance of 'St Monday' was also declining, and was an important factor in the rise of labour input (especially in London). A declining regard for tradition and authority is hard to square with a rapid decline of revelry and slothfulness on Mondays. Since the practice of 'St Monday' had been a source of much complaint by the authorities for centuries, it is difficult to see how increasing 'compliance' with this particular social norm can be interpreted in the same framework as growing disregard for traditional political and religious festivals.

The Sirens of Consumption

According to an anonymous schoolboy cited by T. S. Ashton, 'a wave of gadgets' swept over England at the very time when we observe a marked increase in working hours.[104] Here I argue that there was a causal connection between both phenomena. I shall first examine the extent to which consumption patterns in eighteenth- and early nineteenth-century England changed. Next, the theoretical reasons why one might expect a relationship between the world of goods and labour input are discussed.

The standard-of-living debate saw an extended discussion about the opportunities for workers to enjoy leisure. While the pessimists emphasized that towns offered fewer entertainment opportunities than the countryside,[105] optimists argued the opposite and pointed to rising literacy.[106] Since then, social historians have added a new perspective. According to its proponents, a consumer revolution occurred in England during the eighteenth century. It consisted of four interrelated developments that occurred at the same time:

---

[104] Ashton, *Industrial Revolution, 1760–1830*.

[105] Crafts, *British Economic Growth*, 114; John L. Hammond, 'The Industrial Revolution and Discontent', *Economic History Review*, 2 (1930).

[106] Max Hartwell, 'The Rising Standard of Living in England, 1800–1850', *Economic History Review*, 13 (1961).

1. consumer spending reached an unprecedented level during the eighteenth century—'men, and in particular women, bought as never before'.[107]
2. for the first time, all classes participated in this development in approximately equal measure.
3. rapid changes in fashion only became a general feature of the economy during this period.
4. a 'leisure revolution' provided a multitude of new entertainments— leisure time could be enjoyed more.[108]

The discontinuity occurring during the eighteenth century was emphasized by McKendrick, Brewer, and Plumb, and has subsequently been elaborated by Campbell.[109]

Consumer Spending

Foreign visitors to England marvelled at the frenzy with which its inhabitants seemed to spend their money,[110] and Englishmen from Packwood to Wedgwood shaped and profited from the phenomenon.[111] As early as the 1750s Henry Fielding could write of a 'torrent of luxury which of late years hath poured itself into this nation ...'.[112] Spending on an altogether novel scale, according to McKendrick, was one of the main features of the eighteenth century's consumer revolution. The inclination to buy and enjoy new goods was not new; rather, the means for doing so only then became available. From the perspective of scholars of consumption, there was a 'convulsion of getting and spending, ... an eruption of new prosperity, and such an explosion of new production and marketing techniques, that a greater proportion of the population than in any previous society in human history was able to enjoy the pleasures of buying consumer goods.'[113] Actual spending patterns are emphasized by McKendrick; Campbell argues that the eighteenth century marked the transition from 'traditional' to 'modern' hedonism, with the former aimed at satisfying

---

[107] Neil McKendrick, John Brewer, and J. Plumb, *The Birth of Consumer Society. The Commercialization of Eighteenth-Century England* (London, 1982), 9.

[108] Lawrence Stone, 'Leisure in Eighteenth Century England', paper presented to the Datini Conference Il Tempo Libero, Prato, 18–25 April 1994.

[109] McKendrick, Brewer, and Plumb, *Consumer Society*; Colin Campbell, *The Romantic Ethic and the Spirit of Modern Consumerism* (Oxford, 1987).

[110] McKendrick, Brewer and Plumb, *Consumer Society*, 10.   [111] Ibid., 100 ff., 146–7.

[112] Henry Fielding, *Enquiry into the Causes of the Late Increase in Robbers* (London, 1751), 6.

[113] McKendrick, Brewer, and Plumb, *Consumer Society*, 9.

needs through consumption while the latter emphasizes a pleasurable imbalance between wants and purchases.[114]

Subsequent research has cast doubt on the novelty of these developments as well as the accuracy of the description.[115] Whether or not the birth of a consumer society is best located in eighteenth-century England is a question of definition.[116] Contemporary observations about new and more extravagant spending patterns are largely concerned with the middle of the eighteenth century, when wages were relatively high. The Napoleonic era of high food prices was clearly less a time for unusually high spending on non-essential items. Real wages in many areas were lower at the turn of the century than they had been half a century earlier.[117] Descriptions of a bout of consumer spending during the early stages of the Industrial Revolution are also in stark contrast to the macroeconomic trends inferred from the national accounts. Crafts estimates that, between 1700 and 1831, per capita consumption grew by only 0.39 per cent per annum. This already represents a marked acceleration from the pace during the period 1760–1800, when per capita consumption grew by 0.25 per cent per annum.[118]

Access to Consumer Goods by all Classes

The proponents of the concept of a 'consumer revolution' see the width and depth of change in consumer behaviour as one of its defining characteristics.[119] As a German visitor to England observed in the 1790s: 'All classes enjoy the accumulation of riches, luxury and pleasure.'[120] Contemporary comment is replete with the social repercus-

[114] Campbell, *Romantic Ethic*; J.-C. Agnew, 'Consumer Culture in Historical Perspective', in R. Porter and Brewer (eds.), *Consumption and the World of Goods* (London, 1993), 24–5.
[115] Porter and Brewer, *Consumption and the World of Goods*, 2. Agnew ('Consumer Culture', 27) argues that the 1920s and 1930s are the most convincing dates for the beginning of mass consumerism.   [116] See Agnew, 'Consumer Culture'.
[117] Hatcher, 'Labour, Leisure and Economic Thought', 99. The new Feinstein series, spliced onto the Lindert–Williamson index, also shows a (modest) decline between 1760 and 1801.
[118] Per capita consumption, recalculated from the consumption ratios in Crafts, *British Economic Growth*, and the growth rates in N. F. R. Crafts and Knick Harley, 'Output Growth and the British Industrial Revolution: A Restatement of the Crafts–Harley View', *Economic History Review*, 45 (1992). It should be remembered that such a long-term average is influenced by the exceptionally high prices in 1801. Some periods, such as the 1770s, showed a higher level of per capita spending than 1801. Crafts, *British Economic Growth*, table 5.2, p. 95.   [119] Neil McKendrick, 'Home Demand and Economic Growth', 170 ff.
[120] Archenholz 1791, cit. McKendrick, Brewer, and Plumb, *Consumer Society*, 10.

sions of these developments. The most prominent of these was a heightened desire of the lower classes to emulate their betters.[121] Lamentations abound: 'the nobleman will emulate the grandeur of a Prince, and the gentleman will aspire to the proper state of the nobleman; the tradesman steps from behind the counter into the vacant place of the gentleman, nor doth the confusion end here: it reaches the very dregs of the people ...'[122] Henry Fielding's gloomy assessment serves as an explanation of the 'late increase of robbers' (the title of his pamphlet from 1750), and we partly owe the large number of court records analysed above to such conditions. Not only did the lure of luxury prove increasingly irresistible, the germs of temptation were also spread through more potent channels. Domestic servants were vital in this process of transmitting the attractions of fashion from the higher and middle classes to the rest of the social pyramid. While some of this was undoubtedly nothing more than a continuation of earlier developments,[123] there can be little doubt that this process accelerated markedly during the eighteenth century.[124]

Servants were not the only economically disadvantaged group that began to share in the pleasures of a consumer society. Evidence from probate inventories suggests that a wide range of groups at the lower end of the social scale participated. King has recently compared pauper inventories with probate inventories.[125] Whereas the former were largely drawn up after 1730, the majority of the latter refers to the years before 1710. The probate inventories primarily contain information on the property of husbandmen and labourers. Pauper inventories were produced by parishes when elderly residents became chargeable.[126] In return for regular payments, the parish would

---

[121] The issue is contentious—Colin Campbell ('Understanding Traditional and Modern Patterns of Consumption in Eighteenth-Century England: A Character-action Approach', in Porter and Brewer, *Consumption and the World of Goods*, 40) argues that simple trickle-down of consumption is not necessarily a sign of deliberate emulation.

[122] Fielding, *Enquiry*, 6.

[123] Cf. Peter Earle, *The Making of the English Middle Class: Business, Society and Family Life in London, 1660–1730* (Berkeley, Calif., 1989), 281; Lorna Weatherill, *Consumer Behaviour and Material Culture, 1660–1760* (London, 1988).

[124] J. Jean Hecht, *The Domestic Servant Class in England* (London, 1956); McKendrick, Brewer, and Plumb, *Consumer Society*, 21.

[125] Peter King, 'Pauper Inventories and the Material Lives of the Poor in the Eighteenth and Early Nineteenth Centuries', in T. Hitchcock, P. King, and P. Sharpe, *Chronicling Poverty: The Voices and Strategies of the English Poor* (Basingstoke, 1997).

[126] Ibid., tables 1 and 2.

'inherit' their material possessions. King uses a number of indicators such as the existence of fires in bedrooms and the amount of linen in the inventory to show that pauper inventories refer to a substantially poorer part of the population:

> The eighteenth century pauper inventories may well cover a subgroup of working people that was positioned lower on the social scale than the subgroups whose goods were listed in the probate inventories of husbandmen and labourers ... This makes it all the more interesting that by the mid to late eighteenth century even that relatively low subgroup of the labouring poor owned a much greater variety of household goods and of decorative or semi-luxury items than that seen in the slightly more affluent subgroup of husbandmen and labourers ... A fifth to a quarter of pauper inventories include these items [looking glasses, clocks and watches]. The ownership of earthenware increased threefold. Candlesticks were now owned by half of the households ... , instead of 6 per cent.[127]

Unfortunately, greater equality of spending patterns is hard to substantiate, according to recent work on earnings.[128] Perhaps more importantly, recent work on household budgets demonstrates that only a small share of the new industries' output was actually consumed by the working classes. Horrell calculates that between 1801 and 1841, working class real expenditure on nonessential items grew by 1.1 per cent, whereas average expenditure by all classes grew by 6.1 per annum.[129] Working-class demand was not the main factor driving industrialization.

Fashion

Fashion, of course, was not invented during the eighteenth century.[130] According to McKendrick and others, this period distinguished itself by the speed with which fashions came and went, the extent to which they affected the masses, and, as noted above, the ability to purchase the latest designs. This was partly a self-reinforcing mechanism—new manufacturing processes made the purchase of more varied clothes possible. This led to an even greater taste for fashion; increased fashion consciousness in turn spurred the development of a fashion

---

[127] King, 'Pauper Inventories', sect. V.   [128] Feinstein, 'Pessimism Perpetuated'.

[129] Sara Horrell ('Home Demand and British Industrialization', *Journal of Economic History*, 56 (1996)) notes that the national accounts for 1801 appear inconsistent, and that after suitable correction, aggregate spending may have been rising at a mere 1.5 per cent p.a.—still faster than working-class consumption.

[130] See the enlightening essay by Eric Jones (*Agriculture and the Industrial Revolution* (Oxford, 1974)).

industry.[131] Cotton goods became 'fashion's favourite', in Beverly Lemire's words.[132] Goods that were once expected to last a lifetime (or longer) could now be purchased with such frequency as to become the object of fashion:

What men and women had once hoped to inherit from their parents, they now expected to buy for themselves. ... What were once available only on high days and holidays through the agency of markets, fairs and itinerant peddlers were increasingly made available every day but Sunday through the additional agency of an ever-advancing network of shops and shopkeepers.[133]

Even for those who had to buy their clothes second-hand, there was an enormous variety of manufactured trimmings. Because of the large running stitches and simple cutting of eighteenth-century clothes, alterations could be carried out at home.[134] Fashionable dress did not presuppose the ability to buy new clothes at a high frequency. The diffusion of fashion was partly due to the disseminating influence of the servant class. What added a new quality to the eighteenth century was the importance of publications such as *The Lady's Magazine*.[135] This journal produced its first fashion print in the 1770s; over the following thirty years no fewer than fourteen women's magazines appeared featuring information on the latest fashions.[136]

Leisure Activities

Lawrence Stone has recently argued that the consumer revolution coincided with dramatic changes in leisure activities.[137] Stone describes in great detail the late eighteenth-century boom in spas and playhouses.[138] From newspapers to pleasure gardens, a significant proportion of the economy was employed to serve the leisure of the

[131] See the argument by Toshiho Kusamitsu, 'Novelty, give us novelty': London Agents and Northern Manufacturers', in Maxine Berg (ed.), *Markets and Manufacture in Early Modern Europe* (London, 1991), 117. There were also increased dangers for manufacturers who failed to adopt to the change in attitudes. Cf. ibid., 134–5.

[132] Beverly Lemire, *Fashion's Favourite: The Cotton Trade and the Consumer in Britain, 1660–1800* (Oxford, 1991).

[133] McKendrick, Brewer, and Plumb, *Consumer Society*, 1.

[134] Ben Fine and Ellen Leopold, *The World of Consumption* (London, 1993), 131.

[135] *The Lady's Magazine, or Entertaining Companion for the Fair Sex, Appropriated Solely to their Use and Amusement* was published from 1770 until 1832. See James Laver, *The Concise History of Costume and Fashion* (New York, 1978).

[136] McKendrick, Brewer, and Plumb, *Consumer Society*, 47.

[137] Stone, 'Leisure in Eighteenth Century England', 5.   [138] Ibid., 4 ff.

English. Plumb has described how, during the eighteenth century, books and plays began to find an audience even among lower-paid workers.[139] After the first of its kind was set up in Bath in 1725, subscription libraries spread to all of England.[140] This evidence is partly at variance with the low levels of literacy found by Schofield (as well as the slow rate of increase);[141] one may argue, however, that the diffusion of reading material served to make leisure time more productive for those who could read already. Plumb also argues that the commercialization of gambling and betting[142] occurred at the same time as the diffusion of sport:[143] 'In the early eighteenth century, culture and sport slowly ceased to be élitist and private and became increasingly public.' This led to even wider proliferation: the more publicly visible these activities were, the more frequent social emulation became.

Also, according to Stone, the now larger and wealthier middle class was clearly committed to an aristocratic ideal of noble leisure. The popularity of country outings and watering places led to diminishing differentiation between the landed elite and the middling sorts—both were equally attracted by these supposedly rejuvenating institutions.[144] On average, according, to Stone, leisure time increased,[145] and it could be spent in a more luxurious way. The taste for luxury, according to Stone, had far-reaching consequences:

> This resulted in what can only be called a revolution in the demand for consumer goods and services, on a scale never seen before in world history. These middling sorts could now afford the luxury of leisure and thus begin to merge with the landed elite as major consumers of the products of a growing leisure industry and to contribute by their numbers to its expansion.[146]

According to Stone, demand for the products of the leisure industry led to an increase in urbanization, which in turn stimulated the economy.[147] He asserts that the growth of a popular consumer culture during the Industrial Revolution was no coincidence, but closely related

---

[139] John Plumb, 'The Commercialization of Leisure', in McKendrick, Brewer, and Plumb, *Consumer Society*, 267–76. Lancashire acquired fourteen theatres during the eighteenth century: ibid., 277.

[140] Stone, *Family, Sex and Marriage*, 229.

[141] Roger S. Schofield, 'Dimensions of Illiteracy, 1750–1850', *Explorations in Economic History*, 10 (1973), 447–8.   [142] Plumb, 'The Commercialization of Leisure', 281–2.

[143] Ibid., 284.   [144] Stone, 'Leisure in Eighteenth Century England', 6.

[145] Ibid., 2.   [146] Ibid.

[147] Ibid. This is a variation on a theme that has been prominent in the literature for some time.

to strictly economic developments. In his view, it is the economic growth of the second half of the eighteenth century that is behind changing patterns of recreation. Stone believes that economic growth outstripped the rate of population increase, leading to markedly higher per capita incomes.[148] These higher incomes, according to him, were behind the rise of the middle classes. Shopkeepers, traders, small masters, and the professions did not only grow in number. There was also an increase the wealth each member of the middle classes owned. It is precisely the demand for leisure generated by this group that is central to Stone's interpretation of the Industrial Revolution. The result of this interrelated set of changes, as Stone sees them, was 'to change the face of England, in its values, its social structure and its physical appearance.'[149]

Stone's wider argument suffers from a number of shortcomings. Per capita income did not grow in the way described by him, and the empirical evidence presented in this paper gives no indication of an increase in leisure time between the middle and the end of the eighteenth century. Yet Stone is correct in pointing to the growing number of leisurely pursuits that Englishmen could engage in. Much of the literature on the 'consumer revolution' has focused on consumer durables, on the clothes, pottery, and furniture that the historian encounters in probate inventories. The value of Stone's contribution lies in his emphasis on other, more fleeting forms of consumer spending—the purchase of services. Instead of buying an intermediate good, which yields benefits over a number of years, the bought 'object' is consumed immediately. If a desire for instant gratification was central to the 'consumer revolution', precisely this type of spending should have seen the largest increases. Stone also contributes to the 'standard-of-living-debate'. The large number of new leisure pursuits that became possible in urban environments counterbalances the argument that leisure time in the countryside was inherently richer.

Synthesis

Parts of the case presented by social historians arguing for a consumer revolution appear to be at variance with economic evidence. Is it possible to reconcile these two views?[150] We need not be concerned with

---

[148] Ibid., 1.   [149] Ibid., 2.

[150] For a perceptive overview of the relationship between the economic and the social history approach to the issue of consumption see DeVries, 'Industrial Revolution'.

many of the wider issues raised. What matters in terms of our principal task—explaining the rise in working hours—are three factors on which there is substantial agreement. First, expenditure patterns across all social groups reveal a strong preference for consumer goods. Second, realizing the desire for consumer goods became easier as relative prices changed. Third, diversity increased as markets integrated and manufacturing and distribution processes began to satisfy a taste for variety.

Expenditure on the new consumer goods was rising fast in all strata of society, and it is this particular part of consumer expenditure that McKendrick and other proponents of a 'consumer revolution' have emphasized.[151] Even amongst the working-class households analysed by Horrell and Humphries during the period of high prices in 1787–96, 10.6 per cent of expenditure went on non-essential items, with the largest share spent on clothing.[152] The apparent contradiction between estimates of aggregate consumption and the spending patterns found by social historians can be resolved because only a small percentage of total consumer spending was devoted to durable goods. If, say, 95 per cent of all expenditure was devoted to food, shelter, and services in 1700, then a 6 per cent rise in consumer spending could have allowed a disproportionate increase in consumer good purchases. If income spent on non-durables remained constant, expenditure on consumer goods could have risen by 120 per cent.[153] Horrell records precisely such a mechanism during the period 1789–96/1830–9.[154] She finds an increase of total household spending by 43 per cent over the period, and a rise in spending on non-essential items of 137 per cent. Spending on essential items did also rise, but by a mere 30 per cent.

This increase in spending on consumer goods such as clothing was not only driven by higher incomes (during the first thirty years of the nineteenth century). The rapid decline in the price of durables—espe-

[151] According to standard national accounting definitions, cotton goods etc. are not 'durables', and are counted as if consumed at the time of purchase. This may be a useful convention to follow, but it clearly departs from actual usage. This is important here—most of the fashion items such as pieces of clothing and ceramics were not consumed immediately after the purchase date, but could be expected to last for a longer period.

[152] Horrell, 'Home Demand and British Industrialization'.

[153] Assume that, of 106 units of income in 1801, 95 are devoted to non-durables. Then there will be 11 units of income left for spending on goods. In 1700 only 5 units would have been available for this purpose.

[154] Horrell, 'Home Demand and British Industrialization', table 5.

cially cotton goods—would have induced some change in consumption patterns independent of a change in income.[155] Horrell finds an own-price elasticity of −7.8 for residual spending, using cotton prices.[156] Therefore, for every percentage point reduction in prices, there would be an increase by 7.8 per cent in spending on clothing (and similar goods).[157] This raises an interesting possibility concerning the probate inventory evidence. There may have been more purchases of some consumer durables simply because they became relatively cheaper compared to other items. Any inference about working time may be unsubstantiated—the substitution effect may not have been accompanied by any increase in material abundance. Since historians normally record only some categories of goods contained in inventories, it is possible that a rise in the number of recorded items simply reflects the fact that they more readily fitted into the researcher's classification scheme.[158] DeVries believes that such a shift into certain commodities may partly explain why probate inventories record more and more material possessions without the total attaining a higher value. The size of the effect, however, is probably not large enough to account for the increasing number and variety of some goods found in inventories during the early modern period.[159] For the moment, the exact reasons for the increase in consumer spending on durables need not concern us unduly. What matters is that both probate inventories and contemporary accounts bear witness to a marked increase in the number and variety of material possessions.

Another crucial element of the 'consumer revolution' is the flood of new commodities that descended on the English during the eighteenth century.[160] From the late seventeenth century onwards, there

[155] Komlos (*Nutrition*) discusses how a change in relative prices might have led to a reduction in food intake and a subsequent decline in heights.
[156] Since residual spending is dominated by expenditure on clothing, this is a useful approximation. See Horrell, 'Home Demand and British Industrialization'.
[157] Crafts, *British Economic Growth*, 22 ff; Crafts and Harley, 'Cotton Textiles and Industrial Output Growth'. Cf. J. Cuenca Esteban ('British Textile Prices, 1770–1831: Are British Growth Rates Worth Revising Once More?', *Economic History Review*, 47 (1994); id., 'Further Evidence of Falling Prices of Cotton Cloth, 1768–1816', ibid., 48 (1995)). Even the more pessimistic side in this debate believes in a rapid fall in (real) textile prices.
[158] DeVries, 'Purchasing Power', 107.   [159] Ibid., 106–7.
[160] A consistent model of industrialization, based on goods innovation and a utility function with a taste for variety, can be constructed. See Giovanni Facchini and Hans-Joachim Voth, 'New Goods, More Work: Industrialization and Labour Input in the Long Run', mimeo, Stanford University, 1999.

was growing interest in the more fashionable items of clothing such as calicoes and other cottons wrought in the East Indies.[161] Clothing is the most famous example for the application of new manufacturing technology, leading to price reductions that made fashionable textiles affordable even for the lower classes. For other products, innovations in distribution and a new labour regime were more important. Josiah Wedgwood's successful attempt to impose greater discipline in Burslem,[162] and his new methods of advertising his wares,[163] made pottery a mass product.[164] Nothing attests more eloquently to the increase in diversity than the growing number of different items found in pauper inventories. In King's dataset, it is not just the percentage of households owning certain items such as chairs that is increasing. There is also an increase in the number of categories for which there are recordings from 12 to 19—despite the move in sample composition from normal probates to pauper inventories.[165]

In combination, these three factors markedly changed the range of choices faced by individuals. In 1766 Elizabeth Montagu had been able to remark of the pitmen labouring at Tyneside: 'they know no use of money but to buy much meat and liquor with it.'[166] The world described by McKendrick, Brewer, Plumb, and other social historians differs strongly from that of Hogarth's prints from mid-century, when 'good' or 'bad' consumption were defined by consuming either gin or beer. Even if the concept of a 'consumer revolution' has been subject to debate,[167] there is little doubt that this period saw an unprecedented rise of 'material abundance ... aligned with a general, emulative acquisitiveness by means of commercialized sales promotion and marketing techniques.'[168] The impression of 'material abun-

---

[161] Lemire, *Fashion's Favourite*, 3 ff.

[162] Neil McKendrick, 'Josiah Wedgwood and Factory Discipline', *Historical Journal*, 4 (1961), 30 ff.   [163] McKendrick, Brewer, and Plumb, *Consumer Society*, 124–6.

[164] As McKendrick has noted, Wedgwood often enhanced his brand name by charging more than marginal cost, thus exploiting a 'Veblen effect' (for some goods, demand increases with price because the real commodity on offer is social exclusivity). In most cases, however, innovations in advertising and distribution widened the market. One could even go so far as to see both strategies as complementary—using Veblen pricing was necessary because the ability to buy pottery itself no longer distinguished one from those on the lower rungs of the social ladder.

[165] It is of course possible that accounting procedures simply became more accurate.

[166] Cited in Hatcher ('Labour, Leisure and Economic Thought', 90).

[167] John Styles, 'Manufacturing, Consumption and Design in Eighteenth-Century England', in Porter and Brewer, *Consumption and the World of Goods*, 535.

[168] Ibid.

dance' need not be synonymous with growing per capita incomes[169] nor with stocks of more valuable possessions.[170] As DeVries has stressed, the effects of fashion, together with shorter depreciation periods, may have caused the value of possession to stay static even if there was a rising tide of new goods making its way into the homes of ordinary English people. Even if per capita incomes had been stagnant or slightly falling, the advent of rapidly changing fashions stimulated the senses, enhanced choice and novelty, and provided variety where uniformity had once ruled. This effect was compounded by the arrival of various new goods, such as affordable cotton clothing and pottery. While the number of hours spent in leisure probably did not rise, there were, by the end of the eighteenth century, numerous new ways to spend it in a more varied and stimulating way.

How can these developments help us explain the trend in working hours between 1750 and 1850? Traditionally, the fall in the total number of hours worked during the past 150 years has been explained through changes in the leisure–income trade-off. In the standard microeconomic model, households act as utility-maximizers, trying to attain the most satisfactory combination of income and leisure under the given constraint. Consider Figure 4.8. The budget constraint RQ

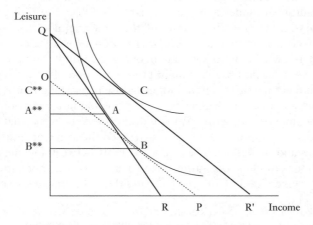

FIGURE 4.8. *Time allocation in traditional household economics*

[169] The latest calculations suggest that per capita income rose from $400 to $430 (US 1970) between 1760 and 1800. Knick Harley, 'Reassessing the Industrial Revolution: A Macro View', in Mokyr (ed.), *British Industrial Revolution*, table 3.4, p. 194.

[170] DeVries, 'Purchasing Power', table 5.1, p. 103.

mirrors the fact that (theoretically) each individual can: 1. either consume only leisure (Q), 2. spend all its time in work (R), or 3. choose a mix of leisure and labour between points R and Q. The convex shape of the indifference curves reflects the fact that, for most people, the extreme solutions (R and Q) are not very appealing—if we devote all our time to work, there would be no opportunity to spend the money earned, whereas in the opposite case, there would be nothing to consume.

With convex indifference curves, households will choose the tangent of the budget constraint and the highest possible indifference curve as their welfare-maximizing allocation of time.[171] If the wage rate now rises, rotating the budget constraint RQ through Q to R'Q, labour supply will decline by (C**-A**). If we draw a parallel (PO) to the second budget constraint R'Q so as to give a tangent on the original indifference curve, we are able to decompose the shift from A to C into a substitution and an income effect. The move from A to B is caused exclusively by the substitution effect, since the household's utility is held constant. The change from B to C is the result of the income effect alone. As our figure demonstrates, normally shaped indifference curves lead us to expect that the income effect will outweigh the substitution effect—working hours will fall.[172]

The traditional model is not particularly useful in explaining the rise in working hours. Falling prices of the 'new commodities' were, in London at least, more than offset by rises in the cost of food;[173] for the nation as a whole, there was a fall between the middle and the end of the eighteenth century, and a modest rise in the period until 1831.[174] The fall in real wages could have induced a rise of working hours, but we have already rejected this factor as the principal interpretation for the reasons mentioned above. We could alternatively argue that the growing attraction of consumer goods changed the shape of indifference curves and thus the nature of the trade-off between income and leisure. If consuming goods rather than leisure becomes more attractive for any given level of income (rotating the indifference curves in

---

[171] See Robert Pindyck and Daniel Rubinfeld, *Microeconomics* (New York, 1989), 502.

[172] The conclusion depends, of course, on the exact shape of indifference curves.

[173] L. D. Schwarz, 'The Standard of Living in the Long Run: London, 1700–1860', *Economic History Review*, 38 (1985). 28. Note that, if the Lindert and Williamson series is used for deflating Schwarz's wage series, 1830 wages appear to be on par with those from the 1750s. Given that the Lindert and Williamson series appears too optimistic (Feinstein, 'Pessimism Perpetuated'), this suggests that London real wages had not fully recovered by the 1830s.   [174] Feinstein, 'Pessimism Perpetuated'.

Figure 4.8 to the right), working hours may rise. Yet explanations that have to assume shifting indifference curves lack theoretical elegance and clear implications—alternative indifference curves in Figure 4.8 would lead to radically different predictions.[175] There is also no direct evidence to support such an interpretation. A more convincing explanation is offered by Becker's model of time allocation (which also encompasses the traditional model as an extreme case).

Becker focuses on the household as a provider of material and immaterial goods.[176] In order to produce 'consumption events',[177] the household combines inputs of goods, services, and time. In this way, time becomes a 'raw material' which is equally vital to the satisfaction of needs as tangible inputs. Note that both consumption and production time now have characteristic productivities. While capital equipment (and human capital) combine with workers' time inputs in the production process, giving rise to a certain output per hour, consumer durables, human capital and leisure time constitute inputs in the consumption process. It is sensible to assume that the productivity of consumption per unit of time increases with the stock of leisure goods, just as output per worker rises with the capital–labour ratio.[178] *Homo oeconomicus* then allocates time, just as any other scarce commodity, to competing activities under the assumption of utility maximization.[179] By taking into account the 'time cost' of activities, some of the findings of traditional microeconomics appear in a different light.

Consider the case of a two-commodity world for some of the implication (Figure 4.9).[180] A household consumes two commodities, Z_1 and Z_2. Let us also assume that Z_1 is the more time-intensive commodity, whereas Z_2 causes higher monetary costs of consumption. The budget constraint now takes the form of S, reflecting the fact that consumption has both a pecuniary- and a time-cost. In the initial situation, the optimum is equal to the tangent P of the full-income opportunity curve S and the indifference curve U(1). Let us now assume that hourly earnings increase, and that this rise is

[175] On the general methodological principle see George Stigler and Gary S. Becker, 'De Gustibus Non Est Disputandum', *American Economic Review*, 67 (1977).

[176] Gary S. Becker, 'A Theory of the Allocation of Time,' *Economic Journal*, 75 (1965); id., *The Economic Approach to Human Behaviour* (Chicago, 1976).

[177] The befitting term is from Alfred Gell, *The Anthropology of Time* (Oxford, 1992), 206.

[178] Juster and Stafford, *Time, Goods, and Well-Being*, 2–3.

[179] Becker, 'Theory', 495.   [180] Ibid., 500.

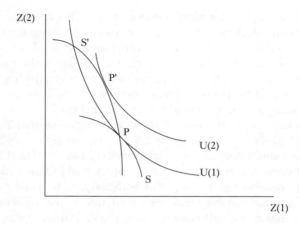

FIGURE 4.9. *Time allocation in the Becker model*

compensated fully by a fall in other income. The old full–income opportunity curve would be rotated clockwise through P so as to give the new full–income opportunity curve S' and the new tangent P'. If the increase in earnings were fully compensated by a decline in other earnings, a household would reduce the consumption of the more earnings–intensive good. This is exactly the same effect as the move from A to B in Figure 4.8.[181] In the uncompensated case, just as in the traditional model, the actual change depends on the magnitudes of the income and substitution effects.

A rise in the productivity of consumption time would have exactly the opposite effects. Rising 'satisfaction' per unit of time spent consuming would raise full income, just as in the case of higher productivity of production, but the direction of the income and substitution effects would be different. The income effect alone suggests longer hours—greater income would raise total demand for goods. Substitution would be induced towards earnings–intensive goods, as

---

[181] The similarity of Becker's and the more traditional approach in this regard has often been overlooked: Gell (*Anthropology*, 208), for example, simply ignores the fact that older interpretations do consider substitution effects, and that Becker postulates exactly the same outcome (in the uncompensated case) as his predecessors: 'Thus, where the conventional labour/leisure indifference curve ... predicts that rising real wages will result in the substitution of labour by leisure, since equivalent levels of psychic satisfaction can now be achieved by working for fewer hours, the Becker model makes the opposite prediction, namely, that rises in real wages will intensify the worker's desire to extend working time at the expense of leisure.'

their relative price falls, reducing hours worked.[182] Actual changes again depend on the exact shape of indifference curves, i.e., the income-elasticity of demand.

How, then, does Becker's theory differ in its implications? The crucial element in his analysis is that not only labour productivity, but also the productivity of consumption matters. The latter measures the amount of utility created per unit of consumption time.[183] Historically, both increased. If this is correct, the secular decline in working hours over the past 100 years has to be interpreted differently. Traditional wisdom has it that a large income effect swamped a smaller substitution effect. In the Becker framework both labour and leisure have to be considered. Since the productivity of both consumption and production grew rapidly, substitution effects would tend to cancel each other out. The income effect, however, is not neutral if the income elasticity of demand is different from unity. In the case of time-intensive commodities, which are normally regarded as luxuries (with an income elasticity of demand for time-intensive goods greater than unity), this is probably incorrect—and the increase in 'leisure' over the past 100 years has to be interpreted as a consequence of this high-income elasticity of demand for earnings-intensive commodities.[184]

Becker's model can help us shed new light on the puzzling trend in total working hours from 1750 to 1800. The 'New Household Economics' has important implications for the interrelationship between labour and leisure precisely because both the productivity of consumption and production matter. As we have briefly described above, labour productivity per head grew at lacklustre rates—especially if the effect of additional working hours is taken into account. At the same time, the 'wave of gadgets' that swept through England during the eighteenth century increased the 'productivity of

---

[182] 'Assume a uniform increase only in the productivity of consumption time... The relative prices of commodities with large forgone earnings would fall, and substitution would be induced towards these and away from other commodities, causing hours of work to fall. Since the increase in productivity would also produce an income effect, the demand for commodities would increase, which, in turn, would induce an increased demand for goods. But since the productivity of working time is assumed not to change, more goods could be obtained only by an increase in work. That is, the higher real income resulting from an advance in the productivity of consumption time would cause hours of work to *increase*.' Becker, 'Theory', 506 (his italics). Real income in this context means the total amount of satisfaction that can be obtained.

[183] Ordinal not cardinal measurement of utility, of course.

[184] Becker, 'Theory', 505 ff., 517.

consumption'. The amount of satisfaction derived per unit of time will grow because of three effects. First, the effects of fashion mean that, for any given stock of material goods, more 'sensual arousal' will be provided. Second, the growing stock of consumer durables will also help to raise the productivity of consumption time. If more durable goods (e.g., clothing) become relatively more attractive than other items of consumption (e.g., food and drink), the induced substitution effects will lead to an increased availability of consumption goods per unit of time. Third, the proliferation of new goods increased variety of choice. It is important to emphasize how these changes were related to the issue of time-use. A quickening pace of consumption means that more goods were being consumed per unit of time—a point that is strikingly illustrated by the declining importance of inherited goods. In a lifetime, per decade or per hour, there was more satisfaction to be derived from 'leisure activities'. In King's dataset, there is an increase of 72 per cent in the number of goods found in inventories from the period 1711–69 to 1770–1812. Leisure time could now be spent more productively in homes much more likely to be equipped with chairs, candlesticks, clocks, or carpets. It is precisely this phenomenon which Becker has termed a rise in the productivity of consumption.

There is therefore every indication that the productivity of consumption grew faster than the productivity of production. Of course, the former can only be hinted at, but the conclusion seems a safe one largely because the productivity of production grew so slowly. In the Becker framework, the consequences are the same as if consumption productivity alone had grown at a somewhat more modest rate. The question then is whether substitution or income effects dominated. This depends on the nature of the goods involved—if the income elasticity of demand for time-intensive commodities was above unity, then total hours would have increased. This is clearly the case, given the income elasticity of demand estimated by Horrell. She finds an income-elasticity for residual spending of 2.32. As this category is dominated by spending on clothing, we can safely assume that the elasticity in the case of clothing was well above unity.[185]

---

[185] A similar argument has been made by Michael Abbott and Orley Ashenfelter ('Labour Supply, Commodity Demand and the Allocation of Time', *Review of Economic Studies*, 43 (1976)), who find that consumer durables and leisure appear to be substitutes and not complements.

The interpretation advanced in this section—that productivity of consumption grew faster than the productivity of production—can also help us understand why the same period that saw a marked increase in the working year also witnessed the rise of a leisure industry. A comprehensive treatment of Stone's concept of a 'leisure revolution' lies beyond the scope of this book. Yet some aspects of Stone's analysis cannot be passed over in a work on time-use in England during the eighteenth century. Our London data provide an ideal test for his hypothesis, since he describes London as the embodiment of the newly emerging leisure culture.[186] If the central argument is correct, we should expect hours to rise first and more rapidly in those places where consumer goods and leisure choices proliferated at the highest rate. This is precisely the case—we find that hours increased sharply in London. The increase in the rest of the country occurred later and was much slower.

The central element in Stone's storyline is that the growing per capita wealth of eighteenth-century England led to increases in the consumption of a luxury commodity—leisure time. We have already found that there is little evidence for growing prosperity in England during the second half of the eighteenth century, and that even the most optimistic accounts show sluggish growth at best. Stone's account of leisure activities during the eighteenth century therefore presents us with a conundrum: how can leisure assume such importance in a society where such long hours of toil prevailed and where incomes hardly grew? One may even be tempted to believe that the most consistent interpretation of these seemingly contradictory tendencies must be that the Old Bailey Sessions Papers and the Northern Assize Depositions only partly allow us to capture patterns of time-use.[187]

Stone's observations do not disprove our findings. Rather, they enforce the explanation offered for the changes we have observed in the working year. The central element in our favoured explanation is a rise in the productivity of consumption. That more active forms of leisure, involving more (and more conspicuous) expenditure should have facilitated the growth of a leisure industry is not surprising. While labour productivity hardly increased at all, the sirens of the world of consumption became increasingly irresistible. Consequently,

---

[186] Stone, 'Leisure in Eighteenth Century England'.
[187] Stone is concerned with the same groups which constitute the majority of our witnesses.

people worked harder, both at their workplaces and at their leisure, than previous generations had done.

The explanation for rising labour input suggested in this section can be summarized as follows: differences in the relative growth rates of the productivity of consumption and production were responsible for the growth in annual working hours. McKendrick's work on the 'consumer revolution' is centred on the equal importance of production and consumption: 'the increased *desire* to spend is accompanied by an increased *ability* to do so.'[188] We argue precisely the opposite— it is the asymmetry between the two that drives one of the most important social transformations, the increase in the number of working days. Narrative accounts of patterns of consumption, a theoretical argument derived from the 'New Household Economics', as well as empirical evidence strongly suggest that the lure of consumer goods was responsible for a longer working year.

When Mokyr dismantled the idea that demand and supply were somehow equally important in engendering economic change during the eighteenth century, he made one exception. His main conclusion, namely that supply was solely responsible for the Industrial Revolution, may have to be modified, if labour supply and consumption were related:

It can indeed be maintained that demand factors mattered insofar as the supply of labor, the demand for leisure, and the demand for goods are simultaneously determined. If there was an increase in the 'demand for income,' economic growth would occur, but only at the expense of leisure.[189]

Therefore, 'rehabilitating the Industrial Revolution'[190] may arguably require less of an emphasis on the world of production, as well as further research into the patterns and productivity of consumption. The present reversal of the secular trend towards shorter working hours (both in America and the UK) may be due to a similar set of factors— a slowdown in productivity growth combined with a wave of new consumer durables.[191]

---

[188] McKendrick, Brewer, and Plumb, *Consumer Society*, 23 (his italics).

[189] Joel Mokyr, 'Demand vs. Supply in the Industrial Revolution', *Journal of Economic History*, 37 (1977), 985.

[190] Berg and Hudson, 'Rehabilitating the Industrial Revolution'.

[191] Cf. the developments described by Juliet Schor (*The Overworked American. The Unexpected Decline of Leisure* (New York, 1991)) and Geoff Mulgan and H. Wilkinson ('Well-being and Time', *Demos Quarterly*, 5 (1995)). They note the growing attraction of consumer goods and the increased amounts of time spent on shopping.

Putting the Arguments to a Test

Testing the competing explanations advanced in this section is not straightforward. Ideally, we would need micro-level data that allow us to model labour-supply decisions at the household level. The information necessary for such a procedure is not available. None the less, the data exploited in earlier parts of this study can be used for a first attempt at empirical testing. The probability of observing individuals at work varied with weekdays, class, and the hour of the day. Did it also vary with the level of real wages,[192] of unemployment,[193] and the dependency ratio?[194] Did years of war and peace matter?[195] Each observation showing an individual at work or not is linked to an additional variable that shows the level of unemployment in the particular year, to the dependency ratio, the real wage, and a dummy variable for war. Table 4.5 gives the results.

Overall explanatory power is satisfactory, with correct classification more than 50 per cent more likely than assignment to the wrong category. Two variables consistently emerge as significant, independent of the chosen specification—real wages and the dependency ratio. The

TABLE 4.5. *Determinants of work frequency*

Regression	(1)	(2)	(3)	(4)	(5)	(6)
Real wage	-0.017^*	-0.018^*	-0.017^*	-0.017^*	-0.013^*	-0.012^*
Unemployment		0.177		-0.006		-0.007
Dependency ratio			0.005^*	0.005^*	0.005^*	0.005^*
War		-0.111			0.144	0.146
χ^2	204.5^*	205.3^*	232.9^*	233.0^*	234.3^*	234.5^*
% correct	62.14	62.2	62.3	62.2	62.2	62.1

Note: * indicates significance at the 99 per cent level. A full set of additional control variables (day of the week, occupational position, gender, hour of the day, sectoral origin) was included, but is not reported.

[192] I used the series in Feinstein ('Pessimism Perpetuated'). Since it only starts in 1770, and we need annual observations for the procedure, I decided to splice it onto the modified Phelps-Brown Hopkins series in Wrigley and Schofield (*Population History*).

[193] The series is the one used in Feinstein ('Pessimism Perpetuated'). It starts in 1760. To derive estimates for earlier years, I estimated an OLS regression using the industrial production index in Crafts and Harley ('Output Growth and the British Industrial Revolution') as an explanatory variable. This was used for 'backcasting' unemployment levels 1749–59.

[194] From Wrigley *et al.*, *English Population History from Family Reconstitution*, app. 9.

[195] Years of war are set equal to 1, zero otherwise. The relevant wars are the Seven Years War and the Napoleonic Wars (counting the Peace of Amiens as a year of peace).

coefficient on the real wage is strongly negative, indicating a tendency towards higher work effort when wages are lower. Increases in the dependency ratio tend to push up work effort. Unemployment enters with a positive or a negative sign, depending on the set of chosen regressors, but is never significant.[196] The same is true of the war dummy, which does not indicate a consistent trend towards longer hours during wartime—an important question, especially when comparing the middle of the eighteenth century with the period of the Napoleonic wars.

Before we proceed to a more detailed examination of the influence of real wages and the dependency ratio, it may be useful to restrict the sample period. This is for two reasons. Real wages and unemployment fluctuate from year to year, but the largest differences are between periods. As our explanatory variables are annual averages, rather than individual wage rates etc., the strong significance of the real wages and the dependency ratio may be driven by large changes in levels over the period when labour input rose most sharply. If we restrict our sample to the period 1799 to 1834, then the large decline in real wages between the first two sample periods is excluded. Second, we can use an additional explanatory variable that may allow us to test one of the arguments advanced earlier—an index of clothing prices, which should capture changes in the relative price of new consumer goods.[197]

TABLE 4.6. *Determinants of work frequency*

Regression	Before 1770			After 1770		
	(1)	(2)	(3)	(4)	(5)	(6)
Real wage	–0.028*	–0.025*	–0.017§	–0.009*	–0.008*	–0.008*
Unemployment		–0.12				
Dependency ratio			0.28*		–0.002	
Rcloth						–0.005
χ^2	73.8*	74.3*	91.6*	138.2*	138.6*	138.7*
Per cent correct	59.5	60.1	60.5	65.1	65.1	64.6

Note: * indicates significance at the 99 per cent level. A full set of additional control variables (day of the week, occupational position, gender, hour of the day, sectoral origin) was included, but is not reported.

[196] This may, of course, reflect possible inaccuracies of the method used.

[197] Data on the price of clothing, using a new index compiled as part of a larger project on the cost of living, were kindly made available by Charles Feinstein. The series begins in 1770, and hence cannot be used for the earlier period. As there is no obvious way of extending the clothing price series before this data, it appeared best not to use alternative price series of markedly lower quality.

The clothing variable does not emerge as significant—despite considerable variation between the beginning and the third decades of the nineteenth century. Note, however, that the real earnings variable is invariably highly collinear with the real price of clothing—both are sticky nominal prices divided by a standard of living index that is dominated by volatile food prices. If the relative price of clothing alone is included, we derive a coefficient of 0.0099, significant at the 13 per cent level. Wages remain highly significant; the size of the coefficient, however, falls by about two-thirds between the first and the second period. Backward-bending labour supply curves—in so far as they existed—were becoming less important, or so many authors have argued, as the nineteenth century wore on.[198] Our estimates lend qualified support to such an assessment. The dependency ratio appears as significant in the first period, but changes sign and becomes insignificant in the second. This should not necessarily be regarded as a sign that long-term demographic trends did not matter. Rather, since demographic variables by their very nature change slowly, we only have quinquennial estimates of the dependency burden. Hence, there are only four different levels for this particular variable in the sample from 1798–1803 and 1828–32. The insignificance of the estimation result could simply reflect a lack of identifying variance.

Which variable is most important in explaining the rise in labour hours between 1760 and 1830? Two variables appear relatively robust—the real wage variable, and the dependency ratio. In determining their influence, we need to take into account the extent to which they changed over the total period. Given the fall in real earnings, labour input should have increased by 1.7 per cent between 1760 and 1800. The overall effect is a decline in labour input by 2.5 per cent. Between 1800 and 1830 it should have fallen by 4.3 per cent. Between the middle and the third decades of the eighteenth century, the dependency burden rose by 16 per cent. Demographic pressure therefore possibly added as much as 14 per cent to labour input (Figure 4.10).[199]

The remaining increase is not easily explained. We observed earlier that it is hard to distinguish between the effect of the real wage variable and the relative price of clothing. Also, the significance level was

---

[198] The most recent statement along these lines is Hatcher, 'Labour, Leisure and Economic Thought'.

[199] Based on the frequency-method in table 3.32, method B.

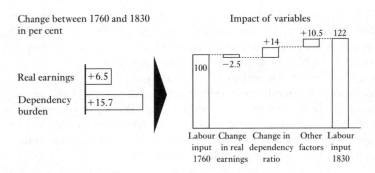

FIGURE 4.10. *Changes in labour input, 1760–1830—determining factors*

only marginally below the conventionally accepted level. Clearly, these empirical results are not sufficiently robust to assign great importance to the decline in the relative price of consumer goods. If we were to use the derived coefficient for calculating the implied impact on labour input, however, the result is large—the fall in the relative price of clothing between the beginning and the third decade of the nineteenth century suggests an increase in labour input by 27 per cent, more than sufficient to account for the full rise of annual hours worked. Given the data available today, this calculation is more illustrative than accurate, but it demonstrates the extent to which 'the sirens of consumption' could have had an impact on labour input.

Firmer conclusions can be drawn in the case of real wages and the dependency ratio. Between the middle and the end of the eighteenth century, the decline in real earnings—driven by the high prices of the Napoleonic period—may have contributed to the overall rise in hours worked. As we argued before when using labour supply elasticities derived from modern studies, the size of the effect is too small to account for a significant part of the total increase in hours. The estimation carried out in the last part of this section confirms this impression. A strong influence on hours appears to be the growing dependency burden. This is surprising in so far as the impact on household consumption has conventionally been regarded as rather low.[200] We have argued that this calculation may be underestimating the true impact of greater dependency ratios. Increasing economic pressures may have been crucial for the rise in labour input, but it may

[200] Wrigley and Schofield, *Population History of England*, 445–9.

have been demographic pressures, rather than lower earnings, that provided the most powerful impetus for additional work.

New Estimates of Labour Input, 1760–1831

Total labour input is determined by four factors—the size of the population, the labour force participation rate, the unemployment rate, and the number of hours worked. In order to derive estimates of changes in labour input, we need to assemble data on these components for the period 1760 to 1831.

Arguably the most reliable evidence on labour input comes from historical demography. Wrigley and Schofield have analysed data from 404 English parishes between 1541 and 1871. On the basis of 'backward projections', they have inferred the total size of England's population. The results substantially revise the demographic figures used by Deane and Cole. On average, the years between 1760 and 1801 saw demographic growth of 0.86 per cent per annum; between 1801 and 1831 growth accelerated to 1.41 per cent per annum[201] Despite some recent objections, the main results do not appear to be too sensitive to changes in the assumptions,[202] and they have served as the basis of all subsequent research into the economics of the Industrial Revolution.

No data on participation rates are available for the eighteenth century.[203] It is only after the first census in 1801 that it becomes possible to estimate the total occupied population. From these calculations, participation ratios can be inferred. No clear-cut trend emerges for the first half of the nineteenth century (Table 4.7). Large as the potential impact of participation rates on labour supply is, for the early decades of the nineteenth century at least, they appear to have contributed but little to the growth in labour input. Mokyr has argued that changes over time were small and can probably be explained by measurement error, stochastic variation, and shifts in the age structure.[204] Figure 4.11 presents Deane and Cole's estimates of

---

[201] Crafts, *British Economic Growth*, 76; Wrigley and Schofield, *Population History of England*, table A9.1, pp. 614–15.

[202] Peter Razzell ('The Growth of Population in Eighteenth-Century England: A Critical Reappraisal', *Journal of Economic History*, 53 (1993)) largely repeats difficulties which Wrigley and Schofield themselves acknowledged in their original contribution.

[203] Joel Mokyr, 'The New Economic History and the Industrial Revolution', in id., *British Industrial Revolution*, 96.   [204] Ibid., 96.

TABLE 4.7. *Labour force participation, 1801–51*

Census	1801	1831	1841	1851
Labour force participation rate (%)	44.9	43.9	45.28	46.5

Source: Deane and Cole, *British Economic Growth*, 8 ff., 143 ff.

participation rates alongside the proportion of the population aged 14–59.[205] There is a high degree of co-movement between the two series.[206]

We can now use the similarity of the two time-series to derive participation ratios before 1801. Crafts was the first to employ the proportion of the population of working age (15–59) as a proxy for labour input during the Industrial Revolution.[207] He thereby improved Feinstein's original calculations, who assumed that the labour force had grown at the same rate as the population at large. Since accelerating population growth boosted the proportion of the population below working age, he arrives at lower rates of increase. In deriving growth rates, Crafts assumes that there is a one-to-one relationship between the labour force and the proportion aged 15–59. Using Deane and Cole's calculations of participation rates between

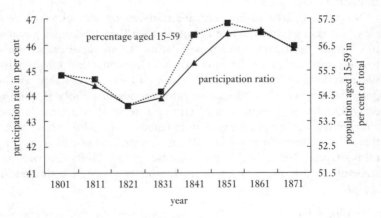

FIGURE 4.11. *Participation ratio and population aged 15–50*

[205] Wrigley and Schofield, *Population History of England*, table A3.1, pp. 528–9.
[206] The correlation coefficient is 0.912.
[207] Taken from Wrigley and Schofield, *Population History of England*, 528–9.

1801 and 1871 as well as the age groups from Wrigley and Schofield, this assumption can be tested econometrically:

$$p = \underset{(0.04414)}{0.3648} + \underset{(5.433)}{0.803A} \qquad (4.3)$$

adj. $R^2 = 0.80$ S.E. $= 0.47$ N $= 8$ F $= 29.52$
[P = labour force participation ratio, A = proportion of the total population aged 15–59, t-statistics in parentheses]

The fraction of total variance explained is high, and the t-statistic on A is sufficiently high to reject the null hypothesis at the 99 per cent level of confidence. This is true despite the rather limited sample size. It has to be stressed that using a regression with 7 degrees of freedom can only be excused because no wider empirical base is available for the period under consideration. Despite the high correlation coefficient, a 1 per cent rise in the fraction of the population aged 15–50 only leads to a 0.8 per cent rise in the participation ratio.[208] Figure 4.12 presents 'best-guess' estimates on the basis of eq. (4.3).

The reliability of the estimate in Figure 4.12 is subject to two qualifications. First, as already mentioned, the regression on which it is based is far from perfect. Second, and perhaps more fundamentally, a 'participation rate' may in itself be a concept of questionable value for the period under consideration. The occupied percentage of the population is difficult to define when a large part of the population works in households, producing goods for autoconsumption.[209] The shift of

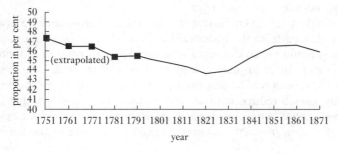

FIGURE 4.12. *Participation ratio, 1751–1871*

[208] It is true that the coefficient—despite the high t-statistic—is not significantly different from unity. However, in deriving a best-guess estimate, it is still sensible to use the most likely value.   [209] Mokyr, 'New Economic History', 96.

employment away from these traditional forms and into the labour market is often seen as one of the era's most salient features.[210] In the absence of information that could shed light on how much work was done outside the market, it is none the less sensible to make no further adjustments.[211] We should also note that the decline in the labour force participation rate induced by demographic change was probably compounded as women gradually withdrew from the labour force. The rise of the 'male breadwinner' family is often associated with the very period with which we are concerned.[212] Horrell and Humphries have assembled evidence that allows us to gauge the possible impact of this effect. They estimate that the percentage of women either recording earnings or having an occupation in their sample of working-class households declined from 65.7 per cent in 1787–1815 to 61.7 per cent in 1821–40. This would imply a decline of 4 per cent over thirty years (taking midpoints of the periods). If the same trend had continued unabated since the 1760s we would have to adjust for a possible decline in female labour force participation of approximately 9 per cent. If we assume that almost all men of working age were employed, the total impact on labour force participation rates would be −5.3 per cent. This would clearly be an important correction of our results, but in the absence of information about the stability of trends before 1800, it would be inappropriate to make any adjustment to our series. It is possible that the high participation rates (and their decline after 1815) is a result of buoyant labour demand during the Napoleonic wars, and that female labour force participation did not decline sharply between 1760 and 1830.

Feinstein's new unemployment series is based on qualitative assessments gleaned from the historical literature. Using the co-movement between economic conditions and unemployment rates in the industrial labour force, he derives estimates of the latter for the period 1760–1871. Between the first two benchmark periods, there appears to be only a small reduction in unemployment rates, from 5.25 per cent to 5 per cent of the labour force in the industrial sector. In the aggregate, it is almost exactly counterbalanced by the rise in the share of

---

[210] Pollard, 'Labour in Great Britain'.

[211] Labour supply decisions are discussed more extensively in the section on working hours because it is unlikely that very many individuals were completely independent of the monetized sector. More probably, change was gradual, leading to longer hours. See below.

[212] Ivy Pinchbeck, *Women Workers in the Industrial Revolution* (New York, 1969).

industrial employment.[213] By 1830 unemployment had increased sharply, to 10 per cent of the industrial labour force. Over the period the share of the labour force employed in industry rose considerably, thereby amplifying the effect of higher unemployment in the manufacturing sector. Thus, we can now correct for the bias resulting from the fact that, during the benchmark years commonly used, the economy was at different stages of the economic cycle.

The second adjustment used by Feinstein concerns agricultural unemployment. After the end of the Napoleonic wars, winter unemployment in predominantly arable counties became widespread. Feinstein argues that winter rates exceeded summer ones by 10 percentage points during the period 1815–1850, and assumes a gradual decline thereafter.[214]

Table 4.8 summarizes the available information on labour input between 1760 and 1831. Crafts and Harley calculated growth rates of 0.8 and 1.4 per cent per annum for the periods 1760–1801 and 1801–31, respectively. This is almost identical with our calculations of the size of the labour force, demonstrating that the use of participation rates rather than the percentage aged 15–59 has little impact on our estimates. Between 1760 and 1801 the impact of changes in unemployment is minute. For the later period, however, using the Feinstein corrections reduces annual labour input growth from 1.36 per cent to 1.25 per cent.[215]

Our estimates of annual working hours have the largest impact for the period 1760–1801, suggesting an upwards revision that almost doubles growth rates, compared to earlier estimates. Unfortunately, trends for the periods 1760–1801 and 1801–1831 are subject to much greater uncertainty than the direction and magnitude of change

[213] Using the figures in Crafts, *British Economic Growth*, 62. I used the average of the years 1760–3, i.e. all the years from our sample for which the Feinstein series contains estimates. In 1800, I used 1799–1803; in 1830 I used 1829–32.

[214] Feinstein, 'Pessimism Perpetuated', 646–7.

[215] Partly, changes in unemployment between commonly used benchmark years are simply the result of chance—volatility in the unemployment series is considerable. Note, however, that there is a general rise in average unemployment rates—between 1770 and the end of the Napoleonic Wars, the mean is approximately 5 per cent, rising to 8 per cent during the period 1815–50 (Feinstein, 'Pessimism Perpetuated', 646). Note that the use of the frequency-based estimates, which may partly capture changes in participation rates and the incidence of unemployment, could result in some partial double counting. However, since the estimation method is more robust than the timing-based approach, the benefits of using this technique outweigh this potential problem. I later test the sensitivity of the magnitudes derived to changes in the estimation method.

TABLE 4.8. *Total labour input, 1760–1830*

		1760	1800	1830
	population size (in 1,000s)	6,127	8,671	13,254
	unemployment (in %)	5.25	5	10
	labour force participation rate (in %)	46.9	44.9	43.9
	hours p.a. (frequency)	2,706	3,523	3,256
	hours p.a. (timing)	2,760	3,115	3,366
	percentage of labour force in industry	23.9	29.5	42.9
Index	population size	100	141.5	216.3
	labour force	100	135.5	202.5
	adjusted for industrial unemployment	100	135.2	196.3
	adjusted for agricultural unemployment	100	135.2	195.5
	adjusted for hours (frequency)	100	176.0	235.2
	adjusted for hours (timing)	100	152.6	238.4

		1760–1800	1800–30	1760–1830
Growth	population	0.85%	1.42%	1.11%
p.a.	labour force	0.74%	1.35%	1.01%
	adjusted for unemployment	0.74%	1.25%	0.97%
	adjusted for agricultural unemployment	0.74%	1.24%	0.96%
	adjusted for hours (frequency)	1.39%	0.97%	1.23%
	adjusted for hours (timing)	1.04%	1.50%	1.25%

between 1760 and 1830. For the first period, both frequency- and timing-based estimates agree on the direction of change; for the latter period, they do not. Table 4.8 uses both estimates. It should be borne in mind that the downward revision for the period 1801–31 hinges on accepting the superiority of this particular approach. The timing-based approach implies a large increase.

Magnitudes of change are less ambiguous for the seventy-year period between 1760 and 1830. Feinstein's calculations tend to reduce the increase in labour input; the new hours estimates have the opposite effect. Even after incorporating Feinstein's adjustments for unemployment, however, the rise in hours is so strong as to suggest a higher midpoint estimate than any previously used. Crafts and Harley's figures, after corrections by Feinstein, imply a figure of 0.97 per cent per annum; taking the longer working year into account, the estimate is now 1.24 per cent. These new estimates of labour input can now be used to cast new light on two issues—the growth of productivity during the Industrial Revolution, and the course of living standards.

Working Hours and Productivity Change

Moments are the elements of profit. (*Report of the Inspectors of Factories* (1860))

The rapid increase in labour input has wider implications for our understanding of economic growth during the Industrial Revolution. It will be the argument of this section that the most important consequence of the changes outlined above was not, however, the additional labour input in the economy. Rather, it was the way in which this supply was extended—the lengthening of the working year—that had important repercussions.

Theoretical Considerations

How is production affected by changes in the number of hours worked? If the benefits of a longer working year were pronounced, contemporaries should have noticed them. This was indeed the case. At the end of the seventeenth century Sir Henry Pollexfen remarked in his *A Discourse of Trade and Coyn*: '2 Millions of Working People at 6*d.* per day, comes to 50,000*l.* which upon a due inquiry from whence our Riches must arise, will appear to be so much Lost to the Nation, by every Holyday that is kept . . .'[216] Sir Henry Pollexfen's estimate of the net welfare loss to England caused by a single holy day is quite large. In calculating the staggering sum of £50,000, Pollexfen simply multiplied an imputed average daily wage with the assumed number of wage-earners. This implies an elasticity of output with respect to labour input of unity—no declining marginal returns exist. If Sir Henry is correct, then he would have illustrated a basic yet important point— even economies with surplus labour (such as the English one during the sixteenth and seventeenth centuries) will experience a notable increase in total output if the length of the working year is extended.[217]

That entrepreneurs paying weekly or daily wages should have every incentive to extend working hours is obvious; longer hours for the

[216] Henry Pollexfen, *A Discourse of Trade and Coyn* (London, 1697), 50.
[217] The surge of vagrancy in the sixteenth century has often been interpreted as a sign of widespread underemployment in the economy. Asa Briggs, *A Social History of England* (Harmondsworth, 1987), 126 ff.

same pay imply a lower cost of labour per hour. A different logic underlies the argument advanced above: it was rational even for those employers who paid piece-rates to be strongly opposed to the allegedly leisurely working habits of their employees. Josiah Wedgwood, for all his skill in managing his men, could not prevent his potters from leaving work for Burslem wakes.[218] Ever since the Industrial Revolution, this struggle about the length of the working day and working year has continued. The first volume of *Das Kapital* is full of observations on the employers' desire to lengthen working hours. Time and again Marx cites the reports of factory inspectors and press articles detailing attempts to shorten lunch breaks by a few minutes or manipulation of factory clocks.[219] As one businessman allegedly told Marx: 'allowing ten minutes of overtime [per day] is equivalent to handing me £1,000 per year'.[220]

The reason for this large impact is simple. Henry Ashworth, a cotton manufacturer, remarked: 'When a labourer lays down his spade, he renders useless, for that period, a capital worth eighteen pence. When one of our people leaves the mill he renders useless, for that period, a capital that has cost £100,000.'[221] The economist Nassau W. Senior, writing on the Factory Act a quarter of a century before Marx, came to the same conclusion. He observed that, as the value of machinery increased, the desire to extend the working day grows stronger since this is the only way to extract a reasonable profit from such a large amount of fixed capital.[222]

There are three reasons why output may not respond to changes in working hours in exactly the same way as if the number of men had

---

[218] Rule, *Labouring Classes*, 216. At Wedgwood's manufactory, wages were either paid on a daily basis or on piece-rate. In either case, the desire to extend the working week cannot be interpreted as an attempt to reduce the cost of labour per hour (or per day). See Anthony Burton, *Josiah Wedgwood. A Biography* (London, 1976) 33, 41.

[219] Karl Marx, *Das Kapital*, i (Berlin, 1983 [1867]), 249 ff. See also E. P. Thompson, 'Time, Work-discipline and Industrial Capitalism', *Past and Present*, 38 (1967) 56–97.

[220] Marx, *Das Kapital*, i. 257.   [221] Ibid., 428.

[222] Nassau Senior, *Letters on the Factory Act* (London, 1837), 11 ff. The economic history of later periods also shows that the economics underlying this desire have remained fairly constant over time. Industrialists in Weimar Germany, for example, were violently opposed to the eight-hour day not only because they had to pay the same daily wage, but also because productivity was sharply reduced. A discussion of the particularly striking example of Siemens can be found in Gerald D. Feldman, *The Great Disorder* (Oxford, 1993), 674. Output had fallen from 9.5 units per day and worker to 6.48 at the same time when daily working hours had been reduced from 9.5 to 8. These productivity and labour input figures given by Bücher, a member of the *Reichsverband der Deutschen Industrie*, imply an elasticity of output with respect to working hours of 2.02, which is strikingly similar to most results in modern empirical studies (see below).

been increased by a similar amount. First, changes in working time also alter the availability of capital services. Second, there are 'overhead' activities, which do not expand in line with total hours. Third, the efficiency of workers may eventually decline as hours are extended. The first two of these arguments suggest that returns to longer hours should be greater than from an increase in the number of men, while the last one is pointing in the opposite direction.

Measuring the flow of capital services is not trivial. Standard practice assumes that the nominal value of the capital invested in a firm is a good proxy.[223] This is correct in most cases, with one exception. If the length of the working year rises (either by new forms of labour organization: e.g., a shift system, or additional hours per day, per week or per year), then capital services can increase without any measured growth of physical capital.[224] Even if a factory installs no new machinery, the flow of services from capital will rise markedly if it operates its equipment for 50 hours a week instead of 30 hours a week. Extending the working week thus provides access to a pool of 'virtual capital'; but instead of having to install new machinery, few additional costs apart from depreciation will accrue to the entrepreneur. Capital input (the number of days machinery is available for use) more or less increases in line with the additional labour input; extensions of working time are equivalent to a rise in all inputs. If depreciation rises by less than the number of hours the capital stock is employed, then longer hours lower the cost per unit of capital services and may boost net output by more than would be expected on the basis of output elasticities with respect to labour.[225] It should be remembered that increased depreciation through longer working hours is less costly if technological progress is comparatively rapid—the faster technological change, the higher the optimal rate of depreciation.[226]

[223] Pindyck and Rubinfeld, *Microeconomics*, 523; Matthew Shapiro, 'Cyclical Productivity and the Workweek of Capital', *American Economic Review*, 83 (1993), 230.
[224] Martin Feldstein, 'Specification of Labour Input in the Aggregate Production Function', *Review of Economic Studies*, 34 (1967), 376 ff.
[225] Depreciation is typically 6–7 per cent of nominal value. This figure constitutes an upper bound, since firms generally make strong use of tax write-offs so as to accumulate silent reserves. See Walter G. Hoffmann, *Das Wachstum der deutschen Wirtschaft seit der Mitte des 19. Jahrhunderts* (Berlin, 1965), 245.
[226] Marx was already aware of this fact, calling it 'moral depreciation' (*moralischen Verschleiß*). See *Das Kapital*, i. 426–7. On the general theoretical background see Roger Betancourt and Christopher Clague, 'An Economic Analysis of Capital Utilization', *Southern Economic Journal*, 42 (1975); Paul Taubman and Margaret Wilkinson, 'User Cost, Capital Utilization and Investment Theory', *International Economic Review*, 11 (1970).

Second, a certain number of hours per working week is spent on activities that are only indirectly related to production—setting-up time, mealtimes, and the minimum of social interaction without which individuals rarely engage in joint activities. If working hours expand, these 'unproductive' activities do not increase to the same extent. The length of time spent in productive activities rises by more than is suggested by the change in official working time.[227]

Third, it has been argued that longer hours reduce output per man hour due to lower concentration, higher fatigue, and, ultimately, deteriorating health.[228] It is sometimes assumed that the optimal working week is defined by biological factors.[229] This would imply that, once a certain level has been surpassed, the elasticity of output with respect to hours should be very small or even negative. Different investigators, using twentieth-century data, have assumed different lengths of the optimum working week, with estimates varying between 40 and 60 hours.[230] Solow and Temin are inclined to agree that sixty hours per week is probably an upper limit beyond which output will rise no further; Matthews, Feinstein, and Oddling-Smee assume that the reduction in weekly hours from 65 to 56 between 1856 and 1873 was fully compensated by rising efficiency of the labour force due to shorter hours. Denison's work on US national accounts incorporated the same assumption.[231] There is one reason why the argument about offsetting efficiency gains is potentially of less relevance to our period. Empirical research into the link between labour efficiency and working hours has normally focused on the working day. The main source of growing labour input, I have argued, was the rising number of days per week and days per year devoted to work. There is no evidence demonstrating that the efficiency effects are the same for all changes in labour schedules. It may sensibly be argued that fatigue etc. will affect output on an additional day of work less than would be the case if the same increase in labour input had come from a longer working day. As Solow and Temin also note, the offsetting-efficiency argument is not supported by the comments of contemporaries. Employers were

[227] Feldstein, 'Specification of Labour Input', 377; Roger Craine, 'On the Service Flow from Labour', *Review of Economic Studies*, 40 (1973), 41.

[228] Maddison, *Dynamic Forces*, 63.

[229] Robert Solow and Peter Temin, 'The Inputs for Growth', in Peter Mathias and M. M. Postan (eds.), *The Cambridge Economic History of Europe*, vii, pt. 1 (Cambridge, 1978), 12.

[230] Ibid.

[231] Edward Denison, *The Sources of Economic Growth in the United States and the Alternatives before Us* (New York, 1962).

almost always opposed to reductions in the working week, which is only sensible if shorter hours significantly reduced output.[232] These theoretical considerations suggest that a relatively wide range of values for η_H is plausible.

These theoretical imply that 'men' and working hours are heterogeneous factors of production, and that the standard production function should be modified to take the form:

$$Y = AK^{\eta_K} N^{\eta_N} H^{\eta_H} \tag{4.4}$$

[N=number of employees, H=number of hours, η_N = elasticity of output with respect to the number of employees, η_H = elasticity of output with respect to the number of working hours]

Empirical studies confirm that output is highly sensitive to changes in working time, and that this elasticity is different from η_H.[233] One of the first to investigate the issue was Feldstein. He estimates the generalized Cobb–Douglas function in log form:

$$\log Y = \log A + \eta_K K + \eta_N N + \eta_H H \tag{4.5}$$

Feldstein uses cross-sectional data on 24 British industries. His estimates for η_H range from 4.6 to 1.1, while estimates of η_N have a range of 0.771 to 0.881. In every case, output elasticities for the number of workers are smaller than for hours worked ($\eta_N < \eta_H$); also, the sum of elasticities for men and capital is almost always smaller than η_H. Declining marginal returns therefore only apply to increases in labour input due to a larger workforce; longer working hours show rising marginal returns. The lowest coefficient found by Feldstein ($\eta_H = 1.1$) also points to the factor that is chiefly responsible for the large elasticities we observe. While all the estimates using specification (4.5) show $\eta_H > 1.5$, smaller values are returned if more direct measures of capital input are added. Elasticities below 1.2 are observed when capacity utilisation or the use of multiple shifts are incorporated into the estimated equation.[234]

Craine presents time-series evidence for US manufacturing 1949–67 that corroborates Feldstein's findings.

$$Y = AK^{\eta_K} N^{\eta_N} H^{\eta_H} e^{t\mu} \tag{4.6}$$

---

[232] Solow and Temin, 'Inputs', 11.

[233] The observed range of hours in these studies is much lower than the efficiency threshold suggested by Denison and others. The results presented below do not contradict their arguments directly.

[234] Feldstein, 'Specification of Labour Input', tables I, II, IV, V, VI, and equations (5), (6), (7), and (8), pp. 379–84.

Using the specification (4.6) to capture technological change by means of a time trend (t) as well, he finds output elasticities with respect to working hours in the range of 1.9 to 2.2.[235] As in Feldstein's study, there were declining marginal returns to the number of employees; η_N was consistently smaller than η_H. There is further evidence of increasing returns to working hours in US manufacturing between 1948 and 1976.[236] Instead of either using only time-series data (Craine) or only cross-sectional estimates (Feldstein), Leslie pools the data from 20 industries, giving a total of 580 observations. For the manufacturing sector as a whole, the estimated elasticity to hours was 1.44 (1.79 if the petroleum industry is included).

A more recent study of 8 Swedish manufacturing sectors between 1980 and 1983 finds that output grew more in response to longer hours than to more men.[237] The authors estimated Cobb–Douglas as well as translog production functions. The results for η_H are in the range of 2.4 to 0.823, whereas η_N varies between 0.61 and 0.75. The elasticity of output with respect to hours is larger than unity if a time-trend is used to capture technological change.[238]

Yet support for the view that $\eta_H > 1$ is not unanimous. For Sweden's private sector between 1963 and 1982 Åberg reports elasticities of hours with respect to per capita output substantially below one. He concedes, however, that these only apply to the very short term, and that long-term elasticities are considerably larger.[239] He also finds that reductions in working hours caused total factor productivity growth to slow by up to 72 per cent.[240] It therefore appears that, had a more stan-

---

[235] The only exception is an equation in which the elasticities are constrained to be equal. See Craine, 'On the Service Flow', 43.

[236] Derek Leslie, 'The Productivity of Hours in U.S. Manufacturing Industries', *Review of Economics and Statistics*, 66 (1984), 489–90.

[237] Dominique Anxo and Arne Bigsten, 'Working Hours and Productivity in Swedish Manufacturing', *Scandinavian Journal of Economics*, 91 (1989).

[238] Ibid., tables 1 and 2, pp. 616–17.

[239] Yngve Åberg, *The Impact of Working Hours and Other Factors on Production and Employment* (Avebury, 1987), 40. The empirical approach is probably fundamentally flawed since it is estimates short-term elasticities. Cf. Feldstein, 'Specification of Labour Input', 377.

[240] Another author who found an elasticity with respect to hours substantially below one is Malinvaud ('Une explication de l'évolution de la productivité horaire du travail', *Economie et Statistique*, 48 (1973), 47–8). Using data on 16,885 enterprises, he finds a coefficient for per capita output of 0.51. No tests of statistical significance are provided, and Malinvaud also fails to give the full specification used. It seems that he neither controlled for the effects of technological change nor of industry-specific effects, both of which influence the estimates of other authors considerably. It is therefore impossible to judge how trustworthy his findings are.

dard specification been employed, increasing returns to working hours would also have been found.

Subsequent research has used the finding of increasing returns to hours to resolve one of the well-known paradoxes of applied economics: procyclical productivity.[241] As mentioned above, we would expect declining marginal returns in the case of Cobb-Douglas technology. The conventional way to resolve this paradox is to assume labour hoarding. Firms incur costs when they attempt to adjust their workforce to rising demand in an economic upturn. They are therefore thought to retain a certain number of underemployed workers during downturns.[242] As output grows, slack is being taken up and labour productivity surges.[243] Amongst the first to address the problem of procyclical productivity by taking hours of work into account was Tatom. He first demonstrates that, on the basis of annual US data from 1948 to 1973, the return to man-hours is significantly larger than one. He then goes on to show that the output elasticity is no longer in excess of unity if a measure of capital utilization is added to the econometric specification.[244] The same result is obtained by Shapiro, who used data on four-digit US manufacturing industries from 1978 to 1988, in the case of total factor productivity. TFP rises with output if it is conventionally defined as the Solow residual.[245] Shapiro shows

[241] Edwin Kuh, 'Cyclical and Secular Labor Productivity in United States Manufacturing', *Review of Economics and Statistics* (1965); Frank Brechling, 'The Relationship between Output and Employment in British Manufacturing Industries', *Review of Economics and Statistics*, 32 (1965); R. Ball and E. St. Cyr, 'Short Term Employment Functions in British Manufacturing Industry', *Review of Economic Studies*, 33 (1966); Robert Coen and Bert Hickman, 'Constrained Joint Estimation of Factor Demand and Production Functions', *Review of Economics and Statistics*, 52 (1970).

[242] Walter Oi, 'Labor as a Quasi-Fixed Factor', *Journal of Political Economy*, 70 (1962); Ronald Soligo, 'The Short-Run Relationship between Employment and Output', *Yale Economic Essays* (1966).

[243] We can explain increasing returns in a competitive framework if we assume externalities (Kevin Murphy, Andrej Shleifer, and Robert Vishny, 'Building Blocks of Market Clearing Business Cycle Models', *NBER Macroeconomics Annual* (1989)). Ricardo Caballero and Richard Lyons ('External Effects in U.S. Procyclical Productivity', *Journal of Monetary Economics*, 29 (1989)) have found some empirical support for this hypothesis in different US industries. Recent work by Domenico Marchetti ('Procyclical Productivity, Externalities and Labor Hoarding: A Reexamination of Evidence from U.S. Manufacturing', *EUI Economics Working Paper*, 13 (1994)) shows that these results may be due to model misspecification.

[244] John Tatom, 'The "Problem" of Procyclical Real Wages and Productivity', *Journal of Political Economy*, 88 (1980), eq. (2) and (4), 389–92.

[245] Robert Solow, 'Technical Change and the Aggregate Production Function', *Review of Economics and Statistics*, 39 (1957), 312–20.

that $\delta TFP/\delta Y$ is not significantly different from zero if the total factor input in the calculation of the Solow residual is adjusted for the work-week of capital. This is in line with findings by Mayshar and Solon that the late-shift share of total employment in the United States exhibits a clear procyclical pattern.[246]

It is conspicuous that η_H is always sharply reduced and not different from unity if changes in capital utilization are measured independently and added as an exogenous variable to the estimated equation. This does not, however, prove that the large effect of working time on output is an illusion, a mere statistical fallacy. If adding an additional independent variable reduces the significance of another regressor greatly, this may either signify that the original regression was misspecified, or that the new variable explains why the original explanatory variable had such a large impact.[247] When the theoretical case for disaggregating labour input was presented, two separate arguments were made for assuming that $\eta_H \neq \eta_N$. Longer hours of work per employee could increase capital services as well, or productive hours per worker could rise disproportionately because of a fixed amount of unproductive time during the working week. The fact that the large (positive) elasticities for working hours are sharply reduced—often to unity or below—when we include measures of capital services demonstrates that the main cause underlying estimates of $\eta_H > 1$ is changes in the service flow from capital.[248] Employers could therefore reap large benefits from longer hours chiefly because their equipment would go unused for shorter periods of time. We can therefore conclude that both theoretical arguments and empirical investigations of present-day data demonstrate that Sir Henry Pollexfen and his contemporaries rightly viewed longer working hours as a key instrument by which the English economy's output could be boosted. There is, however, no indication that this applied to a greater extent in 1800 than in 1750. The potential beneficial effect of extended working hours, proxied by capital/labour ratios, was almost constant. Yet, when other factors diminished the conflict of interest between work-

[246] Joran Mayshar and Gary Solon, 'Shift Work and the Business Cycle', *American Economic Review*, 83 (1993), 225–6.

[247] For a sophisticated application of this methodological principle see Robert Waldmann, 'Inequality, Economic Growth and the Debt Crisis', *EUI Economics Working Paper*, 40 (1994), 4 ff.

[248] This conclusion receives some support from empirical work by Susanto Basu, 'Procyclical Productivity: Overhead Inputs or Cyclical Utilization?', *University of Michigan Center for Research on Economic and Social Theory Working Paper*, 25 (1993).

ers and employers, declining marginal returns could successfully be avoided.

These findings from present-day studies are relevant to our investigation of the English economy at the end of the early modern period. There are strong reasons to assume that contemporaries were correct in thinking that longer working hours would *ceteris paribus* boost output.[249] Second, there is little indication of these advances being offset by adverse employment effects of longer hours. Contrary to public sentiment in some continental European countries, there is also some evidence that employment and normal hours move in the same direction. Having explored the theoretical implications of a longer working year, we now turn to its consequences for the English economy in the eighteenth and nineteenth centuries.

Accounting for Growth

The sources of growth during the Industrial Revolution have been hotly debated for some time.[250] Attention has focused especially on the issue of capital formation and its relationship to output growth. Particular interest attaches to the issue of total factor productivity growth during the century after 1750. TFP is normally calculated as: [251]

$$TFP = \frac{\Delta Y}{Y} - \eta_K \frac{\Delta K}{K} - \eta_L \frac{\Delta L}{L} \qquad (4.7)$$

At present, the historiography of the Industrial Revolution seems to diminish the importance of productivity growth by the decade. For 1760–1801, research during the past fifteen years has halved its importance. For the three decades to 1831, there was a decline from 1.3 per

---

[249] Note also that there is no reason to assume that increases in hours were offset by a commensurate decline in employment. Present-day studies uniformly suggest that, if there is an association between the variables, it often indicates significant (positive) correlation. Cf. Elisabeth Neifer-Dichmann, 'Working Time Reductions in the Former Federal Republic of Germany: A Dead End for Employment Policy', *International Labour Review*, 130 (1991); Wolfgang Konig and Winfried Pohlmeier, 'Employment, Labour Utilization and Procyclical Productivity', *Kyklos*, 41 (1988); Jeremy Atack and Frank Bateman, 'How Long was the Workday in 1880?', *Journal of Economic History*, 51 (1992); Jennifer Hunt, 'Has Work-Sharing Worked in Germany?', *Quarterly Journal of Economics*, 114 (1999), 117–48; Alison Booth and Fabio Schiantarelli, 'The Employment Effects of a Shorter Working Week', *Economica*, 54 (1987); Giorgio Brunello, 'The Employment Effects of Shorter Working Hours: An Application to Japanese Data', *Economica*, 56 (1989).

[250] See Crafts, *British Economic Growth*; id. and Harley, 'Output Growth'.

[251] Crafts, *British Economic Growth*, 78.

cent per annum to 0.35 per cent per annum—a fall equivalent to 73 per cent (see Table 4.9).[252]

Recent work confirms that there was no sudden burst of capital accumulation during a brief period of 10–20 years, no 'take off' in the sense suggested by Rostow and Lewis. Saving, and consequently, investment, made the largest single contribution to output growth during both periods according to Crafts and Harley. Yet the expansion of capital stock was even slower than initially estimated by Feinstein, and it compares unfavourably with growth rates of other industrializing nations at a similar stage of development.[253]

It is conspicuous that all the estimates except the ones for labour input have been revised during the past fifteen years.[254] We can now use the new estimates from Table 4.10 to augment existing calculations. For all factor inputs and output growth, I use the figures from Crafts and Harley.[255] I also use their assumption that capital and labour both have weights of 0.5. The labour input calculations based on the frequency method imply TFP growth rates of −0.2 per cent

TABLE 4.9. *Estimates of TFP growth*

	$\Delta Y/Y$	$\Delta K/K$	$\Delta L/L$	TFP
Feinstein				
1760–1801	1.1	1	0.8	0.2
1801–1831	2.7	1.4	1.4	1.3
Crafts				
1760–1801	1	1	0.8	0.1
1801–1831	2	1.5	1.4	0.55
Crafts/Harley				
1760–1801	1	1	0.8	0.1
1801–1831	1.9	1.7	1.4	0.35

Sources: Crafts, *British Economic Growth*; id. and Harley, 'Output Growth'.

[252] It should be noted that per capita output rose chiefly because of technological change if the Crafts and Harley figures are used. Cf. Mokyr, 'New Economic History', n. 21, p. 25.
[253] Crafts, *British Economic Growth*, 73.
[254] Recently, the issue of human capital has attracted the interest of scholars. See Tranter, 'Labour Supply', 222 ff.; David Mitch, 'The Role of Education and Skill in the British Industrial Revolution', in Mokyr (ed.), *British Industrial Revolution*.
[255] Crafts and Harley, 'Output Growth'.

TABLE 4.10. *Impact of revisions—TFP*

	growth p.a. in per cent			
	$\Delta Y/Y$	$\Delta K/K$	$\Delta L/L$	TFP
Crafts Harley				
1760–1801	1.0	1.0	0.8	0.1
1801–1831	1.9	1.7	1.4	0.35
1760–1831	1.5	1.4	1.1	0.25
Frequency-based				
1760–1801	1.0	1.0	1.4	−0.2
1801–1831	1.9	1.7	0.98	0.56
1760–1831	1.5	1.4	1.24	0.18
Timing-based				
1760–1801	1.0	1.0	1.04	−0.02
1801–1831	1.9	1.7	1.51	0.30
1760–1831	1.5	1.4	1.26	0.17

per annum in the first period, and 0.56 per cent in the second.[256] For the timing method, the respective values are −0.02 and 0.3. The frequency-based estimates would therefore signal an early acceleration of productivity growth, coinciding with the period that saw the end of the Napoleonic Wars.[257] A rate of 0.56 per cent would be higher than the latest reworking of the data by Crafts and Harley suggests, and would approach the original value calculated by Crafts.[258] For the period as a whole, the estimated rate of TFP growth is 0.17 to 0.19 per cent per annum, or approximately one-third less than suggested by Crafts and Harley.[259]

As discussed above, there is some evidence to suggest that hours and workers are not perfect substitutes, as implied by the calculation

---

[256] Ibid., 718.

[257] Jeffrey Williamson ('Why Was British Growth So Slow During the Industrial Revolution?', *Journal of Economic History*, 44 (1984)) argues that high levels of government spending—an immediate consequence of the Napoleonic Wars—were largely to blame for slow growth during the initial phases of Britain's Industrial Revolution.

[258] Crafts (*British Economic Growth*, 81) who uses a three-factor decomposition.

[259] In no way do I wish to suggest that previous authors have not been sufficiently aware of the need to adjust for changes in hours. Crafts (ibid.) in particular has done much to emphasize the need for new estimates. The importance of our revision could be judged more appropriately if it became customary to publish confidence intervals alongside the best-guess estimates (see Feinstein and Thomas, 'A Plea for Errors').

carried out above. The reason is that longer working hours should also have increased the availability of capital *services*—tools, machines, and buildings will no longer go unused on Mondays and holy days, for example. A number of studies indicate that the returns to longer working hours may be much higher than the returns to additional workers. Table 4.11 gives an overview of alternative growth estimates if different values for η_H are used.

If values greater than 0.5 are used, TFP growth is very rapidly reduced to zero or even negative values. The majority of studies indicates an elasticity with respect to working hours in the range from unity to two.[260] It is difficult to understand why the extended availability of capital services should lead to elasticities above unity. Fixed periods for maintenance and setting up of machinery may go some way to explain such high returns. Yet longer hours also have to be balanced against the increased depreciation as well as additional repairs and outlays for maintenance of the capital goods used, a factor that was probably of considerable importance in the eighteenth century.[261] Econometric studies have used data from a wide range of countries and periods, with working hours varying considerably. The results seem to be untouched by such variation. There is, however, a potential problem in applying the coefficients from modern econometric studies. The data used in modern studies refer to a markedly shorter

TABLE 4.11. *TFP growth after adjustments for heterogeneous labour input, 1760–1831*

	growth p.a. in per cent				$\eta_H = 0.5$	1	1.5
	$\Delta Y/Y$	$\Delta K/K$	$\Delta L/L$	$\Delta h/h$		TFP	
Frequency	1.5	1.4	0.97	0.26	0.18	0.055	−0.075
Timing	1.5	1.4	0.97	0.28	0.17	0.035	−0.105

[260] This holds if capital utilization is not controlled for. Since I argued above that longer working hours have such a large impact precisely because capital services rise proportionately, it seems sensible to use the initial estimates.

[261] Charles H. Feinstein and Sidney Pollard (*Studies in Capital Formation in the United Kingdom, 1750–1920* (Oxford, 1988), app., table 1, p. 427) suggest a depreciation of 1.4 per cent of gross stock in 1761–70 and of 1.1 per cent in 1800–10.

working year—the very long hours prevailing around 1800 must have taken their toll in fatigue and decreased efficiency.[262] None the less, for the reasons cited above, I believe a total efficiency offset to be very unlikely. For our historical analysis it therefore seems prudent to assume that η_H was between 0.5 and unity. This implies that the extended use of capital equipment has some positive effect on output over and above the one resulting from the added labour alone. At the same time, we also discount strongly the very large effects present in modern-day industry. Interestingly, even such a conservative assessment has important consequences for our view of economic development between 1760 and 1831—productivity grew barely at all.

In terms of per capita output, rising hours per member of the labour force may have been as important as increases in the capital–labour ratio. While capital stock per worker grew by 25 per cent over the whole period, hours increased by approximately 20 per cent; therefore, elasticities only slightly larger than 0.5 on hours imply that longer hours contributed more to per capita output growth than capital deepening in the economy.

Note, however, that technology may none the less have played an important role. Even if the efficiency with which the economy combined factors of production was falling, we assume in our slightly extended Solow framework that there are positive returns to capital, labour, and working hours. That these still existed at a time of spectacular population growth cannot be taken for granted. It is likely that, in the absence of technological advances, declining (and possibly negative) marginal returns to labour would have rapidly acted to depress the living standard of the population. Such interaction effects are not included in the standard growth accounting framework, and it is unlikely that explicit modelling can be achieved in a satisfactory manner. This potential 'veiled' influence of the adoption of more advanced techniques adds an important note of caution to any analysis of productivity change. Yet it is none the less important that, if hours of work are included in the Solow model, factor inputs grow at a rate that is more or less sufficient to explain all, or almost all of the increase in production.

This section's main contribution to the issue of technological change during the Industrial Revolution therefore lies in the fact that we do not have to attribute a substantial proportion of output growth

[262] Maddison, *Dynamic Forces*, 63.

to a 'residual'. Our calculations confirm Crafts's suspicion that, once labour input is more adequately measured, the contribution of TFP growth will be much reduced.[263] Productivity growth—'ingenuity', in McCloskey's phrase—may have played an even smaller role than is presently assumed in accounts of the British Industrial Revolution.[264] Output growth was largely driven by additional labour input, and it was an 'Industrious Revolution' (DeVries) that overcame the adverse effects of rapid population growth. Abstention seems to have been more important than invention, but it was abstention from leisure—as well as from consumption—that was at the heart of economic growth.[265]

Real Wages and Consumption

For our period, evidence on real wages on the one hand and on patterns of consumption on the other presents a conundrum. Schwarz finds a rapid fall in London real wages between the middle and the end of the eighteenth century.[266] Lindert and Williamson also find a reduction in real wages, but of a much smaller magnitude.[267] Feinstein's new series only starts in 1770, and shows a small improvement between this date and the turn of the century.[268] If his series is spliced onto the Lindert and Williamson series, we again find a fall in real earnings between the middle and the end of the eighteenth century; it is not before 1831 that real earnings are substantially above the level seen in mid-century.

At the same time, calculations of consumption per head of population show a clear gain between 1760 and 1801, and a pronounced improvement between 1801 and 1831. The approach using the macroeconomic accounting identity

---

[263] Crafts, *British Economic Growth*, 82.

[264] D. McCloskey, '1780–1860: A Survey', in R. Floud and ead. (eds.), *The Economic History of Britain Since 1700* (Cambridge, 1994), 267–8.

[265] DeVries, 'Industrial Revolution', 249 ff.

[266] Schwarz, 'Standard of Living', 28–9.

[267] Lindert and Williamson, 'English Workers' Living Standards', table 5, p. 13.

[268] Feinstein uses both weekly and daily data in the compilation of his series. It is not clear to what extent the definition of a 'full working week' may have changed over the period. For the purposes of this section, I assume his series captures daily wages accurately. If changes in the number of actual days worked per year are already reflected in the series (by a clandestine shift in the definition of a normal working week), then our analysis would be invalidated.

$$C \equiv Y + M - I - G - X \qquad (4.8)$$

[C = consumption, Y = domestic output, M = imports, I = investment, G = government spending, X = exports]

was first used by Feinstein to calculate changes in personal consumption during our period.[269] Combined with population estimates, we can easily infer consumption per head if the other variables are known. Crafts, using his new output figures, suggests that consumption rose by almost exactly 10 per cent between 1760 and 1801—if we set the figure for 1851 equal to 100, the respective values are 57.2 and 63.[270] Between 1801 and 1831 the increase is 21.6 per cent, to 76.6 per cent of the 1851 level. New estimates of output growth allow a reworking of the consumption series, using the same ratio of consumption to output as used initially by Crafts. If the new growth figures as recently presented by Crafts and Harley are used, the calculated change in per capita consumption between 1760 and 1801 is 10.6, marginally higher than the original value. Between 1801 and 1831, the rise is reduced to 18.8 per cent. The overall rise between 1760 and 1831 is now calculated as 31.4 per cent instead of the 33.9 per cent initially calculated by Crafts. Rising per capita consumption as inferred from national accounts coincided with probate inventories recording a rising stock of consumer goods being passed on from one generation to the next—at a time when wages were broadly stagnant (or increasing only very slightly).[271] Can the new estimates for labour input help to resolve the puzzle?

Consumption per capita net of saving will equal total wages earned by the labour force, divided by the size of the population.[272] As a first approximation, changes in income per head of population should evolve in line with the sum of changes in hours worked per member of the labour force, the labour force participation ratio, and the real wage. We can combine the new estimates from Chapter 3 with some of the real wage indices in the literature to examine if there is still evidence of conflicting trends. Table 4.12 gives the results. I have

---

[269] Charles H. Feinstein, 'Capital Accumulation and the Industrial Revolution', in Floud and McCloskey (eds.), *Economic History of Britain*, 128 ff.

[270] Crafts, *British Economic Growth*, table 5.2, p. 95.

[271] King, 'Pauper Inventories'. For general trends see DeVries, 'Purchasing Power'.

[272] This only applies, of course, if we disregard consumption financed by profits or income from private wealth. Since I am inferring rates of change over time, my results will only be biased if income from these sources did not fluctuate in parallel with the wage bill.

TABLE 4.12. *Real wages, hours, and consumption*

	C/Y	C p.c. (1760 = 100, revised)	Lindert and Williamson	Feinstein (1780 = 100)	Wage series (1760 = 100)	Hours— frequency	Hours— timing	C p.c implied (frequency, 1760 = 100)	C p.c implied (timing, 1760 = 100)
1760	0.744	100.0	42.74	(109)	100	2,706	2,760	100	100
1780	0.755	99.4	39.24	100	92				
1800	0.768	110.6		103	94	3,523	3,115	112.1	106.6
1831	0.795	131.4		114	105	3,256	3,366	121.6	127.6

Notes: col. 1 from Crafts, *British Economic Growth*, table 5.2, p. 95; col. 2 based on output estimates in id. and Harley, 'Output Growth' and col. 1 (see text); col. 3 from Lindert and Williamson, 'English Workers' Living Standards', table 5, p. 13; col. 4 from Feinstein, 'Pessimism Perpetuated', table 5, p. 648; col. 5 see text; col. 6 sectoral hours estimate from table 12.6; col. 7 timing-based estimate, method B; cols. 8 and 9 see text.

calculated the implied change in consumption per capita between 1760 and 1800, using the Feinstein series spliced onto the Lindert and Williamson estimates.[273] Alternative calculations using the frequency- and the timing-based estimates for labour input from above (p. 126) have been included to give a total of four results.

The Feinstein series implies a fall in per capita consumption of approximately 6 per cent between the middle and the end of the eighteenth centuries, and an increase over the whole period of 5 per cent,[274] whereas the (marginally) revised consumption series suggests an increase of 10.6 per cent between the middle and the end of the eighteenth century, and a rise between 1760 and 1831 of 31.4 per cent. Use of the new estimates for hours worked reduces the discrepancy markedly—the frequency method implies an increase in per capita consumption of 12 per cent for the first period, and 21.6 per cent overall. While no puzzle remains for the second half of the eighteenth century, the implied rate in 1831 is still 10 percentage points below the one inferred from national accounts. The timing-method is less successful during the second half of the nineteenth century, explaining only a 6 percentage points increase. For the period as a whole, it performs better, suggesting a 27.2 per cent increase overall.

The time-use data has further implications for the history of income. Lindert and Williamson recently re-examined Massie's social tables for England in 1759. In addition to revising his estimates for occupational composition, they argue that his guesses of family income at this time are too low.[275] Estimates of mean weekly income appear unconvincing when compared with daily wage rates from other sources. Dividing the former by the latter implies a working week of only 4.79 days.[276] Lindert and Williamson deem this figure much too low since they believe that there is overwhelming evidence for a 6-day working week at this time (or more than 25 per cent more than the implied figure), citing Bienefeld as a source. First, it is important to

---

[273] I used Lindert and Williamson, 'Living Standards', table 5, p. 13 and Feinstein, 'Pessimism Perpetuated', table 5, p. 648.

[274] Assuming that none of the additional factors that impact consumption changed significantly over the period.

[275] Lindert and Williamson, 'Revising England's Social Tables', 395–6.

[276] Their results are 4.9, 4.6, 4.1, and 4.95, giving an average of 4.64. Since one of their sources for daily wage rates (building labourers) actually gives a range of 20–4 d., I calculated an additional observation from the lower bound (equivalent to 5.4 days). Lindert and Williamson simply used the upper bound, thus biasing the result in favour of their argument.

note that Bienefeld was anything but firm on the matter, merely stating that the 6-day week was generally regarded as the norm.[277] Second, they do not take account of the large number of public and religious festivals still prevailing at this date. Converting the frequency-based estimate, assuming 11 hours per day, this suggests 4.73 working days per week. The timing-based estimate is somewhat higher, implying 4.83 working days per week.[278] Our first estimate diverges from Massie's figure only by 1.3 per cent, the second one by a mere 0.8 per cent. Our finding of a comparatively short working week in 1760 resolves the inconsistency in favour of Massie *and* it vindicates the accuracy of the contemporary daily wage estimates.

The value of these calculations is twofold. While it must be stressed that our simplifying assumptions diminish the accuracy of the exercise, and the time-use data only refer to London and a sample of Northern counties, it is none the less reassuring that our revised estimates for labour input go some way towards resolving some of the puzzles posed by conflicting evidence on consumption, income, and real wages. This is important if we believe that economic history should strive for a coherent image of the past. By fitting another piece into the puzzle (and connecting two disparate parts), the existing results and our findings reinforce each other. Further, the calculations in Table 4.12 are also of interest for the historiography of the Industrial Revolution, in that they cast further doubt on some optimistic interpretation of its early years—what limited gains in consumption existed were bought at the price of a reduction in leisure. The next section attempts to quantify the magnitude of this effect.

Welfare implications

Englishmen in 1800 and 1831 worked for longer than their counterparts in 1750. How did this affect the standard of living? Since Pigou, it has been commonplace amongst economists to distinguish a wider concept of social welfare from a more narrow economic one.[279] Here, I shall briefly discuss some of the consequences of increasing working hours on both categories of well-being.

[277] Bienefeld, *Working Hours in British Industry*, 36 ff.

[278] Again, using the timing-based, constant hours estimate under method B.

[279] Richard Easterlin, 'Does Economic Growth Improve the Human Lot?', in P. David and M. Reder (eds.), *Nations and Households in Economic Growth. Essays in Honor of Moses Abramovitz* (New York, 1974), 90.

Under normal circumstances, according to economic theory, work is a disamenity—the less the better.[280] Sametz was amongst the first to suggest that leisure is simply another commodity, that it can be consumed in very much the same way as bread or beer. He added the forgone earnings from leisure to his calculations of real income, assuming a maximum work-week of 78 hours: [281]

$$y_t = w_t h_t + 52w_t(78 - h_t) \qquad (4.9)$$

[Y_t is full income, w_t is the wage rate in year t, and h_t the number of working hours]

Using the Sametz method, we value the leisure consumed in year t by the real wage w_t in this year. Implicit in this is the assumption that leisure becomes more productive as wages increase.

Nordhaus and Tobin attempted to improve this approach by adding time spent in non-work activities.[282] They also augmented the Sametz technique by various assumptions about the relative productivity of non-work and leisure. Three alternatives exist. First, we could value non-market activity and leisure at constant rates. As real wages increase, the leisure and non-market component of total income would become smaller and smaller. Second, we can assume that leisure productivity remains constant over time, but that non-market work (do-it-yourself, housework, etc.) shows the same productivity pattern as market work. The third alternative is an extension of the Sametz approach, which values both time spent in non-market activities and leisure at present wage rates.

A widely used way of valuing leisure was proposed by Usher.[283] Changes in leisure compared to a certain base-year are valued at the wage rate of any given year and added to money income—the productivity of leisure changes with the wage rate:

$$y_t = w_t h_t + w_t(h_0 - h_t) \qquad (4.10)$$

---

[280] An elegant exposition of standard microeconomic theory can be found in Robert Frank, *Microeconomics and Behaviour* (New York, 1991), 484 ff). The assumption that work is a disamenity is rarely confirmed by empirical studies—in many cases, work is experienced as one of the most enjoyable activities. It almost always receives higher process benefit scores. See F. Thomas Juster, 'Preferences for Work and Leisure', in id. and Stafford, *Time*, table 13.1, p. 336.

[281] Dan Usher, *The Measurement of Economic Growth* (Oxford, 1980), 136.

[282] Nordhaus and Tobin 1972, cited ibid., 136.   [283] Ibid., 138 ff.

where h_o is the number of working hours in the base-year. If we use real wages in any given period to value leisure, instead of assuming static leisure productivity, the necessary adjustment of per capita income is smaller. Crafts estimated that the growth rate of real consumption per head between 1750 and 1851 would be reduced from 0.63 to 0.37.[284]

If we undertake an adjustment for changes in leisure alone, the effect is, as Crafts has shown, quite large. Because we impute a value to the time consumed as leisure in the earlier years, full income in 1760 would be raised relative to later periods; income growth would be correspondingly lower.[285] Using real wages in 1851 as an indicator of leisure productivity in earlier years, and assuming that annual labour input increased from 2,500 hours per year to 3,000, Crafts finds that per capita income growth 1760–1851 would only be 0.1 per cent per annum.[286] Thus, the inclusion of leisure lends further support to the revisionist view of the Industrial Revolution as a period of great structural change that was not accompanied by a major increase in per capita output.

The implications of including leisure in calculations of per capita consumption are even more pronounced if our new estimates for labour input are used. The upward movement found in Chapter 3 is larger than the one assumed by Crafts, and it is concentrated in a shorter period of time. Table 4.13 gives the new estimates for the years 1760–1801, using two alternative methods for valuing leisure.

The years 1760–1831 saw only very slow advances in per capita consumption adjusted for leisure if our estimates of annual labour input are used. The range of our estimates is relatively small—the minimum and the maximum of adjusted growth rates are 0.09 to 0.12 per cent per annum Independent of the scenario and assumption used, however, the net result remains positive.[287]

Better information on time-use in 1850 would clearly be welcome. It is unlikely that between 1830 and 1850 labour input changed as radically as it did between 1760 and 1830. Tranter's educated guess for 1850, which served as the basis for Crafts' calculations, would suggest a small reduction of workloads after 1831.[288] Matthews, Feinstein, and

---

[284] Crafts, *British Economic Growth*, 111.   [285] Ibid., ch. 5, app. 2, p. 114.

[286] Crafts' usage equates the wage rate with per capita consumption per hour worked. I follow this practice below.

[287] Note that this is not true for the period 1760–1801, when per capita consumption grew more slowly than working hours (under either method).

[288] Tranter, 'Labour Supply', 220–1.

TABLE 4.13. *Per capita consumption, 1760–1831 (growth in per cent p.a.)*

	Frequency-based estimates	Timing-based estimates
Unadjusted	0.38	0.38
Leisure productivity = Y/h 1831	0.10	0.10
Leisure productivity = Y/h 1760	0.12	0.09

Odling-Smee suggest a figure of 3,185 for 1856, which would imply a reduction of per capita labour input of between 0.09 and 0.22 per cent per annum between 1831 and 1856. Our findings therefore tend to reinforce the view that gains during the Industrial Revolution were minimal during the first seventy years. Improvements in living standards only become clearly visible towards the middle of the eighteenth century, when rising consumption, increasing full-time earnings, and reductions in annual workloads can be observed—arguably a case not of 'pessimism perpetuated', but pessimism reinforced.[289]

When discussing the implications of changes in leisure for living standards, Crafts concluded that the potential revisions were very large compared to the magnitudes of conventional variables. Uncertainty about the direction and size of shifts in labour supply, and difficulties over which valuation method to use, strongly suggested that adjustments for changes in leisure should only be made for illustrative purposes. The evidence on changes in hours presented here is, as has already been stressed, far from certain. Yet it replaces vague conjectures with empirical estimates. Also, because of the specific values derived, issues of valuation methodology are less pertinent—independent of the question if leisure productivity changed over the period or not, for example, the most optimistic estimate of changes in per capita consumption per annum is now only one-third of the value before adjustments for changes in leisure.

[289] Feinstein, 'Pessimism Perpetuated'.

5
Comparisons and Conclusion

Early industrial Britain experienced 'the longest years'—in terms of hours worked per member of the labour force—around 1800. The previous chapter sought to explain the causes underlying the rise in labour input, and discussed some implications for the history of the Industrial Revolution. Yet how do the patterns of time-use found amongst our witnesses compare with patterns of labour and leisure observed in other countries and periods? This is the question that the first part will address, providing comparisons with the sociological and anthropological literature on today's societies, both in the Third World and in industrialized countries. The second part adopts a more historical perspective. Following the work of Crafts, I attempt to establish a 'norm' of time-use relative to the attained level of economic development using cross-country comparisons. Britain's experience is then compared with this standard. Finally, the results obtained in this study are summarized and discussed together with the implications for future research.

How Exceptional was Early Industrial Britain?

The total number of working hours during the first eight decades of Britain's Industrial Revolution—according to our calculations in earlier chapters—was remarkably high. While the estimates for the 1750s are similar to the ones for the third quarter of the nineteenth century, the values for 1830 are higher than any figures for annual labour input either before or after this date. The upper bound for 1800 suggests even longer hours of toil. This section seeks a more comprehensive basis for comparisons. I present data on time-use from 35 individual studies, conducted in areas as diverse as the Upper Amazon of 1975 and 1960s America. Before proceeding to the results of sociological time-budget studies I shall first briefly summarize the anthropological literature.

Societies studied by anthropologists can be categorized according to economic activity. The most 'primitive' groups live by the oldest forms of food production—hunting, gathering, and fishing. While many tribes under this heading move often, some (particularly in coastal regions) are static. The most important characteristic, however, is that no effort at *producing* foodstuffs is made—all the food consumed is provided by nature, without more human intervention than the gathering of fruits. Typically, hunting-gathering communities exist in sparsely populated territories.[1] The other extreme is marked by plough agriculture or irrigated rice cultivation. These forms of food production are not only sedentary, but also require complex ways of working, fertilizing, and harvesting the land. At its most advanced, two or more crops are harvested in the same field each year without any fallow.[2] Between these two extremes of 'permanent fallow' and great intensity of land-use, there exists a wide spectrum of systems supplying food.[3] In what follows, I shall only distinguish between three different forms of agriculture—hunting-gathering, intermediate, and advanced. The last refers to all societies which produce at least one crop per year from the land.

Distinct contrasts in time-use between these societies emerge when this simplified classification scheme is applied.[4] Hunting-gathering communities show a generally low level of total labour input. Initial research had suggested the opposite.[5] From the early 1960s onwards, however, more and more studies emerged that showed just how short the average working day in these societies is. The first indication came from a study by McCarthy and McArthur.[6] There were two groups in their sample: aborigines in Fish Creek and in Hemple Bay (West Arnhem Land, Australia). The latter worked for an average of 5 hours and 8 minutes per day, while the former spent 3 hours and 47 minutes in such activities. Differences between men and women were small. On average, the aborigines in West Arnhem Land spent only 4 hours and 28 minutes in food-related activities.

---

[1] Boserup has argued that the adoption of more advanced techniques is largely driven by population densities. See Esther Boserup, *Population and Technology* (Oxford, 1981); ead., *The Conditions of Agricultural Growth: The Economics of Agrarian Change under Population Pressure* (New York, 1965).　　　　　　　　　　　[2] See ead., *Population and Technology*, 19.

[3] Boserup (ibid., table 3.2, p. 19) presents one possible classification scheme.

[4] Here and below, average values for men and women are presented because our data on London do not allow us to produce accurate estimates of female labour input.

[5] Julian Steward and Lewis Faron, *Native Peoples of South America* (New York, 1959), 60.

[6] F. McCarthy and M. McArthur, 'The Food Quest and the Time Factor in Aboriginal Economic Life', in Charles Pearcy Montfourd (ed.), *Records of the Australian-American Scientific Expedition to Arnhem Land*, ii (Melbourne, 1960).

It was Marshall Sahlins who first related these findings systematically to similar results for !Kung Bushmen in the Kalahari, who work an average of 2 hours and 9 minutes.[7] The consequence has been a reversal of the earlier consensus, which saw hunter-gatherers as engaged in a permanent struggle with nature, only wresting from it with great difficulty the food necessary for survival. Later research has largely endorsed Sahlins's view regarding hours of work—even if not every scholar has shared his assessment of the 'Original Affluent Society'.[8] Subsequent studies are somewhat superior since they often encompass a wider range of work-related activities, rather than restricting 'work' to food-gathering alone. The Kayapo in northern Brazil, who earn their livelihood by hunting and gathering, work for 3.9 hours (men) to 4.9 hours (women).[9] Johnson, studying the Machiguenga in the Upper Amazon who engage in slash-and burn gardening as well as gathering, found an average of 6 hours for men and 7.4 for women in total labour time.[10] These figures are very similar to the ones reported by Hill *et al.* in a study of the Ache of Paraguay. The males in this hunting-gathering community spend 7 hours per day in food-related activities.[11] Even if the variance among different societies of hunter-gatherers is high, average workloads always remain below 8 hours per day—the average is only 4.86.

Much longer hours of toil are registered among societies practising sedentary agriculture. The record number of hours of work per day was found among female French Swiss, who in the 1950s toiled for an average of 13.65 hours per day.[12] Other areas of the Swiss Alps, also engaged in agropastoralism and plough agriculture, show similarly long hours of work. Minge-Klevana finds 9.4 hours for women and

[7] Marshall Sahlins, *Stone Age Economics* (Chicago, 1974), 21 ff; Richard Lee, 'What Hunters Do for a Living, or, How to Make Out on Scarce Resources', in id. and Irven DeVore (eds.), *Man the Hunter* (Chicago, 1968); id., '!Kung Bushman Subsistence: An Input–Output Analysis', in Andrew Vayda (ed.), *Environment and Cultural Behaviour* (New York, 1969).

[8] K. Hill, H. Kaplan, K. Hawkes, and A. Hurtado, 'Men's Time Allocation to Subsistence Work among the Ache of Eastern Paraguay', *Human Ecology*, 13 (1985).

[9] Wanda Minge-Klevana, 'Does Labour Time Decrease with Industrialization? A Survey of Time-Allocation Studies', *Current Anthropology*, 21 (1980), 281.

[10] Allen Johnson, 'Time Allocation in a Machiguenga Community', *Ethnology*, 14 (1975).

[11] Hill *et al.*, 'Men's Time Allocation'.

[12] Jean Nicollier, 'Recherches sur la rénovation de l'organisme de la production dans l'agriculture: l'exemple de Medieres, Valais', in J. Loup (ed.), *Pasteurs et agricultures valaisans* (Grenoble, 1950).

7.2 for men.[13] On the basis of a larger sample, Haffter and Minder observe an average of 11.1 hours per day.[14] Rice cultivation, as found among the Kali Loro of Java, requires 10 hours per day.[15] Coffee and banana growing also makes strong demands on the labour force—the Muhero in Rwanda work for 11.1 hours per day (males) and 11.3 hours per day (females).[16] Nepalese villagers engaged in plough agriculture average 11.4 hours.

Between these two extremes, societies combining sedentary agriculture with forms of hunting and gathering register moderate levels of work. The Tenía Mayo of Mexico work for 9 hours a day in gardening, fishing, hunting, and animal husbandry.[17] Hoe agriculture among the Bemba in Northern Rhodesia, practised in combination with fishing and hunting, requires an average of 4.7 hours per day. Maize agriculture, combined with gathering, took 8.6 hours of the time of female Kikuyu in Kenya.[18] Table 5.1 summarizes the evidence.

The areas in which more advanced forms of agriculture developed also show very long working hours. This is no proof that the arrival of sedentary agriculture in the past caused an increase in working hours—cross-sectional data should not be confused with time-series. The Kali Loro of Java, for example, when they were still engaged in hunting and gathering, may have had to work longer hours than the hunting-gathering communities which still exist today. The latter would then only have continued their traditional lifestyle because it offered such an advantageous combination of working hours and resources. The failure to develop more advanced forms of food production could possibly be the result of favourable economic conditions—as demonstrated by short working hours. Independent of the type of community with which we compare the Old Bailey data, the working day derived in Chapter 3 appears very long. Only the most labour-intensive forms of cultivation require daily working hours similar to those found in eighteenth-century England (10–12 hours).

---

[13] Wanda Minge-Klevana, 'Household Economy During the Peasant-to-Worker Transition in the Swiss Alps', *Ethnology*, 17 (1978).

[14] Andreas Haffter and Barbara Minder, *Arbeitsbeanspruchung und soziale Stellung der Bäuerin: Ergebnisse einer Voruntersuchung auf 25 Ostschweizer Bauernhöfen* (Tanecon, 1973).

[15] Benjamin White, *Problems in Estimating the Value of Work in Peasant Household Economies: An Example from Rural Java* (Bogor, 1979).

[16] Minge-Klevana, 'Does Labour Time Decrease with Industrialization?'.

[17] Charles Erasmus, 'Work Patterns in a Mayo Village' *American Anthropologist*, 57 (1955).

[18] Audrey Richards, *Land, Labour and Diet in Northern Rhodesia* (London, 1939); Minge-Klevana, 'Does Labour Time Decrease with Industrialization?'.

TABLE 5.1. *Working hours in agricultural societies*

Hunting-gathering communities		'Mixed'		Advanced sedentary agriculture	
group	h/day	group	h/day	group	h/day
Fish Creek, West Arnhem Land	5.1	Tenía Mayo, Mexico	9.0	French Swiss (female)	13.7
Hemple Bay, West Arnhem Land	3.8	Bemba, Northern Rhodesia	4.7	Swiss Alps	8.3
!Kung Bushmen, Kalihari	2.2	Kikuyu, Kenya	8.6	Swiss Alps	11.1
Kayapo, Northern Brazil	4.4			Kali Loro, Java	10.0
Machiguenga, Upper Amazon	6.7			Muhero, Rwanda	11.2
Ache, Paraguay	7.0			Nepal	11.4
Average	4.9		7.4		10.9

There is a wealth of information on the gender division of labour in anthropological studies. We can almost always ascertain the length of the working day for both men and women. Unfortunately, the restricted size of our English sample makes it impossible to evaluate female work accurately.[19] Since differences in working and leisure time between the sexes are potentially important indicators of discrimination and gender roles, future additions to our dataset may yield large returns.[20]

One shortcoming of the anthropological literature is evident—we have very little information on the number of working days in the

---

[19] The difference between the times of starting and stopping work, used to infer the length of the working day for men, would be a misleading indicator. In the case of women, this information is scarce; it would also be inaccurate since much additional work is conducted in the household, where no continuous work activities with a clearly defined beginning and end take place.

[20] The number of additional observations would have to be sufficient to move from comparisons of starting and stopping to frequency-based measurement.

year. Many anthropological studies are only carried out over a few days or weeks—annual labour input can only indirectly be inferred from these studies.[21] Even when data collection was carried out during all the months of the year, sampling techniques are often applied—e.g. every eighth day was recorded. Holidays, etc. may easily escape such methods.[22] Yet the most important finding of this thesis concerns not the length of the working day in England, but changes in the weekly and annual distribution of workloads. We may be inclined to think that it is inherently unlikely for any agricultural society to match the 300 + working days per year found in England in 1800–30, but there is little empirical evidence to bolster such an assessment. It is none the less safe to conclude that no society examined by anthropologists registered a higher labour input than the one inferred for eighteenth-century England.

Just how unusual the levels found in Chapter 3 are also emerges from a comparison with modern-day data. All the countries for which we have data are industrialized nations in either the West or in the (then) Communist bloc. I shall first briefly summarize the evidence on daily working hours before discussing annual labour input. Although there is a much larger number of studies, I shall limit comparisons of the 'average working day' to data from the Multinational Comparative Time-Budget Research Project (MCTRP). This is for two reasons. First, only the studies conducted under the auspices of the MCTRP use similar categories and study designs, therefore yielding comparable estimates. Second, the majority of additional studies was conducted after the multinational comparative project had been finished. At a time of generally falling working hours,[23] our standard of comparison will therefore provide a lower-bound on the contrast between eighteenth-century London and the modern period.

[21] The studies on Switzerland are the exceptions that prove the rule.

[22] The only study to avoid such pitfalls (Eva Mueller, 'The Value and Allocation of Time in Rural Botswana', *Journal of Development Economics*, 15 (1984)) unfortunately restricts itself to the number of days in paid employment.

[23] Some recent studies (Juliet Schor, *The Overworked American. The Unexpected Decline of Leisure* (New York, 1991); Geoff Mulgan and H. Wilkinson, 'Well-being and Time', *Demos Quarterly*, 5 (1995)) have argued that hours of work are actually rising rather than falling. The empirical basis of such claims is weak (J. Gershuny *et al.*, 'Time Budgets: Preliminary Analyses of a National Survey', *Quarterly Journal of Social Affairs*, 2 (1986)) and also largely concerns differences between the 1990s and the 1980s. Compared with the 1960s, hours of work have fallen almost everywhere in the industrialized world.

TABLE 5.2. *Working time in Eastern and Western Europe and North America, 1965–6*

	Men	Women	Average
USA (Jackson)	6.50	7.9	7.20
Federal Republic of Germany (Osnabrück)	6.90	8.0	7.45
Federal Republic of Germany (100 districts)	6.80	8.9	7.85
USA (44 cities)	7.50	8.3	7.90
Belgium	7.50	9.1	8.30
Yugoslavia (Kragujevac)	7.20	9.5	8.35
USSR (Pskov)	6.93	10.0	8.45
Bulgaria	7.90	9.8	8.85
Poland	7.80	10.0	8.90
German Democratic Republic	8.10	9.9	9.00
Yugoslavia (Maribor)	7.60	11.0	9.30
Czechoslovakia	8.10	11.1	9.60
Hungary	8.10	11.1	9.60

Table 5.2 summarizes the daily work-schedules from 14 different MCTRP studies.[24] The figures are given for a 7-day week. To make our figures from the Old Bailey and the Northern Assize comparable, we therefore have to multiply by 0.857, assuming a six-day week on average. The lowest figure for daily hours (from London in 1800) is very safely within the range of MCTRP estimates. It is higher than the estimates from any Western country, but lower than the ones for the former Eastern bloc. The highest estimate however (9.85 hours/day, using data from the North in 1830) implies a longer working day than even the one observed in Hungary.

The estimates for England in 1800–30 are even more unusual when we focus on annual labour input. The countries in Table 5.2 provide workers with substantial vacations, and a considerable number of public holidays are observed. Londoners in the early years of the nineteenth century did not enjoy such benefits. Consequently, the working year was 13 to 19 per cent longer than even in the most work-inclined country during the 1960s, Japan, which registered 2,318 hours per year.[25] Even ninety years earlier, Maddison's data suggest that working hours were no more than a maximum of 2,984 hours per

---

[24] Alexander Szalai, *The Use of Time* (The Hague, 1972), vi. 5, 785 ff.
[25] Angus Maddison, *Dynamic Forces in Capitalist Development* (Oxford, 1991), table C. 9, p. 271.

year in any of today's industrialized nations.[26] Our estimate of 3,231 to 3,439 hours in 1830 is therefore higher than any other observed figure for annual labour input. A word of caution is, however, necessary—the reliability of any estimate before the First World War is quite low.[27]

This concludes our brief survey of working hours and comparisons with the length of the working day and year observed in eighteenth-century London. Neither sociological evidence from developed countries nor anthropological studies from the Third World have uncovered societies that knew markedly longer hours of work than the English did during the first three decades of the nineteenth century. Our estimates are consistently close to (or above, depending on the use of upper or lower bounds) the highest figure identified anywhere else. While the daily working schedule is still within the range of other societies, the same is not true of the working year. The tentative estimates derived in the preceding chapter are considerably above the number of working hours identified in other countries and periods. The error band around these figures is substantial, but probably not larger than the margin between the observed levels and our estimates of annual labour input in England in 1830.

While the number of hours worked in England at the beginning of the nineteenth century was unusual, the same cannot be said for hours of sleep. Let us assume that the point estimate for the most extreme observation—in the case of London in 1800, we calculated an average of 6 hours and 35 minutes—accurately reflects experience.[28] Six and a half hours of sleep may seem very short for us. Approximately eight hours are the norm in industrialized countries today.[29] This is not to say that the number of hours of sleep is below the range observed in some countries and for some groups. Japanese college students sleep for 47.6 hours per week or 6 hours and 48 minutes a day; early time-use studies also suggest that Russian peasant women had to make do

---

[26] Ibid. Note that Michael Huberman and Wayne Lewchuk ('Glory Days? Work Hours, Labor Market Regulations and Convergence in Late Nineteenth-Century Europe', paper presented at the All-U.C. Group in Economic History Conference, University of California, Davis, 14–16 November 1997) have presented alternative estimates, which confirm our overall conclusions.

[27] Walter G. Hoffmann (*Das Wachstum der deutschen Wirtschaft seit der Mitte des 19. Jahrhunderts* (Berlin, 1965), table 2, p. 19), on the basis of rough calculations, arrives at somewhat higher figures.

[28] Recall that the difference between the two estimates for hours of sleep was not statistically significant. [29] Szalai, *The Use of Time*, table 1, p. 114.

with even fewer hours of sleep. [30] I showed that annual working hours increased. Today, we can easily observe differences in the number of hours of sleep on weekdays and the weekend. When the demands of work subside, people spend more time on other activities. Sleep is one of these. A recent American study found that, for every 10 minutes less work, people are likely to spend an additional 6.8 minutes on sleep. [31] Such a high elasticity is surprising, particularly since the average for weekdays is already almost eight hours of sleep. If we now assume that exactly the same trade-off between work and sleep was made almost two hundred years ago,[32] we would predict a reduction in sleeping hours of 1 hour and 48 minutes in London between 1760 and 1800, and of 8 minutes in the North over the same period.[33] Clearly, these figures are not identical with the 45 minutes in London and 24 minutes in the North that we find, but the similarity of the order of

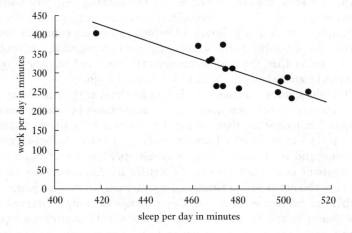

FIGURE 5.1. *Sleep and work in twelve countries*

[30] F. Thomas Juster and Frank Stafford, 'The Allocation of Time: Empirical Findings, Behavioral Models, and Problems of Measurement', *Journal of Economic Literature*, 29 (1991), table 4, p. 480.

[31] M. Hill, 'Patterns of Time Use', in F. Juster and F. Stafford (eds.), *Time, Goods, and Well-Being* (Ann Arbor, Mich., 1985), table 7.9, pp. 167 ff.

[32] Of course, forgoing sleep for a few days is much less difficult than to do so for prolonged periods.

[33] Using the timing-based estimates with varying hours per day. The same calculation for 1800–30 leads to an expected reduction in sleep in the North of 1 hour (versus a calculated change of 40 minutes), and of 14 minutes in London (versus an actual increase of 1 hour and 47 minutes).

magnitude is striking—I compare responses in America during the 1980s with time-series data from the eighteenth century.

I have also regressed the number of hours of sleep from Szalai's multinational study on the number of hours of work (Figure 5.1).[34] The coefficient is −0.35, which would suggest a reduction in sleeping time by 56 and 11 minutes a day in London and the North between 1760 and 1800.[35] Importantly, the order of magnitude never differs markedly from the observed reduction in sleeping hours. Unfortunately, anthropological studies are largely silent on the issue of sleep and rest since most confine themselves to daylight hours. The information on sleep that we do possess from the Third World is concerned with naps and periods of rest during the day.[36] It may also be interesting to note that some of the modern elasticities would suggest an even stronger reduction in sleeping hours than the one that occurred.[37]

Explaining the Unusual: Working Hours and Development

The hours and, in particular, the number of days of work found in industrializing Britain were unusual. This is the conclusion above, where our data were contrasted with results from anthropological and sociological research. Comparisons can be conducted in more than one way. We may ask if a certain property, such as the number of hours of work, has ever been observed in the same range. I used this approach in the preceding section. Alternatively, we can attempt to explain a phenomenon by another factor—e.g., income per head. Comparisons are then no longer restricted to levels alone. If our explanation of the phenomenon under consideration is a good one, we can develop a sense of 'normal' levels under the given circumstances. We may then be able to demonstrate that, even controlling for certain factors, the observed level was or was not unusually high.

This section attempts to apply such an analysis to the issue of working time. As economies developed, average working hours fell. While

---

[34] I used the data in Szalai, *The Use of Time*, table 1, p. 114.

[35] The t-statistic (−4.7) is highly significant, and the total share of variation explained is high (adj. $R^2 = 0.6$). Sample size was close to the acceptable minimum (N = 15; three countries provided data on two sites).

[36] See Sahlins, *Stone Age Economics*, 14, 19, 26; Johnson, 'Time Allocation'; Erasmus, 'Work Patterns'.

[37] It should be borne in mind that we use 'out-of-sample' elasticities—the range of experience (in terms of sleeping hours per day) is substantially above the historical levels.

the average working year during the late nineteenth century had approximately 2,900 hours, this has declined by almost one-half to 1,600 hours per year.[38] This section examines more closely how the length of the working year has varied with stages of development. The aim is to compare time-use in Britain between 1760 and 1800 with the experience of other countries. Following Crafts, the British case is placed in the context of other industrializing nations.

Method

Kuznets was the first to examine a large sample of European nations in the nineteenth century in search of characteristics that were common to the development process.[39] By investigating systematic variations in social and economic indicators normally associated with rising levels of income, his aim was to identify proximate causes of industrialization. Chenery and Syrquin extended Kuznets's approach to the modern world. Using data from 101 countries between 1950 and 1970, they produce tables of typical values for variables such as crude death rates, consumption as a percentage of national expenditure or the proportion of the country's workforce employed in the primary sector at different stages of development. These were estimated on the basis of the following equation:

$$X = \alpha + \beta_1 Y + \beta_2 Y^2 + \gamma_1 N + \gamma_2 N^2 \qquad (5.1)$$

[X = dependent variable, Y = GNP per capita, N = population]

In order to take possible non-linearities into account, the squared values of GNP per capita and population size were also included. The fit was good for most of their regressions. None the less, there was almost always a substantial amount of variation left unexplained by estimates of equation (5.1). The predicted values at different income levels become the 'typical' values for certain socio-economic characteristics at different stages of industrial growth.[40] At an income level of $100 per capita, for example, they find that societies are most likely to register 22 per cent of the population living in towns. The urban share increases to 60.1 per cent when income rises to $800 per head.[41]

---

[38] Maddison, *Dynamic Forces*, appendix C, table 9, pp. 270–1.
[39] Simon Kuznets, *National Income and its Composition* (New York, 1941).
[40] In calculating typical values, they use a population size of 10 million. See Hollis Chenery and Moshe Syrquin, *Patterns of Development, 1950–1970* (London, 1975), table 3, p. 21.　　　　　　　　　　　　　　　　　　　　　　　[41] Ibid., table 3, pp. 20–1.

Crafts has applied the Chenery–Syrquin framework to European industrialization before the First World War.[42] He then compares the British case with the 'typical pattern' of economic development. Several features distinguish economic change in Britain during the Industrial Revolution from the experience of other European nations. First, income growth was markedly slower than on the continent, with most countries needing about 70 per cent less time to move from an income level of $1,100 to $1,500.[43] Second, the shift out of agriculture was much more rapid than could have been expected on the basis of Chenery–Syrquin equations. While merely 39.9 per cent of the labour force worked the land in Britain in 1800, the European norm for the same income level was 62.3 per cent. Further, the sectoral productivity gap was small. While most nations showed a lower proportion of agriculture in national income than in total employment, the same was not true in the British case.[44]

Working Hours in Britain, 1760–1830: A Comparative View

We can apply the Chenery–Syrquin methodology to the case of working hours. Unfortunately, the authors do not include the amount of time devoted to productive uses in their work. I have therefore followed Crafts's example, repeating the exercise for a set of 16 nations between 1870 and 1987.[45]

Several features of the dataset have to be borne in mind. First, the data come exclusively from industrialized countries. Observations on both per capita income levels and working hours over such a long period of time are only available for these nations. Whereas some of Crafts's comparative data goes back to 1840, the starting point for my series is 1870.[46] Data came from Maddison's *Dynamic Forces in Capitalist Development*.[47] The estimates of working hours are of a particularly low quality for the earlier part of the period.[48] Note that

---

[42] N. F. R. Crafts, *British Economic Growth during the Industrial Revolution* (Oxford, 1985), ch. 3, pp. 48 ff; id., 'Patterns of Development in Nineteenth Century Europe', *Oxford Economic Papers*, 36 (1984).

[43] Id., *British Economic Growth*, 61. I converted the 1970$ used by Crafts into 1985$ in order to make the figures compatible with the analysis that is to follow. The original figures cited by Crafts are $400 and $550.   [44] Ibid., 60–1, table 3.6, pp. 62–3.

[45] The countries are Austria, Australia, Belgium, Canada, Denmark, Finland, France, Germany, Italy, Japan, the Netherlands, Norway, Sweden, Switzerland, the United Kingdom, and the United States.   [46] Crafts, *British Economic Growth*, table 3.2, p. 54.

[47] Maddison, *Dynamic Forces*.   [48] Ibid., 255 ff.

Britain's level of per capita GDP in the eighteenth century is fully within the range of experience in the OECD dataset—in 1870, for example, Japan ($618) and Finland ($933) are definitely poorer. None the less, they have fewer hours of annual labour input—a little less than 3,000 per year. Such a consideration can only be a first step in controlling for the various parameters that may influence working hours. The next step therefore is to estimate a Chenery–Syrquin model.

Population size in our sample varied from 1.6 million to 244 million, GDP per capita (in 1985$) from 618 to 17,339, and working hours from 1,387 to 2,984. There was therefore no lack of identifying variance for the Chenery–Syrquin regressions. Table 5.3 presents the results.

TABLE 5.3. *Determinants of working hours*

	REGRESSION	
	1	2
INDEPENDENT VARIABLES		
GDP/CAPITA	-0.197***	-0.118***
	(-10.68)	(-3.77)
(GDP/CAPITA)^2	7.15E-0**	2.33E-06
	(5.91)	(1.09)
N	-0.0016	-0.00056
	(-1.44)	(-0.29)
N^2	8.03E-09	5.35E-09
	(1.28)	(0.56)
CONSTANT	3022.37***	2775.6***
	(55.49)	(24.7)
SUMMARY STATISTICS		
adj. R^2	0.75	0.71
S.E.	220.5	206.75
N	141	40

** and *** significant at the 95 and 99 per cent levels.
Notes: T-statistics in parentheses. Estimation technique: OLS. Eq. 1: full sample. Eq. 2: Germany, Japan, the Netherlands, United Kingdom and the United States, 1890–1987.
Sources: GDP: Maddison, *Dynamic Forces*, App. A, table 2, p. 198; Population: ibid. table B2, p. 228; Hours: ibid. App. C, table 9, pp. 270–1.

Both equations explain a high proportion of the observed variation, and the standard error of the regressions is low.[49] Their quality is very similar to the better ones reported by Chenery and Syrquin.[50] Rising levels of per capita income show a strong and statistically significant association with shorter hours of work. The effect diminishes as incomes grow, suggesting that the additional benefit of extra hours of leisure is also subject to diminishing returns. Note that this non-linearity is only significant for the full sample (eq. 1). Population shows no significant influence on the length of the working year, and there is no evidence of a non-linear association. This directly contradicts the widespread view that longer hours were often the result of population pressure.[51] Figure 5.2 also shows that GDP per capita alone explains a high proportion of changes in time allocation.

The problem with regression (1) is that the error term indicates heteroscedasticity. This is due to the presence of a large number of less-developed nations which had similar lengths of the working year. Because of this and the questionable quality of the data on hours

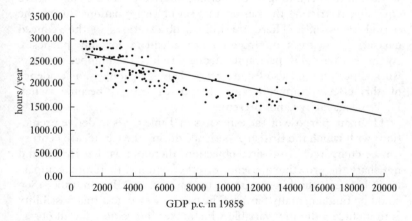

FIGURE 5.2. *Working hours and GDP in sixteen countries, 1870–1989*

[49] Low Durbin–Watson statistics (0.79 and 1.2) indicate serial correlation. After correcting for this source of bias, using the Cochrane–Orcutt method, the parameter estimates were not significantly different from those in table 2.

[50] Chenery and Syrquin, *Patterns of Development*, 200–14.

[51] See E. H. Phelps Brown, *et al.*, 'Labour Hours: Hours of Work', *Encyclopedia of the Social Sciences* 7 (New York, 1968) 487; Boserup, *Population and Technology*, 121–2; ead., *Conditions of Agricultural Growth*. Of course, this may none the less be true in other countries or periods.

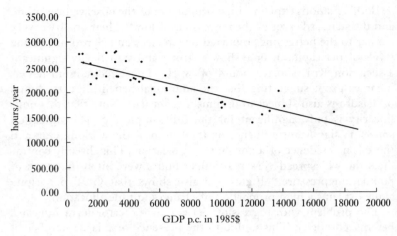

FIGURE 5.3. *Work and GDP in six countries*

worked at the beginning of the period, I have estimated an alternative equation, restricting the sample to a set of larger nations during the period 1890–1987. There are still 40 observations in the reduced dataset; 35 degrees of freedom are adequate for our purposes. Again, rises in GDP per capita strongly reduce the number of hours worked per year (cf. also Figure 5.3). There is no longer any evidence of this effect diminishing in strength as nations become richer. Heteroscedasticity is not present.

The main purpose of the estimates in Table 5.3 is to derive predictions with which the British experience during the eighteenth century can be compared. A possible objection, therefore, is that Britain did not share the growth experience of other nations; therefore, comparisons between the larger sample of nations and Britain 1760–1800 could be fundamentally flawed. The easiest way to test this possibility is to include a dummy variable which takes the value 1 for all observations from the UK, 0 otherwise. When the UK dummy is added to eq. (1), the t-statistic is 0.593, suggesting that it is not significantly different from zero. There is therefore no evidence of Britain *after 1870* constituting a special case.

Before we can proceed, however, it is interesting to consider the range of experience underlying Figures 5.2 and 5.3. At an income level of approximately \$1,500, for example, annual workloads varied between 2,945 hours (France 1870) to 2,166 (Japan 1950). These are

TABLE 5.4. *Working hours at different income levels*

| | Per capita income, $1985 | | | |
	$500	$1,000	$1,800	$2,500
Mean estimate	2,920	2,830	2,690	2,570
Lower bound	2,800	2,680	2,510	2,360
Upper bound	3,050	2,970	2,870	2,790

extreme cases, but it is important to remember that the 'typical' values presented in Table 5.4 are derived from data showing substantial variation that is not associated with GDP per head.[52]

Despite the occasional outlier in the data, the differences between upper and lower bounds are not large. At $500 per capita, the highest possible estimates consistent with 95 per cent confidence intervals around the intercept and the exogenous variables yield a prediction that is only 9 per cent higher than the lower bound.

The latest estimates by Crafts and Harley suggest per capita income of $1,080 in 1760, $1,160 in 1801, and $1,333 in 1831.[53] Two differences between the experience of industrialized counties and Britain during the Industrial Revolution are immediately apparent. First, our estimates for annual working hours in 1801 and 1831 are higher than even the upper bound estimates for similar levels of income. In 1760 the observed levels are safely within the range of experience in other countries. For 1801 they are slightly higher—and in 1831 hundreds of hours higher than even the upper bound from the Chenery–Syrquin regressions suggests.

Second, and perhaps more importantly, we have found a substantial increase in annual workloads at the same time when per capita output was growing.[54] This is the exact reverse of the relationship observed in our large sample of nations.

[52] Since the object of the exercise is to arrive at forecast values and not a causal explanation, eq. (1) was used because of its slightly better fit and despite the heteroscedasticity problem.

[53] Knick Harley, 'Reassessing the Industrial Revolution: A Macro View', in J. Mokyr (ed.), *The British Industrial Revolution: An Economic Perspective* (Boulder, Colo., 1993) table 3.4, p. 194. 1970$ converted into 1985$ at a rate of 1/2.7.

[54] N. F. R. Crafts and Knick Harley, 'Output Growth and the British Industrial Revolution: A Restatement of the Crafts–Harley View', *Economic History Review*, 45 (1992) table 4, p. 715. Critics of the Crafts–Harley view have argued that they *underestimated* growth rates. Cf. Maxine Berg and Pat Hudson, 'Rehabilitating the Industrial Revolution', *Economic History Review*, 45 (1992), 24 ff. Note also that divergences between real earnings growth and GDP growth could potentially be responsible—in the long run, shifts in income shares will have only a small influence, but they can be responsible for short-term divergences. Charles Feinstein ('Wage-earnings in Great Britain during the Industrial

TABLE 5.5. *British working hours and the OECD 'norm'*

		1760	1801	1831
Income (1985 US$)		1,080	1,160	1,333
Implied by Chenery–Syrquin regressions	*upper bound*	2,970	2,960	2,939
	'norm'	2,809	2,790	2,751
	lower bound	2,647	2,619	2,563
Calculated from witnesses' reports	*upper bound*	2,829	3,523	3,483
	lower bound	2,646	2,999	3,231

These findings suggest the possibility that factors inherent in Britain's role as the 'first industrial nation' caused it to be different, and that the divergence from the 'OECD norm' highlights a peculiar characteristic of its growth process. This is the argument of the following section, which develops a slightly more complex theoretical explanation and conducts an empirical test.

The Burden of Being First—A Speculation

It is conspicuous that, compared with Europe in the nineteenth century, working hours in today's Third World are short. The workweek is rarely 25 per cent longer than in the rich OECD countries, where 40 hours or less are the norm. This is in marked contrast with the 60 to 80 hours common in industrializing countries of 100 years ago. In this part, I will argue that the factor which causes this systematic difference is also largely responsible for the outstanding number of working hours found in eighteenth-century England. As the whole world gradually industrializes, the adoption of more advanced manufacturing techniques in one country requires fewer and fewer hours of labour input. First, I briefly discuss the evidence contrasting working time in Europe before the First World War and in today's less developed countries (LDCs). I then develop a simple model that explains why the 'first industrial nation' had to endure particularly long

---

Revolution', in I. Begg (ed.), *Applied Economics and Public Policy* (Cambridge, 1998), 200–2) recently argued that there is growing evidence for increasing income inequality in Britain during the Industrial Revolution.

hours of arduous toil. I conclude with a simple empirical test of this theoretical model.

Table 5.6 gives a more detailed comparison of weekly working hours in developing countries in 1985 and the industrializing

TABLE 5.6. *Weekly working hours in the developing world and industrializing Europe*

Developing countries	GNP p. c. (1985$)	Hours/ week	European countries pre-1913	GDP p.c (1985$)	Hours/ week
	(1)	(2)		(3)	(4)
Sri Lanka, 1985	370	47.4(b)	Germany, 1820/30	937(n)	75(h)
Ecuador, 1985	1,150	44.0(a)	Germany, 1870/80	1,300(j)	72(i)
Korea, 1985	2,260	49.0(a)	Britain, 1856	1,888(m)	65
Thailand, 1985	1,020	48.6(a)	Britain, 1873	2,610(j)	56
Egypt, 1985	620	56.0(b)	France, 1856	1,379(m)	72
Kenya, 1985	300	42.0(b)	France, 1910	2,734(l)	60(k)
Bolivia, 1985	440	44.9(a)	USA, 1832	1,048(n)	67.8
Chile, 1985	1,410	43.1(a)	USA, 1880	2,247(j)	60.5
Uruguay, 1985	1,500	43.4(f, a)			
Paraguay, 1985	1,130	47.0(a)			
Costa Rica, 1985	1,270	43.0(a)			
Poland, 1985	2,020	38.3(a)			
Portugal, 1985	2,220	38.8(a)			
averages	*1,208.5*	*45.0*		*1768*	*66.0*
index (col 1, 2 = 100)	100	100		146	147

Notes: a = actually worked, b = paid for, f = 1986, g = assuming 6 days of work per week, h = textile industry, i = total manufacturing sector, 1875/80, j = 1870, k = 1905, l = 1913, m = 1850, n = 1820. col. (1): gross national product per head, 1985 $ calculated by the Atlas method. (World Bank, *World Tables 1995*, p.); col. (2) working hours per week in the manufacturing sector. col. (3): GDP p. c. in 1985 US$.
Sources: col. (1): World Bank, *World Tables, 1995*, table 2, pp. 6–9. col. (2): International Labour Office, *Yearbook of Labour Statistics*, section 12, pp. 693–9. col. (3): Maddison, *Dynamic Forces*, table 1.1, pp. 6–7, table B1, pp. 226–7, table B3, pp. 232 ff. table A5, p. 206. col. (4): Hoffmann, *Das Wachstum der deutschen Wirtschaft*, table 26, p. 213; Robin Matthews, Charles Feinstein, and John Odling-Smee, *1856–1973* (Oxford, 1982), *British Economic Growth*, table D.1, p. 566; Edouard Dolleans and Gerard Dehove, *Histoire du travail en France*, i (Paris, 1953), 286 ff.; Patrick O'Brien and Caglar Keyder, *Economic Growth in Britain and France 1780–1915* (London, 1978) 85; Jeremy Atack and Frank Bateman, 'How Long was the Workday in 1880?', *Journal of Economic History*, 51 (1992), 136, 138.

economies of Europe and the United States. Data from Egypt and Kenya constitute upper bounds on hours actually worked, since the information on 'hours paid for' includes vacations and other paid holidays. While every effort was made to glean comparable figures, it must be emphasized that our confidence in these figures should not be great. Too many indirect inferences were made, particularly for the historical data. I attempt to match closely the dates for which income and worktime estimates are given, but, as the notes to Table 5.6 show, this was not always possible. Unfortunately, data for the developing world are only available on a weekly basis—not the appropriate level of analysis when we are interested in the relationship of working hours and annual per capita income.[55] The data in Table 5.6 will therefore not be used in econometric exercises; they have been assembled to give an impression of different levels.

On average, the historical data on Germany, France, and Britain indicate weekly workloads of not less than 60 hours.[56] In the developing world only one country shows more than 50 hours per week— Egypt, where paid hours were measured. The difference of the averages is dramatic: Europeans before the First World War worked almost 50 per cent longer per week than their counterparts in today's poor countries. This is all the more remarkable because, on average, they were 47 per cent wealthier. If the generally observed inverse relationship between economic wealth and working hours holds, one would expect the opposite—the work-week in France, Britain, and Germany ought to have been shorter and not longer than the one in LDCs. If we combine this observation with the fact that some of the figures in column (1) are upper bounds, we have to conclude that, whatever the inaccuracies of the data, weekly working hours in the Third World today are markedly shorter than they were in pre-1913 Europe. Note also that growth rates in the Third World do not generally lag behind those achieved in Europe and North America during the nineteenth century.[57]

---

[55] O'Brien and Keyder, *Economic Growth in Britain and France, 1780–1914*, 85.

[56] Walter Schröder ('Die Entwicklung der Arbeitszeit im sekundären Sektor in Deutschland 1871–1913', *Technikgeschichte*, 3 (1980)) finds a rise in weekly working hours in Nuremberg from 61.1 in 1821 to 66.5 in 1870. The study is, however, too narrow in its geographical scope to be used here.

[57] Jeffrey Williamson, 'How Tough are Times in the Third World?', in D. McCloskey (ed.), *Second Thoughts. Myths and Morals of U.S. Economic History* (New York, 1993), 12.

How can we explain this peculiarity? Chenery *et al.* distinguish between three different interpretations of structural change.[58] Trade explanations centre on comparative advantages as productivity and output grow. Technological approaches are based on differences in the rate of productivity growth and the consequent shift in relative prices. Other explanations focus on the composition of demand. Engel's law, the fact that the share of food expenditure takes a smaller and smaller share of expenditure as incomes rise, is central to demand explanations. The factor driving change is exogenous to such models—shifts in demand based on Engel's law obviously require an increase in income originating from a different source. I shall briefly develop a simple model in which industrialization is the outcome of growing human capital. Such an explanation is compatible with the three models mentioned above, but requires no assumptions about trading patterns, Engel's law, or divergent rates of technological growth. The main underlying mechanism is that human capital growth also enlarges the size of the internal market. Consequently, the use of more advanced techniques is encouraged. The model is in the spirit of Murphy *et al.*[59] In the final analysis, the British case appears as a special case determined by an underlying mechanism which also explains the short working hours in today's LDCs.

Let us assume that the economy consists of a large number of sectors. In each one, a potential monopolist decides whether or not to adopt a new manufacturing technique with increasing returns to scale. He will only do so if the internal market is large compared to the fixed costs he has to incur. Total income in the economy is aggregate profits plus the return to labour and human capital:

$$y = \Pi + Lh \qquad (5.2)$$

where Π is corporate profits, L is labour input, and h is human capital. There are a large number of different sectors producing a good q ($q \in [0,1]$). Two types of firm exist in each sector. On the one

[58] Hollis Chenery *et al.*, *Industrialization and Growth: A Comparative Study* (New York, 1986), 39. This section draws on joint work with Jon Temple (Temple and Hans-Joachim Voth, 'Human Capital, Equipment Investment, and Industrialization', *European Economic Review*, 42 (1998)).

[59] Kevin Murphy, Andrej Shleifer, and Robert Vishny, 'Income Distribution, Market Size, and Industrialization', *Quarterly Journal of Economics*, 104 (1989). See also James Buchanan and Yuong Yoon (eds.), *The Return to Increasing Returns* (Ann Arbor, Mich., 1994). An extension of their model, which is used in adapted form in this chapter, can be found in Temple and Voth, 'Human Capital'.

hand, a large number of small, price-taking firms produce output, thereby converting one unit of human labour into h units of output (h represents the average individual's human capital). Further, there exists one firm which has access to a superior production technique with increasing returns to scale. Adoption of this technique results in increased productivity of the average agent, who now converts labour into αh units of output, with $\alpha > 1$. Also, the advanced firm has to incur a cost of $F(q)$ to switch production to the modern process. Let us assume that this fixed cost is a function of q, and that, with rising q, $F(q)$ increases. With a unit-elastic demand curve (for simplicity), the profit of a potential monopolist is

$$\pi(q) = \frac{\alpha - 1}{\alpha} y - F(q) = ay - F(q) \tag{5.3}$$

where $(\alpha - 1/\alpha)$ represents a mark-up for the advanced firm. Let x represent the fraction of firms that industrialize. Total profits can then be inferred as

$$\Pi(x) = xay - \int_0^x F(i)di \tag{5.4}$$

Total income as a function of x can then be derived as:

$$y(x) = \frac{Lh - \int_0^x F(i)di}{1 - ax} \tag{5.5}$$

The potential monopolist in sector q will industrialize if his profit from eq. (5.3) is larger than zero. All other potentially advanced firms in sectors [0,q) will also adopt new techniques—the market's size is untouched by the decision in sector q, and their fixed costs are lower. Consequently, the shift towards increasing returns to scale technology in sector q requires that

$$a = \frac{Lh - \int_0^q F(i)di}{1 - aq} \geq F(q) \tag{5.6}$$

and

$$L \geq \frac{1}{h} \left[\frac{F(q)}{a} (1 - aq) + \int_0^q F(i)di \right] \tag{5.7}$$

The shift to more advanced production methods will therefore only occur if total labour input is sufficient, given the levels of human capital. The higher h, the lower *ceteris paribus* the threshold value for L.

Therefore, if human capital is crucial in explaining the relatively short working year in the LDCs, we would expect proxies for human capital such as school enrolment to be higher there.[60] The primary school enrolment ratio for the countries in column (1), Table 5.6 is indeed high—97.2 per cent on average. Strictly comparable figures for England around 1800 are not available. We do know, however, that enrollment in Sunday schools in 1801 was 200,000, or almost exactly 10 per cent of those aged 5 to 14.[61] Even if total school enrolment was five times this level, school attendance in LDCs would be markedly higher today than it was in industrializing Britain. Crafts's work has also demonstrated that British school enrolment rates were markedly below the 'European norm' derived from Chenery–Syrquin regressions. In 1870, for example, when Britain's school enrolment ratio was 16.8 per cent, the European norm at this level of income was 51.4 per cent.

These effects will be even more pronounced if those nations that shift to more productive techniques first have small populations. Labour (L) in eq. (5.2) was defined as total annual labour input, the result of both annual working hours per member of the workforce and the number of workers. Our model therefore predicts that modernizing changes in production technique are more likely to occur in larger countries—as is indeed the case.[62] It is also noteworthy that population in the countries from Table 5.6 was, on average, 50 per cent larger than the British one in 1800. In our model, the size of the market $y = \Pi + Lh$ is crucial for the adoption of modern technology. To compensate for the effect of a smaller workforce on y, either labour input per individual or the level of human capital has to be higher.

The model also helps us to understand one of the important characteristics of Britain's Industrial Revolution—the importance of structural change in the economy as a whole. The central element of Crafts's reinterpretation of the Industrial Revolution is that overall rates of output growth were lacklustre. Structural factors however,

---

[60] Our approach has stressed the importance of human capital transfer. Schooling may also be important in this context if it allows foreign technology to be profitably employed.

[61] David Mitch, 'The Role of Human Capital in the First Industrial Revolution', in J. Mokyr (ed.), *The British Industrial Revolution: An Economic Perspective* (Boulder, Colo., 1993) 280; Wrigley and Schofield, *Population History*, table A3.1, 529.

[62] Chenery and Syrquin, *Patterns of Development*, 103.

such as the reallocation of labour, affected a very large part of the economy, and not just a few revolutionary industries such as cotton.[63] There is now evidence of traditional sectors such as agriculture having experienced technological change (measured as TFP growth) at a rate close to or above the ones witnessed in the 'leading-edge' sectors.[64] Such an observation can be naturally explained in the framework of our model. It belongs to a group commonly known as 'Big Push models'.[65] By that it is meant that industrialization can either proceed in a large number of sectors simultaneously, or in none at all. We have already demonstrated that, if the conditions in eq. (5.6) and (5.7) are fulfilled for sector q, all the other sectors [o,q) will adopt new technology as well. The relatively good 'performance' of traditional sectors is therefore no surprise if the fixed cost of switching to new production is lower than in the most advanced sector. Further, the revisionist finding that overall growth rates were slow during the Industrial Revolution also fits the story from the 'Big Push' model rather nicely. Lower growth implies that levels of per capita income were higher than previously calculated even before the onset of industrialization in the classical sense.[66] The ability to sustain them—and even improve them somewhat[67]—in the face of rapid population growth during the early years of the Industrial Revolution was also vital in providing the market size necessary for the adoption of more advanced techniques. Wrigley and Schofield have shown how the 'low-pressure' demographic regime of England, which regulated population size through changes in fertility rather than in mortality, helped to secure a higher living standard than would have prevailed otherwise.[68] Technology transfer may also play a role. Chenery and Syrquin found that the adoption of new techniques is strongly influenced by the size of domestic markets. At the same time, technology transfer is a potent force influencing growth rates.[69] The fixed costs for adopting

---

[63] Crafts, *British Economic Growth*, passim.   [64] Ibid., 43–4, 46–7, 83–7.

[65] The concept was originally formulated by Paul Rosenstein-Rodan, 'Problems of Industrialisation of Eastern and South-eastern Europe', *Economic Journal*, 53 (1943).

[66] Crafts and Harley, 'Output Growth', 705.

[67] Output per capita, according to Crafts and Harley (ibid.) clearly grew, even if there was no improvement in output per hour worked.

[68] Wrigley and Schofield, *Population History of England*, 458 ff.

[69] Even if convergence continues to be debated: see William Baumol, 'Productivity Growth, Convergence, and Welfare: What the Long-Run Data Show', *American Economic Review*, 76 (1986); Bradford DeLong, 'Productivity Growth, Convergence, and Welfare: Comment', *American Economic Review*, 78 (1988); Robert Barro, 'Economic Growth in a Cross Section of Countries', *Quarterly Journal of Economics*, 106 (1991).

the new technique have, however, already been paid. Therefore, the follower can increase productivity without having to pay the full cost in terms of 'providing' internal market size. Finally, the small size and rapid disappearance of a productivity gap in agriculture—another feature of English industrialization that sets it apart from the continent—may also be closely connected with the fact that England was first. Our model only takes internal demand into account. Countries that came later found larger, more developed export markets for their produce, and did not have the same need to generate as much demand internally. Consequently, the dispersion of productivity between sectors was wider.[70]

Our model is, of course, not an accurate representation of the English economy between 1750 and 1800.[71] It makes no attempt at comprehensiveness. Further, a large number of our assumptions are clearly not mirror-images of historical reality. Yet they represent simplification, I believe, of important structural aspects. The value of our mathematical speculation is therefore twofold. First, it shows how many salient features of the industrialization process can be captured in a simple 'Big Push' framework. Second, we are able to explain why late developers attain similar stages of industrialization with fewer hours of work per year. It follows that the first nation to undergo the development transition also has to endure the longest work-year. Our brief excursion would, however, be of little value if there were no evidence to support it apart from the strikingly low hours of weekly work in LDC and the exacting schedules identified in Chapter 3.

To test the model empirically, I return to the dataset from 16 countries used to estimate the Chenery–Syrquin equations. As mentioned earlier, the nature of our argument requires annual averages; we therefore cannot use the data from Table 5.6. A simple test of the theoretical explanation advanced above relates working hours (in addition to the standard variables in the Chenery–Syrquin framework) to the GDP p.c. gap in any given country compared with the leading nation. Comparable levels of GDP per head (as an indicator of the adoption of advanced manufacturing) can be attained more easily the

---

[70] This is, of course, just one possible interpretation of differences in agricultural productivity gaps.

[71] On the applicability of 'new growth' models to economic history see Crafts, 'Exogenous or Endogenous Growth? The Industrial Revolution Reconsidered', *Journal of Economic History*, 55 (1995), 767–8; id., 'Endogenous Growth: Lessons for and from Economic History', *CEPR Discussion Paper* 1333 (1996).

more human capital[72] is provided through technological transfer. As countries approach the production frontier, advances require higher levels of labour input. We therefore estimate

$$X = a + \beta_1 Y + \beta_2 Y^2 + \gamma_1 + \gamma_2 N^2 + \rho_1 G + \rho_2 G^2 \qquad (5.8)$$

[X = working hours, Y = GNP per capita, N = population, G = gap vis-à-vis the most advanced country]

If the coefficient on G is strongly negative, we will have shown that, for a given level of per capita income and population size, working hours are shorter the wider the gap between any given country and the most advanced one. This is what our theory predicts. If the reverse is true, with G positive or insignificant, the theoretical framework advanced above receives no support from the empirical evidence. Table 5.7 gives the results.

The equation for the full sample improves markedly with the inclusion of the 'catch-up' variable. The adj. R^2 increases, and the standard error is sharply reduced. GDP p.c. is still inversely related to working hours. This effect tails off when GDP p.c. rises, as demonstrated by the significant coefficient with an opposite sign on (GDP p.c.)². GAP is strongly significant and negative, but there is no evidence of any non-linearity. The coefficient is also large—a nation that lags 50 per cent behind the most advanced country enjoys, all else being equal, a working year that is 349 hours shorter than it was when the advanced nation had the same level of per capita income. Note also that these results are largely robust to changes in the sample—regression (2) gives almost the same results, with an even higher coefficient on GAP. Our estimates are fully in line with the predictions from our small model described above.

We can also test our predictions in a less rigorous fashion. Table 5.8 presents the dates when certain OECD countries reached a GDP per capita of $3,000.[73] If the transfer of human capital from the industrial leader enables countries to modernize without the long hours of arduous toil, and if human capital stock in the world as a whole grows over time, the followers should reach certain income levels with fewer working hours than the most advanced countries. Table 5.8 gives a few examples, showing that this was precisely the case.

---

[72] Defined in our framework as the efficiency of economic agents.

[73] In the World Bank framework, they thereby qualify for the 'middle-income' group. See World Bank, *World Tables*, p. viii.

TABLE 5.7. *Determinants of working hours*

Independent variables	Regression	
	3	4
GDP/capita	-0.27***	-0.34***
	(-17.1)	(-7.86)
(GDP/capita)²	1.04E-05***	2.3E-05***
	(10.8)	(8.4)
N	5.15E-04	0.0047*
	(0.6)	(2.05)
N²	-6.4E-09	-4.7E-08
	(-1.3)	(-4.1)
Gap	-6.97***	-12.2*
	(-3.3)	(-2.3)
Gap²	-0.04	0.06
	(-1.3)	(0.9)
Constant	3,558.7***	3,337.3***
	(57.8)	(19.3)
Summary statistics		
adj. R²	0.87	0.65
S.e.	158.2	230.8
N	141	40

* and *** significant at the 10 and 1 per cent level.
Notes: T-statistics in parentheses. Estimation technique: OLS. Eq. 1: full sample. Eq. 2: Germany, Japan, the Netherlands, United Kingdom, and the United States, 1890–1987.
Sources: GDP: Maddison, *Dynamic Forces*, App. A, table 2, p. 198; Population: ibid. B2, p. 228; Hours: ibid. App. C, table 9, pp. 270–1.

Can our empirical results explain the puzzling length of the working year in Britain at the beginning of the nineteenth century? If we use the estimated coefficients from the 16-nation sample, the prediction for Britain in 1800 is 3,247 hours/year.[74] This is safely within the range of our estimates, and equivalent to 104 per cent of the timing-based figure derived using constant hours. The value calculated for Britain on the basis of observed relationships in other countries between 1870 and 1987 is no longer statistically different from the observed one.

[74] Since Britain wrested industrial leadership from the Dutch at this time (Maddison, *Dynamic Forces*, 30 ff.), I assume a gap of zero.

TABLE 5.8. *Working hours at $3,000 GDP/head*

Country	Date	Hours/year
US	1890	2,789
UK	1890	2,807
Netherlands	1913	2,605
Germany	1950	2,316
Japan	1960	2,318

In this limited sense, we can now 'explain' the long hours of toil that had to prevail in Britain if economic modernization was to proceed. In essence, the unusual level of annual labour input was necessary because there was no scope for 'catch-up' growth. Human capital had to be produced at home, through learning-by-doing processes driven by intensive work. In addition to augmenting human capital, the longer working hours also compensated for the low level of productivity. Only long and exacting work could bolster total income in the economy sufficiently to allow the adoption of more advanced technology.

Conclusion

The commonwealth of learning is not at this time without master-builders, whose mighty designs, in advancing the sciences, will leave lasting monuments to the admiration of posterity ... and in an age that produces such masters ... it is ambition enough to be employed as an under-labourer in clearing the ground a little, and removing some of the rubbish that lies in the way to knowledge. (John Locke, *Essay Concerning Human Understanding* (1690))

During the Industrial Revolution England began to work harder—much harder. The timing and the extent of the rise in annual hours differed by location and social group. None the less, the finding that emerges most consistently from this study is that, by the 1830s, both London and the Northern counties of England had seen a considerable increase in annual working hours. What drove the change was not longer hours per day. Instead, changes in the number of days worked per week, and in the observance of holy days, were largely responsible for the rise in annual hours. In London, the demise of 'St Monday' and of numerous religious and political festivals were the main factors. In the North of England change was less drastic. During the middle of the century 'St Monday' and feast days had not curtailed the length of the working year as much as in London; what old customs had existed faded more slowly as the eighteenth century wore on.[75] In the seventy years between 1760 and 1830 the total number of hours worked per year increased by approximately 20 per cent.

The issue of working time has long been central to the historiography of the Industrial Revolution. Marx saw the long hours in the 'satanic mills' as a glaring indictment of capitalism. Where he led, scholars such as E. P. Thompson followed, arguing that the intensification of work practices and the increasing pressures of the clock had transformed 'merry old England' into a workhouse dominated by an oppressive and arduous routine of work. The nature of the transition they describe has two main components. One is the change from self-determined work, when labourers could time their efforts at their own discretion, to the harsh discipline of the factory and the workhouse. The second concerns the length of the working year, which reached unprecedented levels during the Industrial Revolution. Lack of more detailed information had long prevented any further attempts to quantify the magnitude of the change. The results emerging from the courtroom have implications at two levels. First, they shed some further light on the history of the British Industrial Revolution itself. Second, long-term developments can now be traced on a quantitative and comparable basis.

What emerges is an image of time-use that shows considerable stability for the years 1760–1831. This, in itself, is an important insight—with respect to many forms of time-use, the Industrial Revolution did not mark a watershed.[76] This is partly because the 'revolutionized sector' continued to be relatively small until the middle of the eighteenth century. E. P. Thompson's seminal article on time and work during the Industrial Revolution described the demise of 'merry old England' as a result of economic and technological change. As subsequent work has demonstrated, there was not one uniform, 'preindustrial' work pattern which gave way to the pressures of industrial work. Substantial variation at the local level and by occupation

---

[75] Our findings thus lend indirect support to the conclusions reached by Gregory Clark and Ysbrand van der Werf ('Work in Progress? The Industrious Revolution', *Journal of Economic History*, 58 (1998)), who argue that evidence in favour of an industrious revolution is not as clear for the countryside.

[76] It thus reinforces the argument by Max Hartwell, *The Industrial Revolution and Economic Growth* (London, 1977), 340.

existed in the eighteenth and nineteenth centuries. We found sharp differences not just between cities and agricultural areas, but also between individual professions, between different social classes, and between the sexes. Owing to small sample sizes, these contrasts could only be explored to a limited extent. What emerges clearly is that relatively long hours of work and little sleep had already been a part of the picture in the 1750s. Annual labour input may have been as high as 2,700–2,800 hours per year. The working year was approximately as long as it was in the 1870s in Britain, and equal to those seen on the continent during the height of industrialization. The 'dark satanic mills' of the nineteenth century may have operated for many hours a day, but this was not substantially longer than the workday in traditional occupations during the second half of the eighteenth century. Our findings thus lend qualified support to E. P. Thompson's hypothesis. On the one hand, we find a substantial intensification of work precisely during the period that Thompson analysed. On the other hand, the long hours and substantial annual labour input found for the 1750s suggest that his view of 'merry old England' is, indeed, in McKendrick's words, 'a prelapsarian myth of the golden past'.[77]

Change occurred not in terms of hours of work per day but in the weekly and annual rhythm of work and rest. It is for this reason that annual labour input grew, by between a fifth and a quarter, between 1760 and 1831. Compared to earlier results based entirely on London evidence, the rise in labour input in England now appears more gradual.[78] The 'industrious revolution', in DeVries's words, had largely arrived in the countryside by the 1750s, the time when our first witnesses begin to testify.[79] To a considerable extent, it is its spreading to urban centres that is responsible for the rise in aggregate labour input. The long working year in agriculture is probably one of the factors that distinguishes the industrial revolution in Britain most clearly from later ones. Sizeable productivity gaps between agriculture and the rest of the economy were common; just as in many Third World countries today, there is substantial evidence to suggest that this was partly driven by short working hours (and low intensity) in agricul-

---

[77] Neil McKendrick, 'Home Demand and Economic Growth: A New View of the Role of Women and Children in the Industrial Revolution', in id. (ed.), *Historical Perspectives: Essays in English Thought and Society* (London, 1974) 163.

[78] Using only one of the two methods of analysing courtroom data see Hans-Joachim Voth, 'Time and Work in Eighteenth-Century London', *Journal of Economic History*, 58 (1998).   [79] DeVries, 'Industrial Revolution'.

ture.[80] Attempts to understand the unique qualities of the first industrial revolution should therefore not only examine the factors that
facilitated the release of labour from the land, but should also focus on
the institutional preconditions such as the legal system that helped to
establish a routine of 'dawn-to-dusk' schedules. In any such explanation, the formation of relatively large farms operated by servants
hired on an annual basis, and supported by casual labour, will be
central.

One of the most famous debates in economic history surrounds the
course of living standards during this period. I make no contribution
to the issues that have been most controversial—changes in real
wages, urban disamenities, and variations in inequality.[81] Our findings
none the less suggest a more pessimistic view of changes in living
standards between 1760 and 1830. Higher levels of consumption were
bought at the price of a fall in leisure. Instead of consumption per
capita increasing by 0.38 per cent per annum, this figure needs to be
reduced to a more paltry 0.09 to 0.12 per cent per annum. While these
figures are still positive, they do not take into account the further bur-
dens of urbanization. In the context of more recent revisions to real
wage series, these results strongly suggest that living standards
improved no more than marginally between 1760 and 1830.[82]

To a considerable extent, industrializing Britain experienced
'Stalinist growth'. The phrase, coined by Paul Krugman, emphasizes
that additional factor input, and not greater productivity, is driving
output growth.[83] East Asia over the past three decades as well as
Stalinist Russia are typical examples of factor-intensive growth. If our
results are correct, then Britain falls into the same category. Instead of
using more capital, however, it was further labour input that was crucial in driving output growth. Because annual working hours
increased between the middle of the eighteenth and the middle of the
nineteenth centuries, GDP per hour grew more slowly than GDP per

---

[80] Gregory Clark, 'Productivity Growth without Technological Change in European
Agriculture before 1850', *Journal of Economic History*, 47 (1987). See also John Komlos,
'Agricultural Productivity in America and Eastern Europe: A Comment', *Journal of Economic
History*, 48 (1988) and Gregory Clark, 'Productivity Growth without Technological Change
in European Agriculture: A Reply', *Journal of Economic History*, 49 (1989).

[81] Jeffrey Williamson, 'British Mortality and the Value of Life', *Population Studies*, 38
(1984); id., *Did British Capitalism Breed Inequality?* (Boston, 1985); Charles H. Feinstein,
'The Rise and Fall of the Williamson Curve', *Journal of Economic History*, 48 (1988).

[82] Feinstein, 'Pessimism Perpetuated'.

[83] Paul Krugman, 'The Myth of Asia's Miracle', *Foreign Affairs*, 73 (1994).

capita. A very substantial part of the increase in output was a result of extra toil, and not of rising productivity; it was perspiration, not inspiration that led to higher per-capita incomes during the first industrial revolution. If our estimates of annual hours are even approximately right, the efficiency with which the economy combined factors of production grew barely, if at all. It is in this sense that the First Industrial Revolution was an 'industrious revolution'. Our findings therefore reinforce the main thrust of research over the past twenty years. The radical nature of the First Industrial Revolution is not diminished by these findings—it was rapid structural change, and not productivity growth, that was essential for the discontinuity.[84]

According to McCloskey, '[t]he heart of the matter is twelve. Twelve is the factor by which real income per head nowadays exceeds that around 1780, in Britain and in other countries that have experienced modern economic growth'.[85] She goes on to concede that real income per head does not measure all of human happiness. As was argued in the introductory chapter, the use of time provides a relatively limited but direct indication of one factor important to 'human happiness'. We can now contrast the period of the Industrial Revolution with the present not only in terms of real income, but of time-utilization. Earning a living in Britain in 1996 required, on average, 1,732 hours of work per year.[86] Compared to our (frequency-based) estimate for 1830, there was a reduction by 1,500 hours per year. The heart of the matter, in this sense, is not only twelve, but also close to 50 per cent—this is at least the reduction in working time between 1800 and the present. The order of magnitude of these changes is not a new insight; yet this study is the first to present data that allow the calculation of more precise estimates derived from a large empirical study. The fall in hours is equivalent to approximately one-third of the waking year.[87] Instead of work occupying more than half of 'our' time, making a living now only requires 30 per cent of waking hours. If we were to take other necessary activities such as eating and basic hygiene into account, there would be even less potentially 'free' time; the increase in time-availability would consequently be even larger.

---

[84] Crafts and Harley, 'Output Growth'.
[85] D. McCloskey, '1780–1860: A Survey', in R. Flood and ead. (eds.), *The Economic History of Britain since 1700* (Cambridge, 1994), 242.   [86] Crafts, 'East Asian Escape', table 2.
[87] Assuming, for convenience, eight hours of sleep.

Not all of this massive reduction in working hours is 'consumed' in the same way. We start work between two and two and a half hours later and stop almost two and a half hours earlier.[88] Differences in mealtimes diminish the reduction in effective daily labour input somewhat; it is none the less quite large. The work-week now counts five days, the same number of days as it did in 1750 and one fewer than in 1800. But instead of taking Monday off, Saturday has assumed the role of the 'second Sunday'. Where the working year was once interrupted by holy days, long holidays now leave factories standing idle and offices closed. The combined effect of all these reductions in working time leaves, on average, an additional 5–6 hours per day for activities other than work.[89] This increase in non-work time is used in many ways; a detailed breakdown cannot be given here. It is worthy of note, however, that a substantial proportion is 'consumed' by sleeping longer. Also, this extension of sleeping hours has occurred almost exclusively in the morning, by people rising later.[90] Note how time is immediately relevant to issues of well-being: while the increase in income noted by McCloskey concerns a unit of exchange, an entity that has to be transformed into the ultimate source of satisfaction (i.e., a commodity), time is not a currency but a good itself—it is all we have to spend.

The line of research pursued in this book could be extended most fruitfully by gathering similar data for other countries. An obvious issue that could be addressed is the empirical basis of Max Weber's 'Protestant ethic'. In its original form, he focused on the level of labour input and the savings rate in certain Protestant sects. In its wider sense, his speculation about the origins of capitalism also argues that Catholics and Protestants spent very different amounts of time at their workplaces.[91] For the same reasons as in the case of the British Industrial Revolution, actual hours worked are far less certain than the number of holy days prescribed. At present, we have little direct evidence that administrative changes such as those following the Reformation had an impact on actual labour input. If the method developed in this work uncovers markedly shorter working years in Catholic countries during the early modern period, there might be indirect confirmation of the Weber hypothesis. In another context,

---

[88] BBC Audience Research Department, *Daily Life in the 1980s*, i, iv (London, 1984).
[89] I divided the total annual saving by 365. [90] Cf. above, Chapter 3.
[91] Max Weber, 'Die protestantische Ethik und der Geist des Kapitalismus', in id., *Gesammelte Schriften zur Religionssoziologie*, i (Tübingen, 1920).

our work appears to qualify some of Weber's arguments. We presented a model in the spirit of new growth theory that allows us to understand how variations in individual labour input may have accelerated the adoption of new techniques. From Weber's point of view, it was the increase in the savings rate, driven by incomes rising faster than expenditure because of longer and harder work, that enabled capital accumulation. Instead of emphasizing savings behaviour, we argue that increases in market size due to increased labour input per capita might be responsible. This would shift the emphasis from the role of religious sects, where additional work was 'voluntary', to state-driven intervention in economies as a whole, where additional work was often forced upon an unwilling population.[92]

Progress in understanding the Industrial Revolution has taken two forms.[93] On the one hand, scholars have re-examined data that has long been available. By improving and refining the way this available evidence has been used to infer national aggregates, and by resolving the numerous conceptual issues involved, this line of enquiry has yielded important new insights into the nature of economic growth during Britain's Industrial Revolution. The most prominent example of this approach has been the work of Crafts and Harley. By, for example, properly appraising the importance of cotton in estimates of industrial output, they showed that Hoffman's (as well as Deane and Cole's) calculations of growth were markedly over-optimistic.

The second approach has emphasized the collection of data from new sources, shedding new light in areas where information had been scanty at best. The most prominent example of this approach has been the work of the Cambridge Group for the History of Population and

---

[92] Reforms in the Habsburg monarchy under Maria Theresia are a case in point. The abolition of holy days formed an integral part of this policy. On 9 March 1754, an edict stipulating that 24 holidays be abolished was published (Alfred Ritter von Arneth, *Maria Theresia nach dem Erbfolgekriege* (Vienna, 1870), 58). Intensive diplomatic contacts with the Vatican had enabled the Empress to secure Benedict XIV's consent. Attendance at church was still compulsory but, thereafter, everyone was free to work. These measures were initially not well received. Clergymen agitating against Maria Theresia's policy were sentenced to imprisonment, and the mob of Vienna attacked builders who came to work on an Imperial building in the *Burgplatz*. The government none the less insisted, and even required shopkeepers to open at 11:00 am on the formerly sanctified days. Mounted police patrolled the cities on 24 April 1754, St George's Day, to ensure that compliant shop owners did not fall victim to outraged masses. These incidents demonstrate two aspects. On the one hand, opposition to Maria Theresia's abolition of holy days was strong and widespread. On the other hand, they show clearly that the government was not willing to compromise on the issue.   [93] Wrigley *et al.*, *English Population History from Family Reconstitution*, 545–51.

Social Structure. Thirty years ago it was still possible to argue that little accurate statistical information was available for the period before 1850, and that demographic data was especially poor compared with information on other variables such as output and prices. Deane and Cole, for example, depended crucially on the parish record abstracts, collected by Rickman, and felt that no more than the broad outlines of population trends could be inferred.[94] For some of the crucial issues, much use was made of Swedish data, the assumption being that England's demographic past must have resembled that of its Northern neighbour quite closely.[95] Since the publication of *The Population History of England* and of *English Population History from Family Reconstitution,* England is easily the country with the best historical demographic data in the world.[96] These studies use family reconstitutions from 26 parishes, as well as aggregate tabulations of demographic events from a sample of 404 parishes. The data are then transformed into national totals by one of two new methods, either backward projection or generalized inverse projection.[97] As a result, many old debates have finally been settled, such as the issue of whether fertility or mortality change was more important in explaining population growth after 1850.[98]

The strategy pursued in this book falls firmly into the second category. No attempt is made to apply more sophisticated methods to already existing data, or to resolve any methodological issues in a spirit similar to recent refinements to national income accounting.[99] The task was a more humble one—to use systematically one source that contains a significant number of observations on time-use by witnesses from all strata of society, in a number of locations. In so doing, we have tried to 'clear the ground a little' for the master-builders in the profession. The experiment of using a familiar source in an unfamiliar way has yielded new insights into patterns of time-use in

---

[94] Deane and Cole, *British Economic Growth,* 5.

[95] Wrigley *et al., English Population History from Family Reconstitution,* 545.

[96] Wrigley and Schofield, *Population History of England;* Wrigley *et al., English Population History from Family Reconstitution.*

[97] Backward projection is a more restricted use of the same principle underlying generalized inverse projection.

[98] Peter Razzell ('The Growth of Population in Eighteenth-Century England: A Critical Reappraisal', *Journal of Economic History,* 53 (1993)) still argues that the question is open, but merely repeats some of the theoretical objections already contained in his earlier writings. Most importantly, he fails to demonstrate that his points matter quantitatively.

[99] Differentiating between 'new' and 'old' data is no easy matter. The sources used in this work have been used before, but not for the purpose currently at hand.

industrializing England, 1760–1830. The contours of daily, weekly, and annual time-use can be described on the basis of witnesses' accounts. Shortcomings none the less still abound. It should be remembered that my estimates are conjectures[100]—educated guesses based on a broader empirical basis than previous work, but guesses none the less. Where our witnesses remained silent, we had to proceed in the fashion of good jurors. Despite the attempts to make careful inferences, the uncertainty of many assumptions is only balanced by the limited nature of the judgement passed. One of the main insights derived from our witnesses' accounts concerns changes in labour input. It should be borne in mind that we have not been successful in resolving the issue of labour intensity—the underlying assumption in all our calculations was that this factor did not vary significantly over time.[101] In the absence of information to the contrary, this may be a defensible procedure. None the less, Adam Smith's injunction that 'there may be more labour in an hour's hard work than in two hours' easy business' reminds us that further research is needed.[102]

[100] Cf. Feinstein, 'Capital Formation in Great Britain', 26. My use of the term in a similar context is in no way meant to imply that the reliability of my estimates approaches his.

[101] Another factor ignored in this work is the quality of labour used—cf. Jeffrey Williamson, 'What Do We Know about Skill Accumulation in Nineteenth Century Britain?', unpub. ms, University of Wisconsin (1981); H. M. Boot, 'Salaries and Career Earnings in the Bank of Scotland, 1730–1880', _Economic History Review_, 44 (1991); id., 'How Skilled Were Lancashire Cotton Factory Workers in 1833?', _Economic History Review_, 48 (1995).

[102] Recall also that Matthews, Feinstein, Odling-Smee, _British Economic Growth_, assume that, because of changes in work intensity, reducing the length of the working week during the middle of the eighteenth century had little effect.

STATISTICAL APPENDIX

TABLE A1. *Logistic regressions—Δ odds ratio—London, 1760 (dependent variable: individuals engaged in work—w1, w2, and w3)*

Weekday	ΔOdds Ratio		
	w1	w2	w3
Sunday	0.52**	0.60*	0.67*
Monday	0.59**	0.61**	0.66**
Tuesday	0.89	1.02	1.15
Wednesday	1.26	1.23	1.08
Thursday	1.17	1.38*	1.11
Friday	1.07	0.92	1.19
Saturday	1.54**	1.34**	1.26

Note: * and ** indicate significance at the 90 and 95 per cent levels, respectively. w1, w2, w3: see text.

TABLE A2. *Leisure during the week—Mann-Whitney u-tests—1760*

	U	Z	Probability	Mean Rank
Monday	65,651	−2.54	0.01	28.07
Tuesday	54,638	−1.64	0.11	−20.05
Wednesday	65,663	−0.79	0.43	8.95
Thursday	60,513	−1.30	0.21	−14.67
Friday	61,775	−1.30	0.18	−15.49
Saturday	58,810	−0.97	0.33	11.55
Sunday	40,288	−0.88	0.38	8.11

TABLE A3. *Logistic regressions—ΔOdds Ratio—London 1800 (dependent variable: individuals engaged in work—w1, w2, and w3)*

Weekday	Δ Odds Ratio		
	w1	w2	w3
Sunday	0.53**	0.54**	0.30**
Monday	0.81	0.92	0.92
Tuesday	1.45*	1.37*	1.20
Wednesday	1.13	1.16	1.70**
Thursday	0.89	0.79	0.86
Friday	1.22	1.38*	1.45**
Saturday	1.31	1.24	1.67**

Note: * and ** indicate significance at the 90 and 95 per cent levels, respectively. w1, w2, w3: see text.

TABLE A4. *Mann–Whitney U-tests for work on different days of the week—1800*

	w1				w2				w3			
	U	Z	Probability	Mean Rank	U	Z	Probability	Mean Rank	U	Z	Probability	Mean Rank
Monday	66,498	-0.99	0.32	-19.09	67,728	-0.46	0.64	-9.82	67,561	-0.50	0.62	-11.07
Tuesday	62,346	-1.90*	0.05	37.57	62,449	-1.70*	0.09	36.76	64,176	-1.00	0.30	23.39
Wednesday	63,537	-0.58	0.56	11.41	62,847	-0.78	0.44	16.93	56,139	-3.04**	0.01	70.69
Thursday	64,033	-0.53	0.60	-10.37	62,075	-1.20	0.23	-25.97	62,953	-0.82	0.41	-18.98
Friday	58,513	-0.94	0.35	19.33	56,282	-1.70*	0.09	38.44	55,191	-1.99**	0.04	47.78
Saturday	68,622	-1.40	0.16	26.27	68,843	-1.20	0.23	24.68	63,183	-2.97***	0.01	65.44
Sunday	38,184	-2.10**	0.04	-51.36	37,257	-2.30**	0.02	-62.74	30,559	-5.03***	0.01	-145.04

Note: * and ** indicate significance at the 90 and 95 per cent levels, respectively.
w1, w2, w3: see text.

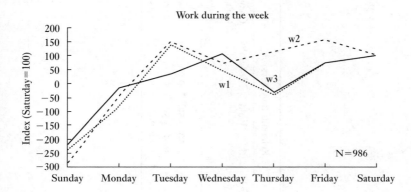

FIGURE A1. *Alternative definitions of work, London 1800*

TABLE A5. *Leisure during the week—Mann-Whitney u-tests—1760*

	U	Z	Probability	Mean Rank
Monday	65,651	-2.54	0.01	28.07
Tuesday	54,638	-1.64	0.11	-20.05
Wednesday	65,663	-0.79	0.43	8.95
Thursday	60,513	-1.30	0.21	-14.67
Friday	61,775	-1.30	0.18	-15.49
Saturday	58,810	-0.97	0.33	11.55
Sunday	40,288	-0.88	0.38	8.11

TABLE A6. *Logistic regressions—work on holy days, London, 1749–63*

Dependent variable	Holy days				Political 'holy days'				Religious holy days			
	B	Wald	Probability	Change in Odds Ratio	B	Wald	Probability	Change in Odds Ratio	B	Wald	Probability	Change in Odds Ratio
w1	-0.63	5.60**	0.018	0.53	-1.18	2.70*	0.09	0.31	-0.52	3.50*	0.06	0.59
w2	-0.40	3.30*	0.068	0.67	0.098	0.05	0.82	1.10	-0.51	4.50**	0.033	0.60
w3	0.14	0.56	0.45	1.15	0.33	0.68	0.41	1.40	0.14	0.47	0.49	1.15

Note: * and ** indicate significance at the 90 and 95 per cent levels, respectively.

TABLE A7. *Logistic regressions for work on political and religious holy days—1800*

	Political 'holy days'			Religious holy days		
	w1	w2	w3	w1	w2	w3
Coefficient on 'Feast'	-0.01	-0.15	0.10	0.23	0.48**	0.42*
Wald	0.0003	0.21	0.13	0.93	4.82	3.50
Probability	0.99	0.64	0.72	0.33	0.028	0.06
Change in Odds Ratio	0.99	0.86	1.10	1.30	1.62	1.52

Note: * and ** indicate significance at the 90 and 95 per cent levels, respectively.

TABLE A8. *Logistic regressions—gender*

Activity	B	Wald	Significance	Δ Odds Ratio
Paid work (w1)	1.20	26.26	0.0001	3.40**
Paid work (w2)	1.00	28.25	0.0001	2.80**
Paid work (w3)	0.75	2.29	0.0001	2.10**
Unpaid work (w3)	-1.58	38.40	0.0001	0.21**
Leisure	0.08	0.09	0.755	1.08

Note: The change in the odds ratio refers to male witnesses.
** indicates significance at the 95 per cent levels.

TABLE A9. *Logistic regressions—gender*

Activity	B	Wald	Significance	Δ Odds Ratio
Paid work (w1)	0.55	7.2	0.0072	1.73**
Paid work (w2)	0.88	21.1	0.0001	2.40**
Paid work (w3)	1.64	89.62	0.0001	5.18**
Unpaid work (w3)	-2.17	81.9	0.0001	0.11**
Leisure	1.51	12.15	0.0005	4.52**

Note: The change in the odds ratio refers to male witnesses.
** indicates significance at the 95 per cent levels.

BIBLIOGRAPHY

PRIMARY SOURCES

Campbell, R., *The London Tradesman* (London, 1747).
FAO, *The Fifth World Food Survey* (Rome, 1985).
—— *The Fourth World Food Survey* (Rome, 1977).
ILO, *Yearbook of Labour Statistics, 1989–90* (Geneva, 1990).
PRO (Kew), ASSI 45 (Northern Assize Depositions).
—— (Kew), Rail 883–189 (Wage Book of the Burnton and Western Canal Company, 1801 ff.).
Whole Proceedings of the Sessions of the Peace, and Oyer and Terminer for the City of London and County of Middlesex (London, var. years).
World Bank, *World Tables, 1995* (Baltimore, 1995).

SECONDARY SOURCES

Abbott, Michael, and Orley Ashenfelter, 'Labour Supply, Commodity Demand and the Allocation of Time', *Review of Economic Studies*, 43 (1976).
Abel, Wilhelm, *Der Pauperismus in Deutschland* (Hanover, 1970).
Åberg, Yngve, *The Impact of Working Hours and Other Factors on Production and Employment* (Avebury, 1987).
Acharya, M., and L. Bennett, 'The Rural Women of Nepal: An Aggregate Analysis and Summary of Eight Village Studies', *The Status of Women in Nepal*, ii, pt. 9 (Kathmandu, 1981).
Agnew, J.-C., 'Consumer Culture in Historical Perspective', in Roy Porter and John Brewer (eds.), *Consumption and the World of Goods* (London, 1993).
Allen, C., 'Photographing the TV Audience', *Journal of Advertising Research*, 8 (1968).
Anxo, Dominique, and Arne Bigsten, 'Working Hours and Productivity in Swedish Manufacturing', *Scandinavian Journal of Economics*, 91 (1989).
Arneth, Alfred Ritter von, *Maria Theresia nach dem Erbfolgekriege* (Vienna, 1870).
Ashton, Thomas Southcliffe, *Economic Fluctuations in England, 1700–1800* (Oxford, 1959).
—— *The Industrial Revolution 1760–1830* (London, 1948).
Atack, Jeremy, and Frank Bateman, 'How Long was the Workday in 1880?', *Journal of Economic History*, 51 (1992).
Atkinson, Anthony B., *The Economics of Inequality* (Oxford, 1975).
Baker, John Hamilton, *An Introduction to English Legal History* (London, 1990).
Ball, R., and E. St. Cyr, 'Short Term Employment Functions in British Manufacturing Industry', *Review of Economic Studies*, 33 (1966).

Barro, Robert, 'Economic Growth in a Cross Section of Countries', *Quarterly Journal of Economics*, 106 (1991).

Basu, Susanto, 'Procyclical Productivity: Overhead Inputs or Cyclical Utilization?', *University of Michigan Center for Research on Economic and Social Theory Working Paper* 25 (1993).

Baumol, William, 'Productivity Growth, Convergence, and Welfare: What the Long-Run Data Show', *American Economic Review*, 76 (1986).

BBC Audience Research Department, *Daily Life in the 1980s*, i, iv (London, 1984).

Beattie, John Maurice, *Crime and the Courts in England, 1660–1800* (Oxford, 1986).

—— 'The Pattern of Crime in England, 1660–1800', *Past and Present*, 62 (1974).

Becker, Gary S., *The Economic Approach to Human Behaviour* (Chicago, 1976).

—— 'A Theory of the Allocation of Time', *Economic Journal*, 75 (1965).

Behrman, Jere, and Anil Deolalikar, 'Is Variety the Spice of Life? Implications for Nutrient Responses to Income', *Harvard Institute of Economic Research Discussion Paper* 1371 (1988).

Berg, Maxine, and Pat Hudson, 'Rehabilitating the Industrial Revolution', *Economic History Review*, 45 (1992).

Berndt, Ernst, *The Practice of Econometrics* (Reading, Mass., 1991).

Betancourt, Roger, and Christopher Clague, 'An Economic Analysis of Capital Utilization', *Southern Economic Journal*, 42 (1975).

Bienefeld, M. A., *Working Hours in British Industry: An Economic History* (London, 1972).

Boot, H. M., 'Salaries and Career Earnings in the Bank of Scotland, 1730–1880', *Economic History Review*, 44 (1991).

—— 'How Skilled were Lancashire Cotton Factory Workers in 1833?', *Economic History Review*, 48 (1995).

Booth, Alison, and Fabio Schiantarelli, 'The Employment Effects of a Shorter Working Week', *Economica*, 54 (1987).

Boserup, Esther, *The Conditions of Agricultural Growth: The Economics of Agrarian Change under Population Pressure* (New York, 1965).

—— *Population and Technology* (Oxford, 1981).

Boulton, Jeremy, 'Economy of Time? Wedding Days and the Working Week in the Past', *Local Population Studies*, 43 (1989).

Bowden, Sue, and Avner Offer, 'Household Appliances and the Use of Time: The United States and Britain since the 1920s', *Economic History Review*, 47 (1994).

Boyer, George, *An Economic History of the English Poor Law* (Cambridge, 1990).

Braudel, Fernand, 'History and the Social Sciences. The *Longue Durée*', in id. (ed.), *On History* (London, 1980).

—— *The Mediterranean and the Mediterranean World in the Age of Philip II* (6th edn., London, 1990).

Brechling, Frank, 'The Relationship between Output and Employment in British Manufacturing Industries', *Review of Economics and Statistics* (1965).

Briggs, Asa, *A Social History of England* (Harmondsworth, 1987).

—— 'Work and Leisure in Industrial Society', *Past and Present*, 30 (1965).

Britnell, R. H., *The Commercialization of English Society 1000–1500* (Cambridge, 1993).

Brunello, Giorgio, 'The Employment Effects of Shorter Working Hours: An Application to Japanese Data', *Economica*, 56 (1989).

Brunt, Liam, 'Providence or Perseverance? Labour Productivity Growth in the Agricultural Revolution 1750–1800', unpub. M.Phil. thesis, Nuffield College, Oxford (1995).

Buchanan, James, and Yuong Yoon (eds.), *The Return to Increasing Returns* (Ann Arbor, Mich., 1994).

Burckhardt, Jacob, *Weltgeschichtliche Betrachtungen* (Stuttgart, 1969).

Burke, Peter, 'The Invention of Leisure in Early Modern Europe', *Past and Present*, 146 (1995).

Burnett, John, 'Trends in Bread Consumption', in T. C. Baker, J. C. Mackenzie, and J. Yudkin (eds.), *Our Changing Fare* (n.p., 1966).

—— David Vincent, and David Mayall, *The Autobiography of the Working Class: An Annotated, Critical Bibliography* (Brighton, 1989).

Burton, Anthony, *Josiah Wedgwood. A Biography* (London, 1976).

Caballero, Ricardo, and Richard Lyons, 'External Effects in U.S. Procyclical Productivity', *Journal of Monetary Economics*, 29 (1989).

Campbell, Colin, *The Romantic Ethic and the Spirit of Modern Consumerism* (Oxford, 1987).

—— 'Understanding Traditional and Modern Patterns of Consumption in Eighteenth-Century England: A Character-action Approach', in R. Porter and J. Brewer (eds.), *Consumption and the World of Goods* (London, 1993).

Cannadine, David, 'The Theory and Practice of the English Leisure Classes', *Historical Journal*, 21 (1978).

Castleden, Rodney, *British History. Chronological Dictionary of Dates* (London, 1994).

Chenery, Hollis, and Moshe Syrquin, *Patterns of Development, 1950–1970* (London, 1975).

—— *et al.*, *Industrialization and Growth: A Comparative Study* (New York, 1986).

Cheney, Christopher Robert (ed.), *Handbook of Dates for Students of English History* (London, 1945).

Clark, Colin, and Margaret Haswell, *The Economics of Subsistence Agriculture*, 4th edn. (London, 1970).

Clark, Gregory, 'Factory Discipline', *Journal of Economic History*, 54 (1994).

—— 'Labour Productivity in English Agriculture, 1300–1860', in B. Campbell and M. Overton (eds.), *Land, Labour and Livestock: Historical Studies in European Agricultural Productivity* (Manchester, 1991).

——'Productivity Growth without Technological Change in European Agriculture before 1850', *Journal of Economic History*, 47 (1987).

——'Productivity Growth without Technological Change in European Agriculture: A Reply', *Journal of Economic History*, 49 (1989).

Clark, Gregory, and Y. van der Werf, 'Work in Progress? The Industrious Revolution', *Journal of Economic History*, 58 (1998).

——M. Huberman, and P. Lindert, 'A British Food Puzzle, 1770–1850', *Economic History Review*, 48 (1995).

Coale, Ansley, and Edgar M. Hoover, *Population Growth and Economic Development in Low-Income Countries* (Princeton, NJ, 1958).

Coen, Robert, and Bert Hickman, 'Constrained Joint Estimation of Factor Demand and Production Functions', *Review of Economics and Statistics*, 52 (1970).

Cornish, William, and Geoffrey Clark, *Law and Society in England, 1750–1950* (London, 1989).

Costa, Dora, 'Height, Weight, Wartime Stress, and Older Age Mortality: Evidence from the Union Army Records', *Explorations in Economic History*, 20 (1993).

Crafts, N. F. R., *British Economic Growth during the Industrial Revolution* (Oxford, 1985).

——'The East Asian Escape from Economic Backwardness', in Paul David and Mark Thomas (eds.), *Economic Challenges of the 21st Century* (London, forthcoming).

——'East Asian Growth Before and After the Crisis', *IMF Staff Papers*, 46 (1999).

——'Endogenous Growth: Lessons for and from Economic History', *CEPR Discussion Paper* 1333 (1996).

——'Exogenous or Endogenous Growth? The Industrial Revolution Reconsidered', *Journal of Economic History*, 55 (1995).

——'Income Elasticities of Demand and the Release of Labour by Agriculture during the British Industrial Revolution', *Journal of European Economic History*, 9 (1980).

——'Patterns of Development in Nineteenth Century Europe', *Oxford Economic Papers*, 36 (1984).

——and Knick Harley, 'Cotton Textiles and Industrial Output Growth During the Industrial Revolution', *Economic History Review*, 48 (1995).

————'Output Growth and the British Industrial Revolution: A Restatement of the Crafts–Harley View', *Economic History Review*, 45 (1992).

Craine, Roger, 'On the Service Flow from Labour', *Review of Economic Studies*, 40 (1973).

Crouzet, François (ed.), *Capital Formation in the Industrial Revolution* (London, 1972).

Cuenca Esteban, J., 'British Textile Prices, 1770–1831: Are British Growth Rates Worth Revising Once More?', *Economic History Review*, 45 (1994).

Cuenca Esteban, Javier, 'Further Evidence of Falling Prices of Cotton Cloth, 1768–1816', *Economic History Review*, 48 (1995).

Dasgupta, Partha, *An Inquiry into Well-Being and Destitution* (Oxford, 1993).

de Grazia, Sebastian, *Of Time, Work and Leisure* (New York, 1962).

De La Paz, Maria, 'Child Labor: Its Implications to Nutrition and Health in the Philippines, unpub. Ph.D. dissertation, Columbia University (1990).

Deane, Phyllis, and W. A. Cole, *British Economic Growth, 1688–1959*, 2nd edn. (Cambridge, 1969).

Deaton, Angus, and John Muellbauer, *Economics and Consumer Behaviour* (Cambridge, 1980).

DeLong, Bradford, 'Productivity Growth, Convergence, and Welfare: Comment,' *American Economic Review*, 78 (1988).

Delsalle, Paul, 'Les Loisiers des ouvriers en France XVIe–XVIIIe siècles', paper presented at the XXVI Settimana di Studi, Istituto F. Datini, Prato, 18–23 April 1994, 4.

Denison, Edward, *The Sources of Economic Growth in the United States and the Alternatives before Us* (New York, 1962).

DeVries, Jan, 'Between Purchasing Power and the World of Goods: Understanding the Household Economy in Early Modern Europe', in R. Porter and J. Brewer (eds.), *Consumption and the World of Goods* (London, 1993).

—— *European Urbanization, 1500–1800* (Cambridge, Mass., 1984).

—— 'The Industrial Revolution and the Industrious Revolution', *Journal of Economic History*, 54 (1994).

Dolleans, Edouard, and Gerard Dehove, *Histoire du travail en France*, i (Paris, 1953).

Dyer, Alan, 'Seasonality of Baptisms: An Urban Approach', *Local Population Studies*, 27 (1981).

Earle, Peter, *The Making of the English Middle Class: Business, Society and Family Life in London, 1660–1730* (Berkeley, Calif., 1989).

Easterlin, Richard, 'Does Economic Growth Improve the Human Lot?', in P. David and M. Reder, *Nations and Households in Economic Growth. Essays in Honor of Moses Abramovitz* (New York, 1974).

Elias, Norbert, *The Civilizing Process*, ii (Oxford, 1982).

—— *Über die Zeit* (Frankfurt am Main, 1984).

Ellis, Christopher, 'The Backward-Bending Supply Curve of Labor in Africa', *Journal of Developing Areas*, 15 (1981).

Engerman, Stanley, and Claudia Goldin, 'Seasonality in Nineteenth Century Labor Markets', *NBER Historical Working Papers Series*, 20 (1991).

Erasmus, Charles, 'Work Patterns in a Mayo Village', *American Anthropologist*, 57 (1955).

Facchini, Giovanni, and Hans-Joachim Voth, 'New Goods, More Work: Industrialization and Labour Input in the Long Run', mimeo, Stanford University (1999).

FAO, *Handbook on Nutritional Requirements* (Rome, 1974).

Feinstein, Charles H., 'Capital Accumulation and the Industrial Revolution', in R. Floud and D. McCloskey (eds.), *The Economic History of Britain since 1700* (Cambridge, 1994).

—— 'Capital Formation in Great Britain', in Peter Mathias and M. M. Postan (eds.), *Cambridge Economic History of Europe*, vii, *The Industrial Economics: Capital, Labour, and Enterprise*, pt. 1 (Cambridge, 1978).

Feinstein, Charles H., 'Pessimism Perpetuated. Real Wages and the Standard of Living in Britain during and after the Industrial Revolution', *Journal of Economic History*, 58 (1998).

—— 'The Rise and Fall of the Williamson Curve', *Journal of Economic History*, 48 (1988).

—— 'Wage-earnings in Great Britain during the Industrial Revolution', in I. Begg and S. Henry (eds.), *Applied Economics and Public Policy* (Cambridge, 1998).

—— and Sidney Pollard (eds.), *Studies in Capital Formation in the United Kingdom, 1750–1920* (Oxford, 1988).

—— and Mark Thomas, 'A Plea for Errors', unpub. ms, All Souls College, Oxford (1999).

Feldman, Gerald D., *The Great Disorder* (Oxford, 1993).

Feldstein, Martin, 'Specification of Labour Input in the Aggregate Production Function', *Review of Economic Studies*, 34 (1967).

Fielding, Henry, *Enquiry into the Causes of the Late Increase in Robbers* (London, 1751).

Fine, Ben, and Elisabeth Leopold, *The World of Consumption* (London, 1993).

Floud, Roderick, Kenneth Wachter, and Annabel Gregory, 'Further Thoughts on the Nutritional Status of the British Population', *Economic History Review*, 46 (1993).

——————— *Height, Health and History. Nutritional Status in the United Kingdom, 1750–1980* (Cambridge, 1990).

——————— 'Measuring Historical Heights: Short Cuts or the Long Way Round: A Reply to Komlos', *Economic History Review*, 46 (1993).

Fogel, Robert, 'The Conquest of High Mortality and Hunger in Europe and America: Timing and Mechanisms', *NBER Historical Working Paper*, 16 (1990).

—— 'Second Thoughts on the European Escape from Hunger: Famines, Chronic Malnutrition, and Mortality Rates', in S. Osmani (ed.), *Nutrition and Poverty* (Oxford, 1992).

—— 'New Sources and New Techniques for the Study of Secular Trends in Nutritional Status, Mortality, and the Process of Aging', *Historical Methods*, 26 (1993).

Frank, Robert, *Microeconomics and Behavior* (New York, 1991).

Freudenberger, Hermann, 'Das Arbeitsjahr', in I. Bog *et al.* (eds.), *Wirtschaftliche und soziale Strukturen im säkularen Wandel. Festschrift für Wilhelm Abel zum 70. Geburtstag*, ii, *The vorindustrielle Zeit: Außeragrarische Probleme* (Hanover, 1974).

Freudenberger, Hermann, and Gaylord Cummins, 'Health, Work and Leisure before the Industrial Revolution', *Explorations in Economic History*, 13 (1976).

Fry, Maxwell, and Andrew Mason, 'The Variable Rate-of-Growth Effect in the Life-Cycle Model', *Economic Inquiry*, 20 (1982).

Gallman, Robert, 'The Agricultural Sector and the Pace of Economic Growth', in David Klingaman and Richard Vedder (eds.), *Essays in Nineteenth Century Economic History: The Old North-West* (Athens, 1975).

Gayer, Arthur D., Walt Rostow, and Anna Schwartz, *The Growth and Fluctuations of the British Economy, 1790–1850* (Oxford, 1953).

Geertz, Clifford, *Agricultural Involution: The Process of Ecological Change in Indonesia* (Berkeley, Calif., 1963).

Gell, Alfred, *The Anthropology of Time* (Oxford, 1992).

George, Mary Dorothy, *English Social Life in the Eighteenth Century* (London, 1925).

Gershuny, Jay, *After Industrial Society? The Emerging Self-Service Economy* (London, 1978).

——'Leisure: Feast or Famine?', *Loisir et Société*, 9 (1986).

——'Post-Industrial Convergence in Time Allocation', *Futures*, 25 (1993).

——'The Time Economy or the Economy of Time. An Essay on the Interdependence of Living and Working Conditions', unpub. ms, Nuffield College, Oxford (1991).

——*et al.*, 'Time-Budgets: Preliminary Analyses of a National Survey', *Quarterly Journal of Social Affairs*, 2 (1986).

Glennie, Paul, and Nigel Thrift, 'The Spaces of Times', mimeo, University of Bristol (1999).

Haffter, Andreas, and Barbara Minder, *Arbeitsbeanspruchung und soziale Stellung der Bäuerin: Ergebnisse einer Voruntersuchung auf 25 Ostschweizer Bauernhöfen* (Tanecon, 1973).

Hammond, John, 'The Industrial Revolution and Discontent', *Economic History Review*, 2 (1930).

Hardy, Melissa, *Regression with Dummy Variables* (Newbury Park, 1993).

Harley, Knick, 'Reassessing the Industrial Revolution: A Macro View', in J. Mokyr (ed.), *The British Industrial Revolution: An Economic Perspective* (Boulder, Colo., 1993).

——and N. F. R. Crafts, 'Cotton Textiles and Industrial Output Growth during the Industrial Revolution', *Economic History Review*, 158 (1995).

————'Productivity Growth during the First Industrial Revolution: Inferences from the Pattern of British External Trade', *LSE Working Papers in Economic History*, 42 (1998).

Harris, Mark, 'Introduction', in *The Old Bailey Proceedings. Pts 1 and 2. A Listing and Guide to the Harvester Microfilm Collection, 1714–1834* (Brighton, 1984).

Harrison, Mark, 'The Ordering of the Urban Environment', *Past and Present*, 110 (1986).

Hartwell, Max, *The Industrial Revolution and Economic Growth* (London, 1977).
—— 'The Rising Standard of Living in England, 1800–1850', *Economic History Review*, 13 (1961).
Hatcher, John, 'Labour, Leisure and Economic Thought before the Nineteenth Century', *Past and Present*, 160 (1998).
Hauck, Walter, and Allan Donner, 'Wald's Test as Applied to Hypotheses in Logit Analysis', *Journal of the American Statistical Association*, 72 (1977).
Hay, Douglas, 'War, Dearth and Theft in the Eighteenth Century', *Past and Present*, 95 (1982).
—— and Francis Snyder, 'Using the Criminal Law, 1750–1850. Policing, Private Prosecution, and the State', in eid., *Policing and Prosecution in Britain, 1750–1850* (Oxford, 1989).
Hecht, J. Jean, *The Domestic Servant Class in England* (London, 1956).
Higgins, Matthew, and Jeffrey Williamson, 'Asian Demography and Foreign Capital Dependence', *NBER Working Paper* 5560 (1996).
Higgs, Eddie, *Making Sense of the Census. The Manuscript Returns for England and Wales, 1801–1901* (London, 1989).
Hill, D., 'Implications of Home Production and Inventory Adjustment Processes for Time-of-Day Demand for Electricity', in F. Thomas Juster and Frank Stafford (eds.), *Time, Goods, and Well-Being* (Ann Arbor, Mich., 1985).
Hill, K., H. Kaplan, K. Hawkes, and A. Hurtado, 'Men's Time Allocation to Subsistence Work among the Ache of Eastern Paraguay', *Human Ecology*, 13 (1985).
Hill, M., 'Patterns of Time Use', in F. Thomas Juster and Frank Stafford (eds.), *Time, Goods, and Well-Being* (Ann Arbor, Mich., 1985).
—— and F. Thomas Juster, 'Constraints and Complementarities in Time Use', in F. Thomas Juster and Frank Stafford (eds.), *Time, Goods, and Well-Being* (Ann Arbor, Mich., 1985).
Hobsbawm, Eric, 'Comment on Asa Briggs, "Work and Leisure in Industrial Society"', *Past and Present*, 30 (1965).
Hoffmann, Walter G., *Das Wachstum der deutschen Wirtschaft seit der Mitte des 19. Jahrhunderts* (Berlin, 1965).
Honeyman, Katarina, 'Review of Periodical Literature, 1700–1850', *Economic History Review*, 48 (1995).
Hopkins, Eric, 'Working Hours and Conditions during the Industrial Revolution: A Re-Appraisal', *Economic History Review*, 35 (1982).
Hoppit, Julian, *Risk and Failure in English Business, 1700–1800* (Cambridge, 1987).
Horrell, Sara, 'Home Demand and British Industrialization', *Journal of Economic History*, 56 (1996).
—— and Jane Humphries, 'Women's Labour Force Participation and the Transition to the Male-Breadwinner Family, 1790–1865', *Economic History Review*, 48 (1995).
—— —— and Hans-Joachim Voth, 'Stature and Relative Deprivation: Fatherless Children in Early Industrial Britain', *Continuity and Change*, 13 (1998).

Huberman, Michael, and Wayne Lewchuck, 'Glory Days? Work Hours, Labor Market Regulations and Convergence in Late Nineteenth Century Europe', paper presented at the All U.C. Group in Economic History Conference, University of California, Davis, 14–16 November 1997.

Humphries, Jane, 'Enclosures, Common Rights, and Women: The Proletarianization of Families in the Late Eighteenth and Early Nineteenth Centuries', *Journal of Economic History*, 50 (1990).

Hunt, Jennifer, 'Has Work-Sharing Worked in Germany?', *Quarterly Journal of Economics*, 114 (1999), 117–48.

Innes, Joanna, and John Styles, 'The Crime Wave: Crime and Criminal Justice in Eighteenth-Century England', in Adrian Wilson (ed.), *Rethinking Social History. English Society and its Interpretation* (Manchester, 1993).

Jackson, J. Edward, *A User's Guide to Principal Components* (New York, 1991).

Johnson, Allen, 'Time Allocation in a Machiguenga Community', *Ethnology*, 14 (1975).

Johnson, Paul, and Steve Nicholas, 'Health and Welfare of Women in the United Kingdom, 1785–1920', paper presented to the NBER conference on health and welfare during industrialization, Cambridge, Mass., 21–2 April 1995.

Jones, Eric, *Agriculture and the Industrial Revolution* (Oxford, 1974).

—— 'The Fashion Manipulators: Consumer Tastes and British Industries, 1660–1800', in L. Cain and P. Uselding (eds.), *Business Enterprise and Economic Change* (London, 1973).

Juster, F. Thomas, 'Response Errors in the Measurement of Time Use', *Journal of the American Statistical Association*, 81 (1986).

—— and Frank Stafford (eds.), *Time, Goods, and Well-Being* (Ann Arbor, Mich., 1985).

—— —— 'The Allocation of Time: Empirical Findings, Behavioral Models, and Problems of Measurement', *Journal of Economic Literature*, 29 (1991).

—— —— Courant, P., and G. Dow, 'A Theoretical Framework for the Measurement of Well-Being', *Review of Income and Wealth*, 27 (1981).

Kalton, G., 'Sample Design Issues in Time Diary Studies', in F. Thomas Juster and Frank Stafford (eds.), *Time, Goods, and Well-Being* (Ann Arbor, Mich., 1985).

Killingsworth, Mark, *Labor Supply* (Cambridge, 1983).

King, Peter, 'Pauper Inventories and the Material Lives of the Poor in the Eighteenth and Early Nineteenth Centuries', in T. Hitchcock, P. King, and P. Sharpe, *Chronicling Poverty: The Voices and Strategies of the English Poor* (Basingstoke, 1997).

Kitson, Peter, 'Festivity and Fertility in English Parish Life, 1558–1713', BA thesis, Cambridge (1999).

Komlos, John, 'Agricultural Productivity in America and Eastern Europe: A Comment', *Journal of Economic History*, 48 (1988).

—— 'The Food Budget of English Workers: A Comment on Shammas', *Journal of Economic History*, 48 (1988).

—— 'Further Thoughts on the Nutritional Status of the British Population', *Economic History Review*, 46 (1993b).

—— *Nutrition and Economic Development in the Eighteenth Century Habsburg Monarchy* (Princeton, NJ, 1989).

—— 'The Secular Trend in the Biological Standard of Living', *Economic History Review*, 44 (1993).

Konig, Wolfgang and Winfried Pohlmeier, 'Employment, Labour Utilization and Procyclical Productivity', *Kyklos*, 41 (1988).

Krengel, Jochen, 'Der Beschäftigungseffekt von Arbeitszeitverkürzungen im sekundären Sektor Deutschlands 1871–1913—ein historisches Beispiel', *Konjunkturpolitik*, 29 (1983).

Krugman, Paul, 'The Myth of Asia's Miracle', *Foreign Affairs*, 73 (1994).

Kuh, Edwin, 'Cyclical and Secular Labor Productivity in United States Manufacturing', *Review of Economics and Statistics* (1965).

Kusamitsu, Toshiho, 'Novelty, give us novelty': London Agents and Northern Manufacturers', in Maxine Berg (ed.), *Markets and Manufacture in Early Modern Europe* (London, 1991).

Kussmaul, Ann, 'England's Industrial Evolution, 1541–1840', unpub ms, Toronto (1990).

—— *A General View of the Rural Economy of England, 1538–1840* (Cambridge, 1990).

Kuznets, Simon, *National Income and its Composition* (New York, 1941).

Landers, John, *Death and the Metropolis. Studies in the Demographic History of London, 1670–1830* (Cambridge, 1993).

—— 'From Colyton to Waterloo: Mortality, Politics and Economics in Historical Demography', in A. Wilson (ed.), *Rethinking Social History: English Society, 1570–1920 and its Interpretation* (Manchester, 1993).

Landes, David, *Revolution in Time. Clocks and the Making of the Modern World* (Cambridge, Mass., 1983).

James Laver, *The Concise History of Costume and Fashion* (New York, 1978).

Le Goff, Jacques, 'Labour Time in the "Crisis" of the Fourteenth Century: From Medieval Time to Modern Time', in id., *Time, Work, and Culture in the Middle Ages* (Chicago, 1980).

Lee, Clive H., *British Regional Employment Statistics, 1841–1971* (Cambridge, 1979).

Lee, Richard, '!Kung Bushman Subsistence: An Input–Output Analysis', in Andrew Vayda (ed.), *Environment and Cultural Behaviour* (New York, 1969).

—— 'What Hunters Do for a Living, or, How to Make Out on Scarce Resources', in id. and Irven DeVore (eds.), *Man the Hunter* (Chicago, 1968).

Lemire, Beverly, *Fashion's Favourite: The Cotton Trade and the Consumer in Britain, 1660–1800* (Oxford, 1991).

Leslie, Derek, 'The Productivity of Hours in U.S. Manufacturing Industries', *Review of Economics and Statistics*, 66 (1984).

Lewis, W. Arthur, 'Economic Development with Unlimited Supplies of Labour', in A. Agarwally and S. Singh, *The Economics of Underdevelopment* (London, 1959).

Lindert, Peter, and Jeffrey Williamson, 'English Workers' Living Standards during the Industrial Revolution: A New Look', *Economic History Review*, 36 (1983).

———— 'Reply to Michael Flinn', *Economic History Review*, 37 (1984).

———— 'Revising England's Social Tables, 1688–1913', *Explorations in Economic History*, 19 (1982).

Lord, Evelyn, 'Fairs, Festivals and Fertility in Alkmaar, North Holland, 1650–1810', *Local Population Studies*, 42 (1989).

McCarthy, F., and M. McArthur, 'The Food Quest and the Time Factor in Aboriginal Economic Life', in Charles Pearcy Montfourd (ed.), *Records of the Australian-American Scientific Expedition to Arnhem Land*, ii (Melbourne, 1960).

McCloskey, D., '1780–1860: A Survey', in R. Floud and ead. (eds.), *The Economic History of Britain since 1700* (Cambridge, 1994).

McKendrick, Neil, 'Home Demand and Economic Growth: A New View of the Role of Women and Children in the Industrial Revolution', in id. (ed.), *Historical Perspectives: Essays in English Thought and Society* (London, 1974).

———— 'Josiah Wedgwood and Factory Discipline', *Historical Journal*, 4 (1961).

———— Brewer, John, and John Harold Plumb, *The Birth of Consumer Society. The Commercialization of Eighteenth-century England* (London, 1982).

Maddison, Angus, *Dynamic Forces in Capitalist Development* (Oxford, 1991).

Malinvaud, Edmond 'Une explication de l'évolution de la productivité horaire du travail', *Economie et Statistique*, 48 (1973).

Marchetti, Domenico, 'Procyclical Productivity, Externalities and Labor Hoarding: A Reexamination of Evidence from U.S. Manufacturing', *EUI Economics Working Paper*, 13 (1994).

Martins, Maria, 'Labor Supply Behavior of Married Women: Theory and Empirical Evidence for Portugal', *Cahiers Economiques de Bruxelles*, 152 (1996).

Marx, Karl, *Capital*, iii (New York, 1967).

———— *Das Kapital*, i (Berlin, 1983 [1867]).

Mathias, Peter, 'Leisure and Wages in Theory and Practice', in id. (ed.), *The Transformation of England* (London, 1979).

Matthews, Robin, Charles Feinstein, and John Odling-Smee, *British Economic Growth, 1856–1973* (Oxford, 1982).

Mayshar, Joran, and Gary Solon, 'Shift Work and the Business Cycle', *American Economic Review*, 83 (1993).

Medick, Hans, Peter Kriedte, and Jürgen Schlumbohm, *Industrialization before Industrialization: Rural Industry in the Genesis of Capitalism* (Cambridge, 1981).

Millan, J., *Coins, Weights and Measure of all Nations Reduced into English* (London, 1749).

Minge-Klevana, Wanda, 'Does Labour Time Decrease with Industrialization? A Survey of Time-Allocation Studies', *Current Anthropology*, 21 (1980).

—— 'Household Economy During the Peasant-to-Worker Transition in the Swiss Alps', *Ethnology*, 17 (1978).

Miracle, M., and B. Fetter, 'Backward-Sloping Labor Supply Functions and African Economic Behavior', *Economic Development and Cultural Change*, 18 (1970).

Mitch, David, 'The Role of Education and Skill in the British Industrial Revolution', in Joel Mokyr (ed.), *The British Industrial Revolution. An Economic Perspective* (Boulder, Colo., 1998).

Mitch, David, 'The Role of Human Capital in the First Industrial Revolution', in Joel Mokyr (ed.), *The British Industrial Revolution. An Economic Perspective* (Boulder, Colo., 1993).

Mokyr, Joel, 'Demand vs. Supply in the Industrial Revolution', *Journal of Economic History*, 37 (1977).

—— 'The Industrial Revolution and the New Economic History', in id. (ed.), *The Economics of the Industrial Revolution* (London, 1985).

—— 'The New Economic History and the Industrial Revolution', in id. (ed.), *The British Industrial Revolution. An Economic Perspective* (Boulder, Colo., 1993).

Mueller, Eva, 'The Value and Allocation of Time in Rural Botswana', *Journal of Development Economics*, 15 (1984).

Mulgan, Geoff, and H. Wilkinson, 'Well-being and Time', *Demos Quarterly*, 5 (1995).

Münch, Peter, *Lebensformen in der frühen Neuzeit* (Frankfurt am Main, 1992).

Murphy, Kevin, Andrej Shleifer, and Robert Vishny, 'Building Blocks of Market Clearing Business Cycle Models', *NBER Macroeconomics Annual* (1989).

—————— 'Income Distribution, Market Size, and Industrialization', *Quarterly Journal of Economics*, 104 (1989).

Neifer-Dichmann, Elisabeth, 'Working Time Reductions in the Former Federal Republic of Germany: A Dead End for Employment Policy', *International Labour Review*, 130 (1991).

Nicollier, Jean, 'Recherches sur la rénovation de l'organisme de la production dans l'agriculture: l'exemple de Medieres, Valais', in J. Loup (ed.), *Pasteurs et agricultures valaisans* (Grenoble, 1950).

Norusis, Marija, *SPSS-X Introductory Statistics Guide for SPSS-X Release 3* (Chicago, 1988).

O'Brien, Patrick, and Caglar Keyder, *Economic Growth in Britain and France, 1780–1914* (London, 1978).

Oi, Walter, 'Labor as a Quasi-Fixed Factor', *Journal of Political Economy* (1962).

Paley, R., 'Thief-takers in London in the Age of the McDaniel Gang, c.1745–1754', in Douglas Hay and Francis Snyder (eds.), *Policing and Prosecution in Britain, 1750–1850* (Oxford, 1989).

Payne, P., 'Public Health and Functional Consequences of Seasonal Hunger and

Malnutrition', in D. Sahn (ed.), *Causes and Implications of Seasonal Variability in Household Food Security* (Washington, DC, 1987).

Persson, Karl-Gunnar, *Pre-Industrial Economic Growth. Social Organization and Technological Progress in Europe* (Oxford, 1988).

Phelps Brown, Ernest Henry, and Sheila V. Hopkins, 'Seven Centuries of the Prices of Consumables, Compared with Builders' Wage-rates', *Economica*, 40 (1955).

—— et al., 'Labour Hours: Hours of Work', *Encyclopedia of the Social Sciences* 7 (New York, 1968).

Pinchbeck, Ivy, *Women Workers in the Industrial Revolution* (New York, 1969).

Pindyck, Robert, and Daniel Rubinfeld, *Microeconomics* (New York, 1989).

Plumb, John, 'The Commercialization of Leisure', in Neil McKendrick, John Brewer, and id., *The Birth of a Consumer Society. The Commercialization of Eighteenth-century England* (London, 1982).

Pollard, Sidney, 'Labour in Great Britain', in Peter Mathias and M. M. Postan (eds.), *The Cambridge Economic History of Europe*, vii, *The Industrial Economies: Capital, Labour, and Enterprise*, pt. 1 (Cambridge, 1978).

Pollexfen, Henry, *A Discourse of Trade and Coyn* (London, 1697).

Porter, Roy, and John Brewer (eds.), *Consumption and the World of Goods* (London, 1993).

Quenouille, M., *et al.* Statistical Studies of Recorded Energy Expenditure in Man, Technical Communication No. 17, Commonwealth Bureau of Animal Nutrition (Aberdeen, 1951).

Radzinowicz, Leon, *History of English Criminal Law and its Administration from 1750*, ii (London, 1956).

Razzell, Peter, 'The Growth of Population in Eighteenth-Century England: A Critical Reappraisal', *Journal of Economic History*, 53 (1993).

Reid, Douglas, 'The Decline of St Monday, 1776–1876', *Past and Present*, 71 (1976).

—— 'Weddings, Weekdays, Work and Leisure in Urban England, 1791–1911', *Past and Present*, 153 (1996).

Richards, Audrey, *Land, Labour and Diet in Northern Rhodesia* (London, 1939).

Riley, James C., 'Disease Without Death: New Sources for a History of Sickness', *Journal of Interdisciplinary History*, 17 (1987).

—— 'Nutrition in Western Europe, 1750–1985: Melioration and Deterioration', Indiana University Population Institute for Research and Training, 92–7 (1991).

—— 'Working Health Time: A Comparison of Preindustrial, Industrial and Postindustrial Experience in Life and Health', *Explorations in Economic History*, 28 (1991).

Robbins, Lionel, 'On the Elasticity of Demand for Income in Terms of Effort', *Economica*, 25 (1930).

Robinson, John, 'The Validity and Reliability of Diaries versus Alternative Time

Use Measures', in F. Thomas Juster and Frank Stafford (eds.), *Time, Goods, and Well-Being* (Ann Arbor, Mich., 1985).

—— 'Changes in Time Use: An Historical Overview', in F. Thomas Juster and Frank Stafford (eds.), *Time, Goods, and Well-Being* (Ann Arbor, Mich., 1985).

Rogers, Thorold, *A History of Prices and Wages* (London, 1884).

Rosenberg, Nathan, *Inside the Black Box. Technology and Economics* (Cambridge, 1982).

Rosenstein-Rodan, Paul, 'Problems of Industrialisation of Eastern and South-eastern Europe', *Economic Journal*, 53 (1943).

Rostow, Walt, *The Stages of Economic Growth: A Non-Communist Manifesto* (Cambridge, 1960).

Rotenberg, Robert, *Time and Order in Metropolitan Vienna: A Seizure of Schedule* (Washington, DC, 1992).

Rudé, George, *Crime and Victim. Crime and Society in Early Nineteenth-century England* (Oxford, 1985).

—— *Hanoverian London, 1714–1808* (London, 1971).

—— 'Prices, Wages and Popular Movements in Paris during the French Revolution', *Economic History Review*, 6 (1953–4).

Rule, John, *The Experience of Labour in Eighteenth Century Industry* (London, 1981).

—— *The Labouring Classes in Early Industrial England, 1750–1850* (London and New York, 1986).

Sahlins, Marshall, *Stone Age Economics* (Chicago, 1974).

Schofield, Roger S., 'Dimensions of Illiteracy, 1750–1850', *Explorations in Economic History*, 10 (1973).

Schor, Juliet, *The Overworked American. The Unexpected Decline of Leisure* (New York, 1991).

Schröder, Walter, 'Die Entwicklung der Arbeitszeit im sekundären Sektor in Deutschland 1871–1913', *Technikgeschichte*, 3 (1980).

Schwarz, L. D., *London in the Age of Industrialization: Entrepreneurs, Labour Force, and Living Conditions, 1700–1850* (Cambridge, 1992).

—— 'Social Class and Social Geography: The Middle Classes in London at the End of the Eighteenth Century', *Social History*, 7 (1982).

—— 'The Standard of Living in the Long Run: London, 1700–1860', *Economic History Review*, 38 (1985).

Seckler, David, 'Malnutrition: An Intellectual Odyssey', *Western Journal of Agricultural Economics* (1980).

Senior, Nassau W., *Letters on the Factory Act* (London, 1837).

Shammas, Carole, 'Food Expenditures and Economic Well-Being in Early Modern England', *Journal of Economic History*, 43 (1983).

—— *The Pre-Industrial Consumer in England and America* (Oxford, 1990).

Shapiro, Matthew, 'Cyclical Productivity and the Workweek of Capital', *American Economic Review*, 83 (1993).

Simons, T. S., 'Working-Days, Holidays, and Vacations in England in the Fourteenth and Fifteenth Centuries', unpub. Ph.D. thesis, University of Boulder at Colorado (1936).

Smith, Adam, *An Inquiry into the Nature and Causes of the Wealth of Nations* (London, 1991 [1776]).

Soligo, Ronald, 'The Short-Run Relationship between Employment and Output', *Yale Economic Essays* (1966).

Solow, Robert, 'Technical Change and the Aggregate Production Function', *Review of Economics and Statistics*, 39 (1957).

—— and Peter Temin, 'The Inputs for Growth', in Peter Mathias and M. M. Postan (eds.), *The Cambridge Economic History of Europe*, vii, *The Industrial Economies: Capital, Labour and Enterprise*, pt. 1 (Cambridge, 1978).

Srinivasan, Thirukodikaval, 'Malnutrition: Some Measurement and Policy Issues', *Journal of Development Economics*, 8 (1981).

—— 'Undernutrition: Concepts, Measurements, and Policy Implications', in S. Osmani (ed.), *Nutrition and Poverty* (Oxford, 1992).

Steckel, Richard, 'Height and Per Capita Income', *Historical Methods*, 16 (1983).

—— 'A Peculiar Population: The Nutrition, Health, and Mortality of American Slaves from Childhood to Maturity', *Journal of Economic History*, 46 (1986).

Steward, Julian, and Lewis Faron, *Native Peoples of South America* (New York, 1959).

Stigler, George, and Gary S. Becker, 'De Gustibus Non Est Disputandum', *American Economic Review*, 67 (1977).

Stone, Lawrence, *Family, Sex and Marriage in England, 1500–1800* (New York, 1977).

—— 'Leisure in Eighteenth Century England', paper presented to the Datini Conference Il Tempo Libero, Prato, 18–25 April 1994.

Styles, John, 'Manufacturing, Consumption and Design in Eighteenth-Century England', in R. Porter and J. Brewer, *Consumption and the World of Goods* (London, 1993).

Sukhatme, Pandurang (ed.), *Newer Concepts in Nutrition and their Implications for Policy* (Pune, 1982).

Szalai, Alexander (ed.), *The Use of Time* (The Hague, 1972).

Tatom, John, 'The "Problem" of Procyclical Real Wages and Productivity', *Journal of Political Economy*, 88 (1980).

Taubman, Paul, and Margaret Wilkinson, 'User Cost, Capital Utilization and Investment Theory', *International Economic Review*, 11 (1970).

Taylor, Alan, and Jeffrey Williamson, 'Capital Flows to the New World as an Intergenerational Transfer', *Journal of Political Economy*, 102 (1994).

Temple, Jon, and Hans-Joachim Voth, 'Human Capital, Equipment Investment, and Industrialization', *European Economic Review*, 42 (1998).

Thirsk, Joan, *Economic Policies and Projects: The Development of a Consumer Society in Early Modern England* (Oxford, 1978).

Thomas, Brinley, 'Food Supply in the United Kingdom during the Industrial Revolution', in Joel Mokyr (ed.), *The Economics of the Industrial Revolution* (London, 1985).

Thomis, Malcolm, *The Town Labourer and the Industrial Revolution* (n.p., 1974).

Thompson, E. P., 'Time, Work-discipline, and Industrial Capitalism', *Past and Present*, 38 (1967).

Tobias, John, *Crime and Police in England, 1700–1900* (Dublin, 1979).

Tobin, James, 'Life-cycle Savings and Balanced Economic Growth', in W. Fellner (ed.), *Ten Essays in the Tradition of Irving Fischer* (New York, 1967).

Toutain, Jean-Claude, 'La Consommation alimentaire en France de 1789 à 1964', *Economies et Sociétés, Cahiers de L'ISEA*, v (1971).

Tranter, Nick, 'The Labour Supply, 1780–1860', in R. Floud and D. McCloskey (eds.), *The Economic History of Britain since 1700* (Cambridge, 1994).

Tversky, Amos, and Daniel Kahneman, 'Judgement Under Uncertainty: Heuristics and Biases', *Science*, 185 (1974).

Usher, Dan, *The Measurement of Economic Growth* (Oxford, 1980).

von Tunzelmann, Nick, 'Technology in the Early Nineteenth Century', in R. Floud and D. McCloskey (eds.), *The Economic History of Britain since 1700* (Cambridge, 1994).

Voth, Hans-Joachim, 'Height, Nutrition, and Labor: Recasting the "Austrian Model"', *Journal of Interdisciplinary History*, 25 (1995).

—— 'Seasonality of Baptisms as a Source for Historical Time-Budget Analysis: Tracing the Disappearance of Holy Days in Early Modern England', *Historical Methods*, 27 (1994).

—— 'Time and Work in Eighteenth-Century London', *Journal of Economic History*, 58 (1998).

—— and Timothy Leunig, 'Did Smallpox Reduce Height? Stature and the Standard of Living in London, 1770–1873', *Economic History Review*, 59 (1996).

Waldmann, Robert, 'Inequality, Economic Growth and the Debt Crisis', *EUI Economics Working Paper*, 40 (1994).

Walter, John, 'The Social Economy of Dearth in Early Modern England', in id. and Roger S. Schofield (eds.), *Famine, Disease and the Social Order in Early Modern Society* (Cambridge, 1989).

Weatherill, Lorna, *Consumer Behaviour and Material Culture, 1660–1760* (London, 1988).

Weber, Max, 'Die Objektivität sozialwissenschaftlicher und sozialpolitischer Erkenntnis', in *Archiv für Sozialwissenschaft und Sozialpolitik*, 19 (1904), repr. in J. Winckelmann (ed.), *Max Weber. Soziologie. Universalgeschichtliche Analysen. Politik* (Stuttgart, 1973).

—— *The Protestant Ethic and the Spirit of Capitalism* (tr. T. Parson, London, 1930).

—— 'Die protestantische Ethik und der Geist des Kapitalismus', in id., *Gesammelte Schriften zur Religionssoziologie*, i (Tübingen, 1920).

Weber, Max, *Wissenschaft als Beruf* (Munich, 1919), repr. in J. Winckelmann (ed.), *Max Weber. Soziologie. Universalgeschichtliche Analysen. Politik* (Stuttgart, 1973).

Wehler, Hans-Ulrich, *Deutsche Gesellschaftsgeschichte*, i (Munich, 1987).

Weiss, C., 'Validity of Welfare Mothers' Interview Responses', *Public Opinion Quarterly*, 32 (1968).

Weiss, Yoram, 'Synchronization of Work Schedules', *Tel Aviv Foerder Institute of Economic Research Working Paper*, 12 (1991).

Wells, Roger, *Wretched Faces. Famine in Wartime England, 1793–1801* (Gloucester, 1988).

White, Benjamin, *Problems in Estimating the Value of Work in Peasant Household Economies: An Example from Rural Java* (Bogor, 1979).

Williamson, Jeffrey, 'British Mortality and the Value of Life', *Population Studies*, 38 (1984).

—— *Did British Capitalism Breed Inequality?* (Boston, 1985).

—— 'How Tough are Times in the Third World?', in D. McCloskey (ed.), *Second Thoughts. Myths and Morals of U.S. Economic History* (New York, 1993).

—— 'What Do We Know about Skill Accumulation in Nineteenth Century Britain?', unpub. ms, University of Wisconsin (1981).

—— 'Why Was British Growth So Slow During the Industrial Revolution?', *Journal of Economic History*, 44 (1984).

Wolfe, Barbara, and Jere Behrman, 'Is Income Overrated in Determining Adequate Nutrition?', *Economic Development and Cultural Change*, 31 (1983).

Woodward, Donald, *Men at Work: Labourers and Building Craftsmen in the Towns of Northern England, 1450–1750* (Cambridge, 1995).

World Bank, *Poverty and Hunger: Issues and Options for Food Security in Developing Countries* (Washington, DC, 1986).

—— *World Tables, 1995* (Baltimore, 1995).

Wrigley, Edward Anthony, 'Energy Availability and Agricultural Productivity', in Mark Overton and Bruce Campbell (eds.), *Land, Labour and Lifestock* (Manchester, 1991).

—— 'Explaining the Rise in Marital Fertility in England in the "Long" Eighteenth Century', *Economic History Review*, 51 (1998).

—— 'The Growth of Population in Eighteenth-Century England: A Conundrum Resolved', *Past and Present*, 98 (1983).

—— 'A Simple Model of London's Importance in Changing English Society and Economy, 1650–1750', *Past and Present*, 37 (1967), repr. in id. (ed.), *People, Cities, and Wealth* (Oxford, 1987).

—— 'Urban Growth and Agricultural Change: England and the Continent in the Early Modern Period', in id. (ed.), *People, Cities, and Wealth* (Oxford, 1987).

—— and Roger Schofield, *The Population History of England, 1541–1871* (London, 1981).

—— R. S. Davies, Jim Oeppen, and Roger Schofield, *English Population History from Family Reconstitution, 1580–1837* (Cambridge, 1997).

Young, Alwyn, 'The Tyranny of Numbers: Confronting the Statistical Realities of the East Asian Growth Experience', *Quarterly Journal of Economics*, 110 (1995).

Zerubavel, Eviatar, *The Seven Day Cycle. The History and Meaning of the Week* (New York, 1985).

INDEX

Index